Building a Radical University

A History of the University of East London

Building a Radical University

A History of the University of East London

Edited by

Michael Rustin and Gavin Poynter

Lawrence Wishart
London 2020

Lawrence and Wishart Limited
Central Books Building
Freshwater Road
Chadwell Heath
RM8 1RX

Typesetting: e-type
Cover design: River Design
Cover artwork: Rachel Whiteread, *Untitled (Stack)*, 1999, photo courtesy of the artist
Printing: Imprint Digital

First published 2020

British Library Cataloguing in Publication Data.
A catalogue record for this book is available from the British Library

ISBN 978-1-912064-99-1
eISBN 978-1-912064-41-0

Contents

INTRODUCTION

UEL – a radical university?

Gavin Poynter and Michael Rustin

The aim of this book is to describe the evolution of a particular institution located in East London, first in its designation from 1968 as a polytechnic, then after 1992 as a 'new university'. Our argument is that this was in many respects a radical and democratic development, in which much of what took place was motivated by explicit ideas and commitments of value, in regard to both education and knowledge. This introduction will describe how the University of East London (UEL) evolved, and the principles which underpinned it. Subsequent chapters will describe the different forms in which this development took place, in the various educational fields of the institution. Finally, some former students will recall their experience of studying in this environment.

There is widespread regret and complaint in present times about what is happening to universities in England and Wales. The complaint is that they have been transformed within the context of neoliberal ideology and governmental policy into corporate institutions, more interested in their balance sheets and their competitive position than in learning as such, or in the development of their students' capabilities and well-being. A considerable amount of critical writing has articulated this view.[1] A sense of disillusion is widespread throughout the university system, among university staff and to a degree among students, who commonly feel that what their universities offer them by way of teaching, stimulation and care is not commensurable with the enormous debts they have to incur to obtain them. There is the further major problem that the 'graduate level' jobs that students had been led to believe would be available to them do not now exist in sufficient numbers. Thus the basis on which students have been invited to define their university experience as an investment in their future employment (rather than as one of intrinsic developmental value) is often felt to be a false one.[2]

The University of East London has not been insulated from these developments, nor from the anxieties which have accompanied them. However this university, from its foundation as the North East London Polytechnic (NELP) in 1968 (this was from three constituent colleges; it became the Polytechnic of East London in 1988 and the University of East London in 1992) originally developed in a spirit, and within an ambience, very different from that of the present day. It grew in a period of rapid expansion of the university system, with the establishment first of the polytechnics and then of the 'new universities', and also with the expansion in student numbers, campuses and resources of the previously existing institutions. The tendency is for the earlier history of an institution like UEL to become dispersed and lost in memories, of what may appear in retrospect to have been better times. However, we suggest that there were substantial elements of value in the culture and practice of those earlier years, which should be recorded and remembered as potential resources for the future development of UEL, and as a contribution to a wider debate about higher education. It is because some elements of the earlier traditions of a university such as UEL remain alive and active (if somewhat overshadowed) in the present day, that we believe that it is worthwhile to describe this history.

Our central argument is that the North East London Polytechnic and the University of East London, which it became, was an institution that was driven by distinctive educational values, rather than by merely instrumental or corporate ambitions. This is in contrast to the definition of purpose which was imposed by the Further and Higher Education Act of 1992. This transformed the then polytechnics into what came to be called 'new universities', but at the same time designated them as 'higher education corporations', removing them from the control of elected local authorities, and instead establishing boards of governors, which were largely composed of 'independent governors' appointed by the secretary of state, and for the most part nominated from the private business sector.[3] Thus a new 'corporate' definition of purpose was inscribed in the constitution of new universities from their inception. The values which motivated different centres of initiative in NELP and UEL were varied, but they had in common some conception of the democratic and radical values often defined at the time against established disciplinary or academic orthodoxies.

The idea that the Polytechnic and then University of East London had a distinctive mission, which set it apart from the orthodoxies of the time, had its inspiration in the early leadership of the institution – from above – as well as from a variety of radical educators and subject-specialists who gathered to work there. Its founding director, Dr George Brosan, and deputy-director, Eric Robinson, were explicitly committed to a vision of the polytechnic as a new kind of higher educational institution, which was to have as its purpose the development of useful and practical knowledge, rather than knowledge understood as the mere reproduction of a traditional elite culture. They were somewhat insurgent figures. Robinson[4] was an educational social democrat, committed to expanding opportunities. Brosan was 'industrial' and entrepreneurial in his outlook – he had earlier, so his *Guardian* obituary tells us, made a fortune through a sale of his successful electrical business.[5] Nevertheless, the two of them encouraged, and sometimes insisted on, innovation in the educational programmes the new polytechnic was to offer.

Here is how Brosan[6] set out the differences between existing universities and what he wished to see the polytechnics become:

> **Purposes**
>
> Universities stand for the preservation of learning and the pursuit of truth for its own sake (i.e. learning in universities is autotelic).
>
> Polytechnics stand for the application of education (i.e. to cause it to be vocationally relevant).
>
> **People**
>
> Universities stand for the nurturing of apprentice scholars (i.e. education in universities is reactive).
>
> Polytechnics stand for the nurturing of apprentice industrialists (i.e. education in polytechnics is proactive). This makes

the one elite and the other comprehensive. The polytechnics expect and are glad to deal with the revolution of rising expectations.

Discipline

Universities stand for the viability and inviolability of separate disciplines, irrespective of application.

Polytechnics stand for a holistic curriculum (i.e. concerned with the unity of diverse disciplines as they are reflected in the real-world situations).

That is, universities are concerned with stating and solving problems within disciplines whatever the situations involved. Polytechnics are concerned with formulation of problems from situations, whatever the disciplines involved.

Inquiry

Universities stand for a mode of inquiry which is speculative (i.e. beginning with a metaphor, elaborating it and developing the hypotheses it yields).

Polytechnics stand for a mode of inquiry which is problematic (i.e. beginning with a problem and searching for metaphor which in its elaboration will yield a hypothesis for solution).

Research

Universities stand for a philosophy of research oriented to be an end in itself (i.e. which has intrinsic value as an activity independent of the results achieved).

Polytechnics stand for a philosophy of research oriented to be problem-solving (i.e. which is specific and may happily have wider implications).

Society

Universities stand for detachment from and for independent criticism of society. This is not to assume that universities must always disagree with society.

> Polytechnics stand for involvement in industry, commerce and society. This is not to assume that polytechnics must always agree with society.
>
> **Entry**
>
> Universities stand for selective admission of students of eighteen years of age or thereabouts, academically screened, and committed to courses of full-time study.
>
> Polytechnics stand for wider age limits and more catholic conditions; the part-time student, the mature student, the student engaged on re-education.

Perhaps the most important step in the refashioning of institutions like the North East London Polytechnic in 1968 was the transfer of responsibility for the design of educational programmes ('courses', as we then called them) from superordinate external authorities to the polytechnics themselves and their staff members. Previously, academics had been employed to teach courses whose syllabuses and examination systems were wholly prescribed by the University of London as its 'external degrees' (but with some courses at West Ham College of Technology, where there were 'recognised teachers', designated as internal degrees). Or, in the case of sub-degree programmes in fields such as technology and business studies prescribed by other qualification-awarding bodies (professional institutions like these retained some authority over some fields in later developments). For the teachers of these degrees, this constituted a kind of apprenticeship on the route to becoming university teachers, which in the University of London could be an 'accredited' status. This system was operated by the University of London with undoubted good intentions, in the cause of extending university education, but it was also distinctly paternalist, conducted under the leadership of its senior professors. Since these external degrees were also taught overseas in territories of the British empire, fast becoming the Commonwealth, the arrangement had a somewhat colonial dimension, though here operating within the United Kingdom.

This transfer of responsibility can be seen, therefore, as a significant act of democratisation of university education. It coincided (not insignificantly) with the ending of the University of London's external degrees worldwide, and, less fortunately, with a broader decline in the extra-mural functions of the established universities, part of a deplorable reduction in non-credentialised adult education more generally. This change was accomplished through a transitional arrangement, the setting-up in 1964 of the Council for National Academic Awards (CNAA) whose role later came to be to guide the new institutions in setting up the replacement or new degree programmes which the polytechnics now needed. (Lionel Robbins, who set up the CNAA, opposed the 'binary divide' and the polytechnic sector, for which it became, after 1966, such a crucial instrument.) But whereas the CNAA might have been established merely as a 'nationalised' substitute for previous university-administered external degrees, prescribing in detail the curricula which the new institutions would be obliged to follow, it came to operate with a different approach, to accredit academic initiatives coming 'from below'. Its system placed the responsibility for initiating and designing courses on to the teaching staff of the new institutions themselves. Its role was to offer the polytechnics, and what came significantly to be called their 'course teams', guidance in how to do this, and crucially to assess the proposals for degrees which were submitted to them from the polytechnics.

This process of 'validation' became an interactive and dialogic one. It involved not only close scrutiny of documentation to ensure its consistency and appropriateness (a task conducted by an expert secretariat), but also the interrogation of course teams and discussion with them of what they were proposing to teach. Many academics from established universities chose to serve on the CNAA's subject panels. However it seems many of those who became involved in this work, and those who took up roles as 'external examiners' to the new programmes, were motivated both by the democratic impulse of extending opportunities to a wider social range of students, and by the wish to encourage innovation and the expansion of their own subject fields. Sometimes this procedure of course design and validation led to the virtual cloning or reproduction of established academic programmes – this was indeed the 'safest' way for an institution to proceed. But it also created, within a compressed period of time, an unusual opportunity for innovation, subject to programmes conforming to established standards of educational provision, in their staff qualifications, staff-student ratios, facilities and resources.[7] Of course, much of the work of course development served to replicate and reproduce established disciplines, mainly enabling them to be taught in new institutional locations. But the system also provided considerable scope for innovation within subject fields, in combinations between them and in the development of virtually new fields, such as those described in later chapters. Only the formation of the new 'plate-glass' universities in the 1960s (Sussex, Essex, Lancaster, Kent, York, etc.) had recently seen a comparable degree of curriculum innovation.[8] These experiences show that for innovation to become possible, new institutions may need to be created.

Another democratic aspect of the operation of polytechnics like the predecessor of the University of East London was the form of governance which was prescribed for it. This contained a detailed specification of where powers were to lie, between boards of governors, their directors and their deputies (the management hierarchy) and the academic staff themselves, whom through nominated and elected academic boards were assigned definite powers to determine academic matters, both through their overall decision-making powers and through devolved faculty boards. This constitutional 'separation of powers' naturally gave rise to conflicts, and the articles of government were sometimes a contentious point of reference. One observed, on one significant occasion, NELP's then rector being overruled by the representatives of the local authorities who controlled the governing body,[9] and, earlier, conflicts between the polytechnic's director (CEO in modern terms) and the constituted academic board.[10] This was, however, a form of *constitutional* government, and one remembers the first director of NELP, Dr Brosan, taking part in these constitutional and political arguments with some relish. Representative government had a reality and substance during the 1970s and early 1980s which it subsequently lost.[11] Another factor of importance in East London was the significant strength of the various trade unions – academic, administrative staff, and sometimes the student union – which reinforced these formal representative processes.

Of course, this situation also corresponds to that which obtained in the wider British society in this period. One can see this development during the 1970s as consonant with wider processes of democratisation then taking place in Britain, indeed as part of a broader development with many social and cultural aspects that followed the Second World War. The CNAA served to enable the new higher education institutions to develop their own autonomy, and in particular that of their academic staff, who had responsibility for the development of their courses. Its validation processes were based on a concept of academic peer review which took account of the knowledge and experience of its participants. Later, from the 1980s onwards, 'professions', as autonomous loci of values and powers, such as teachers, medical doctors and even judges, came under wider political attack.

In this period, universities struggled to retain their autonomy in their relation to government. They had some limited success in this, through establishing practices of academic peer review, both in regard to quality assurance and the allocation of research funding. (The former through the Quality Assurance Agency for Higher Education (QAA) and its systems of regular audit and inspection, and the latter through the research assessment exercises (RAEs) conducted by academics under the auspices of the Higher Education Funding Council, HEFCE.) However, governments exercised increasingly intrusive control over the entire system, demanding the expansion of student numbers and improvements in standards, even while reducing the 'unit of resource' which was to provide for these. The defence of the universities' autonomy became a losing struggle, as the competitive and marketised environment in which they were obliged to operate changed their internal environment, in a managerialist and corporate direction. Managements became compelled to focus on the 'market position' of their institutions, signified by their position in 'league tables', since it was on this that their relative status and resources depended. League tables assess all institutions on a common metric – thus the level and rank of a university has become more salient than the qualities which are specific to it. Universities have become primary allocators of social status, giving Britain's ancient system of class inequalities an ostensibly meritocratic justification.[12] The competition for research funding and reputation led to the creation of a 'transfer market' in professorial staff (analogous to the Premier League in professional football), giving rise to the individualisation of academic life, and an increased differentiation of salaries and conditions of employment. These developments have enhanced the power of university managements, at the expense of the academic professionals. Increasing workloads, precariousness of employment at junior levels, and a culture of 'deliver' (e.g. in terms of research outputs) or else face sanctions leave less scope than before for cooperative intellectual work. Many of the chapters in this book describe how important such collegial activity among academic staff was in the formative days of NELP and UEL.

In some of the new polytechnics, such as the North East London Polytechnic, the management of the institution was itself committed to innovation, and actively encouraged, and sometimes even demanded it, from course teams. Brosan and Robinson insisted on a rapid pace of development, with eighty courses submitted to CNAA in the first two years of the polytechnic's existence.[13] But they also often insisted on innovatory course designs that reflected their commitment to 'useful knowledge', and sometimes gave forceful effect to their antipathy to traditional academic orthodoxies.

This context of a rapid and necessary development of educational programmes in the polytechnics was one in which course development became a primary activity for their academic staff, giving rise to opportunities for them to initiate development and, through this, to achieve influence and seniority. It was only with the abolition of the 'binary division' in British higher education in 1992 and the consequent access of the former polytechnics to research funding from the Higher Education Funding Council that research came to assume a priority for academics approximating to that obtaining in the older universities.[14] This had the effect of somewhat displacing educational development as the most valued professional activity. It can be argued that this change has contributed to the weakening of the original educational mission of the new institutions, and has been one aspect of the process of 'academic drift' to which Tyrrell Burgess and John Pratt drew critical attention.[15]

Another consequence of the abolition of the polytechnics and their integration into a single higher education system was their retreat from vocationally focused education, and the continuing overvaluation of the 'academic' which has long been an attribute of British higher education. The nationwide decline of part-time education was a significant aspect of this change.

Thus at NELP, humanities staff found their original proposal merely to reproduce the University of London's discontinued external degree in humanities rejected, creating the opportunity to develop the first undergraduate degree in cultural studies in the UK. Its authors borrowed substantially from the postgraduate programme that had been established by Richard Hoggart and Stuart Hall at the Centre for Contemporary Cultural Studies at Birmingham University. It was consciously developed as an approach to the humanities which challenged traditional cultural hierarchies. Cultural studies was designed to analyse cultural forms in their social and historical contexts and in relation to wider systems of power, helping students to locate themselves within these systems as 'critical citizens'.

In sociology, a similar initial proposal merely to replicate the London external degree was also rejected. In its place, the course team was encouraged to develop a more vocationally oriented degree, which emerged as a four-year programme in sociology with professional studies, with options in social work, sociological research and vocational guidance, with related placements in the four-year degree structure that was then possible in terms of its funding.

The procedure for course development and validation through the mediation of the CNAA had an inherently democratic potential (although this was not always realised). This is because the responsibility for developing and submitting a course for validation lay with its prospective teachers, and not with higher levels of management, although, of course, the latter held considerable power to determine what was even permitted to be put forward for academic validation. The process of dialogue with the assessors which followed was itself often stimulating and educative, drawing attention to possibilities and practices of which course teams may have been previously unaware. Sometimes validation panels would insist that a whole course team must contribute to the defence of a course proposal, and refused to allow this to be dominated by a single course leader. At NELP, and no doubt in most new institutions, a course development unit was established whose practice was to facilitate the work of the course teams designing the new curricula.[16] The consequence of this system was that throughout the polytechnic and post-1992 'new university' sector (which came to comprise half of the UK higher education system) the degree of diversification and innovation in curricula, teaching and assessment methods far exceeded the tradition-bound practices of most of the older universities. At NELP and UEL in particular, it became the established practice that the principal criterion for assessment of new educational programmes was whether it fulfilled the purposes it had itself defined, not whether it conformed to some pre-defined academic requirement or expectation. Of course, the standard criteria of academic level and quality still obtained, but within a diverse and flexible frame of reference.

To give an example of this open-minded approach, in the 1980s and 1990s, UEL undertook the accreditation and validation of a large number of professional and educational training programmes at the Tavistock Clinic. This was a mental health trust that was the leader in its fields of psychoanalytic and family systemic therapies and their wider community applications, but very few of whose education and training programmes had academic accreditation. These courses often made substantial use of learning methods based on psychoanalytically informed infant and young child observation, and on the individual and group supervision of clinical work. These methods were unlike those used in most conventional taught programmes. The criteria for course development which were by this time established at UEL were well adapted to the issues posed by the Tavistock programmes. 'What are the course objectives, how are they delivered, how can their achievement be appropriately assessed?' were the questions asked in the validation process. While some disciplines at UEL were unsympathetic to the psychoanalytic orientation of many Tavistock courses, and to their qualitative and relational methods of learning, the university's approach as an institution was to engage positively with the Tavistock's approaches. It saw its purpose as to give its programmes adequate academic definition and validity. The outcome of this was a programme in which around a thousand Tavistock postgraduate students were at one time registered with UEL, including many studying at professional doctorate level. These became a high-level expression of the university's vocational mission.

For several years, from its foundation in 1965 to its abolition in 1992, the authority of the polytechnics and other non-university colleges to award degrees remained with the CNAA, although the validated degree programmes were always initiated by the institutions themselves. This model, developed during this exceptional period of change, was then 'internalised' from 1992 by the newly enfranchised universities, and became their own standard practice. However, the routinisation of this initially democratic and innovative practice has come at a price. In the early days, the process of academic and professional peer review, conducted by panels of subject assessors, was an interactive and substantively rich one, in which issues of content, method and purpose were often keenly debated. Validation could be in itself a learning experience leading to the clarification and diffusion of innovative practices. But it seems now to be common for validation and periodic course review processes to have little if any substantive 'subject' content, becoming reduced instead to meeting merely bureaucratic criteria of conformity to rules. This is similar to the way in which course assessment procedures, which also used to have a dialogic, qualitative component in which the particularities of individual students and their circumstances could be taken into account, have become wholly routinised and numerically driven processes.[17]

A radical tradition

What happened at NELP and UEL, as they developed, was an unusual conjunction of educational programmes which were notable for their idiosyncratic, committed and sometimes radical social purposes. Radicalism, however, came in quite different forms. One of the developments for which NELP and UEL is best known, its degree by independent study, was both radically egalitarian *and* individualist in its conception. Students, often from the locality of East London and its region and typically with poor educational qualifications from their schooling, were enabled to design their own curriculum, drawing on the academic resources of the university – its teachers and sometimes its subject-based courses – to do so. Its primary locations of learning were individual supervision by staff members throughout the university, and interactions within the Department for Independent Studies itself.

The students who benefited most from the opportunity to pursue a degree by independent study were often mature students, returning to education after having had other formative experiences in their life and work. Where appropriate supervisors could be found for such students, they were often able to embark on a significant experience of personal and educational development. It was sometimes more difficult for younger students, with a poor previous experience of education, to cope with the degree of individual responsibility that the programme called for, and the 'counter-cultural' atmosphere which developed around it led it eventually into difficulties with the validating authorities.

The opportunity to recruit 'mature students' (at least twenty-five years old) to its degree courses was important in this and in other polytechnics in these early years, as several chapters in this book describe. This provision was a means to enact the principle set out in the Robbins report of 1963 that higher education should be accessible to all those qualified to benefit from it. But this was in a context not anticipated by Robbins, where limitations of schooling had precluded many potential students from obtaining university entrance qualifications, or even aspiring to do so. It was a farsighted decision of the CNAA to allow this exceptional form of 'mature student admission' to university, which was comparable to the open-access provision of the Open University, and with comparably 'democratising' effects. This entitlement, and its flexible interpretation by academic staff, was one of the ways in which NELP and UEL were able to extend educational opportunities to students previously denied them. Many of these students were especially serious about their studies, and found them valuable, not only in opening up future work opportunities for themselves, but also in reflecting on their situations in life and on their personal development. The favourable staff-student ratios in those days permitted a considerable amount of tuition in small groups. These circumstances, and the commitment to learning of both staff and students, gave rise to strong shared commitments to the fields being studied. The relatively 'democratic ethos' of these early days was thus enhanced by the fact that many students brought considerable adult experience into the polytechnic, and were able to actively define the meaning of their education for them.

NELP and UEL's programmes

Many education programmes were developed at NELP and in UEL which had a commitment and orientation to distinct, socially committed values. Here are those, and some fields of research, which are described in later chapters.

- An anthropology degree course, unique in the new university sector, and in its interest in prehistorical social evolution.
- An architecture course exceptional for the freedom of exploration and expression which it encouraged in its students.
- Art and fashion courses, which sought an engagement with the life of local East London communities, as well as seeking to develop a theoretically based understanding of communication design.
- Cultural studies, consciously developed as an approach to the humanities which challenged traditional cultural hierarchies, and saw cultures as locations for learning and argument about the nature and development of societies, both past and present.
- An economics degree course which challenged some of the dominant theoretical assumptions of its subject.
- A European studies course, whose commitment was to enlarging the geographical horizons of study, and experience, for sociology students, and which was able to make use of the European Union Erasmus programme to facilitate student exchange with several European universities.
- Studies in history, embedded mainly in the Cultural Studies programme.
- Independent studies, described above, and one of only

two programmes of its kind in the UK (the other was at the University of Lancaster).

- Innovation studies, whose principal interest was in the social applications and uses of information technology, when this was still at an early stage of development.
- A law school with a distinctive focus on issues of human rights.
- Physiotherapy, which was an early example of the enhancement of education and training of one of the major 'professions allied to medicine'.
- A psychology programme which was notable for its commitment to the development of its students as psychologists, both through its undergraduate pedagogy, and through its development of several different postgraduate professional specialisms, when these were rarely found in what was primarily a location of undergraduate education.
- Psychosocial studies, which emerged as new subject area reflecting an increasing focus on the subjective and personal in society and in the experience of students.
- A refugee studies programme, one of only two of its kind in the UK, responding to the ethnically diverse population of East London and its significant number of refugees.
- Sociology, which focused on the exploration of different lines of social division, successively of class, gender and race, making these a resource for students' explorations of issues of identity relevant to themselves.
- Tavistock and Portman NHS Foundation Trust, developing many postgraduate programmes in fields of community mental health.
- A women's studies programme which reflected the emergence of feminist interests and preoccupations in this period among East London women.

After university status was achieved in 1992, opportunities for research developed across the sector, as the 'new universities' were included in the system for assessing and funding research. At UEL, research tended to be value-oriented in ways similar to its teaching programme. The Centre for Institutional Studies developed a distinctive approach to the evaluation of social policies, based on the social philosophy of Karl Popper, and developed community-based research projects. Research in East London, over many years, sought to map and interpret the 'regeneration' which was taking place in the region, especially seeking to give a voice to those sections of the population whom it was doing least for. In an area of London with a large ethnic minority population, and with many refugees and asylum seekers, migration and refugee studies became a leading field of research. Narrative studies was another area of importance, its innovation being in the development of research methods able to capture the subjective experience of individual subjects, and their forms of agency and participation in society.

This book concludes with three essays which describe the experience at this polytechnic and university of three of its former students, conveying the atmosphere and spirit of those times.

Swimming against the tide: value-oriented education in East London

Rising in the East[18] was the title of a book that sought to capture the difficulties and opportunities facing higher education institutions located in East London in the 1990s. A journal, *Rising East*, and many further books followed it. The area witnessed significant economic and social change with the development of Canary Wharf in the former London Docklands. In the course of a decade, East London became the site of a global financial and business services sector with its attendant wealth and high-rise towers. It emerged alongside areas of significant social and economic deprivation, a legacy from the loss of the docks and traditional processing and manufacturing industries. The changing industrial landscape was accompanied by rapid demographic changes, particularly through the growth in immigrant communities, the expansion of ethnic diversity, the rise of the young as a growing proportion of the local population, and the beginnings of significant gentrification in Docklands and elsewhere in the East London boroughs.

Within the higher education sector in England, the 1990s witnessed significant growth in student numbers, often led by the former polytechnics in the guise of newly incorporated universities. During this period, university funding grew but not at the same pace as the growth in student numbers. The 1990 Education (Student Loans) Act saw the freezing of means-tested maintenance grants (eventually replaced by loans), and in the years that followed, public debate was focused upon the financing of higher education and the expectation that the beneficiary, the student, should be expected to contribute to the costs of their studies. The Conservative government in 1993 introduced a series of charters setting down what recipients could expect to receive from public services. The citizen became a 'service user', the student a 'customer' of the university. In turn, student fees were introduced, this time by a Labour government, in 1998. UEL in the 1990s found itself to be located in an area of significant social and economic change, and within a sector that underwent the series of state interventions that replaced a system of virtually free post-school education with a quasi-market, which now defined the environment for students, and universities and their academic staff.

The university responded to the opportunities presented by East London's 'regeneration' by developing plans to reorganise its estate, closing the Barking campus (formerly the location of the Barking College of Technology) and opening, with HEFCE advice and support, a new Docklands campus in 2000.[19] In turn, staff sought to develop the institution's teaching and research programmes, often finding themselves swimming against the tide of change taking place within the sector. The value-oriented education that inspired staff and students, and which is illustrated in this text, rested uneasily with the creeping marketisation and new managerialist ethos that successive governments sought to introduce in higher education, and more widely within the public sector.

There have been several highly informed and critical examinations of the transformation of the higher education sector in the UK, not least from the perspective of the elite institutions.[20] But there has been little writing specifically about the polytechnics and the 'new universities' to which they were converted in 1992. This book seeks to address this absence, with chapters that describe many of the programmes which were developed in one particular institution. We as its editors, despite having had a very long experience within it (for one of us from 1964), have been taken aback to discover how extensive was the range of creative work that was done during those years, within a shared commitment to education as a public good. There is no chapter in this book which does not report an original development of some kind. It is suggested that the conditions that facilitated such creativity sit in stark contrast to those that currently prevail in the higher education sector in the UK.

We are aware, of course, that parallel developments took place in many other polytechnics and universities whose history is in many ways similar to the University of East London's, and where there was also considerable innovation. We have not been able to gather information for this book on institutions other than ours. We hope that one outcome of this collection may be a broader discussion of the significance and achievement of this large segment – around half of it in fact – of British university education, and of the issues which concern its future development.

Notes

1. R. Brown, *Everything for Sale: the Marketisation of Higher Education*, Society for Research into Higher Education: London, 2013; Stefan Collini, *What Are Universities For?*, Penguin: London, 2012; Stefan Collini, *Speaking of Universities*, Verso: London, 2018; Peter Scott, *The Crisis of the University*, Routledge: Abingdon, 2018. Michael Rustin, 'The Neoliberal University and its Alternatives', *Soundings* 63, 2016, pp147-170, https://www.lwbooks.co.uk/soundings/63/the-neoliberal-university; K. Thomas, 'Universities under Attack', *London Review of Books*, 15 December 2011; G. Poynter, 'Beyond Instrumentalism. Why education is living on borrowed time', in D. Hayes (ed.), *Beyond McDonaldisation*, Visions of Higher Education, Routledge: Abingdon, 2017.
2. An Office of National Statistics survey reported in 2017 that 47 per cent of recent (within five years of leaving higher education), and 35.6 per cent of non-recent graduates, were working in non-graduate roles. A consequence of this 'graduate surplus' may well be to worsen still further the opportunities for those who do not obtain university degrees; https://www.ons.gov.uk/employmentandlabourmarket/peopleinwork/employmentandemployeetypes/adhocs/008381percentageofemployedgraduatesinnongraduaterolespartsoftheuk2015to2017

3. There would have been scope, in a different political climate, to have replaced sole local authority control, which was far from ideal in its operation, with a multiple 'stakeholder' model, in which local authorities, business, professional and non-governmental representatives could have taken shared responsibility for these institutions. In our experience, the current model has created a mode of governance which is largely remote from the functions and purposes of the institutions governed, other than in regard to financial solvency. The fact that vice-chancellor salaries are now determined by reference to corporate rather than educational norms makes clear the now-dominant ethos, with a divisive effect within universities.
4. Eric Robinson, *The New Polytechnics*, Penguin: London, 1968.
5. Tyrrell Burgess, Obituary of George Brosan, *The Guardian*, 16 November 2001, https://www.theguardian.com/news/2001/nov/16/guardianobituaries.highereducation.
6. George Brosan, 'The Development of Polytechnics in the United Kingdom', *Paedagogica Europaea*, Vol. 7, 1972, pp41-53, p46. Brosan once introduced a conference at NELP of the Sociologists in Polytechnics. He asserted the value of sociology as a 'demystifying' field of study, to the astonishment of participants from other polytechnics.
7. Sometimes CNAA subject panels imposed conditions for course validation which in effect supported course teams in obtaining from the institutions the staff and other resource which they needed, in a form of tacit tripartite negotiation.
8. Michael Beloff, *The Plateglass Universities*, Secker and Warburg: London, 1968.
9. This was at a meeting of the board of governors at which the chairman, from one of the local authorities, administered a lesson to the then director in where real power lay, defeating the latter's (commendable) attempt to broaden the composition of the governing body by calling in the councillor members' votes.
10. In a major crisis, in 1981, a director's attempt, with the then support of a committee of governors, to close four departments was defeated in part because of his failure to carry the academic board with him, an outcome which influenced the later decision of the entire governing body. This happened following a time of intense political provocation and conflict, in the course of which in 1977 an injunction was served on the student union president (an active member of the Socialist Workers' Party), the breach of which led to his imprisonment for ten days. Thus the wider conflictual atmosphere of 1970s Britain found its expression in polytechnics like NELP.

11. It is not clear whether this weakening of academic democracy was a direct consequence of formal changes in the principles of governance after 1992, or happened for other reasons.
12. One says 'ostensibly', since social access to universities of different ranks is highly stratified, with approximately half of Oxbridge students recruited from 'public' (that is private) schools.
13. Tyrrell Burgess, Obituary of George Brosan, *The Guardian*, 16 November 2001.
14. Incidentally, the discourse of 'excellence' promulgated in this period flattered the academics just as their autonomy was being undermined.
15. J. Pratt and T. Burgess, *Polytechnics: a Report,* Pitman: London, 1973; T. Burgess, M. Locke, J. Pratt and N. Richards, *Degrees East: The Making of the University of East London 1892-1992.* Athlone Press: London, 1995; J. Pratt, *The Polytechnic Experiment 1965-1992,* Society for Research into Higher Education: London, 1997.
16. Its leading figure, Jim Proctor, should be remembered for his dedication to this work.
17. A university system that could once be characterised as dominated by forms of 'craft' and 'batch' production has moved in the direction of mass production on 'Taylorist' and 'Fordist' principles, just as the wider economic system has been allegedly moving in the 'post-Fordist' direction of 'flexible specialisation.' On these distinctions, see Robin Murray, 'Benetton Britain: The new economic order', *Marxism Today,* November 1985, pp 28-32, www.banmarchive.org.uk/collections/authorsandtitles/mt/85_11_28.htm, and 'Life after Henry (Ford)', *Marxism Today,* October 1988, pp 8-13, www.banmarchive.org.uk/collections/authorsandtitles/mt/88_10_08.htm
18. T. Butler and M. J. Rustin (eds), *Rising in the East: The Regeneration of East London,* Lawrence & Wishart: London, 1996.
19. David Albury and Carole Snee, 'Higher Education and East London: a Case for Social Renewal', in T. Butler and M. Rustin 1996, p353-369.
20. Collini 2012, 2018.

CHAPTER ONE

Anthropology at UEL, 1990-2019

Lionel Sims

In the autumn of 1963, British social anthropologists met at the University College London (UCL) to discuss the implications of the recently published Robbins report on higher education. Daryll Forde, head of department at UCL, persuaded the participants not to engage with the report's recommendation to widen student access to their anthropology courses. Instead, he argued that British social anthropology should concentrate on postgraduate courses and research degrees since, according to him, social anthropology was intrinsically a specialist discipline for a highly selected few. This account was told to me by Mary Douglas in 1993 when she was acting as external reviewer to the accreditation of the new BSc (Hons) Anthropology programme at the University of East London (UEL).[1] Unlike sociology, which enthusiastically embraced the subsequent Robbins expansion, social anthropology remained a minority discipline with few departments and students in British academia, and this continues to be so to this day. Therefore the successful launch of an anthropology degree at UEL in 1993 presents a paradox. Since, as we will see below, the anthropology degree at UEL came out of what is labelled in the Introduction a 'radical and democratic culture' born during its polytechnic origins, then how could this culture embrace such an elitist discipline? The paradox can be resolved by examining the initial conditions, personnel, curriculum, processes and rationale of the anthropology degree at UEL.

The 'radical and democratic culture' at North East London Polytechnic (NELP) was conceived out of the strident radicalism of then director George Brosan's insistence that all degree courses at the new NELP must be revalidated around distinctive new *polytechnic* values, rather than as reheated versions of the old London University external degree courses. But if this culture was then denuded by 1980s Thatcherite neoliberalism, then that would not support the claim of this chapter that the BSc Anthropology programme embodied these radical values, since this course was validated much later in 1993, when NELP had become UEL. But after their conception, pregnancy, birth and maturation, all these founding NELP courses were designed and delivered by newly enlivened academic staff inspired in the spirit of innovation. The locus of the resulting new culture was therefore not the brainchild of the polytechnic director but a *relationship* among the entire staff and student network. And, like all relationships, this new radical and democratic culture had its own history according to the changing political relations in internal and external education policy.

There is a big debate within anthropology on what length of time is required to guarantee immersive knowledge of a culture, and one convincing argument is that twenty years are needed, since on that timescale it is reasonably guaranteed to experience a 'dominance episode' which assaults and lays bare the founding assumptions of a culture.[2] This roughly fits the experience at NELP-PEL-UEL, since our history has been punctuated with two main dominant episodes: one in 1981 provoked by Dr Brosan's attempt to close down four departments and another in 1998 when the vice-chancellor, Frank Gould, attempted his third annual tranche of ninety-or-so compulsory redundancies in a budget-balancing exercise devoid of academic rationale. The resulting staff and student outrage and revolts at both events put a stop to both neoliberal assaults, and protected the staff's confidence and self-esteem to continue to innovate. Our radical and democratic culture therefore had a variable intensity and inhabited different levels at different times. Anthropology at UEL was part of this defence of its radical and democratic culture.

The launch of anthropology at UEL not only came very late but also pivoted on a tiny and radical foundation. Innovation within an existing university social anthropology degree usually begins not as a clean slate but encounters the expectations and traditions of the staff cohorts and generations of anthropologists before it.[3] At UEL, however, the whole enterprise began with one lecture in autumn 1989 smuggled into a discussion on sociological models of the family in a course on the social structure of modern Britain. This course owed much to its own origins in the old external London sociology degree taught previously at West Ham College of Technology and continuing on into NELP-PEL-UEL. The reason for this anthropological discursion was to radically stretch the sociological models of the family in the modern west by comparing them to matrilineal/matrilocal clan formations in some traditional societies. But while this discussion at other universities would commonly stay at the level of cultural relativism, this one lecture introduced methods and data from behavioural ecology, or what was then termed 'sociobiology'. This engagement with the new Darwinism, accompanied by explications from primatology, modern genetics and paleoanthropology, met with great enthusiasm from the students. Unlike the then and now prevalent bio-phobia of many academics in the humanities, this discursion into the 1970s revolution in the natural sciences caught their imagination. They demanded more.

It was on the back of this excitement that it was possible the following year to suggest and win first one option on anthropology within the sociology degree, led by myself, and then another the year after that with the part-time employment of Chris Knight to deliver it. It was the interdisciplinary approach to anthropology that inspired the students, since it allowed for the first time to suggest answers to the discipline's founding question of 'what is it to be human?'. Adopting this American definition of four-field anthropology as integrating social anthropology, biological anthropology, archaeology, linguistics, myth and folklore studies, we also added to it the new discipline of cultural astronomy. Such an approach allowed the conduct of multidisciplinary tests which radically reduced the number of possible narratives for accounting for what made us human. The narrow prescription of twentieth century British social anthropology programmes largely emphasising cultural relativism could not reach this stage of what had been conjectured but not resolved in its nineteenth century formation as 'classical anthropology'. Our aim was, therefore, to return to classical anthropology, but now through the modern methods of the new Darwinism combined with social and cultural anthropology, and start offering testable hypotheses to explain what it is to be human. It was this pan-human project that gained traction among our students and established a radical break with the normal anthropology degree offering.

But the shift from two small option courses into an entirely new anthropology degree needed not just student enthusiasm and one and a quarter members of staff, but a qualitative step change. An opportunity presented itself during the 1992 reorganisation of NELP into the University of East London (UEL). Since all established and new degree courses, now called programmes, had to be validated, it was a time of great flux and open discussions among many staff, frequently outside of the usual disciplinary boundaries. Moments like this are rare in academia, and the prior radical history of NELP had encouraged an open culture which included little reticence to engage with colleagues across the university. Through emails and informal discussions, a call went out for staff with an anthropology background and qualification, but at that time working in another discipline at UEL, to declare an interest in the devising and offering of an anthropology degree. To my surprise, in short order five staff emerged identifying themselves as anthropologists, albeit working in other disciplines, and offered to collaborate. Paul Valentine and later Arnd Schneider from European studies, John McGovern from politics and Gurcharan Virdee and Jayne Ifekwunigwe from sociology all appeared, bringing the total complement to three full-time staff and four fractional staff in a very short time. Later, as the students of the new degree came on stream and progressed through the degree, Camilla Power was appointed as another full-time member of anthropology staff. All of these staff were recent recruits to UEL and had no experience of its polytechnic foundations, yet enthusiastically engaged with and enlarged its radical and democratic culture through sharing the exciting challenge of building a new degree programme.

This self-selected emergence of six other anthropologists allowed the formulation of a full anthropology degree that included, but went beyond, its initial radical niche of an interdisciplinary evolutionary modelling. A common problem we faced was the low profile occupied by anthropology in the public consciousness – the most common misconception being that 'it was something to do with bones'. Our modules therefore had to be translated into accessible punchlines in our publicity material – an example of which is in Box 1.

BOX 1:

In the first year of the degree you will study how cultures both adapt to their environment and adopt their own cosmological and religious concepts, how human culture began in sub-Saharan Africa over one hundred thousand years ago, why the western family does not exist in clan societies, what is sexual morality and is sexual jealousy normal, introductory anthropological theory, carnival from Notting Hill, Rio de Janeiro, Trinidad and Venice, and mask-making and interpretation.

In the second year of the degree you will study more theory, how cultures without governments and political parties nevertheless still have 'politics', why the first kings were dead kings, the system of honour and shame in Mediterranean cultures, how traditional cultures resist the disruption of 'development', how the African diaspora variously influences black identity in many cultures around the world, and the ten-thousand year-old Australasian religion of the rainbow-serpent.

In the third year of the degree you can study whether female biology can empower and whether the human male is a naked ape, what is human language and can chimps and dolphins be trained to talk, how does anthropology construct knowledge, why is it that all around the world persons that monopolise ritual power like priests or shamans frequently adopt an androgynous or gender-ambiguous role, who built Stonehenge, Silbury Hill and Avebury stone circle and why, or you can specialise in the study of traditional societies in Amazonia.

But their integration into an entirely new degree programme was, compared to the usually pre-programmed criteria of traditional anthropology departments, unusually 'open'. All staff were encouraged to devise new anthropology modules that were allied to their own research interests, with the proviso that in their unity they could meet the discipline's understanding of a rounded undergraduate anthropology programme, and which would engage the type of students who enrolled at NELP/UEL and any new student constituency we might attract. The first two of these criteria were contingent factors that, while very unusual, might have happened at any higher education establishment. But it was anthropology staff's understanding of the prospective student intake that, in particular, reveals the radical and democratic stamp of many subject areas at UEL, including that of anthropology.

As mentioned in the Introduction, NELP/PEL/UEL students did not fit the normal academic profile of traditional university entrants. Frequently with poor prior educational experience and success, the mature student entrance requirements gave a second chance to many to continue their education. Early on in the history of NELP, just emerging from the external London degree courses, there was a mismatch between some staff expectations that new students should already possess the study skills associated with traditional university entrants compared to our own students' low confidence to succeed at degree-level study. During this period of West Ham and Barking colleges there was no institutional 'radical or democratic culture', but it emerged from both the director's initial vision and then from lecturing staff rising to the challenge in creating NELP and moving out of the tutelary shadows of London University. This creation of a new confident polytechnic self-identity had many dimensions. In responding and engaging with the management-led insistence on relevance, the vocational applications of many new polytechnic degrees were built into the structure and content of curricula by staff. But down to the very lowest levels of course delivery, radical and democratic innovations were essential to stave off various crises that emerged during the transition from the old external degree to the new polytechnic degrees. The new polytechnic turn to the mature student entry route at first led to very high levels of student dropout during the first few years of some degree courses. Those staff still wedded to the previous external degree culture retained a somewhat detached and under-resourced didactic teaching style unsuited to the expectations of highly motivated but under-equipped anxious polytechnic student entrants. Most staff soon adapted to this by developing new study systems, usually combined with the traditional university didactic pedagogy: studies skills taught within courses, seminar work notes allied to specific provided readings, workshop discussion groups, project work, fieldwork, and dissertations. These required high investment in teaching materials by staff, and drew students into their studies through process-oriented activities within which they drew upon their own life experiences. In turn this mobilised virtual feedback among subject area staff teams that shared the delivery of these new systems.

This new polytechnic culture emphasised high-quality teaching of vocationally relevant courses to mature students. All of this NELP-established 1970s tradition was drawn upon and extended into the new 1990s anthropology degree. For those who are understandably dismayed with the present grade inflation, we struck a radically different course. We ignored the pressure from the way government league table metrics rewarded incentives to drop examinations and, unlike many of our colleagues, devised a diet of assessments that blended assessed coursework, fieldwork, weekly reading and comprehension tests, and end-of-term examinations. Weekly reading tests and marked précis/comprehension for set readings were added as attendance-encouraging marked components of each module. Examinations were retained as a key mode of assessment to maintain the expectations of a high level of student engagement and scholarship. And projects and fieldwork encouraged practical and embodied experience of how to be an anthropologist.

This mixed diet of pedagogies was not typical of anthropology programmes – particularly the emphasis on fieldwork. Ethnographic fieldwork was usually a province for postgraduate or research degrees only, in traditional anthropology courses. This practical engagement with anthropology was much appreciated by students, especially those who at first might be intimidated by the more hypothetico-deductive mode of cultural interpretation associated with the interdisciplinary amalgamation of neo-Darwinism and social anthropology. Starting gently with on-campus ethnographic observation exercises, then as a key part of Paul Valentine's second year anthropological theory course – where a small cultural world was explored and evaluated through the eyes of a paradigm drawn from the anthropological canon – on to a final year dissertation contrasting competing theoretical models through the immersive experience of field data. This mix of high demand testing and high embodied engagement was very successful. Our experience was that this did not lead to high dropout but, on the contrary, a deeply satisfied student body proud of its hard-earned achievements. We found through annual surveys of our students that the most successful were those not with high grade A levels but those who, before coming to UEL, had completed five or more years of continuous employment. This was particularly true of women students. If a year cohort had at least three highly engaged cooperating women students they usually emerged as the informal leadership among all the students,[4] lifting the entire year cohort with them to successful degree completion.

Our BSc Anthropology degree therefore set a requirement for a high level of scholarship from all staff and all students, and successful degree completion required a heavy diet of private study by our students. The curriculum that emerged was shaped not just by individual staff research interests or the expectations of the anthropology profession and university quality assurance requirements, but by paying close attention to the interests of our students. A range of key concepts were raised in the degree. Sex and gender among hunter-gatherers and then all of their many subsequent transformations through power, social class and ethnicity were central themes throughout the degree and in all modules. Seeing gender as a generic transformational template allowed detailed debates on the roots and varieties of social oppression across the full range of human history and regions. Alongside these central themes were subjects informed by staff's specific expertise, as can be seen from some of their publications (Box 2). Through their fieldwork projects, students applied these models to many subcultures, especially those from East London. Over the three years of the degree through participant observation and ethnographic interview by informed consent they were encouraged to carve out a research study route through the degree that would enhance their move to professional outcomes.

BOX 2: SOME PUBLICATIONS BY UEL ANTHROPOLOGY STAFF

Chris Knight, *Blood Relations: Menstruation and the Origins of Culture*, 1995.

Stephen Beckerman and Paul Valentine, *Cultures of Multiple Fathers: The Theory and Practice of Partible Paternity in South America*, 2002.

Lionel Sims, many articles on Stonehenge and origin myths: https://uel.academia.edu/Sims

Camilla Power, many articles on women's power: https://uel.academia.edu/CamillaPower

Arnd Scheider, *Alternative Art and Anthropology: Global Encounters*, 2017.

Jane Ifekwunigwe, *Scattered Belongings: Cultural Paradoxes of Race, Nation and Gender*, 1999.

John McGovern *et al.*, *The Modern State*.

Merl Storr, *Latex and Lingerie*.

Further opportunities for flexibility were built into the degree. We designed the degree around three spines: two compulsory and one optional. Anthropological theory and anthropological practice modules ran through all three years and were compulsory for all BSc-route students. The remaining third of the degree was option courses based on the specialist research areas of staff in which students could choose the areas of anthropology they would like to specialise in. And those students who had demonstrated consistent performance at upper second degree level and above were eligible for applying for the four-year route through the degree by spending one year in an exchange programme with one of the top anthropology departments in the USA at the University of New Mexico. This innovatory programme was devised and managed by Paul Valentine. For every four to eight of our students who a panel of our staff would agree to allow on to this exchange, we would receive an equal number of UNM anthropology students. This allowed both departments to gain from the different suites of skills each had, and was an exciting opportunity for some of our best students.

Many programmes beside anthropology had a small high-performing group among a larger group of average-to-poorly performing students, some of whom might not cope with the initial steep learning curve of degree-level study and possibly drop out of the course within the first year. Looking at anthropology student experience from this other end of those who at first struggled, we made another innovation – a strong emphasis on anthropology field trips during every year of the three-year programme. We found that none of those students who attended the first-year field trip ever failed the degree. This is interesting since the founding circumstances of this field trip were difficult and challenging. Our aim as staff was not to have the usual type of academic field trip where students listen to talking heads in a field somewhere rather than in a classroom – we wanted an experience that in some way simulated the customs of traditional cultures. We knew that this would probably involve music, song, dance, storytelling and reinvented ritual, but felt personally, profoundly ill-equipped to deliver such an experience. We shared these vague ideas with our students in 1995 when we had just first and second year groups moving through the degree, and one mature student suggested a plan. He, like many others during the 1970s and 1980s, had moved out of London and relocated in Wales. Some of his neighbours had set up organic farms and alternative communal living arrangements, and among their number were talented singers, musicians, dancers, storytellers, and they also integrated their communities with various types of re-invented rituals guided by reading books such as *Black Elk Speaks*.[5]

After a weekend trip with this student to meet these people in his network, and booking accommodation for 40 people on a local organic farm, a draft programme was devised, including a Preseli Hills walk, vegetarian cooking by a local chef, circle dancing, singing, storytelling, a sweat lodge ritual and a final evening masquerade feast. The personal dynamic within this programme was strongly egalitarian. The camp was devised and run by a student committee with one or two staff. Crucially, those staff who attended the one-week trip shared and participated in the programme with students and did not lead each session. This was handed over to the local artists and leaders from the Welsh communities who, with payment, were employed to lead and run most of this programme. This became a highly successful formula but only after intense debate among students and staff during the first two field trips. Through argument and laughter, we collectively worked out how to implement what the locals offered and how we should engage with them.

One discovery we made was that the greatest student fear during the week was singing in public. We all learned a lot from this experience and, thankfully, the group brain guided a careful and safeguarding route through all these very new experiences. For most of us, students and staff, coming from a ritually diminished culture many lessons were learned of the need for and demands of building strong cooperative coalitions. The culmination of the week away was a final evening carnivalesque masquerade feast along the theme of the Green Man, with the student election of a carnival king and queen to lead the festival. This field trip was not just confidence building for the students, but for the staff as well. Early on in its design we had saddled ourselves with a rule of no electronic music, only to also discover that we were useless at making our own music. On return to university we therefore filled this gap with a new module on the anthropology of carnival, which included the optional choice of attending samba drumming workshops registered as a student union club. Field trips occurred in each year of the degree tailored to themes emerging from particular modules, ranging from visits to an East End cinema to experience a Bollywood film to visiting the museum of anthropology in Cambridge. In fact one of them, designed as end-of-year and course get-together, still runs with ex-students, staff and others to meet up every summer solstice in the Avebury camp.

One virtue of the intentionally few small university departments was not to over-populate the main professional employments of anthropology graduates in field research in exotic locations, academia, museum curatorship and forensic anthropology. This was such an inbuilt assumption by those trained in this sector that one member of our staff coming from a chequered post-doc career history replied in jest to students who asked for careers advice that 'there was no money in anthropology and if you are after money then become a drug dealer'! To counter this popular misconception of universities teaching irrelevant degrees, we set about devising a comprehensive anthropology careers strategy. The main drift of this strategy was to make explicit throughout the degree how the special skills incorporated in anthropology are eminently transferable to a very wide range of professions (Box 3). The problem was not one of finding a job but building the student's confidence in relating degree success to employment success. This message culminated in a final year session built into the dissertation module on how to get a job. This was a full-day session which would begin with the students being given a photocopy of the latest Wednesday's copy of *The Guardian* graduate job page with the question of which jobs did each of them think they might be eligible for. The invariable response from all the students was that they all felt unable to apply for any of them. From the two to three staff members present came the response – you could apply to *all* of them! The rest of the day was spent demonstrating that they had all the professional and cultural skills to deal with all the advertised jobs.

BOX 3:

Anthropology can provide a route into many professional employments, some of which are:

Health officer, medical researcher and advisor, ecological protection, environment officer, relief and refugee field officer, event management, development planner, race and ethnic relations officer, child protection, care of the elderly officer, human rights officer, tourism and media management, management and projects officer (especially in voluntary and minority rights groups), research (especially in areas of applied evolutionary theory such as health and in social policy and research), teaching (special needs; ESL etc.).

As anthropology trains you to deal with cultural difference, it is particularly suited to prepare you for work abroad, or in special cultural settings in this country.

As I write this chapter in May 2019, the anthropology degree at UEL is being closed down by management. The main intention of the polytechnic initiative by Anthony Crosland in 1963 was to discipline the established private universities' high unit costs and poor vocational relevance.[6] Polytechnics came to deliver degree-qualified students at substantially lower costs and with a far greater emphasis on professional outcomes. The subsequent resulting convergence, with polytechnics becoming universities and universities becoming more like polytechnics, has focused a near-universal acceptance that students not government must pay the costs of degree study, and that there must be explicit focused professional outcomes.[7] While seeming to having done away with the binary system, a new polarisation has emerged between already rich universities and poorly funded new universities. Anthropology degrees in the new universities, and many others in the humanities, do not fit the present management mission for narrowed horizons and narrowly specified vocational outcomes. While I and some other founding staff retired from the university a decade ago, nevertheless for us and those staff now losing the degree and their jobs it is a moment to take stock on whether our work has had some durable value which might inform another possible future.

Our initial conditions of adapting to a non-traditional university intake in the successful delivery of well-taught vocationally relevant degree programmes established a new staff polytechnic culture. Defending this culture against neoliberal assaults in both 1983 and 1998 revealed that, while very senior staff periodically attempted to undermine it, its loyal and true owners had deep roots among staff and students. We developed an innovative curriculum that drew upon the latest research in the life sciences to newly inform the founding concerns of classical anthropology – what is it to be human? And with supportive processes of high scholarly standards, students who would otherwise have not been accepted for degree-level study at traditional universities managed to excel and prove to be an asset to those very same universities when they applied there for masters' courses.

To those concerned at the present trend for grade inflation in degree results, itself an understandable but regrettable response to adapting to the central government grading system, we showed that high standards could be maintained with rigorous assessment techniques which did not artificially boost grades. To those critics who question the worth of mass degree-level provision, we showed that poorly qualified students could unlock their potential through a well-taught and exciting degree course and become a great asset to society when they had graduated. We taught in the spirit that everyone deserves the right to a full education and a lifelong availability of learning and training. Those universities that came through the polytechnic experience have shown how to do this. This would be one way to heal the deep alienation experienced by much of the population of Britain. And to those who view anthropology as a minority interest for a select few, we have shown through the BSc Anthropology degree at UEL what all anthropologists have long known – the psychological unity of all humanity. But we have shown this through the revolution that has taken place over the last fifty years in the life sciences, and through seeing anthropology as the scholarly bridge between science and the humanities – the unifying queen of scholarly disciplines.

Many years ago the French anthropologist Claude Lévi-Strauss left us with a startling image. He asked us to consider what we would do if it was noticed that a planet with intelligent life on it would shortly pass by us, only then to move on and disappear into space forever. Imagine the effort we would make to achieve contact with this civilisation and possibly learn great truths from it. Well, he announced, there are such rapidly disappearing civilisations among us, and they are the traditional cultures that first emerged as hunter-gatherers in the Palaeolithic. One of their truths, expressed by the Trobriand people of the south west Pacific islands and many other traditional cultures, believes that 'a poor man shames us all'.[8] To assist in moving to another possible future we could not do better than ponder upon the implications of the words of these 'primitives'.

Notes

1. See also A. Kuper, *Anthropology and Anthropologists*, Routledge and Kegan Paul: London, 1983, p124.
2. C. Boehm, *Hierarchy in the Forest: The Evolution of Egalitarian Behaviour*, Harvard University Press: London, 2001.

3. Kuper, 1983; A. Barnard, *History and Theory in Anthropology*, Cambridge University Press: Cambridge, 2000.
4. Lionel Sims, 'Course Monitor Project 1985-2000', unpublished.
5. J. Neihardt, *Black Elk Speaks: Being the Life Story of a Holy Man of the Oglala Sioux Holy Man*, State University of New York Press: New York, 1961.
6. M. Shattock, *Making Policy in British Higher Education 1945-2011*, Open University Press: Maidenhead, 2012, pp117-122.
7. J. Pratt, 'Higher education in England and Wales: unification, stratification or diversification?', *Tertium comparationis* 7:1, S, 2001, pp19-27.
8. D. Maybury-Lewis, *Millennium: Tribal Wisdom and the Modern World*, Viking: London, 1992, pp63-90.

CHAPTER TWO

The Architecture School

Christine Hawley

When I started this chapter my first thoughts were to describe as factually as possible the events that transformed the Architecture School at the University of East London (UEL) during the 1980s. It is a 'rags to riches' story of a poor disaffected department becoming one of the most interesting avant-garde workshops of design over a period of ten years. There were many people who contributed to its success but as I was the head of school I wanted to ask myself how much 'nostalgia' would play a part in my description. It is too easy to look back and see everything with a rather rosy glow, or be rather indiscriminate and only remember the positive, so I hope the picture I have painted is fairly honest. There is also the wonderful act of hindsight when, after many years of further experience, you can set its characterisation into a wider context. My observations are not only about the school but also the institution, as I now realise that it is the freedom the institution offers that gives any department a lease of life (or a quick death).

I have taken the precaution of speaking to as many people as I can about their time and experience at UEL, and was reassured that many of my memories were ones that were shared.

There is one other point I would like to draw attention to: in the last thirty-five years methods of representation have changed beyond recognition and the work I talk about in the Architecture School was all done by hand. Both the demands of the industry and the rapid acceleration of digitisation have meant that today's architects (and architectural students) must communicate via the computer. If you are not familiar with digital draughting technology then you are unemployable. Computerised imagery has many great virtues. Its speed and ubiquity makes it indispensable in the construction industry but the software, regardless who is using it, homogenises the information, and the signature that could once be read through a drawing is no longer there – that elusive pencil flourish that characterised the really talented gets lost under the shroud of the computer. There has also been a change in the value system by which the drawing or model could be assessed; there can be of course digital fireworks but these are produced by the very technically competent, not necessarily by the most talented. During the 1980s, all students had to rely on was their own basic skills and their hands, nothing could be disguised by sophisticated software, and for me that made the good work that came from the Architecture School even more special. The illustrations (Figures 1-3, at the end of this chapter) show drawings and models crafted only by hand, perhaps not as slick as contemporary work but I think for that very reason it is much more impressive.

In retrospect I consider my time at the UEL as probably one of the most formative and influential periods of my career. I came to East London (or the North East London Polytechnic as it was then known) in 1982 as a young and fairly inexperienced architectural design teacher. Unlike many traditional disciplines, architecture requires one-to-one teaching over a drawing board with pencil in hand. In many ways there are similarities between architecture and music teaching; it is done demonstrably and through repetition. To say there are enormous cultural differences between architecture schools is something of an understatement. Disciplines such as medicine iron out those discrepancies through a universal demand for faultless A-levels required both by the universities and medicine's regulatory body, but the Royal Institute of British Architects (RIBA) and Architects Registration Board (ARB) who are responsible for setting professional architectural standards have no such strictures. Therefore, the entry requirements are always set by the university – so at Cambridge, the school would demand prohibitively high access criteria and at East London the story was very different.

My own academic background, both as a student and as a teacher, was through the Architectural Association (AA), which was then considered to be the most avant-garde breeding-ground for architectural debate anywhere in the world. By upholding its radical history, it was a place of educational discourse, progressive thinking and political ferment. The people who taught and the visitors who lectured all had a desire, if not to challenge the status quo, then at least to question it. I was simply unaware of just how privileged I was, and when I received an invitation to teach the third year at East London I accepted for a number of reasons. The first was curiosity and probably some subliminal concern about being in a gilded cage which didn't make enough contact with the world outside the doors of the AA at 36 Bedford Square.

I arrived at Holbrook, one of the buildings on the outer fringes of the East London campus, where the floors of the Architecture School were both silent and empty. I could find no staff and no students. After much telephoning I found one student who confidently told me that it was usual to send someone in to get the brief for the term, which was then circulated among the year and the students would then turn up at the end of the term having done the work at home! I had never experienced anything like it. I needed to get everyone to attend and convince them that I was there to give tutorials regularly and on a twice-weekly basis: what I was ignorant of, was that most of them were working because they had to. Unlike the immense privilege of my background, where students were expected and able to study full time, these young people often had dependants of their own, either children or unemployed or disabled parents; they were not only responsible for their own economic survival but also for that of others. The challenge of accommodating and understanding the background of these students was immense and, if I am honest, I struggled. All I was interested in was the quality of work that needed to be produced, but this was all rather academic as my preconceptions and expectations simply did not reflect the extraordinary wealth of experience these young people had.

Architecture relies on a number of attributes and perhaps the most elusive is judgement. Judgement can be acquired over the years through professional experience, academic study and life skills. I was more familiar with those architects who had developed their decision-making skills through professional and academic experience, but the street-wise maturity of the students I now encountered at UEL were like a different tribe, and one to which over time I was to become greatly indebted.

My passage through the school was accelerated by a number of factors. The most important I had known through rumour ever since I started. Due to the RIBA's obsession at the time with 'manpower planning' they were looking to close schools down. I have very little idea whether the reasons were historic or political, but the school at East London was targeted. The Architecture School was to have public funds withdrawn and the school was given three years to die a slow death. It is easy to imagine that no one wanted the job of administering a closure, but the university needed a candidate (as the previous head had departed.) I had no enthusiasm for any form of administration, my job was simply as a design teacher, but (to my horror) I found myself one of two candidates sitting in front of an interview panel chaired by the then rector, Gerry Fowler. Having heard nothing for several days I breathed a sigh of relief, knowing that the poisoned chalice had not been passed in my direction. However, I then received a phone call asking me to return to the Rector's office which I did for yet another interview. The panel seemed to be identical, with identical questions, and at the end I asked why the reprise. Without hesitation, Fowler said the panel and the protocols were identical except for one difference, 'we do not have the chair of governors'. Apparently, this man had objected so vehemently to a female being put in any position of authority, he insisted I be discounted. In retrospect I hugely admired the rector for what he did. This was not simply remedying an injustice, it was demonstrating an act of equality long before its time. I was just aware of his political history as a junior minister in the Labour cabinet, ousted from office with the demise of the Labour government. He was, certainly for me, someone who acted with a set of principles which continued to support the school through what was to be a very testing future.

So the unglamorous job of steering the school through to closure lay ahead, except there was one problem. Since starting, we had drawn to the school a number of brilliant if renegade teachers who would all lose their jobs. Architectural teaching then was largely part time, and young architects eked out a living by patching together practice and part-time jobs in education. So, however little they were earning, it would still represent a significant loss if these jobs were to disappear. However, the most important factor was that the quality of work had materially improved, and students were enthused and motivated, above all in the school.

I had no appetite for closure and so started the long, hard battle, together with colleagues, to regain RIBA accreditation, regain lost UK students and establish the Architecture School at the University of East London as one of the best in the UK. Without dwelling on any of the details here, I need to mention that there was one ambition that unified all the staff, and that was that the quality of education we offered, and that the resulting work should be outstanding. The university system did not grind us to a halt through suffocating, time-wasting bureaucracy, and this simply allowed everyone to get on with their work. I realised many years later what a gift that had been.

As previously mentioned, in the early 1980s RIBA and ARB, in their wisdom, decided to cut the number of architects qualifying, and one of two schools targeted was UEL. This, of course, has catastrophic consequences for any academic department running a professionally validated course, as the government withdraws funds from UK applicants and, if you want to survive financially, you need to attract overseas income. It would be disingenuous to say that the school enjoyed an excellent reputation: it had for many reasons rather 'wilted on the bough'; many who had been employed for years saw the writing on the wall and took early retirement or moved elsewhere, which suddenly gave the school an open door through which some extraordinary teachers and designers entered. It also coincided with a period of economic disruption for the industry, and more good practitioners were available to teach than in previous years. The AA was also a source of fresh 'radical' teaching, and the slightly more attractive remuneration made the school an interesting proposition. Notwithstanding the short-term prospects for everyone, the advantage of the institution was that it was not hide-bound by establishment bureaucracy, and slowly emerged as a ferment of radical marginalised thinkers who were only interested in one thing, and that was the quality of what was produced. It is not an exaggeration to say that for those in any creative field the burden of establishment protocol, unnecessary auditing and time-wasting meetings was an anathema, and so to be liberated from the academic harness that has subsequently emerged was a gift.

I cannot adequately relate how interesting discourse developed, but student work flourished, and staff became involved in work that genuinely pursued the boundaries of knowledge. In hindsight having subsequently moved to University College London, with its panoply of audits, finance committees, health and safety committees – all the framework that, I am sure makes modern educators think an institution 'sound' – it is easy to recognise the freedom we once had and a value system that was not mired in the consequences of career progression.

But life at the school was far from easy. The first cohort of UK students had disappeared and to maintain the critical mass we needed to attract significant numbers of overseas students. The depletion of home students was to last for four years, during which time I, with the support of Gerry Fowler, established campaigns that were to take me to Malaysia, Brunei, India and Singapore. The logistics of such an operation were both difficult and largely unknown, as most architecture schools only considered a tiny handful of overseas applicants. I needed to understand the different religious observances in strict Muslim countries, such as Brunei, and the almost Kafkaesque system of immigration operated by Lunar House in East Croydon. Very slowly the student numbers were stabilising and then slightly increasing, and the wisdom of the management was wonderful in that we were to be left alone to set our house in order.

In parallel with this recruitment strategy was a bid to win back RIBA accreditation, which proved to be a much harder task. However good the apparent results, the prejudice from the profession was deeply ingrained. One also has to remember that context was to play a large part in the shaping of both the staff profile and equally important the burgeoning reputation of the school. For the previous two decades, the Architectural Association had an almost exclusive reputation for being at the forefront of architectural debate, design and radicalism, all of which was expertly propagated and distributed through a range of in-house publications. Sadly the brilliant director of the school died and his legacy began to fade very quickly. This of course was greatly to our advantage as students are always looking over the horizon for 'the next best thing'. Although we had almost lost all our undergraduate UK cohort, we were building the diploma course (post-degree) and attracting brilliant young graduates from

Cambridge, Edinburgh, Liverpool, Bath, and this was changing the culture and the very substance of conversation. While at the beginning of the 1980s UEL's Architecture School was on course for closure, by the end of that decade it had won peons of praise and all the major student awards open to students nationally. UEL had become, quite unwittingly, the alternative to the AA as the 'progressive' school to go to. Success bought some downside in that after Fowler left, the management saw that the Architecture School was not only successful and gathering favourable plaudits, but it was also very profitable financially. And so from a situation of benign neglect, we slowly began to endure a regime that had an altogether tighter grip.

One of the most fascinating things I learned was that exemplary academic exam results were not always the failsafe measure of success. Many of our students had extraordinary practical backgrounds, either from school or from just having to survive, and I felt it was important that we supported the skills they had, rather than force them into a mould they would not comfortably fit. We reopened and expanded our workshop, and it is fair to say that the school pioneered some of the most brilliant model-making in wood, metal, resin, plaster and reconstructed mechanical body parts, together with constructions that were found in skips not only made from objets trouvés but also those made to mechanically function. It is fair to say that the model-making at the Architecture School probably pioneered not only a stylistic course for several decades but also the ways in which architectural discourse could be narrated and demonstrated. This would not have been possible except through the efforts of the staff, who came to the school from diverse and, in some cases, highly unusual backgrounds: painters from Germany, boat-builders and landscape ecologists from the Netherlands, Cambridge historians and, of course, those like me from the AA who had been trained to question the status quo. These people created a community that was in many ways like the Bauhaus but without the formality of acknowledging independent disciplines.

It felt as if the spirit in the school was pioneering and far less regulated than in grander establishments, and it might be reasonable to observe that it was occasionally a bit too much like the wild west for comfort. My approach to bureaucracy was almost nonexistent. I think we operated on the bare minimum of meetings; communication was achieved through personal discussion or group crits in the central space, which became a wonderful lens through which you could see the work of a very special community.

What was started at the Architecture School at UEL at the beginning of the 1980s, and what emerged nearly a decade later, was not the result of a carefully planned and methodically implemented ethos but an organic development that was both intuitive and opportunistic. I believe the word 'opportunity' is important in this school's history as the vacuums that existed and that we took advantage of were just as important as any financial or historic privilege. A school where the academic agenda had little established dogma provided a fertile training ground for the imagination, the ability to think laterally circumnavigating the logical and the sequential – a task made more difficult for some after their blinkered route march through secondary education.

Let me first outline the profile of the students. Many of those who came to the school had dropped through the academic net and were not automatically seeking out exam success. They were open-minded in a very literal sense, willing to experiment and to work in areas that were far beyond their comfort zone. They had also experienced failure or perhaps a feeling that the orthodoxy of schooling held little that was relevant to their future. Having taught students both prior to and subsequent to my employment at East London, I was able to observe an intellectual rigidity from those who had been schooled and disciplined to be conventionally academically outstanding. The education regime within the national system does not seek out eccentricity or original thinking, but an ability to perform prescriptive tasks with predetermined solutions. Therefore, there was a delightful quality of intellectual innocence which many of our students had that liberated them from any ideas of preconceived outcomes. One characteristic of such intellectual liberation is that there is little fear of making mistakes, as the exercises were simply unknown, and this in turn meant that individuals were able to experiment and explore, whether self-consciously or otherwise.

Architecture is unlike many of the classic disciplines – our pursuit of unorthodoxy came through lateral thinking and imagination. The measure of this mental fluidity is hard to quantify, and the response by those who teach tends to be intuitive rather than measured. It was a fortunate set of coincidences that brought together a group of risk-taking academics and an eclectic group of students who were in many ways fearless. Let us be quite candid; neither the staff nor the students were always a match made in heaven. Some young people drifted into the Architecture School out of curiosity, boredom or both, rather than from a passionate commitment to pursue a career in design. Others had wholly mistaken ideas about further education and what a lifetime in architecture might offer. But in the midst of this extraordinary mix were those who would be genuinely surprised by their own talent.

Architecture is a form of visual communication – the production and existence of drawings is central to everything we do – and those experienced architectural teachers know only too well that demonstration and observation are as important as any form of verbal instruction. In the best architectural schools (and offices), the walls, drawing boards and computers are filled with drawings. These drawings are a form of instruction; they are a visible demonstration of what you can and perhaps should not do. The school at UEL had no such precedent, and there was initially very little to look at. However, the building at Holbrook was an absolute gift in that, being designed originally as a Victorian board school, there were classrooms/studios surrounding a large airy space, all of which were double height. We had acquired, completely by accident, the perfect configuration in which to teach and display drawings and models. The 'crit', a universal technique for publicly reviewing student work, is often maligned, as it is public and if it does not go well it can be a humiliating test. The architecture student does not have the luxury of ignominious private exam failure, but the rooms at Holbrook allowed an audience to discreetly view the work without the discomfort of the interviewee being publicly exposed. The central space was, by contrast, a wonderful arena in which to have grand juries, examinations and exhibitions – a fabulous platform where we could exhibit the very best the school could produce. The design was, of course, based around the functional needs of a Victorian school where the classrooms were all light and high ceilinged, with all being clearly visible from the head's office raised on the mezzanine. This was a nuclear spatial arrangement that wasted little space and provided the perfect environment for teaching, both in the nineteenth and the twentieth century.

The student community was not only unusual in its highly varied academic and technical mix but also in the social and ethnic origin of the groups. Many academic communities now strive for a balance of ethnicity and socio-economic backgrounds, but at that time the Architecture School had a very particular reason for pursuing overseas students, and the reasons were not simply to widen cultural diversity. There were absolute financial imperatives; as the RIBA had withdrawn recognition and the government would no longer fund UK students, we were compelled to seek students from overseas to provide funding. Fortunately, the withdrawal of funds from UK students was incremental and, if events had gone to course with no intervention, the school should have taken five years to close down. In reality the school would have closed far sooner than this, because if the critical mass dwindled and the staff numbers dropped, lack of morale would have compelled most students to move elsewhere long before the five years was complete. So, there was a binary choice – either wait for the numbers of both staff and student to wither or try and keep both the staff and student numbers and critical mass intact, not only to survive but to build a creative community that was stronger than before.

The imperative was driven partly through the visceral need to survive and partly through anger at being closed for politically and self-interested professional reasons. It will take an historic overview to understand what the waves of manpower planning did to the professions. It neither worked then nor does it work now.

In the 1980s, the British government established an arrangement named 'the Northern Consortium' where a group of six northern universities actively pursued overseas students, and so the traditional quotas that would have previously been distributed across the HE sector were now concentrated in the northern schools. This situation made overseas recruitment a little more complex and challenging, as we were obliged to adopt a much more proactive policy. The Architecture School needed overseas income if it was going to survive, and in the first year of government withdrawal of funds we needed a complete cohort from outside the UK. As a studio teacher whose interests lay in teaching design, the dark arts practised by the Head of School had been not only a mystery but of little interest to me. Little did I realise that I now not only had responsibility to establish and steer the academic direction but also be the loudest advocate for our small school hidden away in the East End of London. I knew absolutely nothing about recruitment or where are potential markets were, but was fortunate enough to be supported by UEL's International Office who steered me towards the Far East.

Understanding the international academic market is not something I was trained to consider, but it had to become a pivotal part of the school's strategy; without international students for the following four years, the school would simply have had to close. It is an understatement to say we did not have the marketing infrastructure in the school – no publication, no institutional reputation, no subject reputation. It was therefore a piece of political good fortune that the British Council still had a vested interest in furthering British education overseas, for it was through their offices that I was introduced to the education fairs and innumerable secondary schools where relentless promotional discussion took place. It was perhaps for the first time that I had to think not just about architectural ideology but educational ideology, and to persuade young students (and their parents) that travelling thousands of miles to the other side of the world to receive tertiary education would be a good thing. The cultural compatibilities were complex and sometimes strange. Addressing gender-segregated teenagers in Brunei was difficult, and even more difficult was to answer why this would not happen at UEL. I believe we recruited a small number of men from Brunei, but no women. Religious sectarianism was a reality in many of the communities I visited, and it quickly emerged that if we were to have any effect recruiting in this part of the world we needed to acknowledge that provision needed to be made for them in the Architecture School. The consequences of this recruitment policy were unforeseen, yet it introduced a cultural dynamic that few English university schools had then encountered.

The Architecture School slowly acquired a student body that was multilingual, multi-faith and multicultural. This may sound like a recipe for the ultimate politically correct community, but the reality posed some very real challenges about the art of communication for both staff and students. We were seeing a first year that was almost exclusively overseas, and the remaining years almost exclusively home-based students. The teaching structure as you move to the later years was a vertical unit system, so it was vital that our overseas and UK students didn't form ethnic cliques, which with some judicious organisation we managed to avoid. Another sensitive issue that arises with foreign students is that if many of them come from the same community they will speak their native tongue and, over time, it becomes much harder to communicate the subtlety, technicality and the abstraction of language used to steer any architectural narrative. The learning curve was huge for both sides, and utility of the drawn image became an even more critical form of communication. But architects are placed in a myriad of situations where they have to advocate a concept, explain a technicality or a point of law, so linguistic skills needed to be mastered.

One of the great benefits of UEL Architecture School at this time was that the staff were wholly enthusiastic about the challenges we faced, and all manner of devices and demonstration were developed to both communicate and extend the reach of each student. As many of the students did not arrive with a perfect set of A-level results, we exploited the skills that they did have, and many of them were both practical thinkers and hugely creative fabricators. Holbrook had developed a wonderful workshop with truly dedicated staff, and many of the projects were not designed over the drawing board but in the workshop. It is worth noting that in the 1980s, most architecture schools produced work through drawings, with only a cursory nod to white card massing models –very simple models on white cards, with no detail, used primarily to establish the correct scale of a building. Holbrook provided the facilities to saw, bend, weld and caste in timber, metal and plaster. Many of the three-dimensional models went far beyond the orthodoxy of the workshop and included fabric, feathers, leather, cannibalised machine parts – in fact anything that resonated with the story of the design. The pioneering work that emerged from the studios, and especially the workshop, attempted to combine poetic narrative with the hard practicality of fabrication, and I believe that the school was one of the first to introduce electronics, lighting and film into the finished assemblies. One can speculate that much of this 'innovative' work was due to the lack of formal inhibition, because the traditional rules of academe, usually introduced in secondary schools, were not as firmly imprinted, but what there was among many, was an imaginative daring that was often brilliantly created as a three-dimensional object that both performed and worked.

The staff were drawn from disparate backgrounds – Flemish practitioners, artists, German conceptual thinkers, boat-builders, Cambridge graduates, East End builders, film makers and, of course, those who came from local practices. This mix had much greater diversity than many university schools and, because the building was fairly small and the work observable, skills became a vital teaching tool. In some ways I would like to draw some parallels with the short-lived Bauhaus, where a range of creative skills from different craft disciplines had a huge influence over what was produced. It would be quite wrong to say the work became homogenous; each 'unit' maintained its own credibility, but you could make opportunistic absorption. What they learned was to transpose skills demonstrated elsewhere in the school. The power of collective physical demonstration is one of the most forceful influences on the development of architectural work within an academic environment. As with many students in tertiary education, using peer advice and being encouraged to research independently is not only a vital support for the teaching staff but a vital part of each student's self-development. However, the concept and practice of self-driven learning was much more prevalent within the culture of northern Europe than the more closely instructed cultures of the Far East, and persuading some students from the global south that it was acceptable to both question and be opinionated took some time. With some very distinct cultural patterns emerging from this unlikely group of university students, there was work that challenged us as teaching staff, and much of it was outstanding.

As time went on, the number of overseas students in the lower years increased while those in the upper part of the school years four and five we expected to stay UK stable, but this was not quite the case. The withdrawal of UK/EU students was designed to take place over five years (ie the full duration of the course), not all at once. This was to our advantage, as we were able to mount a campaign targeting the RIBA, ARB and HEFCE – all the agencies that were attempting to put us out of business. Therefore we lost students on a year-by- year basis. The campaign was won after the third year when we had maintained the upper years (fourth and fifth), and were then able to reintroduce UK students back into the first year If we were to attract the best students accessible to us we had to demonstrate the quality of work the school was capable of, so another tool in the armoury was a series of modestly collated brochures which I and others could circulate among a wide audience, whether it be school leavers, careers advisers or just a wider community of friends. But the real battle existed with the RIBA and the ARB (who assign architects their professional qualification and title), who at that time were fixated with issues of manpower planning. I had several visits to the senior partners of big- to medium-size practices, all of whom had been concerned by the reduction in work and how architectural practices had to manage. What was rarely discussed within the school was that the profession was going through historical changes in that the traditional role of the architect as the principal designer and absolute authority was being eroded away. Emerging within the construction sector were people who would project- manage, cost control, undertake delivery and supervise on site any complexity sequencing, and the supervision of a plethora of subcontractors.

The world around the architectural profession was changing and the traditional big clients were now going straight to large contractors or to design-and-build companies. In the construction world the balance had changed, and the imperatives were on cost control efficiency and technical speed. The profession I feel (and this is just my view) was not keeping pace with change.

Everyone who came to work at the Architecture School at UEL was aware of its challenges.

When I first arrived at the school it was just about to be closed down and government funding was withdrawn. When I left, the students at UEL had won the RIBA bronze and silver medals, and the work produced from everyone was a testament to its experimental reputation. As the RIBA and ARB finally relented and government funds were reintroduced, the school had become educationally pioneering, proudly demonstrating that in the face of adversity a global reputation could be established.

These illustrations and model show a final-year thesis project by Chris Thurlbourne and Aaron Davies, which was submitted to the RIBA awards and won the top prize of the Silver Medal.

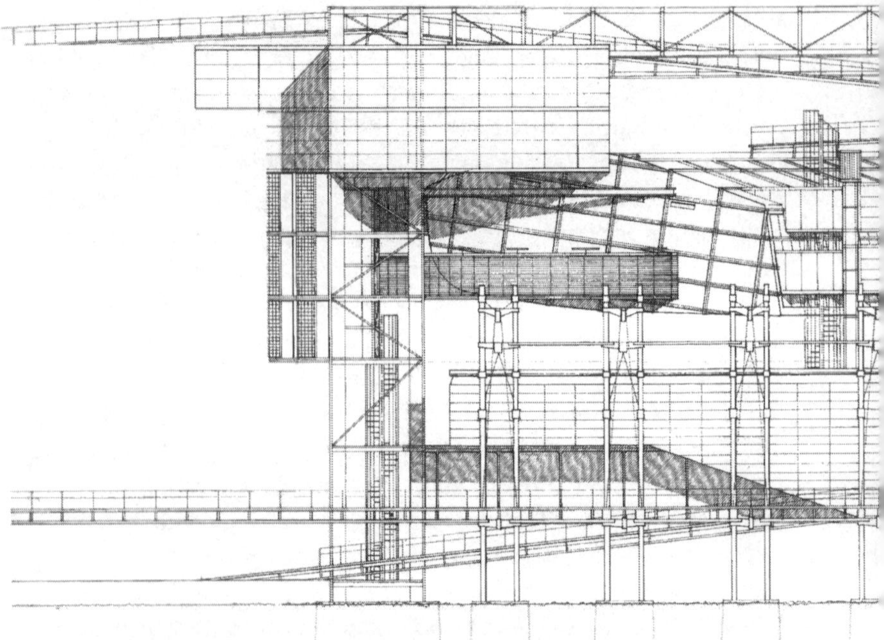

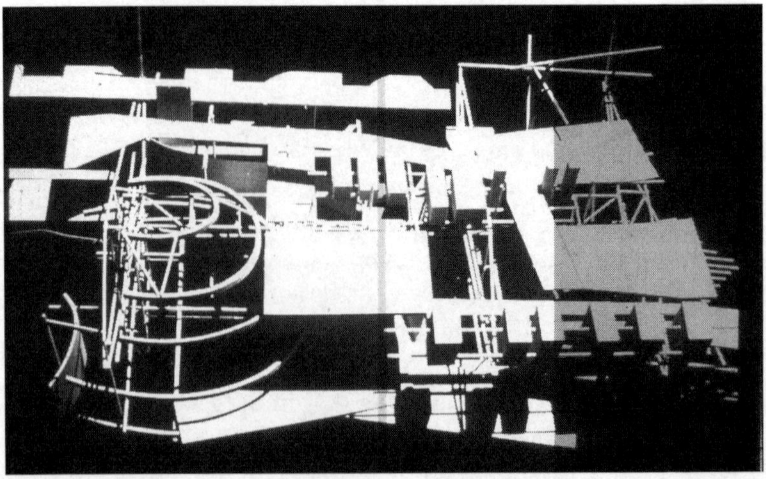

Figure 2 Information Archive and London Assembly by Chris Thurlbourne and Aaron Davies.

Figure 1 Information Archive and London Assembly by Chris Thurlbourne and Aaron Davies.

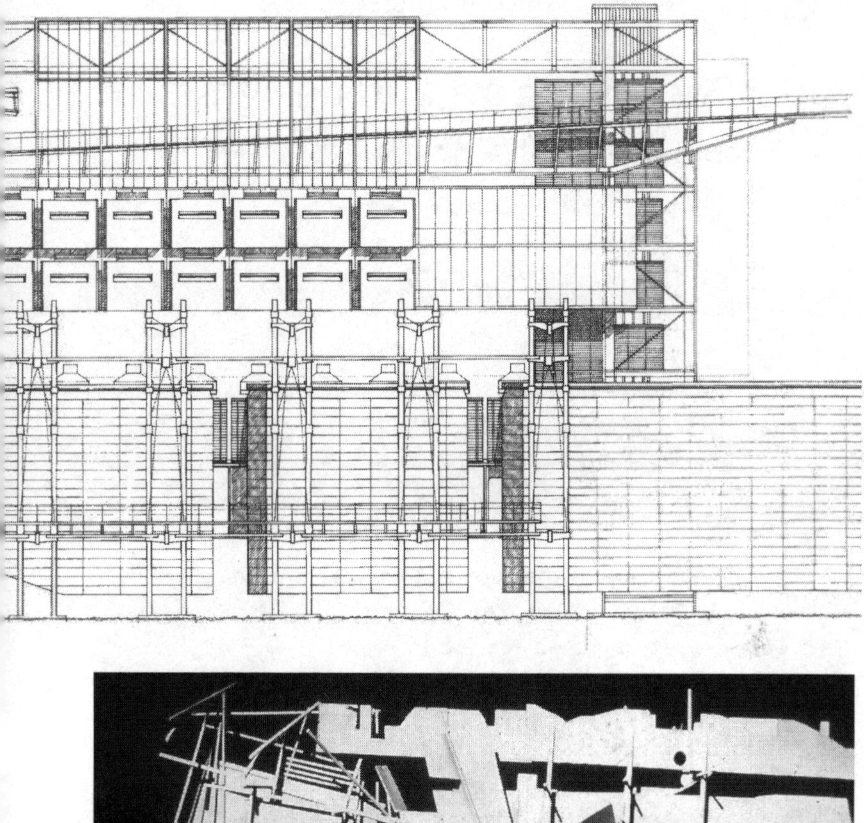

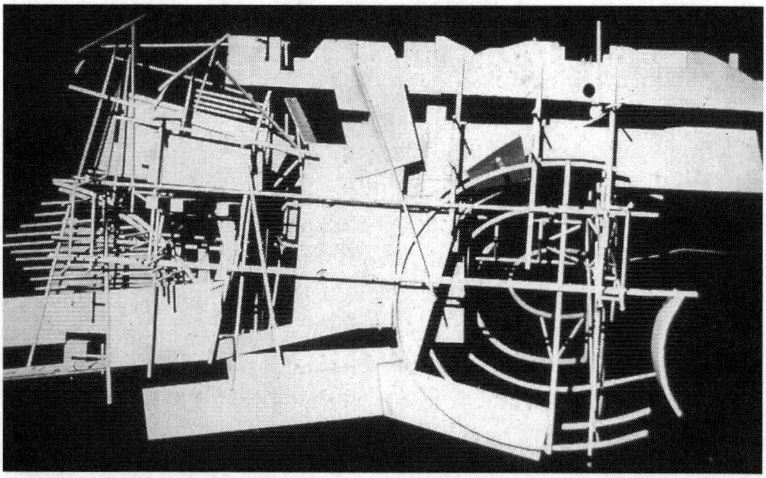

Figure 3 Information Archive and London Assembly by Chris Thurlbourne and Aaron Davies.

CHAPTER THREE

Rethinking art and design in the 1970s

David Page

This is a personal view of art and design in North East London Polytechnic, where I was involved, so it is not a complete or objective account. Many interesting people and fine teachers, and no students, are named. I beg their pardon: I learned a lot from both groups.

> 'Art students occupy a specially chaotic corner in the chaotic scene of higher education', Tom Nairn and Jim Singh-Sandhu in *Student Power,* Penguin Special, 1969.

It was Eric Robinson who encouraged me to come to the North East London Poly (NELP) in 1969. He had addressed a jam-packed meeting of the Association of Members of Hornsey College of Art (AMHCA) in my front room in Hanley Road, N4, in summer 1968, standing proud of the crowd, like the soap-box orator that he enjoyed being. He thought I was in touch with something – and I was.

The Hornsey College of Art revolt in May 1968 had been sparked off by a small, loosely political group of students: it evolved into a much more heterogeneous bulk of students, collaborating with sympathetic staff and technicians. Although it was initiated politically, the event was largely about the deficiencies of art and design education, after eight years of major change in the sector, at all levels, and how to remedy them. Everything had been questioned, structure and content. Six weeks of intense argument and analysis eventually brought it round again to everyday politics, that is to say government, because few of the problems, which were hierarchical, could finally be solved outside the national political arena. To our surprise, national government said there was nothing it could do: either it was someone else's problem, or (Shirley Williams, Secretary of State for Education in this case) that the government could not afford to get another bloody nose interfering in local authority territory. So who exactly was in charge?, we all asked, not knowing that this was an endless-loop problem. In the meantime, however, an AMHCA general meeting was probably the least sectarian debate to be found anywhere in 1968, because it started from highly specific experience and evolved a politics to fit as it went along.

At some point during the sit-in, one of Hornsey's distinguished art historians (Susie Lang), engaging a group of us, radical staff and students, shouted: 'Well, if that's what you want, why don't you go to Mos-kau?'. It was not worth trying to disentangle her assumptions: we went to NELP instead.

Separately, after the Hornsey sit-in, a number of us from Hornsey joined NELP's Art and Design School, with our own perception of the problems of the art and design sector and our own mental version of 'what is to be done?' However, first there was the situation on the ground. Walthamstow School of Art had entered NELP with a foundation course, a two-year graphics course, scientific photography, fine art and fashion/textile courses. The graphics course was run out, since students from a two-year course would not be able to compete on the market against the many from three-year courses, and the (very successful) one-year foundation course was also later closed as part of a local turf war.

Paradoxically, the first job I was given was to bureaucratise art and design (A&D). The national art and design sector had grown up independent of other teaching institutions. Students usually worked in college most of their working day, interacting with a mainly practitioner staff (full and part time), making and doing. Theory was mainly intuited through practice, by learning and applying, skills. One of the graffiti in the Hornsey male student fine art loo read, 'My mind does not work, but my work does not mind'. There was little tradition at staff level of memos, reports, position papers etc., which were common in large academic organisations, and which were mostly viewed in A&D with various degrees of scorn. In return for which the deputy director, Eric Robinson, refused to agree the A&D budget for the coming year. 'I can't get any sense out of them', he said. 'Get them to come up with a coherent understandable statement of what they plan to do; I won't pass their budget until I receive that!'. Accordingly I set out to get an agreed statement, and to generate a sufficient weight of memos, position papers, etc. to convince the poly that we qualified as normal. There was no resistance in A&D so long as somebody else was willing to write the stuff. A rumour reached me that I was Eric's new hatchet-man: the fact was more mundane; I was told to put them to the pen, not the sword.

But old attitudes died hard. At one stage Stuart Ray was in charge of A&D (he had been a worthy head of Walthamstow School of Art prior to the formation of the poly), when we were yet again moved, from custom-built accommodation in Walthamstow to a former YMCA in Plaistow. He hadn't much time for memos, regarding them as redundant verbiage (which they often were), so he put them in his waste-paper basket. His diligent secretary would then go through the basket and re-present the ones which looked important in the next day's in-tray. After a while Stuart twigged what was happening so he slid them out of the window instead. Later on, a visiting deputy director was outraged to run into 'confidential' and 'highly confidential' papers blowing round the carpark.

The back story

The ethos of the schools of art and design was one of the factors which bore on NELP's art and design. The schools had been set up after the report of the Select Committee on Arts and Manufactures, 1836. Britain had been falling badly behind France, Prussia and Bavaria in the 'direct, practical application of the Arts to Manufactures', and so a system was set up which eventually produced schools of art and design in larger towns, particularly in the industrial north.

These were intended to train designers and design technicians, especially to serve the local industries of the time, but also became tangled up with a parallel desire to produce local academies so that fine art should be nurtured as well. From the start this led to confusion – but, as Harry Munn remarked, the fact that the schools had muddled aims also made it hard to shoot them down. Their buildings, whether ample and imposing, like the Norwich School, or mainly Nissen huts, like Southend, were dedicated spaces with attendant facilities. The schools were local and provided for a range of local need well after the second world war, alongside their full-time courses. My mother went to classes in pottery and cabinetmaking at Southend Art School, as well as to afternoon painting classes – known as 'the mums' classes'; I myself went to evening life-drawing classes before I went to university (and was consequently lucky enough to draw Quentin Crisp). The result of this engagement with all levels of the community was a degree of local solidarity. In Southend, when we organised an exhibition of paintings, mostly by Southend Art School graduates, and with a substantial number of abstract paintings, we were denounced on the letter pages of the *Southend Standard* as corrupters of the young (some of us were teachers). But in the next issue there was a strong defence by people who knew the art school because they attended its part-time classes, along the lines of, 'leave them alone: we know them and they're all right!'. Local solidarity, at least in principle, was one of the objectives of the Eric Robinson doctrine.

Much of the temper of the schools derived from the nature of their intake, which reunited those who had been divided by the 11+ examination between high school, secondary mod (the residue) and (if available) secondary tech, along with 11+ 'failures' whose secondary education had been in private schools. Another facet of their nature was that they were broadly gender-balanced, though much of the intake might previously have been in single-sex schools. Most important of all, the schools were a very valuable conduit into further education and employment for working-class kids with visual/tactile ability, particularly since, in spite of the official position, statutory entry requirements were not rigorously applied. At all events, the schools had produced a coherent community locally, and one nationally to which former A&D students felt allegiance.

Structurally, the schools of art and design were, like secondary schools at the time, autocracies, at best benevolent ones, with a principal and heads of department. As late as 1970, the Summerson report (*The Structure of Art and Design Education in the Further Education Sector*) noted its 'ongoing concern' with the nature of governing bodies, without actually specifying how they should be constituted, so naturally it did not specify what the *internal* structures should be. The principal of Hornsey College of Art, being asked by official visitors about his academic board, confected one on the spot out of thin air, to the surprise of senior staff present, who found that they were among its members.

The nationally recognised course taught in the schools of art and design after the second world war had been the National Diploma in Design (NDD), which consisted of a two-year Intermediate followed by a two-year National Diploma in Design course; this had pluses (more inclusive and generalist), and minuses (a clumsy national examination and too craft-based). But the ministry's prime objective was to cut the number of students and courses, and eventually also the length of courses (it assumed that the new one-year foundation course leading to the three year DipAD could ultimately be subsumed by school sixth-forms), and lastly to introduce a class system divided between new quasi-degree graduate courses and cheaper 'technician' courses. (The only difference between Hornsey's DipAD graphics and vocational graphics courses was that the former had stainless steel photographic developing trays and the latter had plastic. Their students emerged to compete for exactly the same jobs.) The 'slimming' objective was quite blatant: Sir William Coldstream told Gordon Lawrence: 'We inherited an enormous number of art schools. We were appointed to get rid of art schools since it was regarded as uneconomic even if the small schools pooled resources'. Gordon Lawrence's study of art education policy-making led him to this conclusion:

> Throughout, it was clear that there would be no attempt to develop a democratic educational structure, which would involve a debate about the educational issues. One can read the minutes of the NACAE ['Coldstream'] and the NCDAD ['Summerson'] committee meetings [the reforming and implementing bodies] and encounter in the ten and twelve years of their respective lives no significant concern with any form of educational issue and certainly no debate about their collective

> purpose in terms other than the politically expedient. What emerges is a sterile debate covertly legitimising fundamental changes in the organisation of the provision, reducing its scope and potential for development. The argument about education never took place.[1]

The Hornsey revolt, which began in a small way over frozen student union funds, ultimately became a wholesale critique of the botched reforms of Coldstream/Summerson. At Hornsey College of Art main building on Crouch End Hill there was a long sequence of seminars discussing aspects of A&D education and proposing new initiatives: these were published locally as Hornsey document one and so on. The author of the chapter in *The Hornsey Affair* on the educational debate, P B-D, (initials were used throughout the book, to avoid the cult of personality), summarised it as follows:

> The principal subjects which dominated all the educational debates ... were, first of all, the conditions of entry into our sphere of higher education; secondly, the problem of beginning studies (and, by implication, of art education in schools); thirdly, the question of specialisation (the old structure was largely ruled by rigid specialisation); fourth, the outdated distinction between 'diploma' and 'vocational' courses in art education; and fifth, the conception of an 'open-ended' type of education with more freedom and flexibility built into it than the old one we were rejecting.[2]

The debate at Hornsey was remarkable in engaging those involved in the sector and many outside it in politics and the arts. For example, Sir John Summerson attended a meeting of staff and students, and joined in the debate. He admitted that the five O-level hurdle to entrance into the DipAD (fiercely resented and contested at the time) was merely 'to make art education respectable'. On the entry loophole he said: 'It's a doorway – but you think it should be a triumphal arch. No one wants to keep talent out of the art schools. I don't think there is any pressure behind the barrier'. When he left he was applauded by the assembly, as much for his willingness to debate as for what he said. Joan Littlewood and Peter Brook sat in (silently) on the seminar that wrote document eleven, while Henry Moore contributed to sit-in funds. Buckminster Fuller came, spoke and answered questions for eight hours.

We need to remember that the five O-level barrier was a high one. *Greater London Statistics* for 1969-70 showed that the percentage of school leavers 'with no GCSEs or CSEs of grade 3 or better' was 38 per cent. This fact did not stop pressure from the authorities to raise it to two A-levels.

The communication design course at NELP

So it was with the concerns of the Hornsey debate fresh in mind that many of us embarked on educational development in NELP. The faculty received external advice that it should devise and prepare for recognition a broad media design course, since the field was already full of straight 'graphic design' courses. Our objective, once we were given the go-ahead, became to create a design course which would primarily equip a generalist, as opposed to a specialist, focused on a basic understanding of the process of communication, rather than on any one communication technology, and which nonetheless equipped a student to work in, or successfully commission work in, those technologies, and which emphasised the extent to which the present and coming communication world required coordinated teamworking by a wide group of workers with individual skills. We anticipated continuous change, though perhaps not the speed at which change would alter the scene. (Computing was at an early stage of development on the NELP Walthamstow site – the computer at that time, programmed in part by a member of NELP fine art, took three hours to draw a table in perspective, seen from an elevated viewpoint!)

Of course there would be problems, partly because our aims did not fit the mindset of the post-Coldstream A&D system. For example, when the Council for National Academic Awards (CNAA) took over the Summerson Council, it failed to reform the heterogenic categories into which courses were sorted (fine art, fashion-textile, interior design and graphic design) and their existing boards, which had already rigidified, quite apart from rethinking the bolt-on studies (art history and complementary studies – undefined – with a dash of fine art) which were, as Summerson said, there for respectability – as if there were no inherent intellectual content in the practice of A&D itself. Hence communication design was classified part of graphic design, whereas we saw this as a subset of communication design.

A more immediate problem was that we had to have a course on the ground before we could submit it for recognition. There was no difficulty attracting students (we advertised in *Time Out*), and many prospective students at the time were very happy to have found a berth. The 1975 submission document grew out of the course practice from its beginnings as a college diploma course. What the course set out to do is described (using the sublegal jargon of submissions) in the Aims and Objectives of the 1980 Resubmission Document for CNAA (revised from the first, successful, submission in 1973).

Aims

The aim of the course is to develop a graduate in Communication Design who:

1. operates in a wide communications framework, working as a designer and/or commissioning and monitoring the work of others
2. through practice can handle a wide range of generally available communication media
3. has the ability to adapt to any future developments
4. understands the social and cultural context in which communication takes place.

Objectives for student achievement of the course are:

Professional competence in handling a design task so as to be able to:

1. identify communication problems and then the means to be used to solve them
2. comprehend the context in which a communication design task is to be carried out
3. define the information need relating to the task

4. gather, select, utilise and present such written, graphical or aural information as are relevant to those needs
5. state possible solutions and evaluate them
6. realise selected solutions and/or supervise their realisation in appropriate media
7. evaluate the success of those realised solutions.

And have the ability to:

8. operate with technical skill and perceptiveness in the areas of photography, video/film/audio, typographics, drawing, written and spoken language
9. commission work in the above areas
10. work successfully in collaboration with others with others and to organise group activity
11. to consider a given communication critically, to relate it to its cultural context, and to evaluate it.

The course set out to provide a student with a basic competence in its areas in the first two years. In the final year the student was to present a programme, to be completed that year, to a course board of studies, which would have to be satisfied that it was properly conceived and achievable. In some cases a group of students would need to combine to carry out the work (creating a video programme, for instance), and all members of the team would then have to commit to it, and be judged by it.

We started new students with a week of communication games (developed from originals devised by John Rae) so that they could explore some of the problems of communication in a simulation, and second so that they got to know one another, and staff, to engender more social coherence right at the start of the first year. These games were meant to be relaxed, but (we found) could become stressful, as when one group of students, after putting some demands according to the game process, locked their partner group in one of the rooms – not appreciated by some students who had fled the Chilean dictatorship.

Later, when we had acquired a second year, we began a practice of interviewing prospective students with a team of two staff and one second-year student, hoping that this would introduce a further social bond into the course. On one occasion, after initial interview the two staff discussed the applicant, who was qualified and whom they thought suitable, but the student member said 'No way'. 'Why not?', asked the staff. 'Because you can't make a sow's ear out of a silk purse'. The applicant was accepted – but did drop out after the first year. When likely applicants came who did not have the necessary qualifications or experience, we sent them away to do some tasks and to come back within a few weeks. Most of those who actually did the work and came back were accepted, keeping open Sir John's triumphal arch, not to mention CNAA's 'ability to benefit'.

Basically the course alternated for the first two years between training blocks, through which students learned skills in communication technologies, and projects which exercised those skills in the context of a communication problem to be solved. The final year consisted of projects proposed by the student to a course board, which scrutinised them for feasibility before endorsing them.

An example of an early staff and student project was entitled 'Problems of patient access to Moorfields Eye Hospital' (1972), carried out with the cooperation of the hospital management and producing a report to them. The hospital was on a busy road (City Road) with pedestrian crossings, subways and bus stops. Many of its patients, by definition, had bad eyesight and encountered difficulties getting to and leaving the hospital. Communication design students had to investigate the site, draw up and administer an (optional) questionnaire for patients, define recommendations, write, design and print a report with recommendations, and make and edit a film.

A later project by two students produced a documentary film about a deaf person in employment, and dealt with the difficulty of understanding the speech of deaf people that might put off a potential employer. The process of watching the film in itself gave members of the audience an incremental ability to understand the speech of the subject, and to appreciate his integration with other workers.

Both these examples show a broad social purpose, but the course accepted that while purposes might range to work carried out without an ulterior motive (i.e. making art), that work should always be able to be judged by its ability to communicate effectively to its proposed audience.

Naturally there were problems at all levels. We were proposing a new kind of course – there was no template and no tradition: we had to feel our way to a process which worked well in practice rather than neatly on paper. We did level with students, explaining to them that this was not like other courses – but for them, this was the only course they were on, their present reality. Another struggle was to find understanding and sympathetic external examiners who would think outside the DipAD box (which the CNAA had uncritically adopted), something we did achieve by 1980. To illustrate the problem: in the case of a piece of student work that had involved considerable historical research and the writing of a radio script, the fact that the script had then been accepted and broadcast by BBC Radio seemed to us to mark that piece of work by definition a First – not so to the external examiner. This problem was not confined to communication design – a fine art student produced a fine thesis composed of interviews with sculptors who had made their reputation in the 1950s. Clearly not understanding the preparatory work, discrimination and finesse required by a successful interview, her external examiner declared, 'Oh no, she just wrote down what they said'. (The interviews were so good that some of the sculptors demanded a cast-iron guarantee from NELP that the work would *not* be published.)

All of this took place in a period of considerable upheaval – NELP in its expansionist phase gave as rough a ride to its members as in the contracting phase which followed. George Brosan went from aspiring to create the Polytechnic of the Outer Circle line, with a continental campus, to closing down departments, perhaps to earn credit from a government which demanded cuts with everything. There were also many moments of surreal comedy. On one occasion in academic board, we were told that we had been validating courses in an institution in Cyprus. Neither the director nor the academic board had known anything about this. On another occasion a deputy director was sent to South Africa to inspect a redundant cruise ship, which, it was suggested, could be sailed back to Docklands to provide student accommodation. The student union duly organised demos with the slogan 'No to the hulks'!

The communication design course started off with serious problems of space, staffing and equipment. Art and Design had a small pre-existing graphics course, but its resources only provided about a quarter of what we needed for the proposed new degree course. The rooms we expected for a first-year intake were not ready on time, so we had to improvise a programme for the time being. In the second year of the new course, Waltham Forest decided to refurbish the central heating system, which took rooms out of service and operated in a seemingly random way. NELP's accommodation planners, grappling with this, seemed not to understand that A&D courses depended on permanently available base rooms and facilities (they were perhaps more familiar with lecture and seminar-based courses, which are inherently more flexible). Staffing allocation was inadequate, and necessary equipment was not in place. Eventually students on the course brought in lawyers, at which point the director found resources and promised more (George Brosan was remarkably cool and pragmatically effective in the meeting about this). These students were also given an extra term's tuition.

To add to the chequered nature of the first years of the course, there was along the way some dissension among staff which, in retrospect, seems to have been primarily about the weight to be given to competence in individual media skills, and a demonstration, on the other hand, that a consciousness of the process of information had informed the pursuit of any particular project. What emerged was the difficulty of keeping these two in balance – perhaps this was the main problem of the course. At all events, there were four changes of course leader in a relatively short period, the household management was for a while not properly carried out, standards fell, and for two years the course was not allowed to recruit a first year.

Closure of the communication design course

By the time of the planned 1980 re-submission to CNAA, most of the major operational course problems had been solved: the rooms, staff and equipment were in place; the staff were agreed about the tenor of the course as presented in the new document; the external examiners were committed and supportive; and we had spent a great deal of staff time preparing the course and its documentation. Some former communication design students agreed to come and support the CNAA course re-application meeting. But the 1980 resubmission never took place, because the director pulled the plug and did not arrange the planned meeting with CNAA. One of the external examiners (Dr Philip Corrigan) wrote to him, saying, among other things:

> I was, frankly, appalled to hear of the closing of the communication design course, for which I have served as an external examiner for some years ... The CD course was one of the few known to me which attempted to hold to a programme of contextually informed practice ... But we also need, and I think CD attempted this, to avoid both the accentuated aesthetics of much film work, or the institutionalised informatics amongst most graphic design and media work, to encourage, in short, design committed to a plurality of aesthetic, communicative and, yes, political modes, if the term informational democracy is to have any real content. (Letter, 2 February 1981)

The director replied:

> I am sorry to hear that you feel the closure of the communication design course has such far-reaching consequences. We all know of course – especially you – of the troubled history it has had. However, it ran out of time administratively, and there is nothing I can do in the present constrained economic environment. It is a pity but I suppose all I can say is that the course was the first to be affected by the cuts. (Letter, 9 February 1981)

Personal postscript

After the demise of communication design I did a variety of teaching and admin. But austerity ruled: it seemed that there would be no improvement in the immediate future. I checked this with Tom Whiteread (a geographer whose wife and daughter were artists) who was at last a first-rate head of department for A&D, and he agreed. Then Tom became visibly very ill. I rang George Brosan and said, 'Tom Whiteread is seriously ill: he's too committed to stay away, but if he's not sent home he'll end up dying on the premises'. George said, 'Good Lord, nobody told me', but he acted on it at once, and Tom went home. Another friend gone.

I couldn't face a life of administration – teaching (and being in turn taught by) students had been what made work worthwhile – so I took 'early retirement'. The package included a year of 'retraining' on full pay, so I opted to enrol on the degree by independent study at NELP – advantageous for the poly as the ministry would pay half my wages that year, which I would spend painting and drawing (I had always been a painter), supervised by my old friend Stuart Ray. Sadly, Stuart died suddenly before he could supervise me.

So I ended up as a NELP student, doing the degree by independent study, a course about which I had some reservations, effectively in the fine art area, about which I had even greater reservations, supervised by a former NELP student union officer who had migrated into the staff, with a degree at the end of it.

Like all fine art students I was allocated a small space in which to paint and draw, where I worked on a painting, and a series of self-portrait drawings wearing a joke-shop false nose. This was my degree-presentation work. I came back one morning to find someone had entered the room, repainted part of my painting and stolen my false nose. I went off to the caretaker and demanded a key. After which I found myself confronted by an indignant deputy director. 'Come along David', she said. 'You can't pull rank now. We don't allow *students* to have keys'. I thought, 'old habits die hard'.

Notes

1. Gordon Lawrence and David Page, 'Art and Design: Time to Think Again', J. Finch and M. Rustin (eds), *A Degree of Choice*, Penguin, 1986, p201.
2. *The Hornsey Affair*, Penguin Education Special, 1969, p10.

CHAPTER FOUR

The Centre for Institutional Studies

Jon Griffith, Michael Locke, John Pratt and Alice Sampson

Origins and intentions

The Centre for Institutional Studies (CIS) was created in September 1970 with the establishment of North East London Polytechnic (NELP), primarily to pursue the polytechnic policy expounded by Eric Robinson[1] and enacted by Anthony Crosland, secretary of state for education and science. NELP director George Brosan and his deputy, Robinson, brought in Tyrrell Burgess and John Pratt from the Higher Education Research Unit at the London School of Economics (LSE), together with Pamela Lewis, to continue and develop their research on policy and economics of higher education, particularly on the polytechnic policy.

Central to Burgess and Pratt's purpose in forming the Centre for Institutional Studies (CIS) was a commitment to influence social policies and institutions with the broad agenda of a 'better world', contending that social sciences is best engaged with solving practical social problems through improving policy.[2] Their concern was with 'how to' questions, such as, how to enable children from disadvantaged backgrounds achieve in the education system, and, in higher education, how to promote programmes to meet the needs of a broad population for employment in industry, commerce and public services.

Burgess and Pratt took their approach for social science from Karl Popper, whose teaching on theory of science at LSE had been formative in their methods and findings for their previous research on the colleges of advanced technology.[3] They took the name of the centre from Popper's proposition that the task of social science should be the study of social institutions as a means of addressing social problems.

Thus, the Centre for Institutional Studies was created on two radical premises:

- the polytechnic policy, committed to egalitarian higher education within local education provision
- an approach to social sciences, based on Karl Popper's theory, committed to improving social policies and institutions for solving social problems.

The CIS approach

Applying scientific knowledge to social policy analysis

The approach adopted by Burgess and Pratt is summarised in Popper's schema for the generation of knowledge,[4] expressed as P1 –>TS –>EE –>P2. TS represents a trial solution, such as a social policy, social institution or programme, to the problem P1, and is tested against the evidence and corrected, summarised as EE, 'error elimination'. This process of critical revision leads to a new problem, P2. That P2 can then generate an improved solution TS2, which is tested and corrected to produce problem P3; a progressive process.[5] The schema is also expressed in terms of TT, a tentative theory in place of TS; an evolutionary view of scientific theory.[6] Popper's hypothetico-deductive method is founded on a process of falsification, in that evidence which refutes a trial solution or tentative theory is accepted provisionally and claims to knowledge are regarded as tentative or provisional. Processes of verification, on the other hand, claim certainty based on a premise that accumulatively collecting 'deep descriptions' represents social reality, even though they are unable to identify contextual features relevant to causal explanations.[7]

A Popperian-informed approach to improving policies and institutions assesses the theories or understandings which have informed them, recognising that all views of the world and observations are theory-laden. This offers the opportunity to consider a multiplicity of formulations of problems and practices, testing them as hypotheses against evidence and eliminating those which are refuted. Accordingly, all practices, policies, proposals and social institutions are regarded as fallible. To reduce error, trial solutions are introduced, tested and improved, leading to a better formulation of the problem and hence a better solution.

This logic encouraged us in our teaching and research to pose the question, 'What is the problem to which the policy or programme is meant to be a solution?' This perspective was, and remains, counter to typical practices that take off from generalisations about problems and jump to declaring solutions; we called this 'solutioneering'. We conjectured that this approach was a reason for government policy intentions falling 'a long way short of original aspirations',[8] and more akin to Lindblom's observation[9] that policymakers' decision-making can be described as 'muddling through', or according to Popper, using a process of trial and error.

Thus, we paid attention to how social problems are formulated, by whom and for what reason, and asked the question 'a problem for whom?' that enabled us to articulate not only the perspectives of policy-makers but also the experiences of people, seldom heard, for whom social policies were intended. We also recognised the role of values in problem formulation.[10] We extended our analysis into the conditions under which aspects of policies or institutions were successful by assessing how context mechanisms were activated, or not activated, to produce desired outcomes[11] and to craft proposals for better policy or institutional arrangements.

Thus, CIS was founded on a premise that greater social improvements can be made using a Popperian-informed approach where effort is put into formulating the problem – P1 – and deliberately considering many different ways of characterising the problem. Further, the approach highlights how social problems are of society's own making; they are neither given nor unchangeable; and how by being better problem-solvers we are better equipped to inform and improve policy-making and practice.[12]

The significance of institutions

A second key idea from Popper was his proposition that the task of social science is the study of institutions. Policies and practices are developed by, and implemented through, institutions which are devised as tentative solutions, taking the TS place in the schema above, to perceived social problems. Urban regeneration initiatives and volunteering programmes may be treated as institutions, as trial solutions, which have purposes, rules and procedures that can be subjected to tests for their aptness and success.[13] A challenge for policy-makers and organisations is to devise institutional forms that redress identified problems by putting in place procedures and practices to achieve 'a transformation from one state of affairs to another'.[14] These transformations are a practical problem,[15] and understanding how and under what conditions an organisation seeks alternative formulations before selecting the most appropriate for the perceived problem is an empirical question.[16]

We used Popper's notion of situational logic and situational analysis[17] to understand how individuals' actions may be shaped by their organisational situation and institutions' actions by their policy environment. We extended this analysis to anticipate how institutions and individuals are likely to respond to policies, programmes or organisations, and we offered trial solutions of the kind, 'If you do this, then that is likely to happen'.

We drew on the work of numerous scholars to enhance our critical reasoning, empirical research and data analysis, including: Hogwood and Gunn[18] for methods of policy analysis, and Majone for understanding the situations from which policies emerged; and for analysing and advising on management to supplement situational logic, March and Simon on organisational development, and Argyris[19] for organisational learning. Through postgraduate teaching, we found how illuminative[20] and participative methodologies produced complementary evidence to improve the quality of our research. Our evaluation research was founded on Popper[21] and informed by realist scholars, notably Sayer,[22] Weiss,[23] and Pawson and Tilley.[24]

Throughout the research process, from constructing initial hypotheses to writing up research findings, we were guided by the

Popperian method that aspires to rigour through testing hypotheses by criticism in the public domain. This public scrutiny relies on open debate and democratic processes that constitutes an 'open society'.[25] Accordingly, we produced series of research reports and commentaries making our findings and ideas available not only to the academic community, but also to policy-makers and practitioners. Our commitment to improving social policies led us to join in policy debates, engaging journalistic as well as political values. We produced guidelines for practitioners based on our research findings,[26] and a pamphlet for a 'Don't shake the baby' campaign.[27]

Teaching and learning

The CIS approach gave us a broad platform on which we could take on a wide variety of topics in research and teaching. It enabled us to be helpful as tutors with new issues put to us by students, and to create courses not bounded by conventional academic definitions and disciplines, from undergraduate to doctoral level. Initially, we taught on existing MEd, MSc (Education Management), Diploma in Management Studies and independent study courses.

In common with other departments and centres at the polytechnic, CIS staff provided tutorial support to independent study students. CIS staff shared with these students the centre's problem-centred approach to policy, to theory-testing and to learning itself. In the mid-1980s, the centre extended this individual support through a timetabled class for a small group of independent study students with a specific interest in community and voluntary organisations. By 1990, centre staff, with colleagues in other departments, had developed postgraduate programmes in education and education management; then, within the independent study framework, a postgraduate programme in management development for community and voluntary organisations, and a further postgraduate programme in institutional studies. By the mid-1990s, we had evolved them into linked postgraduate programmes in public and community service, and voluntary sector studies; undergraduate and postgraduate programmes in social enterprise were added in 2001. We also responded to demands for research-based studies leading to a PhD, both from our MA and MSc students and from others who sought rigorous, in-depth examination of practical problems and potential solutions.

Problems and experience

While research to solve social problems was the centre's raison d'être, the relationship between research and teaching was important to its staff. We thought the centre's approach worth testing in the wide range of situations which students brought to a course. We believed that by sharing the centre's experience of research and evaluation – and our reflections on this experience – it could offer a rich and critically engaged path to learning, more so than subject-based programmes.

We argued the case for institutional studies in the context of the new world of public policy, identifying:

> a particular need to enable the growing body of people, engaged in public and social policy through a wide range of organisations, to evaluate their own work, organisations, and projects in a way that will contribute not only to the requirements of audit and accountability but to the development of a fuller understanding of the effectiveness of policy interventions. (Internal CIS document, circa 2000)

The centre's taught programmes were an attempt to do this. As Tyrrell Burgess wrote: 'Because students are not used to posing problems, they do not know how to do it productively. It is a skill that has to be learnt, and it cannot be learnt without doing it'.[28]

The problems which independent study and postgraduate students brought to our courses from their experience in employment or voluntary action ranged widely, including, for instance, concerns from community hygiene about treatments for head lice (involving a somewhat squeamish seminar), founding stories of voluntary organisations, and the finance of higher education in China.

The portfolio of part-time postgraduate courses we developed during the 1990s attracted people with responsible professional, vocational, voluntary or civic roles, seeking to develop their effectiveness and careers. The courses were not, predominantly, designed or marketed as management programmes:[29] voluntary sector studies was about the sector, its organisations and people; public and community service was about services; and although the postgraduate social enterprise programme had management in its title, it was as much about the development of organisations in a broader policy environment. Aspects of management were included in their curricula, but in an effort to promote questioning of orthodoxies.

The centre adopted the School of Independent Study's approach to learning on its taught postgraduate programmes, through its 'planning, development and synoptic' (PDAS) module. An external examiner noted:

> The PDAS module ... brings together the three modules and the dissertation ... in a framework of planning, self-appraisal, and critical learning ... and could usefully be studied by tutors elsewhere who find that modular work can too easily become a pick and mix ... without coherence or intellectual development.[30]

In keeping with the centre's overall approach, students had been encouraged to think about the problems to which organisations and their policies were an intended solution; even though there was often some tension between the centre's commitment to critical scrutiny, and the demands from the students' institutional worlds. They were there required to learn to manage more efficiently, lead more confidently, and build better business plans (and, preferably, sooner rather than later, from the management studies textbook rather than reflective research).

Higher education policy research

Burgess and Pratt's research into higher education policy was the principal factor in establishing CIS at NELP, and during the following decades we produced a series of studies of the non-university sector in Britain, contributed to international studies of this sector and assisted in the development of policy in other countries. These studies exemplified the centre's approach, testing outcomes of policies in terms of stated intentions and of alternative formulations of problems the policies were intended to solve, analysing the instruments of policy and their consequences, and drawing on our research experience to craft proposals for their successful development.

The CIS approach emerged from Burgess's and Pratt's study of the colleges of advance technology (CATs).[31] Government policy for the CATs had sought to solve the – perceived – problem of a shortage of technologists. The colleges were vocationally and professionally oriented, concerned with teaching rather than research, and, moreover, offered important opportunities for social mobility for working and working-class people; they were open rather than exclusive; and formed part of the local authority further education sector. The CATs were identified with one of two traditions in higher education, contrasting with the university tradition, which was exclusive and theoretical rather than practical. The study revealed, however, a pattern as the CATs founded in the technical college tradition aspired to and adopted university status.

Academic drift

In their subsequent study of the new polytechnics, Pratt and Burgess coined the term 'academic drift' for this pattern of aspiration,[32] and it became widely accepted in the lexicon of higher education policy in Britain and abroad. The development and application of the theory of 'academic drift' was an example of the study of social institutions. We examined how what we called the 'instruments' of policy – such as funding mechanisms, building controls and specifications, and salary structures – had been used to implement policy. Applying Popper's notion of situational logic, we found that many instruments of policy created situations in which the interests of institutions and people within them diverted policy intentions by producing incentives to act in unintended directions. Some policy instruments, however, such as the creation of a national validating body, the Council for National Academic Awards (CNAA), were conducive to desirable policy aims, confounding many expectations. In the end, the polytechnic policy, like the CATs before it, succumbed to academic drift, becoming the universities that they were supposed to be different from.

Situational logic

The procedure of situational logic was particularly apposite for the third of our studies of higher education policy. In 1972, a white paper announced that, because of reduction in the need for teachers, some 200 colleges in England and Wales were to be reorganised. By contrast with the previous policies, the white paper did not prescribe the outcomes. The secretary of state, Margaret Thatcher, rejected an 'architectural' approach to policy in favour of an 'organic' one.[33] The government outlined the opportunities for the colleges and left the outcome to negotiation between individual colleges, the Department for Education and Science (DES), local education authorities and voluntary bodies.

Situational logic for the colleges suggested that different colleges might take different directions. However, our analysis revealed that, despite Mrs Thatcher's antipathy to a centralised approach, there was forceful central management over the negotiations. The DES had its own view of the situations the colleges faced and enforced its conclusions on them. As Locke *et al.* wrote: 'The notion that the DES was setting up a healthy process of diversity and competition and securing the survival of the fittest failed to recognise the administrative structures of the further education system';[34] it failed to recognise the pressures for academic drift. The colleges that emerged mainly espoused traditional and established values, seeking university affiliation. Locke *et al.* concluded that the organic approach was 'a failure of intellect',[35] and, pursuing the notion of situational logic, argued that Darwinian notions of natural selection could not be applied unmodified to social institutions because the environment is human-made and not policy-neutral.

Because our interest was not just explaining how things happened, but in addressing 'how to' questions, we sought – not least to avoid reversals of policy intentions – to put forward propositions or hypotheses of the kind, 'If you want this to happen, you need to do [the following things] and/or avoid doing [other things]'. Our experience had generated a number of lessons of this kind, which we contributed to Organisation for Economic Co-operation and Development (OECD) studies of non-university higher education, and policy-making in Austria, and Finland.[36]

In 1993 the government of Austria created a non-university sector of *Fachhochschulen,* in which courses would be offered by any provider for accreditation by a new body, the *Fachhochschulrat.* The policy broke not only the monopoly of the universities, but also the tradition of government ownership of higher education institutions. Given the radical nature of this policy, the government negotiated with OECD to have a policy review, chaired by Pratt. The review drew heavily on the experience of the British polytechnics and the CNAA on which the *Fachhochschulrat* was modelled. It concluded that the 'accreditation model' was an important mechanism to enable 'a wide variety of courses is possible within strict standards',[37] and the *Fachhochschulen* quickly became a major sector in Austrian higher education.[38]

Volunteering and voluntary organisations

We began our research on volunteering and voluntary organisations in the early 1980s. Michael Locke was inspired by his experience in community action in North Kensington/ Notting Hill[39] and in a consultancy project for Notting Hill Housing Trust (1983-86) with Jon Griffith (a part-time student on the independent study programme) and Graham Parry from NELP's business school. Parry brought theory and processes from organisation development, which we found compatible for problem-solving with voluntary organisations and Popperian theories of situational logic and provisional knowledge. Griffith established a relationship with management development for voluntary organisations in the National Council for Voluntary Organisations (NCVO). Our work in this area was consolidated by our tutorial interaction with independent study students who focused their projects on community organisations, and the synergy led to the creation of CIS postgraduate programmes.

Policy analyses and tests

We undertook a sequence of policy analyses, programme evaluations and action research studies.[40] We created the Institute for Volunteering Research (IVR) in 1997 as a partnership of UEL with the National Centre for Volunteering (later Volunteering England), whose director Andy Kelmanson had gained her BA by Independent Study with CIS supervision.

Through our involvement with IVR and experience in urban regeneration evaluations, we created a research project to explore how community leaders became involved in voluntary action and the consequences for them. We interviewed twelve community leaders in disadvantaged communities in East London to enquire into how individual, institutional and situational factors shaped their involvement.

The study was set in the policy domain of the Blair government (1997-2010) where the role of voluntary action was a central policy for combating social exclusion and creating active communities, according to its concept of the 'third way'.[41] We planned our study to test hypotheses informing these policies.

We took as provisional corroboration of the policy hypothesis the evidence that our interviewees had become more active in their communities and involved with others in organisations. In the words of one interviewee, she had gained 'A lot of friends. A lot of appreciation, and a phone that never stops ringing'.[42]

This government policy was underpinned by social capital theory, particularly following Putnam,[43] that hypothesised that individuals' voluntary action contributed to habits, skills and knowledge, creating a capital of knowhow and experience. We explored this assumption by asking community leaders about the skills and support they had drawn on and about what had kept them going. Here too the evidence broadly and provisionally corroborated the policy hypothesis. Our interviewees, variously, talked of how they had engaged through established associations and voluntary organisations or through informal networks, and their involvement had fostered cooperation. We modified Putnam's title *Bowling Alone* to 'Bowling along' for our journal publication.[44]

Alternative perspectives

The community leaders' accounts, however, raised some doubts about the assumptions of social capital. Several research participants were anxious that 'things would collapse' without them; nor did they perceive their actions as banking ways of working like a capital fund to be drawn on in future. Moreover, they were worried about whether they could continue in their voluntary roles, considering the stress and the limited time they could give. They were concerned about negative effects on their families, and one interviewee felt 'railroaded' into a voluntary role.

Both concepts of social inclusion and social capital were problematised by our findings that some of the community leaders spoke of how it was the supportive responses of local government and police officers which sustained them in their community action. We found this particularly significant, and we hypothesised that central government might be better focusing on the role of local government in providing, in Popper's terms, the situational logic that would shape voluntary action rather than on specific pro-volunteering policies.

We also found complications in findings from national data that a positive feeling about where the individual lived contributed to their motivations for volunteering.[45] Some of our community leaders talked with anger and negativity about their neighbourhood, and we hypothesised that people's commitment to place might be more significant than positivity towards volunteering.

Collaboration

Overall, our study corroborated working hypotheses about individuals' decisions to volunteer in terms of the combination of individual and institutional factors, and our input into joint papers considered the situational logic. Working with colleagues in IVR and the NCVO research team, we saw the need for greater understanding of how these factors functioned across place and time, and we pursued questions about the geographies and histories of people's volunteering, creating a project led by IVR, which produced *Pathways through participation*.[46] Thus, the CIS approach enabled us to be partners in the pragmatic concerns of agencies working in public policy and in the improvement of knowledge underpinning policy and practice.

Problems of violence

East London communities have a reputation for deeply entrenched violence, an issue that has perplexed and frustrated numerous local policy-makers and agencies over the years. We found that our Popperian-informed research was well suited to contributing to social improvement in low income areas with high levels of violence in East London and beyond.

Analysing the formulation of problems

Violence is typically ill defined or ambiguous, evokes many different meanings and responses and is 'at best re-solved over and over again'.[47] Violence can be a response to feelings of injustice, oppression and alienation, an expression of excitement or rebellion; violence can include killings by the state, street robberies, domestic violence and abuse, racist violence, bullying in schools and street riots. In such situations, our research aimed to assist policy-makers and practitioners to characterise this complex problem less ambiguously, and to indicate which problem representations are likely to be more useful in producing effective problem solutions.[48]

In one study in communities with reputations for grooming jihadists, we found that increasingly punitive discourses defined responses to violence and were precluding debates on alternative formulations and courses of preventive action. The anxieties of local authorities, punitive beliefs and moral panics by the UK government, combined with unyielding media rhetoric, were leading to solutions the consequences of which were likely to escalate violence, by, for example, labelling Muslims leaving to fight in Syria as evil – a claim that is irrefutable and lends itself to repressive and ideological solutions. However, among local community and faith leaders there was a considered and realistic analysis of the multi-faceted problem of how to prevent extremism. This recognised contributing factors, including the stigma of living in poverty and racist discrimination, that thwarted aspirations and ambitions. Their practical solutions included English language classes for women, socially inclusive children's centres, outreach youth work and employment opportunities.[49]

Trial, error and refinement

In particular, we were attentive to agencies and their interventions that may be causing harm, and our empirical research identified where mistakes can be rectified, and the modification of social programmes to seek better solutions. In an East London initiative run by the police and social workers to prevent domestic violence, abused women were expected to demonstrate their willingness to leave their violent relationship by attending the project located in a police station. We observed that women heavily in debt with numerous young children were struggling to get on buses and pay their fares, and those with ill-health and disabilities were unable to travel and denied access to the service. Neither the police nor the social workers were willing to adapt the project, and so we recommended the withdrawal of funding.

Our research also facilitated progressive problem-shifts so theories and practice can be adapted to give greater explanatory and predictive power than previous formulations.[50] Our research in violent communities in Jamaica problematised the normalisation of violence by re-conceptualising perceptions of childhood. Perceptions that children are naturally 'bad' and should be controlled with strict discipline and physical punishment were shifted towards an understanding that the children are traumatised and highly stressed by their experiences. Having witnessed so much violence at home, in school and on the streets, they acted out the violence they had seen. From this perspective, promising initiatives included a peace garden in a primary school where children were able to grieve and receive counselling, as well as parenting classes that challenged perceived child-rearing wisdom and promoted love, care and support.

Unplanned consequences

Our approach to evaluation research encouraged us to assess anomalies and unintended consequences and hence increase the potential for contributing to social improvement. In a Brazilian favela where rival drug trafficker gangs patrolled their territory with guns, those who crossed into other territories were shot dead. We observed, however, that young people wearing T-shirts with the logo of a voluntary sector youth organisation were able to cross these 'no-go' boundaries safely on their way to the youth centre. These symbolic actions by young people peacefully challenged the violent community social norms and, in our assessment, were a potentially effective community action not included in the aims and objectives of the peace initiative intended to reduce and prevent violence.[51]

The life course of the centre

The formation of the centre and its approach to research and teaching were rooted in the radical national polytechnic policy, and we sustained the commitment to these values and ethos during – and despite – the changes in the national policy environment and our situation in the institution over the subsequent fifty years or so. Polytechnics were originally situated in local authorities and a democratic local government framework. Our closeness to community structures and organisations laid the foundation for a programme of research with East London community organisations, and for supporting students from local communities. We were well placed to do research with the local community, notably in gaining commissions for evaluating Stratford City Challenge and subsequent urban regeneration initiatives.[52] For the greater part of CIS's life, there were usually somewhere between six and twelve people on contracts working in the centre. They came with a variety of academic and non-academic backgrounds; many had experience relevant to the research topic from their employment, voluntary action or personal lives. Our projects engaged disabled people with experiential knowledge of the problem-field;[53] we hired minority ethnic women, new migrants and those typically under-represented on university payrolls. With our non-elitist ethos we trained local primary-aged schoolchildren to be co-researchers and raised the profile of socially excluded groups in our research, including minority ethnic women survivors of domestic violence[54] and repeat offenders,[55] and neglected fields such as community health.[56]

Our researchers' careers tended to be those of professional workers committed to a field more than of academic staff progressing within a theory-defined subject area. Consequently, we had a strong sense of teamwork and an egalitarian, open ethos about working with each other – a powerful collegiality. However, academic drift was deeply felt – and regretted – in CIS itself. The environment of higher education policy and funding became tighter, restricting scope for non-standard teaching and research, shaping performance towards league tables, and inducing among senior management a compulsion towards command and control. When the new managerialism swept over higher education in the 1980s, their successors restructured and restructured again, including, as fashions changed, CIS within schools, faculties and departments. Customs and practices, such as our open-plan working space with a library, kitchen and seminar room that stimulated discussion between staff, students and visitors, weekly seminars followed by lunch, which had sustained the Centre's values and ethos were eroded. We lost control over our budgets, which were raided annually even though we won prestigious grants, including from the Economic and Social Research Council (ESRC), Arts and Humanities Research Council (AHRC), Home Office, Youth Justice Board and the Department of Education, and experienced researchers had to leave.

A move to a Docklands campus in a location remote from the homes or offices of our students and organisational networks disrupted the flow of people in and out of the centre. The forces of academic drift were encouraging elitist and closed theoretical frameworks, focused on refining theory within discipline boundaries unsympathetic to our commitment to social improvement.

The centre's legacy

The legacy of the Centre for Institutional Studies is a Popperian-based approach to analysis and institutional studies which has been tried and tested in a range of policy areas and contributed to social improvements, ranging from community organisations in East London to volunteering policy for the UK, the higher education system in Austria and Finland, community action on gang violence in Brazil, and the prevention of youth violence in Jamaica. Our research and teaching emphasised the importance of learning from mistakes,[57] and the practice of criticism necessary for problem-solving. Students graduated with an understanding that the formulation of real-world problems leads to strong theories that produces knowledge relevant to policy-making and practitioners, that eliminates errors and improves the problem-solving capabilities of institutions.[58] This approach offered an alternative to current governments who persist with social policies which are obviously not working and are causing harm.[59]

The centre's formation was, and remained, rooted in the ethos and principles of the radical polytechnic project. Like all ideas, we subjected radicalism to a social process of critical discussion to reduce errors and stimulate problem-solving. In practice our method may be considered as one kind of radicalism among a plurality of radicalisms. Our preoccupations were with practical problems in everyday lived realities, and learning how to best move from 'one state of affairs to another' through a process of trial and error and incremental change to minimise the possibility of harm, particularly for those with limited life opportunities through no fault of their own. Perhaps, our type of radicalism lies in an understanding that social policies, institutions and social programmes are tentative solutions, which are provisional and which can always be altered to bring about social improvement. We proposed that some policies, institutions and social programmes may be best abandoned or dismantled, others modified and reduced, or invested in and strengthened. Thus, our approach offers a plurality of perspectives that minimises dogma and steadfast adherence to policies clearly causing harm, and it is, in essence, an optimistic and proactive 'can do better' approach to research, teaching and learning.

Acknowledgments

A grant from the Karl Popper Charitable Foundation, to whom we are very grateful.

Notes

1. Eric Robinson, *The New Polytechnics*, Penguin: Harmondsworth, 1968.
2. Karl Popper, *The Myth of the Framework: In Defence of Science and Rationality*, Routledge: London, 1994; Popper, *In search of a better world: Lectures and essays from thirty years*, Routledge: London, 1994.
3. T. Burgess and J. Pratt, *Policy and Practice: The Colleges of Advanced Technology*, Allen Lane The Penguin Press: London, 1970.
4. Popper, *Unended Quest; An Intellectual Autobiography*, Fontana: London, 1976, p132.
5. Tyrrell Burgess, 'P1-TT-EE-P2', *New Society*, 23 January 1975.
6. J. Swann, *Learning, Teaching and Education Research in the 21st Century*, Continuum: London, 2012.
7. M. Hammersley, *Questioning qualitative inquiry*, Sage: London, 2008; J. Pratt, 'Grounded - or tested - theory?', *Higher Education Review*, 2011, Vol 43 (2) Summer pp90-96.
8. S. Barrett and C. Fudge (eds), *Policy and Action: Essays on the Implementation of Public Policy*, Methuen: London, 1981, p3.
9. C. E. Lindblom, 'The science of 'muddling through', *Public Administration Review*, 1959, 19 (2), pp79-88.
10. G. Majone, 'Policies as Theories', *Omega: The International Journal of Management Science* 1980, 8 (2), pp 151-162.
11. R. Pawson and N. Tilley, *Realistic Evaluation*, Sage: London, 1997; A. Sampson, 'Developing robust approaches to evaluating social programmes', *Evaluation Journal*, 2007, Vol. 13, No. 4, pp469-485.
12. Majone, 1980; G. Majone and A. Wildavsky, 'Implementation as Evolution (1979)', J. Pressman and A. Wildavsky (eds), *Implementation*, University of California Press: Berkeley, 1984, pp163-180.
13. Tyrrell Burgess. 'Towards a social science: A comment on Karl Popper's "twenty-seven theses"', J. Pratt, M. Locke and T. Burgess, *Readings in Institutional Studies: Book 1: Popper and problems, problems with Popper.* Working paper 64, Centre for Institutional Studies, University of East London, 1994, p64.
14. E. V. Krick, *An Introduction to Engineering and Engineering Design*, John Wiley and Sons: New York, 1969, p3.

15. J. Pratt, 'Testing Policy', J. Swann and J. Pratt (eds), *Improving Education: Realist Approaches to Teaching and Research,* Cassell: London, 1999, p40.
16. D. Chisholm, 'Problem-solving and Institutional Design', *Journal of Public Administration Research and Theory,* J_PART, 1995, 4, pp451-491.
17. Popper 1979, p179.
18. B. Hogwood and L. Gunn, *Policy Analysis for the Real World,* Oxford University Press: Oxford, 1984.
19. C. Argyris, 'Good communication that blocks learning', *Harvard Business Review,* Harvard Business Review: Boston, Vol. 72/4, 1994.
20. M. Parlett and D. Hamilton, 'Evaluation as illumination: A new approach to the study of innovatory programmes', R. Murphy and H. Torrance (eds), *Evaluating education: Issues and methods,* Paul Chapman Publishing: London, 1988.
21. Popper, *The Logic of Scientific Discovery,* Hutchison: London, 1959; Popper, *Conjectures and Refutations: The Growth of Scientific Knowledge,* Routledge and Kegan Paul: London, 1963.
22. A. Sayer, *Method in Social Science: A Realist Approach,* Routledge, Shaw and Crompton: London, 1992, 2nd edition.
23. C. Weiss, 'Nothing as practical as good theory: exploring theory-based evaluation for Comprehensive Community Initiatives for children and families', J. Connell, A. Kubisch, L. Schorr and C. Weiss (eds), *New Approaches to Evaluating Community Initiatives: Concepts, Methods, and Contexts,* Aspen Institute: Washington, 1995, pp65-92.
24. Pawson and Tilley, 1997.
25. Popper, *The Open Society and its Enemies, Vol 1 Plato, Vol 11 Hegel and Marx.* Routledge: London, 4th edition, 1962; Bernard Crick, *In Defence of Politics,* Penguin: Harmondsworth, 1964.
26. Social Care Institute for Excellence (SCIE), 'Seldom heard: Developing inclusive participation in social care', Position paper 10, Summary, Social Care Institute for Excellence: London, September 2008, and L. Hernandez, P. Robson and A. Sampson, 'Towards integrated participation: Involving seldom heard users of social care services', *British Journal of Social Work,* 2010, 40, 3, pp714-736; A. Parmar and A. Sampson, 'Evaluating domestic violence initiatives', *British Journal of Criminology,* 2007, 47, pp671-691; A. Parmar and A. Sampson, 'Tackling Domestic Violence: Providing Advocacy and Support to Survivors of Domestic Violence', Home Office, Good Practice Guide, 2005(a); A. Parmar and A. Sampson, 'Tackling Domestic Violence: Providing Advocacy and Support to Survivors from Black and other Minority Ethnic Communities', Home Office, Good Practice Guide, 2005 (b); M. Locke, P. Robson and N. Begum, *Developing user involve-*

ment: Working towards user-centred practice in voluntary organisations, Policy Press: Bristol, 2003.

27. J. Shepherd and A. Sampson, 'Don't Shake the Baby: Towards a Prevention Strategy', *British Journal of Social Work*, 2000, 30,6, pp721-735.
28. Tyrrell Burgess, 'The Philosophy of Karl Popper and the Improvement of Educational Practice: The Implication of Popper for Formal Education'. Paper presented at the Scottish Educational Research Association Annual Conference, 24-26 September 1998.
29. J. Griffith, 'From Voluntary Sector Studies to Social Enterprise: Development and Management: What Happened, Why, and Where Next?', *Learning for Democracy* 2006, Vol 2 No 3.
30. J. Pratt and J. Cocking, 'Making Modularity Work.' *Teaching in Higher Education*, 1999, Vol 4 No 1.
31. Burgess and Pratt, 1970.
32. J. Pratt and T. Burgess, *Polytechnics: A Report*, Pitman: London, 1974, p23.
33. M. Locke, J. Pratt and T. Burgess, *The Colleges of Higher Education: 1972 to 1982*, Critical Press: Croydon, 1985, p152.
34. *ibid*. p154.
35. *ibid*. p155.
36. Organisation for Economic Co-operation and Development, *Innovation in Higher Education: Technical Education in the United Kingdom*, OECD: Paris, 1971; Organisation for Economic Co-operation and Development, *Alternatives to Universities*, OECD: Paris, 1991; Organisation for Economic Co-operation and Development, *Reviews of National Policies for Education: Austria*, OECD: Paris, 1995; Organisation for Economic Co-operation and Development, *Reviews of National Policies for Education: Finland*, OECD: Paris, 2003; J. Pratt, T. Kekale, P. Maassen, I. Papp, J. Perellon and M. Uitte, *Different but Equal: An Evaluation of the Postgraduate Polytechnic Experiment in Finland*, Finnish Higher Education Evaluation Council: Helsinki, 2004.
37. OECD, 1995, p104.
38. J. Pratt (ed.), *The 'Accreditation Model': Policy Transfer in Higher Education in Austria and Britain*, Symposium Books: Didcot, 2004.
39. Mike Locke, 'Reflections on community action', 2016. http://maxillaarchive.com/wp-content/uploads/2016/05/Reflections-on-community-action-by-Mike-Locke.pdf.
40. See for example: S. Howlett and M. Locke, 'Volunteering for Blair: The Third Way', *Voluntary Action*, 1999,1.2, pp67-76; M. Locke, N. Richards, L. Down, J. Griffith and R. Worgan, *Local information*

points for volunteers, Home Office: London, 1995; and Locke, Robson and Begum, 2003.

41. Howlett and Locke, 1999.
42. M. Locke, A. Sampson and J. Shepherd, '"A lot of friends. A lot of appreciation and a phone that never stops ringing: Voluntary action and social exclusion in East London – a pilot study', *CIS Commentary*, Centre for Institutional Studies, University of East London: London, No 96, 2000.
43. R. Putnam, *Making democracy work: civic traditions in modern Italy*, Princeton University Press: Princeton, 1993; R. D. Putnam, *Bowling Alone: The Collapse and Revival of American Community*, Simon & Schuster: New York, 2000.
44. M. Locke, A. Sampson and J. Shepherd, 'Bowling along: Community leaders in East London', *Voluntary Action*, 2001, 3.2: pp27-45 accessible at: https://www.bl.uk/collection-items/bowling-along.
45. J. Davis Smith, *The 1997 National Survey of Volunteering*, Institute for Volunteering Research: London, 1998.
46. E. Brodie, T. Hughes, V. Jochum, S. Miller, N. Ockenden, and D. Warburton, *Pathways through participation: What creates and sustains active citizenship?*, NCVO: London, 2011.
47. H. W. J. Rittel and M. M. Webber, 'Dilemmas in a general theory of planning', *Policy Sciences* 1973, 4, p160.
48. Chisholm, 1995, pp475-6.
49. A. Sampson, 'From Paki-bashing to Muslim bashing: Extremism policies considered', Dick Hobbs (ed.), *Mischief, Morality and Mobs: Essays in Honour of Geoffrey Pearson*. Routledge Advances in Ethnography: Abingdon, 2017, pp 44-60.
50. P. Watzlawick, J. Weakland and R. Fisch, *Change: Principles of Problem Formulation and Problem Resolution*, Norton & Company: London, 1974; Majone, 1980.
51. A. Sampson and M. Villela, 'How young people peacefully challenge community norms embedded with violence in a Brazilian favela', *British Journal of Criminology*, 2017, 57,3, pp684-703.
52. See for example: J. Pratt and R. Fearnley, 'Stratford City Challenge', T. Butler and M. Rustin (eds), *Rising in the East: The Regeneration of East London*, Lawrence & Wishart: London, 1996 pp327 -352; R. Fearnley, D. Gordon, A. Sampson, 'Problems on the Training Ground: Tackling unemployment in East London', *Rising East*, 1997 1, 2, pp73-88; A. Sampson, 'The lessons of Winsor Park; creating a new community; the role of the LDDC', *Rising East*, 1998, 2, 2, pp142-159.
53. Hernandez *et al.*, 2010.
54. Parmar and Sampson, 2007.

55. A. Sampson and S. Themelis, 'Working in the community with young people who offend', *Journal of Youth Studies*, 2009, 12, 2, pp121-137.
56. S. Riordan, *Discovering the power to make a difference*, Beckton Community Health Project: London, 2000.
57. Popper, 1969.
58. Popper, 1968; Burgess 1994.
59. B. Tuchman, *The March of Folly*, Michael Joseph: London, 1984; Y. Dror, *Policymaking under Adversity*, Transaction Books: Oxford, 1986.

CHAPTER FIVE

The Centre for Narrative Research

Molly Andrews and Corinne Squire with
Cigdem Esin and Aura Lounasmaa

This chapter tells the story of the Centre for Narrative Research (CNR): where the inspiration for its formation came from, how it was situated within the political and intellectual culture of the University of East London (UEL) and its broader academic and socioeconomic context, and how it has developed over the twenty years of its existence. The chapter closes with a few thoughts about the future: about the kind of work for which we hope to have laid some foundation, and about the continuing obstacles to that kind of work.

Background: what and who we are

The Centre for Narrative Research was officially created in 1999 by Molly Andrews, Shelley Day Sclater and Corinne Squire, all of whom at that time worked in the UEL undergraduate degree programme of psychosocial studies. All three of us had in different contexts spent a lot of time listening to stories people told about their lives, and had positioned ourselves as psychologists who framed our work more broadly than was then common within the western psychological mainstream. For us, the discipline was and is a social science, concerned fundamentally with the social and political world. The immediate impetus for CNR, though, was also a reactive one. It is ironic to think that in some ways we have Mrs Thatcher and her introduction of the Research Assessment Exercise (the RAE, forerunner of the Research Excellence Framework, REF), the university research audit process which came to dominate much academic life, to thank for CNR. The research community of CNR was both an alternative to this auditisation, asserting and maintaining scholarship as collaboration and engagement, rather than output production, and more superficially, a contribution to it, as it helped us justify our existence as researchers in terms of events hosted, grants gained, networks created and graduate students taught.

The 1990s expansion in student numbers generated heavy teaching loads at UEL. Research was backgrounded, and we had few postgraduate students. Nonetheless, through CNR we were able to organise a series of research seminars, and later workshops, postgraduate seminars, summer schools and postgraduate courses. At the same time, we were teaching an undergraduate module on life histories, so synergies between the different levels of teaching, and between teaching and our research, were there from the start, and developed steadily.

This incorporation of teaching at all levels with the narrative scholarship of the centre has always been an important part of the work we do. For instance, one of the projects on which we originally focused was a series of intensive one-day workshops on topics such as 'education and narrative', 'politics and narrative', 'sexuality and narrative' and 'refugee' narratives'. These events were exhilarating – research-based, but often also 'walking through' the research in a pedagogically informed way. They formed the basis for our first edited book, *Lines of narrative* (Andrews *et al.*, 2000). Our later volumes, the edited *Doing narrative research* (Andrews *et al.*, 2013), and the co-authored *What is narrative research*? (Squire *et al.*, 2014 – written with some of our many internal UEL CNR members and external CNR advisors) approached the research-teaching synergy from another direction, setting out to guide researchers through possible approaches to and questions about narrative research.

While we focused our efforts on creating a scholarly and creative space for narrative work, we were nonetheless building on what had come before us at UEL, particularly in psychosocial studies, sociology and cultural studies. Indeed we have found throughout the two decades of our existence that there has always been strong collaboration with colleagues from many different disciplines. Such collaboration is, moreover, the deliberate aim and not just the happy product of CNR. For us, the term 'narrative research' was indeed less a research identity, more a placeholder for concerns with qualitative research, language, research contexts, and participatory and transformative research that could bring together colleagues from different subject areas and schools. 'Narrative' was thus a contingent term, not an agenda.

Within a few years of creating CNR, Maria Tamboukou arrived at UEL, with an ambitious and far-reaching feminist research programme around written narratives, and very quickly became an integral part of the centre. (Around this time, Shelley Day Sclater left UEL.) We decided that we would continue to have three co-directors of the centre – Squire, Andrews and Tamboukou – and this structure of feminist co-leadership has remained ever since. Often we were asked by the university who was the 'real' director, as it had difficulty computing that three people could lead a centre collaboratively. We refused its efforts to place us within its expected management structure, and even had a triple professorial inaugural together. Cigdem Esin, who came to UEL as a CNR PhD student, eventually became a co-director, interjecting her creative energy and passion into many aspects of our work, particularly around reflexivity and multimedia narratives. Maria's work coordinating UEL's Feminist Research Group and other commitments eventually led to her stepping aside from the co-director role. Early on, she had developed an annual conference for postgraduate narrative students from across the UK and internationally, 'To think is to experiment'. The coordination of this event, now running for 15 years, was taken on by Cigdem. Research fellow Aura Lounasmaa, who first came to CNR through the 'To think is to experiment' postgraduate conference, joined CNR in 2014 and has been a vital part of the 'narrative sisterhood' since that time, leading on many of the projects connected to our engagement with refugee issues.

The experience of CNR and the values that shape it

Having outlined briefly how CNR developed over the twenty years of its existence, we now turn to the less tangible question of what the experience was like for us and what values frame the work we have done. As this book demonstrates, we were at the tail end of an important time in the history of the university. In that period, there are countless examples of innovative and radical ways of teaching and doing research which were practised and promoted by colleagues across the university. While not aware of all of these at the time – they have become much more apparent to us in retrospect, and in particular in preparing this book – we were nonetheless clear that we were part of something much bigger than ourselves. Not only were we part of the social research 'wave' now referred to as 'the turn to narrative', in addition, within our own institution, there was much collegial, if not institutional, interest in and support for the kind of work we were doing.

We have been asked to describe the values which shaped what we did. Five broad areas emerge as being particularly important.

Process – As with many political projects, at the core of CNR was a concern not only with particular topics, but also with the processes by which we operated. It has already been mentioned that our feminist co-leadership defied the expectations of the university, and troubled box-ticking exercises. It was always clear to us that this was not only a preferable way to operate, but for us the only way possible. When we tried to extend this organic process beyond the co-director group to others connected to the centre, we had less success. While we always held AGMs linked with seminars and receptions, in hopes of attracting people who would like to contribute their ideas for future events, what mostly happened was that few people attended and those who did, for the most part, were content to hear a summary of what we had done the previous year and our plans for the next. While we emailed members and advisors regularly to ask for feedback and suggestions, our collaborative events were generally planned through more direct contacts with colleagues interested in specific issues – for instance, narratives in relation to visual arts, or the family, or crime. These processual limitations indicate the impact of limited time and thinking resources in an increasingly marketised university – limitations with which CNR has always had to deal. However, the successes of our more directed collaborations – for instance: a popular Economic and Social Research Council (ESRC) seminar series, 'Methods in dialogue'; a long-running Erasmus programme with colleagues at Linkoping University; a European summer school, 'Narrative Innovations', developed and delivered with Monash University colleagues; and a National Centre for Research Methods programme, led by the Institute of Education alongside CNR and centres from Sussex and Oxford universities, 'Narratives of Everyday Life and Linked Approaches', or NOVELLA – all demonstrate the successes of CNR's consistently dialogic, engaged, and 'slow scholarship' approach to intellectual work.[1]

Transnationalism – The work of CNR has always had an international reach, as indicated by the nationality and the research interests of its co-directors, members, visiting scholars and postgraduate students. Moreover, we have always sought to address ourselves to an international community. One effective means of reaching researchers from outside the UK has been through our e-list, which has grown through the years to include more than 1000 narrative scholars situated around the word. We also ensure that our postgraduate module, narrative research, is available online, and have whenever possible endeavoured to reduce fees for students – again, something that contemporary evaluations of teaching predominantly in terms of the profits accruing from it have made increasingly difficult. We have also taught methodology schools in many countries where narrative research is developing or little known. Finally, the recent focus of many CNR activities has been the 'refugee crisis', and this new focus has led us to collaborate with others both within and beyond the UK who share this commitment, including with many asylum-seekers and refugees. 'Educating without borders' (https://educatingwithoutborders.wordpress.com/) is representative of such commitment to transnational collaboration.

Intergenerationality – As co-directors of the Centre for Narrative Research, we have always regarded our work as building on the scholarship and political engagement of many of those who were established academics long before us, some of whom are contributors to this volume. Equally, we believe it is our duty to provide the necessary support and skills to enable our younger colleagues and students to flourish as scholars in their own right. As already mentioned, this means that our teaching extends to all levels of higher education, and we are proud that one of our co-directors began her association with CNR as our PhD student. Similarly, we have had undergraduate students from our life histories module carry on to do PhDs with us, and then to become established academics in their own right. Some non-UK students enrolled in our postgraduate modules or summer schools have established narrative networks in their own countries, with which we remain closely affiliated. In this way, the 'family' of CNR has grown exponentially through the decades of its existence. Annual gatherings of CNR member and advisors with PhD students and other young researchers at 'To think is to experiment' can sometimes take on the feeling of a reunion.

Multidisciplinarity – CNR has always regarded itself as an inclusive organisation which brings together a wide range of narrative work. It supports research on spoken, written and visual narratives, and it draws from psychological, sociological, anthropological and cultural studies research traditions. CNR members work on issues that include: 'race', racism and ethnicities; multilingualism; young masculinities; sexual abuse; popular culture; e-culture; ageing; the 'thirtysomething' generation; political engagement; teaching and education; clinical practice; and artistic practice. An example of this multidisciplinary work is the project 'Hard edges – lives behind the numbers' (https://hardedgesthestories.com/), which explored student homelessness through animation, activism and design.

Working beyond the academy – CNR has adopted a broad conceptualisation of what constitutes 'legitimate' academic work, including but extending beyond the academy. We have collaborated with artists, photographers, gerontologists and therapists, and been associated with numerous public exhibitions. An example is Chila Kumari Burman's 2009 Leverhulme artist in residency at CNR, during which she developed a project, 'You are here: East London self-portraits', which investigated students' visual and verbal self-representations across a range of East London environments. Burman worked with social science students and staff to explore autobiographical materials and ideas visually, drawing on students' academic work, personal histories, and social and political understandings. The centre's work is also increasingly informed by principles of participatory and transformative research, about which we've learned a great deal from our ESRC international visiting scholar collaborations with US and South African colleagues. Recent work with refugees has involved refugee-led photography, art and poetry workshops, and has often been open to the public. Although CNR co-directors and members publish extensively in international, peer-reviewed journals, they also write for and talk with more general audiences. For instance, they co-edited *Voices from the 'Jungle'* (Africa *et al.*, 2017), a collection of life stories written by residents of the Calais refugee camp, most of whom had been engaged with the life stories short university course taught by CNR members and advisors in the camp.

Ideas for the future

2019 marks the twentieth anniversary of the creation of the Centre for Narrative Research. While we feel proud of what we have been able to build together with colleagues in these years, we are also acutely aware of the effects of the attacks on higher education and academic research in the UK on what we can do currently and perhaps in the future. Most concretely, universities rarely now provide consistent funding for research centres, expecting them to fundraise for costs such as administration, researchers' own time, and sometimes also room costs and utilities. Not only are research centres judged largely by annual cost-benefit analyses, all but the most obvious and easily quantifiable benefits tend to be dismissed. To help sustain another, parallel university within the university, CNR has developed collaborative, work-sharing, low-expenditure practices that allow us to pursue our research relatively independent of funding. Even funding bodies' cost-cutting has had some positive impact, as their resultant insistence on institutions working together to reduce expenses and to rationalise has encouraged our already collaborative practices. The human 'costs' of marketised academic labour are harder for us to deal with. At the same time, though, the centre and similar initiatives were and are what enable us to continue academic work that itself tries to sustain and create progressive university practices.

As we write, we contemplate the meaning of radicalism in the university sector. The marketisation of universities has undoubtedly been a radical shift, although not a progressive one. We ask ourselves whether what we were able to do over these two decades was 'radical' in another, progressive way. We know that we have been fortunate to be academics at a certain period of time when there was flexibility in the system to create new and innovative ways to pursue the topics of our interest. We also know that those doors did not open for us; often we had to push very hard to open them ourselves. We feel fortunate that we were able to transcend traditional boundaries between the academy and the 'real world', to collaborate with colleagues from a vast array of disciplines, and to feel part of an international community. For this and much more we know we are lucky. We know, too, that younger scholars are beginning their careers in a very difficult context.

At the same time, there are helpful aspects of that new context. Feminist understandings and practices are much more embedded than they were, albeit still precariously, across academic work. The discourse of 'slow scholarship' has become widespread. Inequalities in university access at all levels – exacerbated by cuts and tuition fee increases – have generated strong and ubiquitous, although not always effective, concern and activism. Colleagues working on decoloniality projects in universities worldwide, especially in middle- and low-income countries, are building powerful progressive movements in higher education; CNR's links with such scholarship are crucial for us. In the UK, instances of progressive higher education practices surround us – for instance, in the universities of sanctuary movement, the Free University of Brighton, Lincoln's Public University, the Cooperative College, and many other programmes operating in and outside of universities, as well as internal programmes of varying levels of radicalism, from Athena Swan to campaigns for more black and minority ethnic professors and other academics. CNR can try, in the coming years, to contribute to what Achille Mbembe has called 'pluriversities', institutions characterised by epistemic openness and dialogue which are also aware of the affordances and limits of the power relations with and within which they operate. CNR and other progressive elements of universities will continue to search out routes to move away from the university as a market, towards the university as a collective of scholars working for knowledge and social justice.

Edited volumes by CNR

Africa *et al.*, *Voices from the 'Jungle'*, Pluto Press: London, 2017.
M. Andrews, S. Day Sclater, C. Squire and A. Treacher, *Lines of narrative*, Routledge: London, 2000.
M. Andrews, C. Squire and M. Tamboukou, *Doing narrative research*, Sage: London, 2013 (2nd edition).
C. Squire, M. Davis, C. Esin, M. Andrews, B. Harrison, L-C. Hyden and M. Hyden, *What is narrative research?*, Bloomsbury: London, 2014.

Additional works by CNR co-directors and fellows

https://repository.uel.ac.uk/researcher/80670/prof-molly-andrews
https://repository.uel.ac.uk/researcher/80682/prof-corinne-squire
https://mariatamboukou.org
https://repository.uel.ac.uk/researcher/81415/dr-aura-lounasmaa
https://repository.uel.ac.uk/researcher/80693/dr-cigdem-esin

Notes

1. Our website provides more information on many such projects: https://www.uel.ac.uk/research/centre-for-narrative-research

CHAPTER SIX

Creating cultural studies

Alan O'Shea

Introduction

The North East London Polytechnic (NELP) was the first institution to introduce a full undergraduate honours degree in cultural studies. This project might never have happened had not a proposal to the Council for National Academic Awards (CNAA) for a BA Humanities degree been rejected. As a consequence, a team led by Ken Parker, the existing chair of the BA General degree, and Michael Rustin, the head of sociology, with support from Tom Whiteread, the head of humanities, seized the opportunity of developing a more adventurous course in cultural studies. The Sociology Department had several staff who had studied at the Centre for Contemporary Cultural Studies at Birmingham University; they were recruited to help develop the core cultural studies elements (Paul Willis, Phil Corrigan, Brian Roberts) and Michael Rustin himself. The existing humanities staff could cover history, English and philosophy, and they drew upon individual staff from applied economics, science and society and applied philosophy. We were fortunate that some members of this team were already well attuned to a cultural studies approach – particularly Bob Chase, Peter Horne, Couze Venn, and Judy Greenaway – and stayed with us for twenty years or more. The course was approved in December 1979 and commenced in September 1980. This paved the way for two more appointments, both having studied at the Centre for Contemporary Cultural Studies at Birmingham University for a few years and strengthened the areas of cultural history, cultural theory and popular culture. Bill Schwarz arrived in September 1979 and Alan O'Shea (myself) in January 1980.

The rise of cultural studies

Some readers of this chapter may be unfamiliar with this relatively new field of study, so it is appropriate to start with a summary of why it arose and flourished at this point in history.

The first formal use of the name 'cultural studies' as a field of study was when Richard Hoggart, professor of English at Birmingham University, established a postgraduate Centre for Contemporary Cultural Studies (CCCS) in 1964.

The social conditions which eventually led to the formation of cultural studies lay in the rapid expansion of working and lower-middle class populations in the late nineteenth and early twentieth century, alongside the expansion of the education system and the growth of literacy. The cultural responses to this included the rise of the mass media, giving these social classes the means to create and participate in new forms of culture – popular fiction, new popular newspapers, the cinema and other 'mass' forms of entertainment. The upper-class establishment and its intelligentsia had long been anxious about the potential political power that this section of the population could wield, but continued to dehumanise it as undifferentiated 'masses', and characterised their new cultural forms as, according to literary critic F. R. Leavis, arousing: 'the cheapest emotional responses. Films, newspapers, publicity in all its forms, commercially-catered fiction – all offer satisfaction at the lowest level'.

In 1957, Hoggart had published *The Uses of Literacy*[1] – again prompted by the rapid growth of the mass media. He was concerned that the culture of working-class communities, their rich sense of neighbourliness, their self-respect, good humour and loyalty to each other, might be disrupted by magazines full of 'gaiety', 'slickness' and 'hedonism'. He argued for a critical valuation of the output of these mass media. Shortly after, Raymond Williams in his book *Culture and Society 1760-1950* (1958) developed a critique of the English literary tradition and philosophical writings in terms of the social and political values enshrined in these works. He too was critical of the repeated representation of the lower classes as 'the masses' and went on to argue that the popular classes possessed their own cultural forms worthy of the name. He proposed that the study of culture cannot be achieved via literary criticism alone but must become interdisciplinary and grounded in its social context. This project of identifying with working-class experience was also being conducted with the publication of E. P. Thompson's *The Making of the English Working Class* (1963) and in the influential pages of the socialist *New Left Review*, edited until 1962 by Stuart Hall. Hall was then invited by Hoggart to join him in Birmingham to help develop the CCCS, and eventually took over as director in 1969.

The mid-to-late 1960s were an ideal moment for the Birmingham centre with its emphasis on interdisciplinary critical analysis. Social movements challenged the political and cultural order: CND, the women's liberation movement, gay liberation, abortion reform, civil rights, countercultures and the anti-Vietnam war movement from the USA, and student strikes for educational reform. These were movements which some analysts have argued were founded on the affluence and the new visibility of the young.[2] National liberation movements since the end of the Second World War accelerated the decline of the British empire, the transition to commonwealth and the immigration of colonial populations who were invited by governments, and believed in the UK as their mother country. By the late 1960s, questions of race, xenophobia and discrimination were high up the political agenda; the gross racism of Enoch Powell and 'the question of numbers' contaminated the development of 'multiculturalism' in Britain.

This conjuncture was ideal for a discipline which analysed the power relations implicit in media forms, and the politicisation of social and cultural relations more generally. Students at CCCS were soon working on the ethnography of contemporary youth cultures, case studies in cultural history, mass media forms and their audiences, the analysis of literary forms and visual cultures, forms of racism, sexism and sexuality, and the rise of the new right.

The centre was now increasingly drawing upon critical thinkers from outside Britain, and its own work was gradually becoming known overseas, especially in the USA, but also in Australia and some European countries, and an international dialogue was established. The centre set up a journal, *Working Papers in Cultural Studies,* and published a number of jointly written books, including: *Resistance through rituals: Youth subcultures in post-war Britain; The Empire strikes back: Race and racism in 70s Britain; Policing the crisis: Mugging, the state, and law and order*; and *Women take issue.* Each of these became widely read and referenced.

So, during the 1970s and 1980s, the field of cultural studies became an international field of work. As Wikipedia puts it, it had become:

> A field of theoretically, politically, and empirically engaged cultural analysis that concentrates upon the political dynamics of contemporary culture, its historical foundations, defining traits, conflicts, and contingencies and relations to wider systems of power. It is multidisciplinary and draws upon literary analysis, history, semiotics/discourse analysis, sociology, psychoanalysis, epistemology and political and cultural theory. It views cultures not as fixed, bounded, stable, and discrete entities, but rather as constantly interacting and changing sets of practices and processes. (Cultural Studies: https://en.wikipedia.org/wiki/Cultural_studies)

This definition captures perfectly the field of work as enacted at the CCCS in Birmingham and as proposed by the NELP/UEL course. This is not to say that it provides a strict orthodoxy. It constitutes a field of debate with different emphases from within this broad set of features, giving rise to fierce contestations both within and between institutions.

The NELP/UEL course

The original course rationale as set out in the approval document stands up well today. Here are some extracts:

> In the design of this course 'culture' is taken to refer to the variety of symbolic forms in which human beings interpret,

> order and give meaning to their experience. It is understood as a means of making sense of life, for individuals, groups and societies. The study of culture, by enabling students to appreciate the diversity of forms and meanings that retain contemporary force, is intended to develop their capacity to find and give meaning to their own situation.
>
> In these present circumstances of great cultural and intellectual diversity and conflict it is held that to clarify the meanings of forms in an historical and situational way may make them more available to students' own experiences.
>
> The course will seek students who have an active commitment to making sense of their world ... The course will encourage wide cultural interests and will seek autonomy and initiative from the students. It will also require of them capacity for sustained intellectual work. The course is seen as relevant for a variety of vocations, but also to other aspects of students' personal and public lives. A student entry to the course that was varied in age and experience would be most consistent with its philosophy.
>
> The choice of teaching methods and modes of assessment reflects this combined concern for students to achieve a grasp of existing disciplines of thought, in their evolving state of development, and a capacity to work autonomously from their own observation and experience. There is also a concern that students learn to work constructively with others.

In short, the course seeks to provide students with the tools to examine cultural phenomena *critically*. What is going on in this particular context? How does it tie into wider systems of power? Which perspectives are being reinforced, and which are challenged? What social values are in play, however implicit?

Outline of the course

Given the background of the initial group of staff, at first the course could be seen as a compromise between humanities and cultural studies, and the team needed to become more familiar with their colleagues' different specialisms and more comfortable with the course's interdisciplinary approach.

The course was structured into six lecture/seminar strands plus a cultural workshop. All students took structural history, cultural history, cultural theory and the workshop throughout, and there were three options: literary culture, philosophy and society, and popular culture. Here students took all three in the first year and then chose one to specialise in for the final two years.

In the first year, each student was allocated a seminar group led by their personal tutor, which gave added support to the students. The seminars which followed each lecture were all run by that same tutor. In these early years this was a learning experience for tutors as well as students – they had come mainly from single subject backgrounds, but now had to chair seminars on all the material of the first year course. The theorists had to come to grips with previously uncharted historical ground, and historians and literature tutors had to take on cultural and political theory. Initially many of us felt inadequate but, with mutual support, ended up as members of a cohesive and spirited team. In fact, this collective mode of working continued throughout the years, and dialogue within the teaching group helped to keep our material updated, especially on the core courses, and also helped our research and publications.

The course had a strong historical frame, focusing on the seventeenth and eighteenth centuries in year one, the nineteenth century in year two and the twentieth century in year three. This reflected our view that, to fully understand cultural phenomena, they should be located in their specific historical context. The course content was constructed so that the students could make connections across these six strands. The history courses were not a continuous linear history of social, political and cultural history, but selected case studies which also resonated with aspects of present-day culture.

Year one was framed by Christopher Hill's book *The World Turned Upside Down*, reflecting on the break-up of feudalism and the rise of radical versions of Protestantism, the Levellers, the Diggers, the Ranters, etc., and the struggles for independence within a religiously-framed universe, and the beginnings of secular rationalism.

Year two was framed around the Industrial Revolution, the movement of the working population into cities, the growth of the middle classes and the struggles of the industrial working class (men and women) to participate in civil society, and gain access to education and literacy, and alongside this the expansion of the British empire.

Year three focused first on the idea of modernity – the excitement of city life, the cinema and the mass media in general, the motor car, new art movements such as futurism and surrealism, and the consolidation of an urban working-class culture. The second half focused on the establishment of the welfare state and the spread of affluence to the lower classes, the decline of the empire and large-scale immigration from the former colonies and the cultural consequences of this, and then the long premiership of Margaret Thatcher, deindustrialisation, financial capitalism, globalisation and the return of competitive individualism.

In each of these courses the question of power relations loomed large – struggles between classes, gender issues, forms of racism and other oppressed groups. And they foregrounded 'history from below' and drew on insights from the optional courses – philosophy, literary cultures and popular culture.

The cultural workshop

Alongside the lecture/seminar-based courses students were required to participate in a weekly cultural workshop. This was conceived as a space for students to be creative in response to themes on the course, contemporary issues or other cultural phenomena, using any kind of written, visual or audio form – we had poetry, plays, music, tape/slide presentations, videos, installations, montages, etc. The polytechnic's resources were rather primitive at first but gradually improved over the years, and as the department of cultural studies expanded its courses to include media studies, the facilities developed into a state-of-the-art media centre, enabling professional recording and digital forms of expression as well (I will return to the media centre later).

Group work was encouraged, but solo work was also permitted. Alongside reports and presentations students were required to keep up a cultural diary which recorded and commented on their week-by-week activity in the workshop. In the final year, students were required to present a substantial project. If they chose to work in a group, we gave the same mark to the whole group, but also, on the basis of their cultural diaries, a smaller separate mark for their own individual input (or lack of it!).

In the early years there were funds to take first year students out for the day to provide material for their projects, and each year we took the whole year group for a weekend project – we visited Folkestone, the Isle of Wight, Conway, Ironbridge, etc. The task was to use their workshop skills to respond to their environment in some way. These events enhanced the relationships between students, and they came to know their tutors on a more informal basis.

During the 1980s the Conservative government began to cut our allocation of funds and we had to terminate such events by about 1986 and, in any case, student numbers grew too large to make this kind of experience manageable. But the presence of this creative/workshop space was kept open more locally, and most students benefited from the regular experience of working in groups, supporting each other, researching cultural phenomena and reporting on this material in a creative way throughout the life of the course.

The growth of the course

By the time the first intake to the BA Cultural Studies had graduated, the annual intake of students over the three years had grown considerably. This expansion enabled more staff appointments to be made in 1982 and 1983, and this helped us to correct a missing element on the course: the original syllabus had rarely touched on feminist perspectives. We were fortunate to make three significant appointments, each having researched and published in this field: Catherine Hall and Sally Alexander are feminist historians, and Mica Nava a feminist sociologist researching at that time on youth subcultures and, later on, consumerism and cosmopolitanism. All three took leading roles in developing the course, and stayed with UEL for many years, even though they could have moved on more quickly to more prestigious institutions.

The course team was constantly working to improve the course. To give an example, when we had seen our first intake through their three years, we held a review of the course to identify what changes we needed to make. By this time I was course tutor and have, by chance, found notes on this meeting. There were different responses depending on each tutor's field of expertise. One commented that we were covering too much content, especially in the history strands, encouraging students to see historical description as background material rather than trying to get the students to 'think historically' and engage in discussion about different interpretations. There was a proposal to introduce a historiographical case study in year one, so that students could better understand that historians are always 'partial' – that is, interpreters of history, and that they select sources which address their particular agendas. Conversely, a literature tutor was worried that literary texts were being reduced to historical material rather than simultaneously being engaged with as a cultural form. Another tutor felt we had not brought out the contemporary relevance of each historical case study strongly enough for students. The students had, after all, chosen a course that states that it 'will seek students who have an active commitment to making sense of their world ...'.

Over the following years we gradually moved towards the direction indicated in this review. Year by year we debated how to clarify the connections between history, theory and cultural forms coherently. By the year 2000, the chronological approach to history had been, in part, replaced by a greater focus on introducing the concepts and methods of cultural studies via more contemporary case studies of phenomena already familiar to the students, but still historicised. We also began to introduce research methods and dissertation training from year two onwards. These changes were facilitated by the fact that the course team stayed together and were constantly engaged in improving the course over the first fifteen years, and that very few moved on after that. The frequent team planning meetings were a great educational experience in themselves, if not always consensual! In a couple of instances in the 1990s, this collaboration on the course turned into research groups and publications: the teams produced two collective books on the themes of the courses they were teaching, each of them deploying about eight contributors.[3]

As the decade went on, and into the 1990s and 2000s, more

lecturers were needed. By then, the high reputation of the department had spread, boosted by top ratings for teaching and research, and we were able to attract remarkably good young – and not so young – well-qualified academics who were fully tuned into the field of cultural studies, and at the same time excellent teachers, researchers, colleagues and friends.

Looking back, we can see most of our discussions were innovative in terms of course content, but our teaching and learning strategies remained quite traditional. Lectures, seminars, tutorials and essays all focused on grasping new knowledge and demonstrating that the students have understood the material and can engage in debates about different interpretations. But cultural studies is also about intervention, about caring about and engaging with, the world you live in. Henry Giroux argues for a 'critical pedagogy' educating people 'to be active and critical citizens capable of fighting for and reconstructing democratic public life'.[4] This involves students 'finding a voice', with a curriculum in which they negotiate both course content and modes of assessment and build confidence in the process. Some of our students certainly achieved something like this, but I wonder now if we could have encouraged more to do so, say, by freeing up the final year of the course and making it more student-centred.

The students

The aim to recruit a mixed range of students in terms of age and experience was met without difficulty for the first decade of teaching on the course. The CNAA had recently waived the academic requirement of two A-levels for higher education entry for over twenty-five-year-olds. These 'mature students' had to apply by making their case for acceptance and coming for an interview. As a result, about two-thirds of the first intake to the cultural studies degree were mature students. These turned out to be mainly intelligent and literate students who, for one reason or another, had not completed sixth-form courses but were keen to resume their education a few years later. Most were in their twenties and thirties, with a few more in their forties and one or two in their fifties. In many cases they had to make financial sacrifices to attend the course and were determined to make the most of it. About one-third of the intake were school-leavers and many said they were attracted by the broad and unique nature of the course. This mix benefited both mature and younger students. The older students' diligence set a standard for the school-leavers in terms of regular attendance, reading for the seminars and taking their turn to present the topic, and delivering work on time. Most of those without the required A-levels (two C grades) had come via access courses provided by further education colleges. We also made allowances for students with some, but not enough, A-levels, etc.

In the first year of the course we were able to nurture the students well. They stayed in the same seminar group for all the discussions and were led by the same tutor. In fact, the first intake missed the target of fifty to sixty students but reached about thirty-five to forty, so we were able to keep seminar size down to seven or eight students. The second intake in 1981 reached over sixty and kept above that level every year after that.

Towards the end of the 1980s the proportion of mature students diminished gradually. It looked as though the pool of mature students – those who had, for one reason or another, failed to acquire their A-levels – was drying up. Alongside this the number of eighteen-plus students rapidly expanded. This changed the atmosphere somewhat. Many of our students had minimal entry qualifications and needed more help with essay writing. We had to introduce more study skills provision and also stronger checks on attendance and delivering work on time.

After tuition fees were introduced in 1998, some students felt this gave them more rights. One morning I walked into the department office and found a student who had not finished his essay on time, justifying his request to have a few days extension on the ground that, as he paid fees, he was a customer and that the customer is always right! The thin end of the neoliberal wedge?

Against this, a good many of our former students have made their mark in different ways. A number became successful academics themselves, some via gaining PhDs in our own department, others doing research degrees elsewhere and then returning. These included Susannah Radstone, UEL and Australia, Amal Treacher,

UEL and Nottingham, Jeremy Gilbert, UEL and 'public intellectual'. Other claims to fame include two successful novelists, Scarlett Thomas and Gilda O'Neill, Daljit Dhaliwal, TV news presenter, David Lawson, film maker, Stuart Bamforth, NGO worker, and Rupa Huq, Member of Parliament.

From course to department

Cultural studies began as a single course, but because of its success became a department in 1985 and I was appointed head. When the courses were modularised, the department became the home for a range of additional courses or 'subject areas', some as spin-offs from the cultural studies degree, such as history, literature, gender and women's studies, and media studies. We also imported communication studies from the school of education as its subject matter is adjacent to both cultural and media studies, and we were able to share units across courses. In addition, we took in third world development – a course constructed from across several departments but keen to join cultural studies. Each of these subject areas had a single honours degree, but also combined pathways, and the cultural studies degree was enabled to continue its core programme but to offer a wider choice of options.

The university introduced a modular scheme in 1990 which standardised all courses into six units a year, thus enabling the cultural studies department to develop new courses and two subject degrees, with some modules open to students from different courses. Some of us working on the cultural studies degree were apprehensive about the introduction of modularisation, on the grounds that if students were freer to choose modules, we would not be able to get them to the same advanced level of understanding and capacity by their third year. But we found that by making core units compulsory and prerequisites for the following year, we could protect the coherence of the core course, while enabling students to select a wider range of options close to their own interests.

Of these new programmes, the media studies degree was the biggest recruiter, partly because students saw the course as making a career in the media more attainable. The cultural studies workshop was still operating, but this surge of media studies students allowed us to make a successful bid for a new purpose-built media centre as part of the move to a new Docklands campus, with three technicians and up-to-date equipment.

In 1991 we also established a part-time MA in Cultural Studies and began taking on research students, mainly by outside application, but with some continuing on from the BA course. The third world development team developed a very successful MA in Refugee Studies and this was followed by a MA in Women's Studies beginning in 1996.

Enter politics

The rapid expansion of the university sector began in the early 1960s and, following the Robbins report, the government had endorsed the principle that courses in higher education should be available for all those who were qualified by ability and attainment. The sector was well funded up to the moment when the Thatcher government set out to 'rationalise' the sector – which included cutting costs from 1982, setting performance indicators and introducing league tables for both teaching and research output. Furthermore this 'rationalisation' was carried out at the high point of the promotion of the 'enterprise culture', which pressurised universities towards favouring courses that equip students for the future workforce rather than those which broadened the mind and produced educated citizens.[5]

In the face of each of these pressures, we had to devise ways of minimising their impact on the morale of the department. Let's look at each in turn.

1. *'The enterprise culture'*

Work placements were encouraged for all students, and some of ours used their workshop slot as material for a report/critique of the experience. The business sector was asked to recommend the qualities they would look for in job interviews. The response was that for candidates to be 'enterprising' they should be able to 'work collaboratively with others, to communicate effectively, and to identify imaginative ways of solving problems and achieving goals'. The irony is that these are precisely the qualities that we tried to develop in cultural studies but with a critical, deconstructive edge in addition. These skills would certainly help any student to have a good chance of gaining employment, but they chimed oddly with the job market. The bulk of available jobs do not require these skills but rather the ability to be reliable and follow a set of procedures (such as in banking) or to have trained for a particular vocation. I will return to this issue later in the chapter.

2. *Performance indicators*

The university introduced performance-related pay for 'managers' – i.e. heads of departments and deans of faculty. It is a process which encourages competition rather than collaboration and peer solidarity. Fortunately, the proposal to extend this to all academic staff was vigorously challenged by our trades union and eventually dropped. In any case, we already had in the department (consistent with our faculty's approach) a more informal system for an annual review for each academic member of staff with the head of department – discussing any changes the tutor would like to see, agreeing a timetable for the following year, asking how their research was proceeding and whether they needed any support. The emphasis was on supporting staff rather than measuring them against each other, and was carried out with a minimum amount of bureaucracy.

3. *Teaching quality assessment*

In 1995-96 a new peer-reviewed teaching quality assessment scheme was introduced, again competitive and published in a league table. Fortunately, the field of cultural and communication studies was a new and fairly small world, and collectively we already knew many of our peers, and that they were on the same wavelength and shared the kinds of practice that we were trying to achieve – collaborative, analytical and pedagogically innovative. The event was time-consuming – a lot of paperwork was required to show that we had mechanisms of our own for evaluating how and what we teach. But what most impressed the assessors was the quality of classroom teaching. As I indicated earlier, by then the department had expanded and been able to recruit a succession of staff, some already well-known, who were both excellent researchers and impressive teachers. We succeeded in achieving the top band six 'excellent' rating.

4. Research and the Research Assessment Exercise

In the late 1980s, in its obsession with measuring and quantifying performance, the Higher Education Funding Council for England (HEFCE) introduced a new system for evaluating and funding research – a Research Assessment Exercise (RAE), primarily based on the published output of individual scholars.

Since the funding for teaching was fixed, winning research funding was the only way of buying time away from teaching and administration. By then we had in the department a strong group of academics, several with international reputations and good publishing records. We had already developed a system of allocating permanent lecturers a semester off every four years to develop their research, and covered their teaching from research income, frequently employing our own PhD students, thereby giving them some teaching experience at the same time.

The assessors for our research were our peers from other universities and, like ourselves, critical of canonisation and how it can be sustained through a pecking order of established journals. However, the assessors were required to assess the national and international influence of research output and could not but reward what is already dominant. This is problematic for a new and innovating subject area. Journals focused on cultural studies were now proliferating but not yet 'established'. We were still building our international reputations.

The RAE itself depended on fine judgement: how many staff do we want to include in the assessment? On the one hand, the more inclusive the better, on the other, too long a 'tail' of lesser outputs will pull down the grade. Our first entry to the RAE was in 1992. We were just learning the ropes then and our entry was incomplete, but we still scored 3a, and were happy to settle for that. But by the

1996 RAE we had done our homework properly and scored a top-rating five ('excellent'). It is remarkable that we achieved this at UEL. By this time, the richer universities were recruiting highly rated researchers as quickly as they could, but we held our own by achieving another 'excellent' grade in 2001. Overall, though, the greater amount of research funding continued to be awarded to older established universities.

We also achieved one of the top aggregates in our subject area in 2008, enabling us throughout this period to increase research time for all permanent tutors. In terms of our careers, our reputation opened up chances for some of us to transfer to more prestigious institutions. There were losses, but a cohort of younger academics were keen to join us and have since taken leading roles in the department.

There is also a potential downside to this incentive to prioritise research and publication. The point at which a vigorous commitment to teaching and research can tip into a careerism – in which external recognition and personal promotion becomes the major motivation – is an imperceptible one. It is not surprising that one's energy goes into conferences and publishing – no bad thing in itself, simply that it reduces one's attention to the education of students. And if the former activities build careers, it is in the latter, in their teaching, that academics can lend their weight most effectively to opening up new perspectives to their students. We were fortunate that all our strong researchers were dedicated to their students and were also helped by the sabbaticals that the RAE funds enabled.

Although the RAE was competitive, there was some distribution of wealth towards the newer, poorer universities rather than continued donations towards the traditional top-rated universities. The sector became more meritocratic – it was not enough to rest on a high reputation, you had to be turning out new and innovative work. However, an effect of incentivising research in this way was to take attention away from the course development and teaching work which had up to then been our principal concern, and had some divisive implications.

In addition to publications, several staff were on the editorial boards of journals, such as *Feminist Review* (Catherine Hall and Mica Nava), *History Workshop Journal* (Sally Alexander and Bill

Schwarz), *Ideology and Consciousness* (Couze Venn), *Theory, Culture and Society* (Couze Venn and Mica Nava), *New Formations* (Bill Schwarz and Jeremy Gilbert).

We also established three research groups. First, in 1992, we recruited as a resident researcher Phil Cohen, formerly working at the Birmingham CCCS, who then founded a Centre for New Ethnicities Research with a series of projects, mainly on race and youth cultures, mostly funded by external bodies. The centre has continued until very recently with the help of younger colleagues, including Roshini Kempadoo, Ashwani Sharma and Jeremy Gilbert. Alongside this, Phil Cohen has been on the editorial advisory board of the London East Research Institute – participating in its projects and publishing in its collective books, the *Rising East* volumes and *Eastern Promise*.[6] He has managed to gain funding himself for most of his projects, and has continued to publish prolifically. In 2000 he established and developed the London East Research Institute for the next seven years. Phil Cohen is still active as an emeritus professor of cultural studies.[7]

Second, we established an East London History Centre when Raphael Samuel, who established the influential History Workshop movement at Ruskin College, Oxford, agreed to join UEL as a research professor. His aim was to continue his lifelong project of encouraging the widest possible participation in historical study and debate. After his death in 1996, the centre was renamed the Raphael Samuel History Centre, and was curated by John Marriott for a short period, and then directed by Barbara Taylor, who continued this role until 2016 after moving to Queen Mary University.

Third, in 2007, a group of the staff from a by then much expanded school (the terms used to describe the university units were constantly changing) organised a huge four-day conference attended by over 450 people from forty-three different countries. This was a high point of our achievement. Stuart Hall gave the keynote speech, which was as inspiring as ever. Following the conference, the organising group, invigorated by the success of the conference, founded the UEL Centre for Cultural Studies Research (CCSR). The centre ran a programme of guest speakers including several of international renown, such as Homi Bhabha, Richard

Sennett and Jacqueline Rose. During the last decade, CCSR firmed up its connections with Iniva, the Institute of International Visual Arts, whose board of trustees was chaired by Stuart Hall during the formative years.

Endgame – the millennium and beyond

Despite these neoliberal pressures towards competition and more vocational outcomes, the department in 2000 was flourishing on all fronts, with all its degree programmes examining cultural and social phenomena with a critical edge, and its research output still growing. And, despite the still increasing volume of workload, most of us kept updating our courses, and this kept our teaching refreshed.

Endnote: neoliberalism triumphs

On a personal note, I retired from my post in 2002, and the department became part of a school the following year. I understand that this was the first of three organisational changes by 2019, and that each change saw a slow drift towards vocationalism.

The undergraduate programme in cultural studies was closed a few years ago, though the Centre for Cultural Studies Research still exists. The BAs in history and English were closed in 2018 and are currently running down their last intake. Gender and women's studies have also been dropped, and third world development is now renamed international development and moved into the School of Sociology.

The remnants of our other programmes have had various fortunes. Much is now located in the Department of Media, Fashion and Communication within the School of Arts and Digital Industries. The head of the school was formerly head of entrepreneurship at Solent University. Before this she had a background as a practising journalist.

The current offer of courses within the Department of Media, Fashion and Communication include the following: media and communication (which still maintains a cultural studies approach, alongside practical work); film; creative and professional writing; journalism; sports journalism; advertising; and computer game development. These are all substantially vocational training courses, though there are vestiges of a cultural studies approach in film and in advertising. They are now all housed in a new building – the College of Arts and Innovation.

Effectively the university has discarded all humanities subjects – cultural studies, history, geography, literary studies, philosophy, semiotics/linguistics and theory of any kind. Feminism has disappeared, along with any other politically related subjects. UEL must now be one of the very few universities without any humanities courses.

The reason for this fundamental shift is that the newly appointed vice-chancellor has made a requirement for all programmes in the university to be much more 'outward facing', to build links with industry and be much more practice-driven. Effectively that means that five out of six modules each year are built around practice, work experience, technical skills and with, at best, one module more theory-based. Essays are discouraged and, if allowed, can be no more than 1500 words.

This is all directed towards improving UEL's 'employability metric' – the percentage of students in graduate jobs six months after graduation. On this measure UEL is very weak in comparison with equivalent universities. The careers office is now called the Centre for Student Success.

Of course, getting our graduates employed is a positive thing. The problem is that UEL management is equating vocational-style training with employability. This takes us back to the earlier section on the 'enterprise culture' and the employers' view that for candidates to be 'enterprising' they should be able to 'work collaboratively with others, to communicate effectively, and to identify imaginative ways of solving problems and achieving goals'. This is calling for critical and imaginative thinking, writing skills and wide reading. But the UEL courses appear to prioritise technical skills with little room for any of the broader intelligence that employers are looking for in graduates.

Could it be that immediate employment is rising up the list of priorities for universities' league tables, and so that UEL will get more students into work by awarding degrees for a vocational education? If so, this is doing the students a great disservice when it comes to competing with other graduates with a broader education.

Acknowledgements and selected staff profiles

Many thanks to Bob Chase, Mica Nava, Catherine Hall, Sally Alexander, Bill Schwarz and Ash Sharma for support and advice on this chapter.

Also, in memory of those who are no longer with us: Ken Parker, Peter Horne, Couze Venn, Raphael Samuel, Mike Holly and Vivian Schelling.

The following profiles provide an indication of the range of research and our contributions to the development of cultural studies within the UK and internationally:

Sally Alexander

Sally joined the department in 1983. She had studied history at Ruskin College and UCL, helped to organise the United Kingdom's first national women's liberation movement conference at Ruskin College in 1970, and was involved in several London women's liberation workshops, as well as the night cleaners' campaign (1970-72) She was a founding editor of the *History Workshop Journal* (established in 1976). Her first major publication was *Becoming a Woman: And Other Essays in 19th and 20th Century Feminist History*, Virago, 1994. Her other interests are the history of other social movements, of memory, and of psychoanalysis. These interests added new dimensions to her teaching and later she organised the core course in the final year. This was closely aligned to the teaching team's collective book *Modern Times: Reflections on a Century of English Modernity* (1996). In the late 1990s she was appointed as professor of modern history at Goldsmiths University and has co-edited (with Barbara Taylor) *History and Psyche: Culture, Psychoanalysis, and the Past*, Palgrave Macmillan, 2012.

Bob Chase

Bob arrived from the USA via Germany with a PhD from Yale, and was teaching German at NELP when the cultural studies degree was set up. He joined the team from the beginning, teaching across various part of the course, but mainly in the literature strand. The support he gave to his students was excellent – he always had time for them. As for research, he focused on the enlightenment, and was able to participate in Barbara Taylor's project. His publications took the form of substantial essays: 'History and poststructuralism: Hayden White and Fredric Jameson' and 'Walter Scott: a new historical paradigm', both in Bill Schwarz (ed.), *The Expansion of England: Race, ethnicity and cultural history* (1996); 'John Locke and cultural relativism', *Interpretation*, Fall 1997, Vol. 25, No. 1; 'Herder and the postcolonial reconfiguring of the Enlightenment', Greg Clingham (ed.), *Questioning History: The Postmodern Turn to the Eighteenth Century* (*Bucknell Review*), Associated University Presses, 1999, Volume XLI, Number 2; plus other shorter pieces in the *History Workshop Journal*.

Later in the 1990s, Bob took on the role, very effectively, of overseeing and coordinating all the undergraduate programmes in the department. He took retirement in 2003.

Jeremy Gilbert

Jeremy came to UEL as an undergraduate, already capable of understanding even the most difficult material, and achieved a good first. He chose to do his postgraduate studies at Sussex University but on completing his PhD he applied to come back to take a teaching post at UEL. He was, and still is, a DJ and the first book he published (with Ewan Pearson) was *Discographies: Dance Music Culture and the Politics of Sound*, Routledge, 1999, and he still teaches a class on this subject. He is keen to make cultural studies available outside academia and regularly organises free courses open to all. His second book is *Anticapitalism and Culture: radical theory and popular politics*, Berg: 2011, and his third is based on his PhD, *Common Ground: Democracy and Collectivity in an Age of Individualism*, Pluto Press, 2014. He is also the editor of the journal *New Formations* and has written in *Open Democracy* and various other journals and in *The Guardian*. He is now professor of cultural and political theory, still at UEL, and his publications are widely read – he has become, in effect, a public intellectual. Power to your elbow, Jeremy!

Catherine Hall

Catherine joined the department in 1983 and strengthened our expertise in cultural, social and feminist history, and quickly became a year tutor, and a central voice in our course development discussions. She was already working on her first book with Leonore Davidoff: *Family Fortunes: Men and Women of the English Middle Class 1780-1850* (1987, new edition 2002); and followed that with *White, Male and Middle-Class: Explorations in Feminism and History*, Polity Press, 1992. She focused increasingly on slavery and slave ownership; as she put it 'the slavery business in its many manifestations was part of British life – not something that belonged to the Caribbean, but part of the everyday fabric of life in the metropole'. Her following books included: *Gendered Nations: Nationalisms and Gender Order in the Long Nineteenth Century* (editor, with Ida Blom and Karen Hagemann, 2000); *Defining the Victorian Nation: Class, Race, Gender and the British Reform Act of 1867* (editor, with Keith McClelland and Jane Rendall, 2000); *Civilising Subjects: Metropole and Colony in the English Imagination, 1830-1867* (2002). Having left UEL in 2009, she became professor of modern British social and cultural history at University College London and became the principal investigator on the 'Legacies of British slave-ownership' project. She is now retired but remains in close contact to her former colleagues at UEL, and is still writing.

Kate Hodgkin

Kate joined us in the 1990s and has taught both history (especially early modern) and literature, with great commitment to both her students and her colleagues, and soon took over the coordination of the literature strand. Her research focused on:

witchcraft and the history of madness and melancholia; madness and gender; madness in autobiographic writing; and also issues around historical memory. She became the UEL director of the Raphael Samuel History Centre – in a partnership with Birkbeck and Queen Mary's. She has also convened two seminars at the Institute of Historical Research, and has been promoted to a professorship of cultural history. Her books include: *Women, Madness and Sin in Early Modern England: the autobiographical writings of Dionys Fitzherbert*, Ashgate, 2010; *Madness in Autobiography*, Palgrave, 2006; and *Witches*, Reaktion Publishers, 2017. She also co-edited the Routledge series on 'Memory and Narrative' with Susannah Radstone, including *Memory, History, Nation: Contested past*s and *Memory Cultures: Memory, Subjectivity and Recognition*, both Transaction Publishers, 2005.

Mica Nava

Mica joined the cultural studies programme in 1983 in order to strengthen our courses on popular culture and to bring a feminist perspective to all aspects of our curriculum. Her publications include: *Gender and Generation* (1984); *Changing Cultures: Feminism, Youth and Consumerism* (1992); *Modern Times: A Century of English Modernity*, co-edited with Alan O'Shea (1996); *Buy This Book* (1997); and *Visceral Cosmopolitanism: Gender Culture and the Normalisation of Difference* (2007). Since the 1980s her work has been widely cited and reprinted, and she has been invited to give keynote conference papers and/or special lectures on her research all over the world. She participated fully in the teaching programme and was involved in setting up the MA in Cultural Studies, and taking on PhD students. Mica was a key organiser of a very successful four-day conference in 2007, including an inspiring keynote speech by Stuart Hall and attended by over 450 people from forty-three countries. Enthused by this, she and her colleagues established the UEL Centre for Cultural Studies Research. Mica is now emeritus professor of cultural studies and, like many of us, keeps in touch with UEL.

Ken Parker

Ken was a key figure in setting up the cultural studies degree and leading it through the validation process in 1979. Born in South Africa, he became a leading anti-apartheid activist and was forced to leave in 1964. He settled in the UK and found a teaching post in NELP (as it was then). He became chair of the BA General Degree, but then took over the leadership of the new BA Cultural Studies course. His specialisms were South African literature, and early modern literature and Shakespeare, and he also coordinated the literature strand of the degree. Later he oversaw the department's research profile and managed the first Research Assessment Exercise. His own research output was vast. His books included: *Brief Chronicles: South African Literatures in Historical Context,* UNISA & Koninglijke Brill; *Shakespeare: Antony and Cleopatra,* Northcote House; *Early Modern Tales of Orient. A critical anthology,* Routledge, (ed. with Elleke Boehmer and Laura Chrisman); *Altered State? Writing and South Africa,* Mundelstrup; *Dangaroo,* Dorothy Osborne (ed.); *Letters to Sir William Temple,* Penguin Classics; (ed.), *The South African Novel in English: Essays in Criticism and Society,* Macmillan. He also contributed to our collaborative book, Bill Schwarz (ed.), 'Fertile Land, Romantic Spaces, Uncivilized Peoples: English Travel Writing about the Cape of Good Hope, 1800-1850', in *The Expansion of England. Essays in the Cultural History of Race and Ethnicity,* Routledge.

Ken retired from UEL in 1998 as emeritus professor in cultural studies, and later became a senior research fellow at the Institute of English Studies. He died after a long illness in March 2019.

Susannah Radstone

Susannah was a student in the first intake of the cultural studies degree, and one of our best students, obtaining a first. She decided to stay with us for postgraduate work, and then was appointed as a teaching member of the department, specialising in the film studies strand. Her first publication was *The Women's Companion to International Film,* University of California Press, 1994, co-edited with Annette Kuhn. She then turned to the issue of memory and narrative in *The Sexual Politics of Time: Confession, Nostalgia, Memory*, Routledge, 2007. Routledge launched a series on 'Memory and Narrative' jointly edited with Kate Hodgkin, and in one case Bill Schwarz, including: *Memory, History, Nation: Contested Paths* with Kate Hodgkin (2005); *Memory: Histories, Theories, Debates*, co-edited with Bill Schwarz (2010); *Memory Cultures: Memory, Subjectivity and Recognition*. Susannah is now working on a book on trauma.

Bill Schwarz

Bill joined UEL following postgraduate work at the Centre for Contemporary Cultural Studies at Birmingham University, one year before the cultural studies degree was launched, and played a large part in refining the initial direction of the degree and throughout our course reviews. Alongside this he embarked on an ambitious programme of research on postcolonial history, exploring Britain at the end of empire. He began on a three-volume history entitled *Memories of Empire*; the first volume, *The White Man's World*, Oxford University Press, 2011, won the Longman-*History Today* prize for 2013. The second volume, *West Indians*, Oxford University Press, was completed in 2015. Bill is still working on the third volume. He also co-edited with Susannah Radstone *Memory: Histories, Theories, Debates*, Fordham University Press: New York, 2010, which is part of a series on historical memory. Bill was also an editor of, and frequent contributor to, the *History Workshop Journal* throughout this period, made many contributions to other books and journals, and edited our collaborative volume, *The Expansion of England: Essays in the Cultural History of Race and Ethnicity*, Routledge.

Throughout this time, Bill had been a close friend of Stuart Hall, and when Stuart fell ill, he took on the role of ensuring that nothing was lost from Stuart's legacy: he organised collections of Stuart's major writings, and helped Stuart to write a political memoir from his childhood onwards: *Familiar Stranger: A Life Between Two Islands*, Duke University Press, 2017. He is a member of the editorial board of *Soundings*.

Barbara Taylor

Barbara joined UEL in 1993 after mental illness and applied to UEL because she already had good colleagues there. She already had an international reputation through her book *Eve and the New Jerusalem: Socialism and Feminism in the Nineteenth Century*, Virago, 1983; Harvard University Press, 1992, and republished with a new introduction, Virago, 2016. Soon after joining us she set up an international research group on the enlightenment, and managed to secure grants and fellowships from the Leverhulme Trust, the Nuffield Foundation, the Guggenheim Foundation (1996), the Social Science and Humanities Council of Canada, and the Wellcome Trust while remaining dedicated to her teaching, even at first year level. This project resulted in *Women, Gender and Enlightenment*, edited with Sara Knott, Palgrave, 2005. She also completed her book *Mary Wollstonecraft and the Feminist Imagination*, Cambridge University Press, 2003. She wrote *The Last Asylum: A Memoir of Madness in Our Times* describing her years at Friern hospital, and co-authored with Adam Phillips *On Kindness*, Penguin, 2009. She co-edited with Sally Alexander *History and Psyche: Culture, Psychoanalysis and the Past*, Palgrave, 2005. She moved to Queen Mary in 2012 as professor of humanities.

Couze Venn

Couze joined the cultural studies degree at its inception and taught the course on philosophy, science and ideology during the whole of his eighteen years at UEL. He had already been developing the journal *Ideology and Consciousness* during the 1970s, which introduced European theorists to a British readership. He co-edited *Changing the Subject*, Methuen, 1984, on subjectivity. He also wrote prolifically for *Theory, Culture and Society, Body and Society* and other journals, while also caring about, and inspiring, his students. He eventually left UEL in 1998 to become deputy director of the Theory, Culture and Society Centre at Nottingham Trent University. When the centre moved to Goldsmiths in 2004, he moved with it. His first book, *Occidentalism: Modernity and*

Subjectivity (2000), addressed the making of Europe as the 'modern west', arguing that postmodernism was inseparable from and underpinned by the suffering of postcoloniality. His 2005 book, *The Postcolonial Challenge,* further developed this idea, exploring the place of neoliberalism within global poverty and the developing world. In *Poverty, Inequality, Education* (2014), written with his wife, Francesca Ashurst, he confronted the history of the pathologisation and criminalisation of poverty. Despite the onset of prostate cancer, he wrote *After Capital* (2018), which offered innovative ways of thinking about capitalism and making the case for 'creating a means of living together beyond profit, wealth or exploitation'. He passed away in March 2019.

Notes

1. Richard Hoggart, *The Uses of Literacy,* Penguin, 1957.
2. D. Robins and P. Cohen, *Knuckle Sandwich,* Penguin Books, 1978; D. Hebdige, *Subculture: the meaning of style,* Methuen & Co, 1979.
3. Bill Schwarz (ed.), *The Expansion of England: Race, Ethnicity and Cultural History,* Routledge, 1996. Mica Nava and Alan O'Shea (eds), *Modern Times: Reflections on a Century of English Modernity*: Routledge, 1996. We rethought the nineteenth century through anti-slavery, family fortunes, empire, suffrage, popular memory, liberalism (Mill to New Liberals), invented a sort of twentieth century European history – modernism, revolution, war memories etc. – and introduced psychoanalysis as a source of meaning across the curriculum by the early 1900s.
4. H. Giroux, 'Resisting difference: Cultural Studies and the discourse of critical pedagogy', L. Grossburg, C. Nelson and P. Treicher (eds), *Cultural Studies,* Routledge: London and New York, 1992.
5. For a full account of the marketisation of our universities, see Stefan Collini, 'Sold Out', *London Review of Books,* Vol 35 No 20, 2013.
6. For more detail on the LERI, see Chapter 7.
7. See Chapter 7.

CHAPTER SEVEN

East London research

Penny Bernstock and Gavin Poynter

The context

As civic engagement, knowledge exchange and evidence-based practice become the new mantra of higher education, universities are increasingly attempting to embed themselves in their local communities as a central part of their mission. This approach has been firmly rooted at UEL for more than four decades, generating cutting-edge research in disciplines ranging from history to social policy. East London is undoubtedly an interesting place to study – a central destination for migrants coming to the UK, marred by extensive poverty and deprivation and a testbed for national regeneration initiatives, including the Thatcherite approach applied in London Docklands and London 2012. This has resulted in the development of a range of centres whose intellectual influence stretches beyond the UK, ranging from the London East Research Institute and the Centre for Institutional Studies through to the Raphael Samuel Centre and Centre for Sustainability, working collaboratively with other universities and driven, fortuitously, by key figures with a passion for promoting social justice and inclusivity in its broadest sense. Here we focus on the development of our East London-related research.

Introduction

John Marriott's[1] accomplished history of East London commences with the story of the American radical journalist and author Jack

London's attempts in 1902 to find East London. He visited the esteemed Thomas Cook & Son at its Cheapside branch. Cook's reputation was founded upon its capacity to organise tours for its wealthy clients to all parts of the world. But, East London, 'they knew nothing whatsoever about the place'.[2] Marriott uses this fable to illustrate the distinctive working-class character of East London, which was, from the Victorian period to the mid-twentieth century, the industrial and commercial 'other side' of the metropolis. The decline and eventual closure of London's vast docklands and its related manufacturing industries from the 1960s to the early 1980s appeared to confirm that the East would retain its character as a poor other side to the city's rich 'West End'.

The half century since, however, has witnessed state-led cycles of urban renewal or regeneration as East London has taken centre stage in a number of national regeneration projects. The first being the expansion of the City's financial services industries to its location on former docklands at Canary Wharf. The second was the ambitious but flawed 'Thames Gateway' programme that envisaged urban housing and business developments that stretched to the eastern edges of Essex and North Kent. And the most recent and costly public investment has arisen from the location of the 2012 summer Olympic Games at Stratford, in the lower Lea valley. The games organisers promised that the sporting spectacle would provide significant economic and social benefits to local communities as its legacy. The legacy, seven years after the games, in and around the location of the Queen Elizabeth Olympic Park, continues to be created. These cycles of change have drawn the city eastwards, improved transport links, attracted significant inward migration and population growth, but have also created new pockets of wealth alongside areas in which social deprivation persists. Regarded as one of Europe's largest regeneration projects, East London in recent decades has been a laboratory for the study of urban renewal.

While John Marriott's main focus has been its history, many other groups and individuals at the university have applied themselves and their respective disciplines to undertake in-depth research into the laboratory that is East London. The result is, we submit, a distinctive and diverse range of research projects and publications that reveal the deep and sustained affinity of their authors to the area.

Affinity has arisen for several reasons. First, the university is itself part of the region's regeneration, having opened a new Docklands campus in 2000 and a new shared location with Birkbeck College in the centre of Stratford. Second, the university's student intake is mainly local from within East London and surrounding areas. Understanding their social and educational background is vital to both staff and students for the latter to benefit genuinely from their university education. Finally, our East London research has and continues to be informed by a deep social commitment to creating 'a better quality of life for those living and working in the area'.[3] This chapter illustrates some of our projects and programmes of work.

Rising in the East

The first publication emanating from scholars at UEL was an extensive survey of the history, culture and economy of East London, aptly named *Rising in the East*.[4] Its contributors captured the significant social changes taking place within the area, taking up themes that have largely defined our research on the region in subsequent decades, including demographic change, trends in the labour market and the increasing polarisation of the labour market between the white-collar professions and those in lower, far less secure employment. The discussion anticipated more recent debates on gentrification and the rise of precarious work, the so-called gig economy. The book explores both continuity and change in class structures, gender and ethnicity, and the consequences of deindustrialisation and policy responses to it. Contributors identify the key tension that has lain at the heart of debates about the regeneration of East London for more than forty years – the conflict between corporate interests and local needs and aspirations, anticipating many of the issues and debates that have taken place since, not least in the construction of East London's Olympic 'legacy'.

In retrospect, *Rising in the East* captured the diversity of social research conducted in the period of the polytechnic's transition to university status. It also anticipated fairly accurately the agenda for the social research on East London that followed. Perhaps most importantly, the book sought to combine high-quality social research with a policy orientation. It was designed to create discussion and debate with those agencies that had the power and political responsibility to 'transform' East London. The book was followed by a journal, *Rising East,* first published in May 1997. Tim Butler stated in its opening edition that its intention was 'to give a voice to the region'. Coinciding with the opening of the university's Docklands campus in 2000, a further publication, *Eastern Promise,* discussed the university's role as a potential resource in support of the area's social renewal.

The Sociology Department, located for many years in a Faculty of Social Sciences, provided the home for East London research, although contributors to the books and journals referred to included staff from other academic disciplines within and outside the university, including local politicians, community activists and policy-makers. Two former chief executives of London boroughs, Anna Whyatt and Drew Stevenson, at different times were appointed to take responsibility for the department's East London research, with the aim of strengthening its links with the local communities and their public bodies. The period of Docklands redevelopment into a major financial centre in the course of the 1990s, and plans of successive quasi-government agencies for the development of localities such as Stratford, the Royal Docks and the Thames Gateway, provided much of the context for the research on social change. It was not long, however, before a second wave of urban renewal was spurred by London's successful bid (in 2005) to host the 2012 summer Olympic Games.

Race, racism and cultural identity

Parallel to the Sociology Department members' research into East London, Professor Phil Cohen, who moved to the university in 1992, set up and directed the Centre for New Ethnicities Research (CNER), which was initially located in Cultural Studies. The centre developed an ambitious programme of research and community engagement in East London around issues of race, racism and cultural identity. This included ethnographic studies of frontline situations of racial conflict in East London, and a funded research programme on young people's perceptions of class, gender and ethnicity in two areas of London and Hamburg, whose results were published as *Finding the Way Home*.[5] In addition, the centre organised a major conference 'Front lines, backyards' (1998), curated Rich Mix, an exhibition of multicultural art in Tower Hamlets (2001), ran an extensive programme of seminars and public lectures, and published a series of working papers. Some of this material was collected in *New Ethnicities, Old Racisms*.[6] The centre's work was influential, especially in directing attention to the deeper, more unconscious, reaches of the popular racist imaginary.

Olympic legacies

In 2004, Phil Cohen set up the London East Research Institute (LERI), with the aim of coordinating the university's research on the regeneration of East London. This became an element in the university's civic engagement agenda, and was supported by John Lock, a former Newham councillor, who was a member of UEL's civic engagement team. By this time, the university's humanities and social sciences fields of study, including sociology, had co-located to the university's new Docklands campus, thus bringing many of the researchers on East London together. Initially the research concentrated on the Thames Gateway, the largest regeneration project in Europe at the time, and this led to the publication of *London's Turning* (P. Cohen and M. Rustin (eds), Routledge 2006), a collection of studies of different aspects of the eastwards turn in London's growth.

With the announcement of London's bid for the 2012 Olympics and the decision to locate the main venue at Stratford, East London, the focus of LERI's work inevitably shifted to evaluating the impact of the games on local communities. Several edited texts appeared over the course of the pre- to post-phases of the games: Gavin Poynter and Iain MacRury (eds), *Olympic Cities and the remaking of London*, Ashgate, 2009; Gavin Poynter, Yang Li and Valerie Viehoff (eds), *The London Olympics and Urban Development*, Routledge, 2015;

and G. Poynter and V. Viehoff (eds), *Mega-event Cities: Urban Legacies of Global Sports Events*, Routledge, 2016.

Phil Cohen conducted an ethnographic study of the initial 'dig, design and demolish' site construction process, and established ongoing focus groups with local residents and young people to chart their response to the unfolding impact of the Olympic delivery process. This material formed the basis of his book on the 2012 games, *On the Wrong Side of the Track?*, Lawrence and Wishart, 2013, which was widely reviewed and praised. The legacy impact of 2012 was the subject of a follow-up study and included a book co-edited by Cohen with Paul Watt, *London 2012 and the Post Olympic City: A Hollow Legacy?*, Palgrave Macmillan, 2017.

UEL, as a centre of research on the urban impact of the games, was widely recognised by local, city-wide, national and international institutions. Iain MacRury and Gavin Poynter were invited to write a 'think piece' on 'London's Olympic legacy' for the Organisation for Economic Co-operation and Development and Department for Communities and Local Government (November 2009), and Penny Bernstock to broadcast for the BBC on housing legacy. A UEL cross-disciplinary research team led by Professor Allan Brimicombe (head of the Centre for Geo-Information Studies) produced the Olympic Games Impact Studies (ESRC/LOCOG) – *Pre-Games Report* (October 2010) and *Post-Games Legacy* (November 2012). These impact studies, a contractual requirement placed on host nations by the International Olympic Committee (IOC), provided government with longitudinal data and analysis of the effects of public investment. Professor Brimicombe was also appointed to the House of Lords special committee on Olympic legacy as its expert advisor.[7] While this investigation drew mainly on quantitative datasets, scholars working with LERI have continued to explore legacy impacts in the fields of employment and housing, enabling a longitudinal interrogation of legacy across the period 2000-18. What is perhaps most surprising is that much of this work was done despite UEL's rather limited involvement, at that time, in the communities of East London. However, this contribution was awarded with a four* 'impact' rating in the Research Excellence Framework (REF) competitive evaluation of research in 2014.

By 2015, a number of staff associated with the London East

Research Institute had left, leading to a rethink of ways that the work could be continued. Minutes of an inaugural meeting in March 2015 indicated that staff had felt unsupported in the past, but that East London research work was now to be given greater priority as part of a new university corporate plan that put civic engagement at its core. The institute moved back to something like its first home (it had been for a while a university-wide research centre) in a newly formed School of Social Sciences, and returned to its original name, the Centre for East London Studies (CELS). The centre sought to serve the wider community through an engaged public sociology that would contribute to the university's identity and its role in the wider community. The centre continued to focus on the dissemination of knowledge and the stimulation of debate on key issues related to urban regeneration and social change in East London. The new centre became a laboratory for undergraduate students to engage with East London issues. It was co-directed by Andrew Calcutt and Penny Bernstock. Andrew was also programme leader for journalism and editor of *Rising East*, which was revamped as an online news magazine produced by University of East London students in collaboration with university staff. Penny Bernstock was head of sociology and involved undergraduates in generating East London research with a clear focus on gentrification and urban change.

The Olympic legacy work continued with a national conference on legacy in 2016 to mark four years since hosting the games. The centre, keen to engage local people in East London-related issues, organised a range of seminars exploring East London old and new, with an array of guest speakers attracting a mix of policy-makers, researchers and local residents to consider a range of issues – from Booth's approach to measuring poverty through to providing an explanatory framework for, and the changing fortunes of, East London on the index of multiple deprivation. The centre continued to foster connections and a network of scholars and students working on issues broadly associated with the regeneration of East London and its governance, thus reflecting its commitment to policy-making.

Both LERI and CELS were commissioned to undertake research on a range of topics. For example: Shelter commissioned LERI to explore new neighbourhoods in Thames Gateway and the voices of 'hard to reach' groups; the London Borough of Newham commissioned us to explore Newham's night time economy; and the Canal and Riverways Trust commissioned us to evaluate the impact of the renovated Carpenters Road Lock on the Olympic Park on local people, their heritage and communities. This research often included a training element; for example, UEL undergraduates were provided with training in ethnographic research methods and paid the London living wage to work on the evaluation of the Carpenters Road Lock. In 2016 we established a YouTube channel that enabled the wider dissemination of information, ranging from conferences and seminars through to 'talking heads' on a range of East London-related issues. We supported PEACH (People's Empowerment Action for Custom House) to disseminate knowledge and promote understanding about the development of community-led housing.

In 2017, we were encouraged to tender for an evaluation of a major initiative led by Citizens UK and funded by Trust for London aimed at promoting a citizens-led housing agenda. Housing on the Olympic Park was one of four case studies. This was a four-year study, but UEL's reluctance to fully support the bid resulted in the contract being awarded to another university. CELS' leading housing researcher initiated talks with Citizens UK East London branch TELCO (The East London Communities Organisation) and moved from a relatively independent academic role to working directly with a campaign group to ensure adherence to original policy commitments on a meaningful legacy. Penny Bernstock, the researcher, took on the role of co-chair of Citizens UK Olympic Legacy Committee. The university's reinvigorated commitment to civic engagement was short lived, and most staff involved with the centre have since left UEL to continue their East London research work elsewhere. The value of our research was reinforced in those years by the extent of media coverage, with researchers and our research publications cited in a range of international, national and local media, ranging from BBC's *Newsnight* to CNN.

Conclusion

Research on East London, as this brief survey suggests, has produced a series of books, journal articles and reports that span three decades of change in East London – the social, cultural and economic effects of deindustrialisation and post-industrial renewal. In its academic context, the publications and engagement with our locality contributed to strong performances in various rounds of the higher education sector's Research Assessment Exercises. In turn, the research was integrated into undergraduate and postgraduate curricula in sociology, cultural studies and other fields in the social sciences (see, for example, Chapter 19 by Tim Butler and Barbara Harrison on sociology). Postgraduate researchers were given the opportunity to publish chapters and contribute to journal papers. Several publications included contributions from colleagues who worked outside the academy – politicians, civil and public servants, and community activists. It could be claimed that the research programme lent a reasoned and critical voice in support of the communities of East London.

Within the polytechnic/university the reception and support for the research has varied. It was typically strongly supported at the level of faculty/school management, particularly by Professor Michael Rustin, over many years with relatively modest financial support, enabling sabbaticals to be given and research centres to function. At senior levels of the university's management, the research programme on East London was supported by colleagues responsible for developing the Docklands campus and the institution's relations with local communities, most notably Carole Snee and John Lock.[8] However, it is to be noted that despite the amount of project funding, and the favourable ratings in research assessment exercises that were achieved, it proved difficult to establish the substantial funding from external sources which are required to sustain a research centre's development. We believe that our origins as a former polytechnic, in a highly status-conscious academic universe, may have been a limitation in this respect.

But East London research was not consistently viewed as an integral part of the institution's role within the region by its most senior staff. This was particularly evident in the years following the transition to university status. The locality was conceived largely in transactional terms as a market for student recruitment, and its new campuses as the means to attract them (particularly from overseas). Such an orientation tended to overlook the institution's academic and intellectual role in helping to shape public debate and inform the policies that sought to manage successive waves of the region's renewal. Perhaps our failure to achieve a sustained influence within the institution was at least partly offset by the research's reception in the world outside. Moreover, it is impressive to realise that such a huge body of work was generated in the main by a small number of scholars committed to ensuring that the university engaged in meaningful ways with the communities in which they were based, making a very real impact on knowledge exchange and understanding about East London. The research was characterised by continual innovation in its methods while retaining its commitment to socially just outcomes for local residents. This was achieved with a very limited infrastructure. In 1984 Doreen Massey gave a lecture at Toynbee Hall observing that urban change in East London was a microcosm of broader economic and social trends, and this was the lens through which our approach operated. This defined a model for analysing urban change that firmly connected the local with the global, in the process providing a valuable information resource for academia, policy-makers and East London communities. At the time of writing, the centre remains relatively inactive. While academics in different fields at UEL continue to undertake research on aspects of local life, the clear focus on East London as an object of study, which characterised the work of the research centres discussed in this chapter, has been for the time being lost, with its former scholars continuing this work elsewhere.

Notes

1. John Marriott was professor and fellow of the Raphael Samuel Centre, Cultural Studies, University of East London.
2. John Marriott, *Beyond the Tower: A History of East London,* Yale University Press, 2011, p1.
3. Tim Butler and Michael Rustin, *Rising in the East: The Regeneration of East London,* Lawrence & Wishart, 1996, pvi.
4. *Ibid.*
5. Phil Cohen, *Finding the Way Home,* V&R Press: Hamburg, 2004.
6. Phil Cohen (ed.), *New Ethnicities, Old Racisms,* Zed Books, 1999.

7. See House of Lords Select Committee on Olympic Legacy, Report of Session 2013-4: https://publications.parliament.uk/pa/ld201314/ldselect/ldolympic/78/78.pdf
8. Carole Snee led the university's creation of the Docklands campus, opened in 2000, and was head of external relations at UEL. John Lock was director of policy. Sadly, John died in 2017. He was posthumously awarded the freedom of Newham, his home borough, for his many years of public service to Newham, and for his work to secure a strong community legacy from the Olympic Games.

CHAPTER EIGHT

A new approach to economics

Frank Skuse and Peter Howells

Preamble

In this chapter, we concentrate on the 1970s and 1980s, a period in which the economics programme offered at North East London Polytechnic (NELP) was at its most radically different from the offering in the subject across the rest of the higher education sector. One paragraph (see 'Subsequent developments' below) briefly moves forward into the 1990s.

In the beginning

A degree in economics was an early addition to the emerging portfolio of courses offered by the then North East London Polytechnic. The small economics team already had some experience of teaching the subject as it offered classes leading to the part-time external BSc (Economics) degree awarded by the University of London, and on the BA (General) course. However, it was felt that an in-house programme was a better proposition, allowing control over the syllabus, assessment etc. Encouraged in part by informal contact with Professor Bernard Corry of Queen Mary College, who was a forceful advocate of economics within the newly designated polytechnics, and an East Londoner himself, the team designed a degree programme, subsequently approved by the Council for National Academic Awards (CNAA), leading to the first intake of students in September 1971.

This first programme, leading to the award of a BSc Applied Economics to distinguish it from economics degrees in the university sector, was nevertheless fairly conventional in terms of structure, content and assessment. Built around a core of macro- and micro- economics over all three years, with quantitative methods and economic history compulsory in the first year and history of economic thought in second year, it justified its title by, in the final year, offering a range of options that were more application- and policy-oriented across a range of areas. In spite of its title, however, it was not that dissimilar to many degrees available across the country.

Assessment too was conventional, being almost entirely exam-based, with diagnostic exams at the end of year one, little contributory assessment in year two and final assessment, including determination of the degree classification, at the end of year three. Teaching methods too were standard – a mixture of lectures and tutorials/seminars, involving twelve hours' class contact per week.

The radical years

In the early 1970s, the course team expanded, gaining staff who had education and/or teaching experiences outside the UK, notably Australia and USA. The result was to introduce rather greater heterogeneity into the teaching staff. The result of this manifested itself in the version of the degree that was approved by CNAA in 1976. Three areas in particular meant that the new offering can be described as radical compared with most other institutions, both then and now.

The first element was a completely revamped syllabus in the first year. The quantitative methods course remained, but the rest of the teaching was split across two large blocks, economics, and economy and society. The former was a complete break with standard structures. In a way that was influenced by the ideas of Imre Lakatos and his methodology of scientific research programmes,[1] which argued that scientific disciplines exhibited simultaneously a plurality of possible approaches, albeit some of them being more progressive and fruitful than others, the team proposed a pluralistic approach. This provided the basis for the economics unit to be broken into four schools of thought: neo-classical microeconomics, Keynesian macroeconomics, marxist economics and institutional economics. This did not represent an attempt to introduce a modified form of history of economic thought, but rather aimed to show that there were competing views among contemporary economists. Inevitably there was reference back to important figures, especially in the areas of marxist and institutional economics, and the syllabus began with a short introduction to the ideas of the classical economists, namely Smith and Ricardo.

The aim was to provide a basis for students to contextualise the disagreements for which economists are (perhaps overly!) famous. The 1970s were rich in debates among economists on a number of then current issues, the causes of inflation and of unemployment being two such examples. Two quotes here provide a summary of the rationale for explicitly building this into the syllabus:

> These debates cannot be seen as mere quibbles concerning matters of policy or fine detail within the context of a generally agreed frame of reference for economic science. Rather they are the reflection of important differences between groups of economists concerning the very nature of their discipline.
>
> Furthermore, the regular student retort that theory does not reflect the real world can also be answered more satisfactorily when the student has some knowledge of the broad framework of which a particular idea forms a part, and has some awareness of the development of that framework.[2]

The economy and society block provided a formation in terms of the background within which economic affairs occur, involving areas such as some economic history, sociology and politics.

The introduction of these two subjects involved a radical restructuring of the teaching: they each occupied 40 per cent of the teaching timetable, with quantitative methods accounting for the remaining 20 per cent.

The second element which distinguished the 1976 submission was an important change in the nature of assessment. As indicated above, the original programme involved diagnostic exams at the end of the first year, very limited assessment at the end of the second year, and a full programme of exams at the end of the third year. The course team was concerned that, for a significant number, this form of assessment encouraged students to drift through the second year, placed an undue burden on the final diet of exams and was implicitly concerned uniquely with 'exit velocity'.

Certainly, students were required to submit essays throughout the year, but these did not count formally in an evaluation of their attainment. Additionally, there was no formal sanction were a student not to submit a piece of work, thereby missing out on the potential diagnostic benefit that would have followed from its submission.

Consequently, two major changes were introduced which, at the time, were effectively radical departures from the norm, within NELP and across economics degree courses elsewhere. The first was to introduce a measure of contributory, continuous assessment, counting 40 per cent towards the student's final grades, but clearly still giving greater weight to exit velocity. Second, units in the second year were assessed at the end of that year, with the joint benefits of providing the student with an evaluation of their progress, and of lowering the burden of the exam load in the final year. Such second-year results contributed towards the final degree classification, but with a lower weighting than those of the following year.

The continuous assessment element was considered sufficiently innovative that Keith Bain, instrumental in constructing, with student participation, the proposal and defending it, had an article published in the *Times Higher Education Supplement,* which unfortunately has proved untraceable. Such a form of assessment became commonplace in subsequent years, on many courses and in many institutions, but at the time was considered innovative and needing a robust defence.

The third element that represented an innovation was the introduction of a unit concerned with post-Keynesian political economy. This area was little taught at the time in other institutions, and was often classified as being merely an element of heterodox economics, and hence outside the mainstream. This was particularly true in

US universities, where contributors to that research programme often suffered professional disadvantage. For example, Alfred Eichner at Rutgers, a key contributor to post-Keynesian economics, was prevented from teaching on postgraduate programmes as the result of his adherence to the approach.

The unit explored the alternative insights offered by this growing school and, over the years, developed a more robust theoretical background, borrowing from the ideas of J. M. Keynes often ignored by readers only of his *General Theory,* and from those of Michal Kalecki. Two areas where it arrived at conclusions radically different from the mainstream were in the behaviour of oligopoly markets and the nature of the money supply.

As regards the former, Kalecki argued that the standard analysis in terms of supply and demand provides a plausible explanation for certain types of market: agriculture, raw materials, the stock market are good examples. But it does not fit markets dominated by a few large firms, i.e. oligopolies. Here firms enjoy what he called a 'degree of monopoly', enabling them to determine prices and allow the market to decide the *quantity* traded rather than its *price.* This market power is not unconstrained, and will vary according to a firm's estimation of its extent.

Oligopolistic markets pose problems for analysis. Participants enjoy a degree of power because they normally produce differentiated products. Such differentiation may be real, that is, demonstrably different product specifications and qualities, such as, for example, the car market, or based on brand and advertising, designed to induce consumer loyalty. A further feature of such markets is that firms have a degree of interdependence, in that decisions of one participant will have a noticeable effect on others. For example, in the UK supermarket industry, growth of market share by one firm will be at the expense of a noticeable loss of share by other participants. This means that a firm's decisions cannot be taken in isolation, and must try to estimate the potential reactions from competitors.

There are two further limitations to the extent of this market power. The first is the threat of entry into the market of new rivals. The UK supermarket industry is again an excellent example: the arrival of discount stores Aldi and Lidl has had a noticeable impact on the growth and dominance of the incumbent firms and, as suggested above, produced reactions from them, for example in the introduction of cut-price ranges or, in the case of Tesco, the introduction of its own range of discount stores under the Jack's brand. The other limitation comes from the threat of government intervention. Here we need look no further than the UK energy market, where Ofgem imposes price caps on suppliers.

Eichner[3] and Wood[4] modelled the pricing decision by large firms by linking it to the need for investment funds. In the oligopoly sector, these funds are, for the most part, internally generated from profits, supplemented by borrowing. Firms' managements attempt the delicate operation of balancing the perceived need for such funds against the threat of losing market share as the result of any price increases. Wood's model is arguably the richer in that it builds into the constraints on firms not only their market power but also their objective in terms of financial structure and gearing, taking into explicit account the dangers of an excessive indebtedness through over-borrowing.

Such investment may take many forms: physical investment in productive capacity; research and development and new product development; advertising and attempts to enhance brand reputation, to cite three examples. All are designed to reinforce the degree of monopoly enjoyed by the firms and sustain their market power.

An appealing feature of both of these potential explanations of oligopoly behaviour is that they link the static question of price determination directly to the dynamic behaviour of markets and development through time. This link can be seen clearly in a number of cases. For example, UK utilities such as energy and water regularly justify price increases to consumers on the grounds of the need to finance modifications and improvements to infrastructure, a clear demonstration of the relevance of the starting point for the models of both Eichner and Wood. Other examples abound.

Turning to the question of the second area, the money supply, the orthodox view of money began with something called the 'quantity theory of money' which, *inter alia*, viewed inflation/deflation as caused by the extent to which the money stock expanded more quickly/slowly than the growth of the economy's output. For this to make any sense, it had to be the case that the growth of the money supply was exogenous to (determined outside of) other events in the economy. The common explanation for this was an assumption of a more or less fixed coefficient between the quantity of notes and coin and the volume of bank deposits (which make up more than 95 per cent of the money supply in most modern economies). This relationship was crucial since the central bank could conceivably control the former directly (by instructions to the mint and the printing press) while the latter were the outcome of commercial banks' day-to-day decisions to lend.[5] As an account of money supply determination this suffered from the fact that no central bank had ever tried to control the monetary base (notes and coin) directly, realising that banks would quickly find ways of economising on notes and coin (changing the size of the coefficient) and fearing the chaos that a shortage (for example) of currency would cause if banks failed to get round the restriction.[6]

The Bank of England experimented during the 1960s and 1970s with various devices intended to restrict bank lending directly but these were either ineffective or, where they had the desired impact, simply led to the predictable consequences of any form of non-price rationing – a combination of inefficiency and inequity accompanied by an explosion of innovative activity to get round the rules. This was finally abandoned in 1971. The new arrangements, titled 'competition and credit control', released banks from these direct controls in exchange for the end to a number of restrictive practices. So far as monetary policy was concerned, this was to consist, in future, of changes in the bank rate (the rate at which commercial banks can borrow from the central bank) in the hope that these changes would be passed through to the rate charged on bank loans, and therefore influencing the *demand* for loans rather than their *supply*. In these circumstances, the quantity of money becomes *endogenous* since the flow of bank credit, of which money is a by-product, is itself the consequence of the state of the economy or, as it was often said in heterodox circles, by 'the state of trade'. Causalities are reversed. Far from monetary growth being an independent cause of inflation, money is itself the result of inflation and output.

In 1981, the Conservative government introduced what it called the 'medium-term financial strategy' (MTFS). Wedded still to a 'quantity theory' view of inflation, it envisaged progressive reductions in money supply growth accompanied by falling rates of inflation. But *in practice* reducing monetary growth meant reducing the growth in bank lending by raising interest rates to whatever level was necessary. This Mrs Thatcher was allegedly reluctant to do because of the effect on 'our people' through the cost of mortgages, an attitude sometimes described as 'willing the ends but not the means'. In the event inflation *did* come down but not because monetary growth slowed (the targets were largely missed), but as a result of the recession induced by high interest rates. The MTFS episode is interesting in demonstrating that the quantity of money could not be easily controlled at the same time that it revealed that this did not matter anyway (at least for inflation).

That NELP was in the vanguard when it came to the teaching of monetary economics is evidenced by the reception given to the textbook, *Monetary Economics: Policy and its Theoretical Basis*, by Keith Bain and Peter Howells. This originated in their difficulty as teachers of trying to reconcile the existing textbook accounts with real-world events as reported in, for example, the *Financial Times.* The first edition (2004) was condemned by one critic for its excessively polemical style (no doubt the result of the authors' frustration). By the time of its second edition (2009), it was widely praised for its realistic account of the way that central banks actually behaved – i.e. treating the money stock as endogenously determined.[7]

The preparations for the 1981 re-approval for the economics degree took place under a cloud. Early in 1980, the director of NELP announced that the departments of applied economics, sociology, cultural studies and mathematics were to be closed. The ostensible reason given for this decision was that these areas were not sufficiently career- and employment-oriented and, especially within the ethos of the Thatcher government, did not fit with the perceived purposes of the polytechnic sector, the 'applied' designation notwithstanding. This, however, was widely seen as a smokescreen for an entirely different, and hidden agenda, the true nature of which was the subject of considerable speculation. This speculation need not concern us here. Despite the decision to phase out economics, and its corollary that the required 1981 re-approval of economics was not to take place, the then head of department, Thanos Skouras, approved the preparation of a new submission, as part of the resistance to the proposed closure, and in the hope that the decision would be reversed. The new degree was little changed, maintaining the innovative first year course, alongside the continuation of a post-Keynesian political economy unit in year two of the programme. Changes that did occur hardly fitted the radical theme referred to in previous paragraphs above, and consisted of introducing units which could be seen a potentially more career-oriented.

In the event, a CNAA panel visited the polytechnic in the spring of 1981 and approved the offering for the standard five-year period. The director appeared before the panel and publicly withdrew the threat of closure.

The degree structure that followed five years later involved further major changes. The department had changed its name from applied economics to that simply of economics, in line with usage throughout the higher education sector, and this allowed a differentiation within the range of programmes. Alternative pathways were constructed, leading to the award of different degree titles. The BA Economics resembled the traditional route of study; the business economics pathway required the compulsory study of business-oriented units (basic financial accounting, managerial economics, corporate finance among them). The BSc Applied Economics title was retained but required units in quantitative methods and econometrics to be studied beyond the first year by students opting for that particular pathway.

Subsequent developments

Later, pathways leading to a BSc Financial Economics and a BA Political Economy were developed. These were designed to increase the attractiveness of the offering to a wider range of students, particularly in the light of falling enrolments in economics across the sector.

Despite the more mainstream elements embodied in these pathways, sight was not lost of the more radical elements referred to in previous pages. The appointment in 1988 of Philip Arestis as head of department strengthened the department's credentials in the area of post-Keynesian economics, still regarded at that stage as outside the mainstream, despite its appearance by then in a limited number of UK institutions, notably from the ex-polytechnic sector. In particular, the research and publication profile of the department was raised, especially, though not uniquely, in the post-Keynesian area. The result was that the department was rated in the 1996 Research Assessment Exercise as equal to the best rating achieved in economics among institutions from the ex-polytechnic sector.

But by this stage, North East London Polytechnic had changed its name, first to Polytechnic of East London and then, in 1992, to University of East London, in the wave of the creation of the so-called new universities.

In retrospect

Given the legendary benefits of hindsight, we would be missing a valuable opportunity to appreciate this experimental period if we were not to consider other attempts to offer a different, more radical, curriculum both at the time and, especially, more recently, following the financial crisis of 2008-09.

At a strictly practical level, a major problem faced by the designers of any course that breaks away from the consensus is the availability of teaching materials. In the 1970s, before the internet, before CDs even, and before interactive simulation packages, 'teaching materials' meant a textbook (in a few cases accompanied by a 'workbook'). For the NELP course, this difficulty was partly overcome by the course team writing a series of essays, organised into two volumes, typed, copied and bound 'in house'. This had the advantage that *all* students had access to a text that followed the lectures closely, but outside of that text there was little help available to them, except from the journals and specialist monographs. This made it heavy-going for any student who found parts of the in-house text difficult. It was also difficult to encourage students to 'read widely' as part of their general education and training.

A book that might have helped us appeared in July 1973. This was the *Introduction to Modern Economics* by Joan Robinson and John Eatwell.[8] A reviewer in the *Economic Journal* referred to: 'the highly critical analysis they present of industrial capitalist societies and the apologetic economic theory that largely serves the dominant classes in those societies'.[9] With this clearly radical focus, it might have been thought an obvious candidate for our programme. But its structure was very different and would have required students to pick very selectively, and to have tackled parts in a completely different order from that intended by Robinson and Eatwell themselves. And, although it was a book that was lavishly designed and presented by the standards of its time, it contained little or no pedagogic support (exercises etc.) for students. It seemed uncertain as to whether it was offering a potential course of study to readers who knew little or nothing of economics or a radical reinterpretation of economics for those who were already well-versed in its conventional foundations (a critical observation made by a number of reviewers).

The most powerful message for teachers of economics that emerged from the Robinson and Eatwell episode was that the forces of inertia in the economics establishment were enormous. Notwithstanding the huge expense to which McGraw-Hill went with their publicity and mailing of free copies to virtually every teacher of economics in the land – and in spite even of some reviews that were sympathetic to its radicalism – it had no discernible impact on the design of undergraduate courses. Clearly, at that time at least, NELP really was pushing a very heavy cart up a very steep hill with its innovations.

Since November 2008, when the Queen famously asked why economists did not see the crisis coming, many academic economists (and their students) have felt obliged to reflect on the nature of the economics curriculum.[10] The Royal Economic Society, the Bank of England and the Government Economic Service have all hosted meetings at which the need for reform has been discussed. The Association for Heterodox Economics,[11] the Post-Crash Economics Society,[12] the Post-Autistic Economics Network,[13] among others, have published explicit proposals, and the Economics Network[14] conducts large-scale annual surveys of economics students to elicit their views on the programmes they are offered. Inevitably, there are many proposals for modification of the conventional curriculum (some of them contradictory and tending to confirm the public's view of economists as a disputatious lot), but it is interesting in the light of NELP's experience to note that the two most popular proposals since the crisis are for 'more economic history' and a 'recognition of plurality'.

The latter, of course, was central to NELP economics in the 1970s and so, to a lesser extent, was the former. The shift from the initial (conventional) programme at NELP to the subsequent radical model reveals an interesting lesson about the treatment of economic history in an economics degree. As we explained earlier, the initial programme had a compulsory economic history unit that ranked, *pari passu,* with other compulsory units. Students at the time, however, frequently expressed the feeling that they were being asked to spend considerable time (20 per cent) on the study of material whose relevance they found limited. This points to the need for the history to be much more closely integrated with the economics, rather than being contained in a parallel unit that inevitably develops its own momentum and narrative. It is instructive to see the way in which the very successful CORE project[15] has integrated economic history into its internet-based economics foundation course – historical episodes are introduced only when they illustrate something of direct relevance to the topic.[16]

However, any reviewer of undergraduate economics courses at present will be struck by the extent to which 'the mainstream' continues to dominate the menu. And this applies not just to the UK but also to Western Europe and (even more so) to the USA. The CORE project itself, while it is much more open to history and evidence, devotes more attention to market failures and rejects 'equilibrium' as the inevitable norm; it is still denounced in heterodox circles as an attempt to 'patch-up' the conventional wisdom: 'a better approach to orthodox economics' as it is sometimes described. The resilience of the mainstream, especially in the light of the financial crisis in 2008-09, is truly astonishing and worthy of study in its own right. Part of the explanation no doubt lies with 'economic' forces themselves. We mentioned earlier the problem of teaching materials for innovative courses. This is a much bigger hurdle now when such materials involve interactive websites and a wide range of supportive materials. The effects of this can be seen even within mainstream economics, where US textbooks are widely used outside the US because economies of scale allow them to be produced in a more attractive and generous format than their counterparts in the UK and Europe. It is significant also that the CORE project, which shows at least *some* willingness to forsake the more manifestly unrealistic components of orthodox economics and to use concepts familiar to the heterodox wing of the profession,[17] and is proving attractive to many universities and students around the world,[18] receives funding from an astonishing range of international bodies.[19]

Nonetheless, the inertia remains. The economics of publishing are unlikely to be the whole story. To understand this fully, we may have to go back to the critique by Robinson and Eatwell. An 'apologetic economic theory that largely serves the dominant classes in those societies' (see above) is unlikely to be readily abandoned by those classes so long as their power continues. In this big picture, NELP's experiment with a more radical, relevant economics education in the 1970s looks heroic.

Notes

1. See I. Lakatos, 'Falsification and Methodology of Scientific Research Programmes', Lakatos, Imre and Musgrave (eds), *Criticism and the Growth of Knowledge,* Cambridge University Press: Cambridge, 1970.
2. F. E. Skuse and J. C. Ure, 'An Alternative Introduction to Economics', *British Review of Economic Issues* Vol. 2, No. 4, May 1979.
3. A. Eichner, *The Megacorp and Oligopoly: Micro Foundations of Macro Dynamics,* Cambridge University Press: Cambridge, 1976.
4. A. Wood, *A Theory of Profits,* Cambridge University Press: Cambridge, 1975.
5. The bank grants a customer the authority to spend funds they do not have. The moment they spend, a loan is created and also, and *inevitably,* the payee receives an increase in their bank deposits. Hence the phrase 'loans create deposits', a standard proposition of heterodox economics.
6. From 2001 to 2005, Frank Skuse was the external economist member of two day-long panels established by the UK Cabinet Office to assess candidates for appointment as fast-track economists. The majority of candidates were from the established university sector. During the economics interview, potential appointees regularly alluded to the exogenous nature of money supply. These candidates were not entirely to blame given the prevailing textbook accounts. *As late as*

1984, Charles Goodhart ex-chief economist at the Bank and professor of economics at LSE, denounced the textbook consensus as '... such an incomplete way of describing the process of the determination of the stock of money that it amounts to misinstruction'. C.A.E. Goodhart, *Monetary Theory and Practice*, Macmillan: Basingstoke, 1984, p188.

7. K. Bain and P.G.A. Howells, *Monetary Economics: Policy and its Theoretical Basis*, Macmillan: Basingstoke, 2009.
8. J. Robinson and J. Eatwell, *An Introduction to Modern Economics*, McGraw-Hill: London, 1973.
9. Review of Robinson and Eatwell, *Economic Journal*, no. 84, 1974, 334, p447.
10. Many, but not all. 'Why should we go around beating our breasts just because some US bankers behaved stupidly?' is a sentiment frequently heard at conferences.
11. See https://hetecon.net/
12. Based at Manchester University. See http://www.post-crasheconomics.com/economics-education-and-unlearning/
13. http://www.paecon.net/petitions/a-e-petition.htm
14. E.g. https://www.economicsnetwork.ac.uk/sites/default/files/Ashley/Survey%20report%202012.pdf
15. CORE is 'An open-access platform for anyone who wants to understand the economics of innovation, inequality, environmental sustainability, and more'. See https://www.core-econ org/
16. Chapter 2 of the textbook (https://core-econ.org/the-economy/book/text/02.html) is titled 'Technology, Population and Growth' and provides a good example of the way in which theory and history (and history of thought) can be integrated. Basic concepts like costs, prices and innovation rents are explained against a background of the British Industrial Revolution, and the outcome (rising productivity) is used to resolve debates between Smith, Ricardo and Malthus.
17. For example, Chapter 20 of *Economics of the Environment* contrasts 'positive feedback' with the negative feedback that underlies the cherished notion of 'equilibrium' in orthodox economics. In effect, it is formalising Veblen's concept of 'circular cumulative causation', to which the NELP programme gave considerable attention.
18. 'CORE is now used in 206 countries, with more than 78,000 registered users and more than 7300 teachers. We are in touch with 128 universities from thirty-three countries around the world that are using CORE in instruction'. *CORE Newsletter* 1.3.19.
19. See https://www.core-econ.org/funders/

CHAPTER NINE

Fashion and textile futures

Sara Bowman

North East London Polytechnic (NELP)'s Art and Design School had radical roots from its inception, as it built on Walthamstow School of Art's outstanding creative history and reputation. This ensured NELP had the heritage to develop a dynamic art and design school when Walthamstow Technical Institute merged into what became NELP in 1970.[1]

Pop artists Sir Peter Blake and Derek Boshier, Royal Academicians Olwyn Bowey, Fred Cuming, Ken Howard and Bill Jacklin, musicians Ian Dury and Terry Day, fashion designers Foale and Tuffin, and Celia Birtwell, film-makers Ken Russell and Peter Greenaway, and costume designer Shirley Russell all taught or studied there.[2]

Its origins go even further back to West Ham Technical Institute, established in 1892 as 'a people's university' to serve the local community, offering science, engineering and art. By the late 1960s, there was little evidence of art teaching at West Ham until the merger with Walthamstow and Dagenham technical institutes in 1970 ensured that art and design flourished and developed in NELP.

In 1979 I was working for Ted Southcott at Worthing College of Art and invited to NELP's fashion department because I was a fashion history person. Fashion history was a new and developing field, and I became responsible for fashion contextual studies.[3]

I also had the added benefit of having been a politics student at the new La Trobe University, Melbourne, then came to the UK where I was an MA student on the history of dress and textiles course established at the Courtauld Institute by the doyenne dress historian Stella Mary Newton. I was able to use my broad insight into textiles, fashion and theatre in teaching fashion history and contextual studies degree courses at NELP.[4]

Drawing on my own experiences at NELP/UEL to write this piece, I also had discussions with Doreen Dyall, first head of the fashion and textiles diploma courses at NELP 1970-78, later head of textiles 1978-89, Valerie Goodworth, who joined the fashion design and marketing course team in 1983 and became head of fashion design and marketing 1993-2002, and conversations with former staff and students.

Walthamstow School of Art and Design

The radical Walthamstow School of Art was committed to the inclusiveness of the arts for all.

> 'The school exists to give a complete and balanced training to those students who are going to earn their living as craftsmen, painters, and designers, or by the profession of teaching. But the cultural needs of the community are not less important and the school provides evening classes in drawing, painting and instruction in the crafts for all those whose interest is non-professional'. Prospectus, 1960.
>
> 'There was a socialistic ethos of giving opportunities to people with talent even if they did not have the exact qualifications'. Brian Harris, artist and millinery tutor, Walthamstow 1960s.

The head of Walthamstow School of Art, Stuart Ray, had been so impressed by some life drawings executed by a road mender he met in the street that he offered him a place at the art school on the spot.[5] This ethos was carried over to NELP School of Art and Design when Stuart Ray became head of school.

Fashion and art and design at Walthamstow

Walthamstow was regarded as a successful point of entry to the Royal College of Art (RCA) for both art and fashion students. In 1960, twenty-five out of thirty-nine art and design staff were graduates from RCA, and in 1964, thirty-four former Walthamstow students were studying at RCA.[6] These included painting student Marion Foale, who later went on to study fashion at the RCA, and fashion student Sally Tuffin who together went on to set up the fashion label Foale and Tuffin. Other students included Ken Russell, Peter Greenaway and Ian Dury.

The 1960 Walthamstow prospectus recognised the growing importance of dress design and fashion because: 'The work of fashion houses commands considerable attention and they provide employment for great numbers of people and great opportunities for designers with talent'.[7]

Some heads of department and tutors were developing stellar careers. Walthamstow alumnus tutor Peter Blake, 1961, completed his painting *Self Portrait with Badges 1961* while teaching there; it won the John Moores painting prize. Joanne Brogden was head of fashion at Walthamstow and in 1968 became professor of fashion at the RCA.

NELP Art and Design School

In 1970, most of the NELP Art and Design School was housed in Greengate House, Plaistow E13, with fashion and textiles based at Holbrook, a former school a quarter of a mile away. In 1980, fashion and textiles moved into Greengate House. Both buildings were outposts, physically separated from the main NELP sites in Barking and Stratford, several miles away.

Greengate House with its particular ambience – an ad hoc meanwhile space – was not purpose-built for student use. A former YMCA building, it was a fine example of facadism converted in the 1980s into art and design studios for graphics, pattern-cutting, sewing rooms, fine art, sculpture, painting, textile print studios and teaching rooms. It had an excellent art and design library. It retained its art school culture, and the layout of the building enabled staff and students to walk past open studios. It was a creative environment: pop-up installations were not uncommon; a lift was converted into a miniature sitting room; and a gallery space in the foyer exhibited staff and students' work.[8]

It became an incubator and catalyst for change for new beginnings and collaboration, driven by a passion for innovation and excellence in art and design education, as well as creating important community gains.

Fashion and textiles at NELP

Doreen Dyall was both an acclaimed young textile designer and RCA alumna[9] when she became head of fashion and textiles at NELP after leading the textile vocational course at Walthamstow School of Art.

Like many of her contemporaries, Dyall had combined her professional design practice with part-time teaching. 'The interaction of my design practice gave me confidence in developing courses when the art school became part of NELP with recognised degrees'.

In the 1970s, students entered the course with a free spirit and desire to experiment. Dyall recollects:

> I would enjoy the surprise inventiveness of going into studios seeing lengths of knitting cloth not, as one might expect, being constructed into fashion garments but brushed with resin and shaped into 4ft x 6ft sculptures alongside another student designing and constructing a chair which she would upholsterer from fabric she had printed, and being tutored by a member of the fine art staff co-opted in on the project as he had experience of undertaking such work.

In the landscape of the new textile courses, NELP had its own unique signature. NELP's textile portfolio focused on textile design for both furnishing and fashion. The courses offered a breadth of experience of textiles and fibres; some students were interested in technical aspects, others wanted to print, others wanted to experiment and work in a more art-based way.[10] Designer and academic Simon Ungless said: 'The programme set me up to move between fashion, textiles, art direction, styling and even copy writing'. After NELP, he went to Central St Martins, then collaborated with

Alexander McQueen on the first ten collections.[11] Textile DipHE Textile innovator and designer Trish Belford later developed innovative screen-printing techniques for Vivienne Westwood, Alexander McQueen, Georgina von Etzdorf, Neisha Crosland, Helen Storey, Liberty Prints, English Eccentrics and Zandra Rhodes. In 2004 she returned to Ulster and established the Tactility factory to produce concrete and fabric wall installations.[12]

The professional practice/business studies strand was an essential tenet of the course programmes and enabled students to understand industry requirements, working to specific briefs, and to industry-led textile competitions – such as annual Royal Society of Arts (RSA) textile student bursaries sponsored by leading textile manufacturers and retailers, and specific industry-led competitions. This strand of the course was highly innovative and is now an essential feature of many textile degree courses.

Dyall developed a portfolio of textile design courses, including an integrated fashion and textile diploma course in 1970, and in the 1980s, with Andrew Ruffhead and their team, was responsible for developing multi-subject Textile Dip HE strand and modular degree in textiles BA Hons and MA individual programmes. Dyall recollects:

> In the early days an overview of teaching was especially rewarding. It was a precious time to inculcate a strong work ethic with students which would be lasting, to open out the individuality and horizon of each student, encourage confidence and creativity of ideas, backed equally with creative technical skills over a wide range of applications These remained core values throughout my approach to teaching design and were integral in the planning and development of future courses.

Additional access to textiles came through the independent studies degrees and diplomas. Cadence Martin, a local homeworking machinist, said:

> When I started the course I knew nothing about printing ... Seeing the print room gave me ideas, and talking to tutors

> helped. Because I couldn't draw I tear paper to form things I want or I use a paint brush. I really enjoy hand painting and when I saw the Raoul Duffy exhibition, I realised he was using the same kind of brush strokes as I did. That was exciting. Many of my designs are of West Indian scenes ... The beauty about it is seeing the things you've done, you never believed you could do.[13]

The creative textile course team of full- and part-time staff included many leaders in their fields, at the forefront of new research, among them Doreen Dyall, head of textiles, and Andrew Ruffhead, who led the textile printing workshop.[14] Visiting lecturers included: Celia Birtwell, the renowned textile designer who also collaborated with Ossie Clark; Brian Harris, artist/milliner and fashion creative; David Jamison, the renowned printer; Victor Herbert, working in the forefront of experimental textiles; and Jacqui McLennan, fashion textile designer.

The importance of industry

The business studies strand was an integral part of the textile courses because it was assumed most students would work free-lance or in industry. They had to understand the industry and changes in the market, develop market research skills, produce design development concepts, make presentations. They benefited from studio visits, attending textile and trade fairs in London and Paris, and heard from industry experts from commercial and high-end individual designers, such as Paul Smith, Timney Fowler Studio and Honour Taft, working as a textile/designer agent in the USA and Europe, in order to understand different business models and aspects of the industry.

As part of their coursework, first and second year students developed and applied for RSA bursaries funded by major leading retailers and manufacturers, such as John Lewis Partnership, Sekers Fabrics etc. Designer student project briefs included creating six-page spreads comparing designers such as Liberty/Next, or Katharine Hamnet/Jean Muir, for magazines such as *World of Interiors* or *Vogue*. This was a third-year market research comparative study.

The course values included collaborative working, technical excellence, experimentation, design development and ability to design for different markets, and the development of individual design signatures. Key were the development of professional practice skills with a strong work ethic, and an awareness of the opportunity, where appropriate, for community gains.

In 1974 after a house/studio fire, Dyall refocused her professional design practice on fashion textiles, which were highly acclaimed and sought out by international buyers.[15] By the late 1970s, Wenda Southcott became the course leader for the fashion diploma course.

Fashion design with marketing

In the 1970s and into the 1980s, there was evidence of some small-scale fashion manufacturing in Plaistow and an invisible network of homeworkers, which the industry relied on. On Thursdays, Ida's, a factory sample outlet store, saw queues of local women waiting to buy samples of cut-price high-end and fast fashion. It was here that one could meet homeworker machinists and women in the local community.

It was timely and appropriate that NELP's new fashion design and marketing courses reflected and acknowledged the fashion history of East London. Over the past fifty years, this has gone on to grow into an important cultural hub.

In 1974, opportunities arose for polytechnics and other higher educational institutions to propose new degree courses validated by the Council for National Academic Awards (CNAA), which ensured the expansion and development of art and design degree courses at NELP. There was a moment of time to conceptually develop new art and design courses with distinct signatures. This led to a climate of great optimism, experimentation and enthusiasm, with the opportunity to create new courses. Art and design, being geographically separate, did not begin to feel institutional pressures from 'the centre' until the mid to late 1980s.

The fashion design with marketing (FDM) course was a radical pioneering new course, validated in 1981, one of the first, if not the first, course of its kind. The course, developed by fashion diploma course tutor Wenda Southcott, Lyndsay Rosenhead, fashion industry/marketing specialist, and David Morris, head of contextual studies, with the fashion course team including Richard Cawley,[16] Graham Price and NELP academic marketing staff such as Allan Hoskins and Colin Madill. The contextual studies team recognised the importance of art, design and fashion history, the changing nature of the fashion industry, and the need for a sociological critique of aspects of the industry, especially in relation to new technology. Thus the course document referenced these.

The course document understood the importance and integral place of both fashion design and marketing, and contextual studies to fashion design education and within the globalisation of the fashion industry.[17] It also understood the importance of student placements within the industry, such as in fashion design, marketing, production or retail. These placements were radical and innovative at this time, and now are mainstream. The structure of the course was made up of three components: fashion design, marketing and contextual studies. The course pioneered integrated fashion design and marketing units that took place in the second and third year, which became the vehicle for students to undertake projects where fashion design and marketing were integrated, and involved industry participation and, in some cases, live industry projects.

The course structure was a four-year degree with two placements – a six-week retail placement[18] at the end of the second year, and a nine-month placement in the third year.[19] This course, along with one other, helped pioneer a fashion course sandwich model. What was different about NELP was that fashion design and marketing were integrated so students left with both a very rich education and a high-level skill set. Their education included theoretical, critical and practical fashion design and marketing experience, and a critique and history of the industry.

Fashion marketing *per se* was a new and developing field and, until the late 1980s, did not exist as a specific subject skill set.[20] In order to teach marketing in the fashion design and marketing degree, staff who had an academic economics focus were recruited from the business school – some of them had little or no practical marketing experience. As a result, there was a culture divide between the art and design focus of fashion staff and those teaching marketing, who had a more academic orientation. The gap was bridged by ensuring that staff understood that: 'Marketing and design must not be perceived as separate activities, nor can they be successfully taught as disparate subjects'.[21]

After a first year which provided an introduction to aspects of fashion design and marketing delivered as discrete separate units, the students undertook project work with specific outcomes/skill sets. From then on in the second and fourth year, students worked on integrated fashion design and marketing projects – a new and innovative vehicle in which they were required to produce, design, make solutions in line with a marketing plan, and develop the creativity and skills to interpret marketing plans and develop the product accordingly.[22] 'This [approach] enabled designers to provide commercially viable solutions, whether working for mass production retailers or individual high street SMEs'.[23]

These integrated projects were additionally linked with industry input, which could vary from basic practitioner input to live design and market research. They were both innovative and highly successful.

The FDM approach also benefited designers planning to start new businesses, ensuring they had marketing and design skills. This was essential, as so many start-ups fail because they don't have a team to support them and to market their products. NELP FDM students won first and second place in 'The Design into Business' national competition in both 1987 and in 1989, which highlighted the success of the FDM course pedagogy, its approach and its programme.[24]

Debbie Johnson Smith came to NELP as a mature student in 1985, went on to work in industry and became a visiting lecturer, teaching at the London College of Fashion, University of the Arts and at Hertfordshire University. She was attracted to a fashion marketing degree course, with a diploma issued by the Chartered Institute of Marketing.

> Competition was very fierce ... with over 300 applicants for thirty places. When we left, we all had a formal marketing qualification as well as a degree, and I believe this gave NELP

graduates the unique edge. In marketing speak we had a unique selling point. [25]

Angela Stockwell, who also graduated in 1989 recollects that the fashion, design and marketing degree:

> Helped us to understand garment technology and pattern-cutting, to aid pricing and production of garments in factory settings ... the course made us understand cash flows, spreadsheets, marketing positioning of customer profiles. Once in industry I was shocked at how little some buyers knew ... because they had not had the NELP course knowledge we had.[26]

The nine-month industrial placements took place in the third year of the course and included buying, brand management, merchandising, production, fashion design, pattern-cutting and workroom placements, as well as PR, styling, and marketing.

Dr Beth Butterwick, former CEO of Karen Millen and Coast, said she wanted a career in fashion and business: 'The opportunity to do a nine-month placement with an organisation/person that offered a specialism ... I ended up at M&S, loved it and was subsequently offered a place on the graduate programme'. She worked for M&S clothing division for sixteen years before moving to Gap as part of the senior management team, Bon Marché and other high profile companies. She is convinced that her successful career was in part due to her 'incredible NELP training'. In 2017 she was awarded an honorary doctorate by Huddersfield University for services to retail, as well as other industry awards. [27]

The industrial placement portfolio was extended to include six-week retail placements and nine-month fashion design and marketing placements in the third year. Industry placements were sourced, monitored and developed initially by Valerie Goodworth.[28] Her contribution to FDM was highly regarded by her students and by industry.[29]

The fashion, design and marketing focus in the fourth year was the development of the final year individual student collection, together with a detailed marketing plan, shown as an entire NELP graduate collection at the end of the year.[30] Initially these shows took place in central London locations, such as the Courtauld's textile showrooms. However by 1991 a graduate fashion week, which still continues today, was set up by Jeff Banks and was held for many years at the Business Design Centre in Islington with national fashion and textile degree courses showcasing their work.

Contextual studies

Contextual studies worked across art and design, with specialist staff: art, fashion and design historians and later film historians who primarily worked within the designated course specialisms and also offered programmes open to students in the art and design school.

For a time (1980-87), with the development of new areas of research alongside new art and design courses, there was a lot of scope for innovation and collaboration. The particular layout of Greengate House and its *ad hoc* nature made this easier. Collaboration with colleagues, as well as visiting lecturers, ensured that students benefited from a range of expertise, especially within the portfolio of contextual studies and women's studies. Many of us had both theoretical expertise as well as our own art practice, which ensured a depth of commitment, radical research and respect for teaching and learning.

During the 1970s and 1980s, fashion and dress history was a new and developing field. Museum curators, academics and fashion writers made major contributions to the history of dress and twentieth century fashion history, which has developed so that it is now an intrinsic part of popular culture.[31]

Simultaneously, a number of pioneering individuals and organisations successfully sought to develop the infrastructure for London as a major fashion capital. In 1975, the London Designer Collections were held in Montcalm Hotel, later moving to the Inn on the Park for five years and then to Hyde Park Hotel. *Women's Wear Daily,* writing about it afterwards, declared: 'the Great has been put back into Britain'. It became the showcase for young designers with talent, who were selected to join and participate in the London Designer Collections.[32] The British Fashion Council, incorporated in 1986, would go on to represent designers by way of a designer subcommittee.[33] These initiatives provided a framework, foundation and focus for the development of London as a major fashion capital, and for London Fashion Week today.

Within the framework of FDM contextual studies, it was possible to innovate, provide a critique of the industry, and create fashion and dress history courses in new and expanding fields. The art and fashion course option focused on a number of key periods within twentieth century visual and decorative arts to include art deco, constructivism, surrealism and postmodernism. Case studies of particular artists and fashion designers sought to explore artists' and craft people's collaboration and contribution to twentieth century fashion. The course referenced Paris haute couture and contemporary practice, and included studio visits to textile artists, embroiderers, museum collections and archives.

In the 1980s, it was possible to access museum stores where the curator selected examples of historic dress and haute couture from the collections for small groups of students to view. This included the V&A, Museum of London and Kensington Palace. We also visited theatrical costumiers and preview sales of dress and textiles at Sotheby's and Christie's auction houses, as well as visits to private collections. These visits enabled students to understand and appreciate the cut and construction, choice of fabrics used, decorative details, trimmings and embroidery, linings, buttons and ties used in both historic dress and Paris haute couture.

Anita Lad, who graduated in 1989, joined the BBC costume department after graduating with a BA Hons, before developing her successful career as a freelance costume designer in TV and films.[34] She recollects that every aspect of the course, including costume history, gave her skills that she draws on in her work.

Contemporary fashion history courses included industry professionals, editors of leading fashion magazines, such as Landels, editor of *Harpers* and *Queen*, and leading designers, as well as pioneering expert researchers, including the economist Professor Swasti Mitter and Professor Ursula Huws, who provided a critique of aspects of new technology, the globalisation of the fashion and textile industry and its impact on women's employment. Homeworking campaigners and collectives were also involved.[35]

The speed of technological change in terms of retail, manufacture and marketing was such that in the early 1980s and 1990s attending the retail technology exhibition in London, and the textile machinery exhibitions in Milan and Harrogate was essential.[36] This ensured students were kept abreast of rapid changes in the industry. Fashion design and marketing staff also attended national and international fashion/dress history conferences, marketing conferences and fashion exhibitions, contributing research papers. Students visited London, Paris, Milan and Florence to see fashion/textile collections, the major fashion/textile fairs, expos, exhibitions and art galleries, and met major department store buyers.[37]

The fashion contextual studies visiting lecturer team included the fashion sociologist Professor Helen Thomas, the fashion anthropologist Ted Polhemus,[38] artist and design historian Mina Thornton, fashion historian of hair Caroline Cox, and designer and fashion historian Michael Dillon.

Enterprise development funds were secured in the early 1990s to fund a new contextual studies course, to enable students to conduct fashion research in the V&A archives at Blythe House. Once marginal, this is now mainstream. They worked on a number of then recent acquisitions of archive collections, including those of fashion illustrator Francis Marshall and the fashion photographer John French, in order to acquire archival experience and knowledge of research methods.

During the 1970s and 1980s, as the fashion specialist in the contextual studies department, much of my research was concerned with celebrating and documenting the hidden world of women artists and embroiderers who contributed to haute couture in Paris in the 1920s,[39] and sharing this with students. Later, focusing on contemporary textile art practice – specifically women and textiles, their lives and their work, including artists, craft workers and homeworkers working on the machine – resulted in a ground-breaking 1983 exhibition and the conference *Women and Textiles, their lives and work.*[40] Subsequently I wrote and directed the documentary *Embroidery and Women's Lives Today.*[41]

Responses to institutional change

In 1988, NELP became a higher education institution and was renamed the Polytechnic of East London in 1989, and then in in 1992 became the University of East London. In 1999 the Docklands campus was opened, the first new campus built in London in fifty years.[42]

During the early 1980s, any constraints imposed by management were managed adeptly by Tom Whiteread, a man of great integrity and kindness, regarded by many as one of the best heads of school in the university.[43] One of the first actions that he undertook was to ensure staff contracts in contextual studies and other areas were at the appropriate grade and were permanent.[44]

In the mid-1980s, the organisational growing pains began to be felt within art and design at Greengate House, despite its location as an outpost. With the expansion of new degree courses and higher student numbers in areas of art and design, it was apparent that there were serious issues of space and inadequate levels of administrative support staff. There was talk of taking over the car park at Greengate House or building in the boarded-up, former swimming pool in the atrium to provide additional studios.

Following her successful career in industry, Ann Priest joined FDM as course leader[45] in 1987. By 1989, she was so concerned about issues of space that she successfully negotiated the transfer of the fashion design and marketing course to the Business School. It was relocated to a former RAF building on the Barking site, renovated to the course requirements, and separate from the main 1930s buildings on the site. The new premises provided room for growth and expansion. There was also an opportunity to increase the proportion of overseas students.

Ann Priest ensured that facilities were available on site for computer aided design (CAD) for textiles and pattern-cutting. Senior lecturer Sheridan Tandy researched CAD and pattern-cutting systems developed by Investronica, and became an expert in CAD for textiles, as well as developing the innovative print dye sublimation process.

These innovations responded both to changes in the industry and demand for student and industry access. The initiatives were an important marker for future collaboration with industry, and became part of the technology hubs that are evident at UEL's Docklands campus today.

In 1991 the FDM course, under Priest's leadership, was so highly regarded by the HM inspectors that it was recognised as a course of national excellence, receiving double stars, both from the design and business inspectors, the highest award that could be given. Ann Priest's contributions to FDM were considerable and highly regarded, and she has had a distinguished career, making contributions to fashion education nationally and internationally.[46]

There was a lot of structural, institutional change in the university, and also site changes. In the late 1980s, pro-vice-chancellor Professor Gould, later vice-chancellor, was developing strategies for the future and provided opportunities for part-time secondment in order to develop a Docklands strategy and plans for international students.[47] I was seconded and co-wrote with David Albury the university strategy, 'Scale and Hype: Scoping the Role of Higher Education in Docklands', which was presented to and adopted by the board of governors.[48] This was later developed and implemented when the Docklands campus opened in 1999.

Community gains

FDM and textiles were constantly developing local, national and international networks as part of their everyday engagement with new developments in fashion design and marketing, culture and industry. For example, between 1988 and 1989, Ann Priest advised and supported the development of the National Institute of Fashion Technology in India and was developing training and education for the Indian fashion industry. In 1989 and 1991, she delivered industrial training programmes for SENAI CETIQT Textile Institute in Rio de Janeiro.[49] FDM staff contributed their expertise as members of boards,[50] gave national and international conference papers,[51] and served on educational panels, including the CNAA, and as external examiners. This engagement enhanced teaching and learning. This was very much the culture of NELP's Art and Design School from its inception. This meant there was substantial community gain.

Student involvement in external professional projects became part of the student FDM and textile experience at NELP.

In the Year of the Child in 1979, Doreen Dyall, and Eve Latimer – the Great Ormond Street Hospital play coordinator responsible for the children's unit in the hospital – were keen to develop the hospital environment and initiated the Great Ormond Street Hospital project to upgrade it, especially the isolation wards. Dyall invited a small selected, diverse working team of interested people to join a working group which, as well as herself, included two industrial design students from the RCA, Stuart Aitken from Medway College and David Rodway, a mature student from NELP fine art. NELP second year fashion and textile students had the opportunity to join the project and redesign the nursery nurses' uniforms and aprons. The designs went into production, and a prototype wendy house was also produced. Following presentations to the hospital staff, it was also agreed to focus on new designs for hospital screens in the isolation unit. The student designs for the hospital screens formed part of NELP's fashion and textile exhibition at the Courtauld's showroom,[52] alongside the annual NELP fashion show.[53]

In 1991, as a direct consequence of my liaison while developing links in Docklands, Olympia and York, the developers of Canary Wharf, sponsored a fashion show in Cubitt Hall. First and second year FDM students designed a printed dye sublimation collection of sequined evening dresses sponsored by Brody's, the established East London-based sequin fabric manufacturer. A collection of twenty-five evening dresses were judged by Helen Storey, the then young designer of the year. The fashion show became the front-page news in *Fashion Weekly,* the leading trade industry paper. The project was led and devised by Sheridan Tandy, the first-year senior tutor. Later this work was displayed in the yet-to-be let retail units at Canary Wharf as *Windows on the Wharf.* [54] This later expanded in 1992 to include exhibitions and installations for fine art and art in architecture students' work, successfully promoting both the University of East London and Olympia and York.

My approaches to the London Docklands Development Corporation (LDDC) enabled us to pilot a series of temporary sculpture projects as the first phase of a proposed sculpture park in Docklands.[55] This led to four sculpture initiatives: 'Art in the Gardens' (1993), 'Tidal Basin

Summer Exhibition' (1994 and 1995) and the successful realisation of the Docklands schools sculpture project. 'They act as a footprint of a wider vision for our urban Docklands sculpture park, which will provide a unique resource for Docklands schools and the wider community'.[56] The Docklands school sculpture project, developed by Jane Riches, course tutor for Art in Architecture MA (a radical new course), involved two Docklands schools, Calverton Primary and Langdon Park Secondary, and three artists in residence (former UEL MA Art in Architecture students).[57] They worked with children as young as six and seven to realise three pieces of sculpture which formed part of 'Tidal Basin 11', a sculpture exhibition sited at the gateway to the Royal Docks in 1995. The exhibition also profiled twenty-one works from the MA Art in Architecture course students. Tony Banks MP said:

> This is just the kind of pioneering work we have come to expect from the collaboration with artists, schools and the University of East London. It symbolises a unique way of working that creates important educational and community gains. These small-scale interventions are laying the foundations for urban renewal and regeneration.[58]

The 'Magic Hoover Sculpture' symbolised the children's response to their changing Docklands environment, as well as involving reference to the local city farm, Canary Wharf, tower blocks, City Airport, the Docklands light railway, bridges and flyovers. They added in mermaids, rainbows and magic Hoovers that reflected their aspirations to be part of a cleaner and friendlier environment. Ms Hollows, head teacher of Calverton School said:

> The most special thing about the school sculpture project is that the sculpture is here in our courtyard and the children made it. It was a wonderful experience. We were delighted by the quality of support given by the scheme. The artists were not only talented but were able to work with children in a very professional way that facilitated the production of excellent work. The artists related well to the teaching and increased the teacher's confidence and skills in the teaching of art.[59]

Conclusion

The move to Docklands in 1999 enabled fashion design with marketing, which had already rejoined the School of Art and Design, while still sited at Barking, to co-locate with art and design, reconnecting to its roots. At the Docklands campus today there is now a flagship cluster of seven fashion degree courses, including fashion textiles. This is a remarkable success story, which has involved a number of site and institutional changes over the last forty years. Fashion has a very high presence in the university and connects to its East London fashion heritage. More importantly, it connects to the developing fashion, technological and cultural hub centred around the new V&A East. The 2019 Positive Fashion Institute, promoted by the British Fashion Council, will focus on opportunities to work more sustainably, and this will create new models of working locally, nationally and internationally.

Students are the greatest ambassadors for the university and will continue to be so. Many alumni are in prominent positions in the fashion design and fashion marketing, and the culture and media industries, as well as in education. They are the success story, and will continue to be so.

References

S. Bowman (ed.), *Feminist Arts News 1983 Fashion Textiles.*

Notes

1. The merger into NELP was fortuitous for Walthamstow, which lost its expected funding for a three-year diploma course as part of the government's consolidation of art schools. In 1964 the newly appointed National Council for Diplomas in Art and Design approved only twenty-nine out of seventy-three art schools which had applied to teach the three-year diploma in art and design. 'Walthamstow takes its place in a wider narrative of the decline in local art education – a precipitous tumble – which meant by 2011 the country had gone from 180 recognised art schools to just eleven, closing a vital space where exploratory creative practice could be sited inside the

everyday, positioned both as an extension of and as a challenge to the quotidian', Will Ashon, *The Guardian* 9 June 2017 quoting from John Beck and Matthew Cornford, The Art School and the Culture Shed, Kingston University and University of Brighton, 2014.

2. *Be Magnificent,* exhibition at the William Morris Gallery 2017.
3. Later, I became principal lecturer.
4. I trained as a tapestry weaver at West Dean College in 1975 (a radical new course) and later set up a studio weaving tapestries in silk. These were exhibited nationally and internationally with the 62 Group of textile artists, including a touring exhibition to Japan and Korea. Textile awards include the International Miniature Textile Exhibition, Hungary 1983 most outstanding achievement award. During the 1970s I had also worked for Inter-action Trust and in fringe theatre.
5. Ian Collins, *Two Lives in Colour: Fred Dubery and Joanne Brogden,* Unicorn Publishing Group: London, 2019.
6. *Ibid.*
7. Walthamstow School of Art 1960 prospectus.
8. Jake Chapman, of Jake and Dinos Chapman, was another NELP fine art student 1980-83, before joining his brother Dinos at the RCA. Sam Taylor-Johnson, Sue Stamp and Simon Ungless were also there at the same time.
9. 'Dyall's desk at the RCA sat in a sea of encrusted varnish and paint ... Dyall was one of the many Pollock-inspired young pattern designers who enthusiastically collaborated with textile and wallpaper manufacturers on leaving college ... such as Heals Fabrics', Lesley Jackson, *The Independent*, 6 March 1999.
10. Doreen Dyall was on a CNAA panel for the validation of textile degrees, so knew the relevant criteria for course validation. She was part of a team, with Clive Latimer, which surveyed textile courses nationally, and her knowledge of course development nationally fed back into NELP's unique portfolio of textile courses.
11. Simon Ungless is executive director, School of Fashion, Academy of Art University, San Francisco. When teaching at Central St Martins he personally introduced Sarah Burton (now head of McQueen) to Alexander McQueen.
12. Alchemy of Screen Print Exploration, 31 October 2019, Fashion and Textile Museum, London, https://www.womenfolk.co/tactilityfactory_
13. Gillian Elinor, Sue Richardson, Sue Scott, Angharad Thomas, Kate Walker (eds), *Women and Craft,* Virago: London, 1987, p124.
14. Andrew Ruffhead became head of textiles after she left.

15. Dyall worked for a range of international clients over many years, including Yves St Laurent, Lanvin, Dior and Jean Louis Sherrer, Fiorucci, Speedo, Mitsui. Dyall's work has been widely exhibited and is in the V&A and Whitworth Art Gallery collections.
16. Richard Cawley was a visiting lecturer to NELP fashion diploma course and FDM BA Hons course. He was designer for London fashion house Bellville Sassoon, a former alumnus 'Ecole de la Syndicale de la Couture Parisienne in Paris (founded by the great couturiers to carry on their treasured traditions), and a design RCA alumnus. In 1984 he won the Mouton Cadet cookery competition and, overnight, exchanged a career in fashion for one in food (Wikipedia). Later Sheridan Tandy DRCA, Norma Gosling DRCA, Caryl Court BA Hons, and Darla Jane Gilroy (now professor, London College of Fashion University of the Arts) joined the design team.
17. Lyndsay Rosenhead had extensive fashion marketing experience gained through working in fashion in Paris and London and for Vogue patterns. She went on to become head of fashion at Harrow School of Art.
18. In the 1980s, retail placements included Fenwick, Next, Richards, BHS and independent designers such as Darla Jane Gilroy.
19. The placements included fashion design, pattern-cutting, workroom placements or marketing, such as PR, branding, styling; or buying at Richards, BHS, M&S and smaller labels, such as Hobbs.
20. Valerie Goodworth (1997) *Role of Design in Marketing: Bridging the Gap in Course Provision,* Manchester Metropolitan University conference (unpublished paper); and 'Reflecting on teaching and learning practice in the UK Fashion & Textile sector of HE and implications for developing student centred learning opportunities', paper at 1998 ELIA conference; *Where are we going: The artist as communicator in the 3rd millennium,* Changing Needs Publication, Manchester Metropolitan University.
21. Valerie Goodworth,1997, *ibid.*
22. Dawn Branigan joined the FDM course team in 1992 as senior lecturer in marketing, working closely with the fashion design team and FDM course students.
23. Valerie Goodworth, 1997, *op.cit.*
24. *Ibid.*
25. In response to a short questionnaire (2019) to the graduate cohort 1989, Debbie Johnson Smith explained why NELP's course was unique.
26. Angela Stockwell's career went on to include children's wear buyer

for BHS and House of Fraser. After many years working in fashion buying, Angela now works in asset management.

27. Butterwick has completed three successful 'turn arounds', three sale processes and one IPO (initial public offering) in her retail career to date. She was named *Drapers Record* retail personality of the year 2015, and Barclays businesswoman of the year 2015. Latterly she was CEO of Karen Millen, a global brand with 400 shops in 65 countries.
28. A former Walthamstow alumna and visiting lecturer to NELP, joining the FDM team in 1982, Valerie Goodworth had substantial industry experience. She developed the integrated fashion marketing course projects and integrated approach to industry participation, including BHS and Hyper Hyper.
29. Valerie Goodworth later became head of fashion in 1993 when Ann Priest left to become dean of fashion management at London College of Fashion, University of the Arts.
30. The marketing plans and marketing material that students produced as an intrinsic part of their collection were also on display at the Business Design Centre for buyers and visitors to view.
31. In 1971 *Fashion: An anthology by Cecil Beaton* was shown at the V&A, the first major exhibition focusing on twentieth century fashion held at the museum. In 1974 the Jacquemart-Andre Museum in Paris held the first major exhibition of Paul Poiret fashion, *Poiret le Magnifique*. These were landmark exhibitions in terms of celebrating and recognising the importance of twentieth century fashion.
32. R. O'Byrne and A. Worsley-Taylor, *Style City: How London Became a Fashion Capital,* Frances Lincoln Ltd: London, 2009.
33. *Ibid.*
34. Anita Lad; IMDb lists all her credits.
35. Bowman in S. Mitter (ed.), *Computer-aided Manufacturing and Women's Employment: the clothing industry in four EC Countries,* Springer-Verlag, 1990; Bowman in Elinor, 1987.
36. It was at the national and international exhibitions, such as the textile machinery exhibition in Milan and the retail technology exhibition in London, in the 1980s and 1990s where one met leading professionals, who were invited in as visiting lecturers. These included M&S clothing technologists, designers, manufacturers such as Brinton Carpets, and retail technology experts, such as Gill Jones who established the retail technology exhibition in London in the 1980s.
37. Students visiting Paris in 1985 were invited to the couture house of Madame Gres, the iconic couturier whose publicist Elaine Kennedy had arranged a private couture show for the students.

38. Anthropologist Ted Polhemus's fashion and street style course involved students working in very small groups to research various street styles and present their group findings to Amy De La Haye, then fashion curator at the V&A, and her team who were undertaking preliminary research for the *Street Style* exhibition curated by Polhemus /De La Haye in 1994. De La Haye is now professor of dress history and curatorship at London College of Fashion, University of the Arts.
39. S. Bowman and M. Molinare, *Fashion for Extravagance*, Bell Hyman: London, 1985.
40. A special edition of *Feminist Arts News* on fashion textiles, edited by S. Bowman, was published in 1983 to coincide with this exhibition.
41. S. Bowman, *Embroidery and Women's Lives Today*, Cable London, BBC 2, Cinenova Distributors, 1992.
42. Wikipedia, East London University.
43. Tom Whiteread trained as a geographer, and had been head of department of humanities before becoming head of the School of Art and Design. His wife Pat was an artist, as is their famous daughter, Dame Rachel Whiteread.
44. Doreen Dyall recollects there were only 2.5-equivalent secretaries for the entire building. Course leaders had to be largely self-servicing, generally without the benefit of computers. Pat Dear was the FDM secretary for 36 years.
45. During her time in industry, Ann Priest worked for a number of high street companies and designer labels, including Wallis, Juliet, Dunn and Jeff Banks, as a designer, pattern-cutter, and later as product developer and buyer responsible for a significant range of products sourced internationally for the Mulberry Company. She was an active member of a number of industry and professional bodies, the Textile Strategy Board, the Textile Institute, London Fashion Forum and Westminster Council fashion steering group.
46. Honorary professor Nottingham Trent University 2019, Ann Priest is also currently visiting international dean, Beijing Institute of Fashion Technology. She retired as pro-vice-chancellor, head of College of Art and Design and Built Environment, Nottingham Trent University in 2019. Previously dean, fashion management, London College of Fashion for thirteen years. Priest was head of fashion NELP/UEL from 1987 to 1993.
47. Three members of the fashion staff were independently seconded, and contributed to their area of interest as well as enabling the department to increase the number of visiting lecturers during these secondments. Ann Priest was seconded to the International

Office and Valerie Goodworth to the Enterprise in Higher Education team. I was seconded to develop the initial Docklands strategy.

48. D. Albury and S. Bowman, 'Scale and Hype: Scoping the role of a Higher Education Institution in Docklands', unpublished paper, University of East London, c.1989-90.
49. Ann Priest also delivered keynote and conference papers and presentations on fashion, fashion forecasting and education in India, Brazil, Hong Kong, China, Taiwan, Australia and Pakistan, as well as to industry events in the UK.
50. Valerie Goodworth, with Tower Hamlets and Newham City Challenge, 1991-92, created links to and developed strategies for local garment producers, including training opportunities, obtaining funding for this. Her consultancy portfolio and contribution to local and national fashion initiatives were considerable.
51. Sara Bowman presented papers on the place of women's design and craft within the clothing industries' competitive strategy, with special reference to aspects of indigenous Australian and Indonesian textiles, including: UNU/INtech Maastricht 1992; Ars Textrina 13th Conference at Leeds University; 14th Conference at Lincoln University Nebraska 1995; also presentations on temporary sculpture and arts interventions in urban regeneration in East London, including the International Youth Culture Conference, Rome 1995.
52. The hospital project installation was designed by fashion artist Brian Harris who was a visiting lecturer in the NELP textile department. The installation was sited to the side of the main entrance to the Courtauld's showroom. Dyall recalls: 'A hospital bed was made up with sheets and a blanket. A white form was created which lay in the bed of a child. Screen structures were covered with several layers of fine white muslin and formed a large square enclosure around the bed which became a rather beautiful diffused image. On two screens students' working drawings of their ideas were displayed. Overall it made a great impact and people responded, and as a result made generous donations to the hospital'. Clive Latimer, in his capacity as head of school, introduced Eve Latimer to Doreen Dyall, who both went on to develop and realise the project.
53. Subsequently, Heal's put into production a group of Dyall's textile furnishing collection, including a set of designs for children's hospital screens.
54. Conceptual developer/curator, myself.
55. As the conceptual developer of the NELP/UEL sculpture park proposal and pilot sculpture projects, I secured LDDC and Paul Hamlyn

Trust funds for a number of pilot projects to enable the Art into Architecture MA course students to create temporary public art works in Docklands, under the direction of course leader Jane Riches.

56. Sara Bowman, Artists in Docklands Schools Sculpture Project.
57. The school sculpture project centred on two schools, attracted 1320 participants and involved forty-four workshops between January and March 1995.
58. *Artists in Docklands Schools Sculpture Project,* UEL's Design and the Built Environment Docklands Arts Initiative, 1995.
59. The artists working on the project were Kirstein Bunting, Sean Cronin and Margaret Wood.

CHAPTER TEN

Feminism in the academy: women's studies

Maggie Humm

Introduction

Academic feminism is facing a historical watershed brought about by the Tory government's mishandling of Brexit, and the subsequent loss of European Union finance and networks – the lifeblood of gender and women's studies; and by the increasingly regulatory framework of the Research Excellence Framework and teaching excellence frameworks, which privilege single disciplines rather than multidisciplinary areas like women's studies, and inhibit staff who take maternity or caring career breaks (primarily women). Finally, Tory austerity discourages working-class and black and minority ethnic students and has a harder impact on poorer women more fearful of lifelong debt. In 2018, the banning of gender studies by Victor Orbán, prime minister of Hungary, along with its university – the Central European University – and the Brazilian president Jair Bolsonaro's 2019 promise to stop the 'ideology' of gender being taught in schools, illustrate an important lesson – that feminist gains are not necessarily progressive and ever advancing, but can slide quickly backwards. It is particularly important, therefore, to remember education's feminist histories, even very small examples like UEL's women's studies, which grew from two units in 1983 to the first full undergraduate women's studies degree in the UK in 1991.

Nostalgia is necessarily selective. It encourages us to remember positives rather than negatives. Memory is a responsibility, and history is never simple. The University of East London (UEL)'s women's studies was not entirely a golden past but did contain some important examples of radical education that might offer pointers and ideas for future change. In simple terms, UEL's women's studies was based on a feminism that assumed women share, but differently experience, discriminations, many of which are unrecognised. The principal category of analysis in women's studies is gender, in a complex matrix with class, race, sexual identities and disability, among other issues. Women's studies is about the retrieval of women's histories, the production of new knowledges and frameworks, and aims to help women understand the dynamics of their lives and engage in social and personal transformations. All of this differentiates women's studies from other disciplines because women's studies involves reconceptualising education itself. Student goals may be initially instrumental – the gaining of a degree – but women's studies encourages students to construct new social identities. Feminism is a new way of being in the world. As a UEL first year women's studies student put it, when interviewed by a visiting US Fulbright scholar, Frinde Maher: 'I even want to get a PhD. I want to go all the way. For as long as I can: teach, write and stay a feminist activist. Women's studies is a way of articulating myself to myself; it is in my bloodstream.'[1]

History and context

The historical background that encouraged UEL's women's studies dates to 1970 and the founding of women's studies at San Diego State University in the USA. By UEL's full degree in 1991, there were over 600 undergraduate programmes in the US. First as an exchange professor at the University of Massachusetts in 1971, then as a visiting scholar at San Diego State and Stanford institutes and centres for gender research (1986) and Rutgers University Institute for Research on Women (1997), I learned a great deal, feeding this back into UEL's women's studies.

In the UK, the first women's studies MA was founded at the University of Kent in 1980, but it took a decade for undergraduate courses to grow. The series of UN sponsored women's conferences, particularly Beijing in 1995, energised women's international networks, and changed women's studies' world view. Institutional support has varied widely in Europe, from Denmark's generous provision of twenty women's studies professors nationwide by the year 2000 to very little support at all, as in the UK beginning with its one professor (Celia Davis, University of Ulster) in 1993. When I was promoted to professor at UEL in 1995 I was only UEL's second woman professor.

Ex-academic support has always been crucial. The UK public face of feminism in journals such as *Trouble and Strife, Feminist Review, Spare Rib* and *Women's Studies International Forum*, spurred on more focused journals such as *Women's History Review*, all of which provided course materials. We had our own bookshops, for example, Sisterwrite in north London and Silver Moon in Charing Cross Road, which hosted two of my book launches. Women's activism in local communities and in the Greater London Council was shaped by a variety of feminisms, from marxism and socialism to small consciousness-raising groups, and ensured that UK women's studies always had a political edge, illustrated by the title of early liberation publications – *Women's Struggle* and *The Big Flame*. Even *Women's Studies* in its first issue would only print articles on marxism-feminism and political action.

From the beginning then, UK women's studies related to larger feminist political issues encompassing health, the media and sexual violence, and explored women's histories to provide ammunition for campaigns, notably the National Abortion Campaign. Women's studies has always been inside and outside the academy, from the first UK women's studies classes by Juliet Mitchell at London's Anti-University 1968-69, and the first national women's conference at Ruskin College, Oxford 1970, then a trade union-financed college. This differentiates women's studies' values from some other disciplines. Those of us devising UEL's women's studies were engaged, therefore, not only in trying to reshape knowledge but also in the politics of change. For example, like many women's studies staff elsewhere, I gave free Saturday classes about feminist ideas in community centres, in my case at Deptford's Albany Arts Centre.

Development

Initially in 1983, UEL's women's studies was only two units in a multi-subject diploma of higher education. With twenty-three units by 1991, it was part of a combined studies degree, enabling it to grow slowly. We could never have developed women's studies if we had been required to present a full degree for validation *ab initio*. Garnering teaching staff, with myself as the only full-time women's studies academic, was a drawn-out process of persuading supportive academics to add women's studies teaching to their existing portfolios, and then persuading their departmental heads to agree. By 1991, only two of the twenty-three units were drawn from outside the subject area (from social sciences and psychosocial studies).

The course consistently attracted many students from local further education access courses. Ours were first-generation students, disparate demographically (aged eighteen to seventy) and ethnically (Hindu, Bengali, Jamaican, Sri Lankan, Pakistani, white and others). On arrival most were active community women, if not yet actively student women. They were experts in the sociology of single parenthood, battered wives and homeless women. They did not lack knowledge and skills, since they could often outmanoeuvre benefit and housing officials, but they were suspicious of handed-down explanations, including academic ones. For example, battered wives knew they did not 'seek out' battering partners. On the other hand, their lack of formal educational skills (an access course substituted for school qualifications) robbed them of confidence in their explanatory ability. They wanted and needed to acquire professional expertise to become professionals themselves.

Starting their first class with an apparently banal question – what were your mother and your grandmother doing at this exact moment in their lives? – and sharing an extract from Alice Walker, raised issues which stayed with us throughout the three years. For example, by year three 'Ellen' had constructed a black women's archive. The question directly challenged the ethnocentricity of traditional sources of evidence. Such family histories were important 'documents' given the paucity of Asian and black materials in most libraries at that time. When describing personal histories, students made connections between private and public personas, questioning the authenticity of constructed public selves. One external examiner, rather patronisingly, reported in 1989, 'it was remarkable how students from a wide-range of cultural backgrounds and differing ages were achieving good results,' although she did conclude that the course was at 'a cutting edge of an expanding subject area'.[2]

When we started in 1983, most women's studies publications and materials were US-focused, and very quickly I spent the decade writing many appropriate feminist textbooks.[3] Our course guides drew on a variety of existing models, including from the Open University and the US catalogue system. We organised units in three pathways, women and the arts, women and socio-historic processes and women and technology, mainly because our staff had these specialisms. The units covered a range of skills, including audio-visual work, creative writing, social surveys, archive research, creative arts, computer modelling and external placements. All our teaching derived from a desire to contextualise the situation of women historically and socially within a feminist praxis. 1991 saw the addition of a third-year unit, lesbian and gay cultures, the first gay course to be publicly advertised in a UK university student brochure, a Scottish student said on entry. Students themselves made major contributions to course materials. For example, in 1996 K. Jdaliad and P. Parker self-published a hundred-page guide to women and the visual arts for incoming students, with information ranging from art galleries to the nitty-gritty costs of 'chinograph pencils £4.00'.[4]

Academic validations involved enduring school interrogations, a central validation committee with an external advisor from the Council for Academic Awards (CNAA). Necessarily descriptions of women's studies had to be as jargon heavy as validation guides to pass. We were required to be an 'area study' and promised 'to give a sound practical and vocational base to students gaining employment'. Although European Social Fund grants were intended for 'mature women in long-term unemployment', I won £8,852 to fund student placements at Cinenova, Roman Road, London which ticked the box of vocationalism.[5] Our politicising and action research were hidden in validations, although self-evidently lesbian and gay cultures was a good example of the politics of knowledge-making in a homophobic society at that time bound by local government section 28 (forbidding the promotion of homosexuality in education as a 'normal' family relationship). Arts projects such as tape-slide and autobiographies were equally political. For example, 'Chris's' media work about male violence ran alongside her political activity in a woman's refuge. Perhaps not surprisingly, it was women's studies students who led a UEL student campus occupation in May 1998, organised to protest at the cutbacks of eighty staff. This leadership role suggested to Maher, interviewing the students: 'that above and beyond the demands of the strike itself, the women saw their involvement as a natural outgrowth of their university education. They viewed it as both self- and institution-transforming in ways suggested by the early women's studies founders'.[6]

Values and practice

For students, the aim of UEL women's studies is best described as a rhizomatic formation of collectivity, multiplicities and connections that undid notions of individual disciplines, geniuses and thinkers. As bell hooks, the African-American writer, notes: 'sisterhood [is] where all our realities could be spoken'.[7] Similarly the act of historical retrieval, an important feature of all our units, was itself a form of feminist activism.

The student presentation replaced traditional exams from day one. That UEL's women's studies was exam-free came as a shock to Jenni Murray of BBC *Women's Hour* who invited me, in 1991, to discuss this feature with a conservative academic from the London School of Economics. However, a greater initial problem was persuading students that the presentation was genuinely more worthwhile than the 'banking' method of education they had expected. In *The Feminist Classroom*, Maher and Tetreault call this expectation 'dualism', which is when students become impatient with discussions, seeing them as a roundabout way of discovering what they think the teacher should have told them in the first place.[8]

Presentations encouraged students not only to include their autobiographies along with analysis, but to include dialogue with others in the different contexts of the classroom and the social context of their research. The seminar provided a framework where analysis, experience and theory projected beyond the bound of individual research. 'Watchful listening' encouraged empathy for diverse experiences, including lesbian and multi-ethnic understandings. 'Active understanding' focused our attention on the form as well as the content of each presentation. For example, I asked students to consider work that would directly speak to (interpellate) other students in the group, rather than simply giving an account of a researched area, like ageing or health.

Students did not hand in presentations immediately, because the completion of their analysis was judged on its social and intellectual interaction with the seminar contributions of other students. Women's studies was thus opposed to how academics normally define 'originality'. Difference was represented when a student enlarged her analysis in recognition of other student experiences not, as traditionally, responding to what she thought I, as a teacher, was likely to assess. 'Women's studies knowledge depends on ongoing analysis of the power relations of difference'.[9]

Organising teaching around discrete blocks, such as 'women and the family', 'women and sexuality', and trying to give a balanced account – one week Asian, another week Afro-Caribbean – was clearly problematic. Students' autobiographies had a much livelier notion of continuous cultural moments. The idea that students in women's studies can enjoy the authority of their experience was not new, but it was important for students writing their autobiographies to understand that their experience was psychosocially constructed, shot through with historical binaries of 'natural' and 'unnatural'. In addition, the act of witnessing, of telling it like it is to a mixed audience can imply a distancing, seeing oneself as oneself. The question of self-representation is a problem not a solution. The issue was not how and why women spoke about themselves, but how and why they listened; and how the written autobiography must be listened to as an issue of politics as much as of consciousness, of theoretical problems not ethnographic simplicities.

Problems and contradictions

At a structural, university level all these subtleties are rarely addressed. The first problem was the sheer difficulty of constructing and managing a cross-departmental, cross-campus programme (then on four UEL campuses), which depended on the willingness of staff to undergo sometimes excessive teaching and counselling work, and students to travel. While heads of school were sometimes supportive (most of all the two editors of this volume), other UEL staff thought women's studies a 'Mickey Mouse' subject. If we welcome subjective experiences than how could the course be at the same time rigorous and objective? 'Nira' was furious at this charge. 'A woman said, oh women's studies might be easy. So I showed her my unit card. I said can you do these questions? It is as hard as other courses'.[10]

The issue of academic rigour surfaced again when, alarmingly, in November 1991 Her Majesty's Inspectors (HMIs), the precursor of the Higher Education Funding Council for England (HEFCE) quality assurance agency, decided to inspect UK women's studies courses, including ours. The HMIs' *In Pursuit of Quality* states that the purpose of scrutiny was to assess the national performance of a subject, identify good practice and provide advice to institutions.[11] Courses were given grades from one to five – the highest being one. UEL's response is an illuminating case study in miniature of the problems feminist teaching faces in a patriarchal education system. The acting rector, Professor Frank Gould, was convinced that the course would fail inspection with its women and one gay male staff who would be judged of poor quality. He instituted a draconian regime of meetings with myself, heads of departments and line managers, all men, to interrogate my preparations. He set up a 'mock HMI visit,' and appointed Professor Mike Slade from the Law School, with no declared gender interests, research or teaching, to assess our abilities, and other staff to sit in on our classes. Professor Slade's report was damaging: 'I tread now on more delicate ground'. Although he notes that 'the courses have been validated and assessors convinced, I would personally not be convinced that the third-level courses and particularly their assessment was of sufficient rigour'.[12]

Trying to maintain staff morale amid these onslaughts, in a pre-email world, was exhausting. One women's studies staff member threatened to absent herself from the visit. But Professor Gould had a problem. He was 'acting', not confirmed as rector, and desperately needed a good HMI grade, even if his methods of achieving success – top-down management riding roughshod over empathetic, cooperative women staff – were likely to produce the opposite. The two HMIs were women. I quickly demanded a budget (women's studies had no designated budget) to create a welcoming environment: a secure room; good art installations with displays of student work on all campuses; colour-coded documentation; seminar plans and staff biographies; personalised signage; flowers; even tissue boxes. To ease the strain of cross-campus travel, I commandeered Professor Gould's personal car and chauffeur (known as Captain Birdseye due to his hirsute appearance) for the HMIs. Everything was cross-referenced, every minute coordinated.[13]

We gained a grade two. The top grade of one was unavailable, the HMIs said, due to 'poor accommodation', and the lack of 'financial resources', the fault of the university, not women's studies. Professor Gould was forced to admit in a letter: 'in debriefing after the event, the HMIs were very complimentary and especially about the staff and course tutor'.[14] We scored a higher grade than many other courses, including Middlesex and Wolverhampton polytechnics. The *Times Higher*'s report on the HMI visits overall was 'the most glowing ever seen at the *Higher*', a reporter noted.[15] We were secure, albeit for a time.

Another problem is that women in education often lose their identity when assessment becomes closure, as marriage in novels is so often for fictional women heroines. The working over of personal experience into dissertation formats often narrows possibilities. Dissertational rhetoric authorises identification with the subject of the topic, not the authorial subject. External examiners prefer a legal-juridical discourse of 'evidence' to 'identify' problems – like Virginia Woolf's characterisation of patriarchy as an anonymous voice 'imprinting on the faces of the clerks'.[16] However, examiner reports, unlike novels, are not fiction. Reports influence teaching and admissions when teachers come to interpret their teaching in examiners' terms. Yet year after year, women's studies students often gained the greatest number of firsts in combined studies, and examiners came to support our approach. In 1988 one wrote: 'I was especially impressed by the way the courses had been fashioned to encourage students from ethnic minorities to utilise their differences positively'.[17]

It was external economic exigencies, however, which impacted most. The 1988 Education Reform Act affected adult education and access courses by placing these in competition with sixth forms through the transfer of funding.[18] The consequent cutbacks in adult courses gradually eliminated several access and feminist courses, whose students often went on to become UEL women's studies students.

During this period, government university funding was diminishing, and universities were encouraged into private sector research funding, and student over-recruitment. The effect, at a granular level at UEL, was that few businesses were interested in women's studies, and on the first day of one academic year my class, usually of twenty-five to thirty students and for which I prepared handouts of that number, in a room seating only thirty, was eighty-five. The institutionalisation of recession planning encouraged management to spend more on appraisal schemes and validations while cutting library budgets, impacting most on impoverished women students. Education was becoming a saleable commodity. The university principles of 'performance indicators', and the division of courses into priority and non-priority, based on 'market productivity', bore down most heavily on women's studies. The symbolic order of the university, then, was a rich source of gender messages, from the under-representation of women in senior positions, the timing of meetings late in the day, making childcare difficult, to process-led documentation ignoring the subtleties of women's studies pedagogy.

By 1999, the university decided to change our nomenclature to 'gender and women's studies' and parcelled up different units into three degree titles – BA Women's Studies, BA Media and Gender,

BA Gender and Literature – to increase applications. But feminism didn't die. The very first intake to the full degree in 1991 were astonishingly determined women. By their first Christmas they demanded that we provide them with an MA in Women's Studies for them on graduation since, unlike younger students, they had to be locally based due to family care. After three years of intensive reading, course construction, multiple meetings and validation we (just) had the MA all set up and ready for their applications. Sadly, by the summer of 1999 the university cancelled the course, claiming a low intake, although we consistently achieved ten to twelve entry students, a figure regarded by other institutions as a viable intake. The closure of the undergraduate degree soon followed.

Contribution to the field

Comparisons with courses elsewhere are difficult. The majority were MAs. One other undergraduate course at North London Polytechnic contributed only a half degree. There were further differences of content. Most women's studies had a strong sociological focus, supplemented by history. Our degree was unique in focusing on the creative arts, including textiles, and on computing technologies. The latter, far in advance of other universities, enabled women to be computer literate in programming, an immense confidence booster, and fed into the university ethos of career development.

Our main contribution to the field lay in placing UEL women's studies, its practices and ideology at the centre of educational structures in the UK and Europe. As co-chair for three years of the Women's Studies Network UK (now Feminist and Women's Studies Association), I successfully gained Arts and Humanities Research Council (AHRC) approval for AHRC-funded women's studies PhDs and post-doctoral awards. I also gained approval for a HEFCE Research Assessment Exercise (RAE, now Research Excellence Framework, REF) women's studies sub-panel, on which I sat twice. In general, the RAE/REF, as noted, inculcates a narrow discipline-based model of research which devalues praxis. My aim was, by encouraging universities to cross-refer submissions with an element of gender research to the sub-panel, that such multidisciplinary work would be better valued when it gained a good rating from our sub-panel and accrued research funding. The field would grow in time.

At UEL I was responsible for our RAE submission to cultural studies and requested cross-referral to the women's studies sub-panel, gaining us a top five* from that panel. The HEFCE research monies are a crucial source of income for new universities like UEL, and endow sabbaticals, studentships, conferences and further research. Perhaps, not surprisingly, the sub-panel existed for only three years before being absorbed into sociology. Supported by this research income, I took UEL into European networks, Women's Studies International Europe (WISE), and the European Network of Women's Studies (ENWS), which enabled us to share ideas and funding across Europe in Athena programmes, coordinated by the University of Utrecht. Due to these collaborations, including an Erasmus exchange with the University of Bologna, several Erasmus students were attracted to UEL. A Dutch proposal to set up a European Network of Women's Studies was formally approved by the Committee of Ministers of Foreign Affairs of the Council of Europe on 1 March 1989, requesting all EU members to 'provide policy-makers with recommendations, among these training programmes' addressing women's issues'.[19]

With our belief in the full integration of research and pedagogy, academic exchanges were an important contribution of UEL women studies. I set up a British Council-funded three-year exchange with the University of Karachi's women's studies, enabling staff from UEL to give workshops and lectures in Karachi, and Karachi staff to work with our students. Given the paucity of black and minority ethnic staff in the university, the sight of wonderful Pakistani role models in our classes had an obvious impact. The exchange also enabled Karachi women staff to escape, if only for a short period, the misogyny and violence of their current Pakistan context. We also set up a similar link with Antioch University, New York London summer programme. Other US academics from Arizona and Massachusetts came to study our innovative pedagogy.[20]

More conventional contributions included student success outcomes, for example, a women's studies PhD student became a pro-vice-master Birkbeck College, University of London. One student wrote and directed an opera, *Pope Joan*, based on a coursework topic, for the English National Opera Youth Group. Another, entering with only access qualifications, ended up on an MFA in creative writing at the University of California, Riverside. Our course was recognised by the Women's Press (after many rejections to my begging letters from other women's organisations, including the editor of *The Guardian*'s women's page) with an annual award of books and certificate to the top graduating student each year. Not surprisingly, with continuous, frenetic course development encouraging thinking and discussions, our women's studies publications proliferated, and we were included in most major edited collections in the field, alongside our single-authored publications.

Conclusion

Historians who indulge in the romance of educational experiments often balance such enthusiasms with the inevitability of failure in new symbolic orders. UEL women's studies was eventually closed. Memories of our work could be seen then through the lens of failure but, equally, histories can speak across decades, and ripples of educational resistance have a way of enlarging academic ponds. We did manage to transcend institutional and economic restraints and develop innovative pedagogy and research for a wider world. As one of our students said:

> After I finish, I am preparing with my husband to go back to Pakistan. I want to be a social worker. There are lots of women who are the same as me, at home, being a woman, as a wife, as a mother, so I just want to tell them they have all these abilities, they just don't know how to explore these abilities. I think I have to fight, I have got the ability to fight. Before I was, even I didn't go to the shopping myself, when I was in Pakistan.[21]

Women's studies is not only a study but a catalyst. It destabilises psychological and historical paradigms, transforming women into activists. Remembering the past of UEL women's studies is not intended then to be nostalgic or romantic, but to offer a history of possible futures. 'Women's studies has been the best part of my life. I am a lot stronger than I ever gave myself credit for'.[22]

Notes

1. F. Maher, 'Women's Studies in England: Mature Women Students and their Educational Vision', *Gender and Education*, 13:1, 2001, pp7-23, p20.
2. AC/2011/16, Women's Studies Papers and Ephemera, University of East London, Archives.
3. Maggie Humm, https://www.amazon.co.uk/Maggie-Humm/e/B001H6UJ34/ref=sr_tc_2_0?qid=1516787028&sr=1-2-ent.
4. AC/2011/16.
5. *Ibid.*
6. Maher 2001, p8.
7. bell hooks, *Feminism is for Everybody: Passionate Politics*. South End Press: Boston, 2000, p58.
8. F. Maher and M.K. Tetreault, *The Feminist Classroom*, Basic Books: New York, 1994.
9. Maher 2001, p14.
10. *Ibid.*, p12.
11. AC/2011/16.
12. *Ibid.*
13. *Ibid.*
14. *Ibid.*
15. J. Brookman, 'Victory for Women's Studies', *The Times Higher Education Supplement*, 5 February 1993, p2.
16. Virginia Woolf, *Jacob's Room*, K. Flint (ed.), Oxford University Press: Oxford, 1992, p240.
17. AC/2011/16.
18. A. Köster-Lossak and T. Levin, 'Editorial', *Women's Studies Quarterly*, Fall/Winter, vol. XX, 3 & 4, 1992, pp3-14.
19. T. Levin, 'Women's Studies Networking in Europe', *Women's Studies Quarterly*, Fall/Winter, vol. XX, 3 & 4, 1992, p154.
20. Maher 2001.
21. *Ibid.*, p10.
22. Student questionnaire, AC/2011/16.

CHAPTER ELEVEN

An Outpost of History: A Conversation

Sally Alexander, Catherine Hall and Bill Schwarz

Introduction

The time that the three of us shared at the North East London Polytechnic – subsequently the Polytechnic of East London and thence the University of East London; here, generically, NELP – more or less lasted through the 1980s to the early or middle 1990s. This largely coincided with the years that Mrs Thatcher was prime minister. The finances were rocky; the threat of redundancies ever-present; and memory suggests that many hours were spent in the dark and the cold on successive picket lines. This itself proved an education for us.

To begin with, the external authorities which oversaw the institution appeared to us to operate with the proverbial light touch. We principally came into contact with the three East End local authorities, which managed the polytechnic, on account of whatever funding strategy happened to be uppermost. In moments of crisis this local-authority presence pressed in closely. But otherwise, day to day, there was little evidence of the micro-management of our professional lives to which we have since become accustomed. In terms of the content and delivery of the teaching, oversight fell to the Council for National Academic Awards (CNAA) which, once a particular course had received approval, required only intermittent contact. In truth, at NELP many of the courses in the social sciences and humanities were also sheltered by the benign, supportive figure of Michael Rustin, who did much to protect us from untoward managerial intrusion and who engaged intellectually with what we were doing. Pretty much we had a free hand to organise our own affairs.

This was so with the shaping of the curriculum. We also had great autonomy in awarding places, with much leeway in considering students who had few or no formal qualifications. Our first intakes were older than students on comparable degrees, and perhaps – we liked to think – rather more worldly.

Our daily working lives were orchestrated by the mise en scène of the building in which we were billeted, Livingstone House. This was located on the edge of Stratford in East London, long before the Olympic Stadium and the Westfield Shopping Centre were envisaged, even in the Thatcherite optic. Run-down streets, high-rise public housing, and the conspicuous signs of the termination of the docks and local small manufacturing composed our familiar landscape. Many polys of the time had their own Livingstone House: once a commercial building taken over at rock-bottom prices by the local authority, reluctantly re-equipped for its new purpose. Our building had originally housed the production of Kensitas cigarettes, a historic company remembered now only by way of the sale of the old collectors' cigarette cards on eBay. It was ramshackle, with none of the amenities associated with higher education. There was perched on the top floor an improvised canteen which – a sign of more heavily unionised times – closed for lunch in order for the canteen staff to have an opportunity to eat. The building, home to sociology and cultural studies, was relatively insulated from the rest of the institution. It set us apart. Visits from the hierarchy were rare. Yet ramshackle though it was, it was ours, home to incessant intellectual disputation. Later we moved deeper into East London, to the old further education campus at Barking.

Looking back we can see that we found ourselves operating in a particular historical interregnum. While many of the key institutions of the state were moving into the hands of the Thatcherites or – as with the Greater London Council and its successors – were becoming the immediate site for open political warfare, for a long while the polytechnics occupied an outpost in the social world which appeared to require no urgent attention from the incoming personnel of the new government, intent on turning the world upside down. Polytechnics were hardly the priority. Indeed, in a strange paradox, Mrs Thatcher herself rather favoured them as they provided tertiary education on the cheap. While the political field was being recast, the polys remained pretty much as they were, unreformed. The currents of dissent they generated, while no doubt unwelcome to the Thatcher loyalists, and on occasion flaring into the light of day, were not in the opening years of Thatcherism a pressing issue for the new government. These circumstances signalled an unexpected historical intermission, in which new collective, intellectual work could flourish relatively unimpeded.

Like a number of cultural institutions at the outset of the Thatcher years (Channel 4, for example, launched in 1982), the polytechnics, precisely due to their putatively inferior position in the given educational hierarchy, were peculiarly receptive to various currents of dissent. NELP itself, like many such locales for higher learning, was not intimately known to the apostles of high Toryism. For long, the commodification of higher education never obviously appeared as a virtue decreed by nature. For the new social values associated with Mrs Thatcher to prevail, a long political struggle – a prolonged war of position, in Antonio Gramsci's terms – was required.

Cultural studies at NELP began life in just this conjuncture, with the evolving Thatcherite offensive palpable but not yet – so far as NELP was concerned – immediately or insistently operational.

For the most part, we focus in these reminiscences on the early moments of cultural studies at NELP.

Bill

In common with every component of the cultural studies we taught, the history we pursued aimed high intellectually, founded on an expectation of serious engagement from the students. Looking back, the ambition seems to have been unrestrained. Not only did we hope the students would familiarise themselves with the full gamut of debate originating from cultural studies – itself complex and demanding – but, in addition, to imagine cultural-studies perspectives in which a feel for history lay at the very core of the students' intellectual discovery.

I'd come from Birmingham cultural studies where at the time the dominant means, although not exclusively so, for grasping symbolic life was through variants of high structuralism, privileging language and linguistics. Ferdinand de Saussure, Claude Lévi-Strauss and Roland Barthes were powerful influences. To imagine that history could become a defining intellectual paradigm for thinking about culture, well, there was barely anything like it.

Perhaps some of the work of cultural studies at Portsmouth Polytechnic, under the inspiration of Robbie Gray, was comparable. But I think the determined analytical centrality of history to NELP's cultural studies was pretty much unparalleled. Eventually a succession of fine historians found themselves attracted to NELP.

Although remarkable, an unexpected consequence of the less vigilant circumstances of higher education in the polys was that they attracted disparate and lively staff who never felt at home in more conventional university departments, where the imperatives of academic disciplines were much tighter. At NELP, even before cultural studies was ever on the books, the disparate elements of something resembling cultural studies were already visible.

To begin with, alongside the core course in cultural history (or more properly, 'cultural history/cultural theory') there existed an ancillary core module designated as 'structural' history, paying greater attention to social and material factors. After a while this seemed overambitious for both the students and for us, although it was also the case that the conversation between this kind of social-economic history and cultural history was not easily developed. Eventually, after maybe two or three years, structural history was dropped and cultural history became the organising intellectual principle.

Sally

Yes, cultural studies at NELP wrote history into its structure and analysis from the beginning, didn't it?

I remember soon after I'd arrived hearing Stuart Hall come to speak to the students about Rastafarianism. This made a powerful impression on me.

I was utterly gripped, because he was making these – to me – bold historical moves, moving from the United States to the Caribbean, to Africa, to London, and back again, which became a characteristic of many of the nineteenth and twentieth century courses that we taught – and a feature of the multi-faceted forms of global history then emerging. The result of new research questions historians – including both of you – were asking, partly under the impulse of thinkers like Stuart about race, the movement of capital (Winifred Stokes had a sharp eye for the forms of capital accumulation), sexual difference and suffrage history, each of which pressed towards a global history. Paul Gilroy's *The Black Atlantic* came out of that political moment too.

I think, cultural studies then, in the 1980s – to many – meant literature, philosophy, cultural theory. But it didn't always mean historical thinking. Hearing Stuart Hall's reading of Rastafarianism I soon discovered that his approach was always historical.

It is interesting that cultural history and structural history were two foundations of historical thinking on the degree because in the outside world among historians, in history departments, while social history was influential and ubiquitous, especially through the marxist historians – against whom we feminist historians had long before cut our teeth – and through past and present, cultural history was only just on the horizon. NELP's cultural history came to life, as you say Bill, through the intellectual challenge of structuralism and poststructuralism: Ferdinand de Saussure, Barthes (a lesser influence among historians) – and especially Michel Foucault. Edward Said's *Orientalism*, first published in 1978, made the most powerful impression on the students' minds: it was everywhere in essays and presentations.

Catherine

Yet much of what we were actually doing as feminist historians was combining the economic with the cultural. I came to the polytechnic, I think, in 1982 and I was still doing the work with Leonore Davidoff, which became our book *Family Fortunes*. This is actually structural history and cultural history, that's exactly what we were doing. But we weren't calling it that.

We were looking at the structure and organisation of the family of business and the culture of the middle-class home. That was such a different kind of work from what I had done as a student in the Birmingham history department. It was a big adventure to go into a cultural studies department because I'd never taught cultural studies. So, then, I arrive in this department where it's possible to teach history, but within this bigger frame of culture, which, of course, suited me absolutely down to the ground, but would have been impossible to do in a history department.

I think it was unique what we were doing, both for cultural studies and for history. We were putting things together that hadn't been put together in terms of university syllabuses. This was a time when there was a greater interest in interdisciplinary work, but not many people were actually doing it and it was difficult. We had an ongoing discussion all the years I was there about the problems of teaching a course from an interdisciplinary base when you only have a base in a discipline – and the students didn't have that.

All of us who were teaching came from a discipline and we all knew our own disciplines and then we were trying to do this work, which was interdisciplinary. That's partly why we worked together so closely, constantly listening to each other and learning from each other about what it would mean to teach literature, theory, philosophy, history, politics as related subjects of inquiry. What did it mean to address seventeenth-century England in this way? What were the elements we needed to bring in to make sense of a whole social and economic formation?

So, we truly did work together: philosophers, cultural theorists, historians, literary critics, art historians.

Sally

Peter Horne was an art historian, as well as a philosopher.

The feminism which you were mentioning Catherine was a great intellectual driving force. For me, being at NELP felt like a continuation of the work that we had been doing as feminist historians for the previous fifteen years, breaking down categories of thought, opening up – we hoped – new forms of historical process; we found new sources because of the questions we asked, about the relations between the sexes, patriarchy, everyday life, the making of the self as well as the nation, and so on.

Feminist history gave us the drive and confidence to ask new questions, pursue new historical narratives. Yet at the same time, poststructuralists challenged the value of historical inquiry itself by questioning the credibility of the concept 'the past', and – especially – the value of an empirical method.

Catherine

Remember, also, that I don't think there was a single university history department teaching feminist history or gender history at this time.

Sally

No.

Catherine

I mean, none of us was in an orthodox university department. So the joy of being in a department where not only were we working with these other people, but with feminist approaches to historical work, or to literature or to whatever it might have been, were absolutely welcomed.

The left culture of the department, the critical engagement all the time with the political world that we lived with and the educational experiment we were engaged with, working also with a large number of mature students and with students who'd come in through non-orthodox routes, all this dominated our thinking. The students we taught proved challenging. It was a heady, experimental moment.

Sally

Intellectual history, the history of ideas, was a huge part of the work of the department, wasn't it? Through Couze Venn, a philosopher, and Peter Horne. Peter and Judy Greenway's work on gay lives, Peter and Couze's lectures on classical and continental philosophy made students think about the relation between culture and the individual in new ways.

I simply learned so much while teaching at NELP. Michael Rustin's lectures on Keynes, Beveridge, Melanie Klein were the spine of third-year teaching. My notes are with me still.

When in the 1990s Barbara Taylor joined the department, Mary Wollstonecraft and women thinkers of the enlightenment added a further dimension to our work on eighteenth-century political thought. Women writers – from Wollstonecraft to Toni Morrison – reconfigured the English-speaking worlds through the modern period. I remember the vigour with which we taught Virginia Woolf's London essays and *To the Lighthouse*, and Toni Morrison's *Beloved*, or Doris Lessing's southern African fiction and *The Golden Notebook*.

Bill

To clarify: we should point out, as Alan has already described in his chapter on cultural studies, that the first year was organised around the seventeenth and eighteenth centuries, the second year, the nineteenth and the third year, the twentieth century. Even though we all had our notional specialisms, all was cross-fertilised because we were teaching in different years.

I remember when I started teaching at NELP I was having to read not just Christopher Hill, *The World Turned Upside Down* and *The Century of Revolution*, which I found homely enough, but also Milton and Hobbes. It was as taxing as it was wonderful. I think my first lecture involved introducing the students to Keith Thomas, *Religion and the Decline of Magic*, which I'd never read before.

This inducted me into what you were calling, Sally, the history of ideas, historical context and history as a way of thinking. Something along these lines ran through the entire course.

Sally

Esther Leslie, who joined the department during the early 1990s, strengthened exactly this approach, while focusing on the twentieth century.

Revisiting my own and others' notes from the mid-1980s, we

anguished over whether Brecht and Lukács arguing over the relation between ideology and forms of representation could mean anything without students learning more of the Russian revolution. Bob Chase was one of drivers of conceptual clarity in this context. His notes on Brecht and Lukács remain indispensable. Just as he insisted on using the 'war between German historians' to orientate the meaning and memory of Nazism in post-war social democracy.

Bill

I can't remember if Esther arrived as a media theorist, because there were three different options for the students, taken alongside the core courses. There was popular culture, philosophy, and literature. I can't remember if she came in as a media theorist or as a literature person, but either way she thinks in a beguilingly philosophical manner. Like Bob Chase, she was absolutely inside the Adorno-Brecht-Benjamin debates about early twentieth-century modernism.

Catherine

I was just remembering the many hours we spent discussing in our course teams what we were going to teach and how we were going to do it. It's unimaginable now to think about a group of people in a department sitting down, having the time to discuss team teaching in that way. We went to each other's lectures, we thought together about what the seminar readings were going to be, we had hours and hours of talk. What a privilege!

Bill

From choice or not we found ourselves lecturing on things which fell outside our specialisms. This was double-edged, of course, but it offered a kind of vibrant intellectual buzz: the sense that, in theory, nothing was off-limits. Towards the end of my time at NELP, once the cultural studies department had expanded, I taught on the third world studies degree, teaching twentieth-century history from what we would call now a subaltern perspective.

Catherine

In a way, what's even more extraordinary is that we had this coordinated course, which was a development over three years – from the seventeenth century to the eighteenth century to the nineteenth century to the twentieth century. It was meant to grow organically and that's what we were trying to do with it, though I am sure it didn't always work. It was a collaborative project for everybody. Now students pick and choose. Our hope was for an integrated course. I wonder if they exist anymore?

Sally

We didn't only plan and work collaboratively, but we attended each other's lectures, and taught in twos or threes. Does that happen sometimes still in universities? I made sure I arrived in time to hear Mike Rustin's lectures – on John Stuart Mill, or John Maynard Keynes or Freud's Vienna.

Bill

And on Karl Popper, he gave wonderful lectures on Popper.

Sally

He sat up all night reading the Carl Schorske book on Vienna at the turn of the twentieth century but then substituted Schorske for a straight lecture on Freud because, he told us, it's about how Vienna itself shaped Freud's choice of profession. This was extraordinarily rich intellectually.

Psychoanalysis was a powerful, influential, if perhaps an intermittent, intellectual presence on the cultural studies degree. This undoubtedly chimed with my own work. For our work on the twentieth century we were all reading Freud on Dora! And then eventually, from the NELP origins, there developed the University of East London/Tavistock Psychoanalytic Studies MA course, which overlapped at some points with cultural studies.

Bill

Even if students now sign up for a good and adventurous literature course or an unorthodox history course, there is in front of you, or at least in sight, 'the curriculum', spoken or not. Over the years it has materialised, and, to various degrees, it shapes our assumptions of how the pedagogy is organised. Basically, with variations, you'll begin with Chaucer, if it's literature, and work up to Seamus Heaney, Zadie Smith, or whoever.

Even though the course at NELP was organised historically, century by century, there was no curriculum addressing literature and philosophy and the media through the lens of history. It just didn't exist. This may have had its drawbacks. But it encouraged us to think thematically, from contrary tangents. There was more space to devise the teaching in relation to the students, on the ground, and with greater opportunity for contingency and spontaneity.

Sally

Yes, you could, but, Bill, I think it was different for first and second years. But for third year it seemed as though we invented the twentieth century. We introduced British history after the Versailles peace congress in 1919 through the debates about modernism and modernity.

My contribution to the twentieth century was to encourage the students to think about shell shock and memory, followed by women's suffrage, women's work in the new industries, unemployment, and the voices of the unemployed during the 1930s.

Bill

It's also significant, Sally, that you introduced your work on, memory, bringing memory as a dimension of historical thought into the department. Later, memory became a critical dimension of cultural studies and cultural history.

We should say in this context that right at the end of his life, Raphael Samuel joined the department, after he'd written *Theatres of Memory*. And earlier Susannah Radstone, one of our first students, moved from teaching film studies at Warwick to work with us.

Sally, can you talk us through the ways that memory cross-fertilised with historical studies?

Sally

Memory was present in so much of the nineteenth-century history that we taught: John Burnett's two edited volumes of working-class autobiography, *Useful Toil* and *Destiny Obscure*, and then later Mary Prince's memoir of slavery, for instance. The history that I'd been writing owed everything to Henry Mayhew's four volumes on the London poor, the blue books – Royal Commissions and Select Committees on needlewomen, handloom weavers, coalminers, children's employment. The Royal Commissions and Select Committees interviewed working people and their representatives; careful reading could elicit truths about the realities of working lives and the mental worlds of the speakers which otherwise were out of reach.

I used oral history in my own research, on travelling showmen and working women in particular. Students were inspired by oral history. Many student essays or dissertations used oral histories, especially for late twentieth-century subjects, or for exploring the symbolic and hidden meanings of political and cultural issues. Memory and oral history broke silences in the more orthodox literary or historical archives; students could create their own archives.

Later, in the early 1990s, I wrote a first-year course on the history of the self and subjectivity, from St Augustine to Freud, which owed something to the course Jim Clifford had created in the University of California at Santa Cruz in the early 1980s. Augustine's fascination with his own capacity to love, or the infant at the mother's breast, could have been written ten minutes ago. I remember one student using St Augustine to present his father's memories of arriving in Lancashire in the 1950s or 1960s to work ankle-deep in water in the mills.

I think NELP was the first university to introduce an MA in Psychoanalysis, which was run through with memory.

Bill

In this context can I also ask you, Sally, how you experienced the interactions between the history you were working on at NELP and *History Workshop Journal*?

Sally

I spoke with other historians on the journal about cultural studies, how it was constituted and whether our historical approach was going to be swallowed by cultural theory and cultural studies.

Yet it soon became clear that Freud is indispensable for the study of memory, and of the meanings of war, group psychology, the sources of violence – questions which dominated European history through the twentieth century. As I read more psychoanalysis I realised how very much of its time it was, and how writers like Freud, Winnicott, Rivière and even Klein were writing about twentieth century realities. I struggled to use unconscious phantasy and memory as a way of opening up historical notions of consciousness and experience, and I think Mike Rustin must have been a subliminal influence because for him the unconscious is second nature – whereas for historians at the time, psychoanalysis was a marginal, beleaguered set of ideas. I have to admit it was not popular among history students either! Perhaps because it's about the unknown and hidden, about uncertainty and doubt, rather than the historian's wishful terrain of empirical and narrative truths.

Catherine

One of the other big new developments was that feminist historians had been gendering history for a long time, but the project of 'race-ing' history was slower to get established. I think it really developed in the degree course over the late 1980s and 1990s.

For Sally, *History Workshop* was indeed another point of connection. For me, it was *Feminist Review* and working on that editorial collective and the huge political debates between white feminists and black feminists in the late 1980s was certainly shifting the way I was thinking about the kind of work that I wanted to do. That shift was also being driven by what was going on in the cultural studies department.

I remember very distinctly being angrily challenged by a student. We were reading Thomas Carlyle and she couldn't understand why we were not dealing with the question of race in relation to Carlyle. I'd never read *Shooting Niagara* until she said, 'You should have!' It was a wake-up call. We started to introduce a new set of texts on the nineteenth century, thinking about what it meant to race English history. We were both listening to the students and what they're bringing to us and demanding from us, but also there was the outside political work, editorial work and research work that we were doing. It was all connected and I've never again had that experience in a university department.

I went to Essex and then I went to UCL and there was never that sense of connection between all the different parts of your life in a way that was so satisfying. It was a unique experience.

Sally

I remember another occasion when we were challenged by the students to think about language: about what constituted the English language, what kind of writing counted and whether Caribbean dialects counted as English in an academic context which prided itself on difference and creativity. I think we came down in favour of orthodox English sentences, standard English, received pronunciations, and so on.

I remember students knocking on my door, coming to see me in a little group to ask me not to argue with them so vigorously, and to acknowledge the power relation between student and tutor ...

Bill

Catherine, when you were talking about race in history, I am interested to hear your thoughts, and then, Sally, your thoughts, about the books you've written. I'm interested to hear your reflections on your publications and your experiences as teachers at NELP.

Catherine

By the late 1980s, the questions about being black and British were so present – forcing us to think about what this meant historically. I don't remember at which point we had Kobena Mercer come in and he was with us for a year, I think, and he had a big impact. The challenges from black students, black feminists, the puzzles about how to re-think an established historiography that took almost no account of race or colonialism and denied the significance of empire to British domestic history – these were big issues. It took me time to come to the understanding that a narrative of nineteenth-century England which ignored the history of empire would be fundamentally lacking. In the 1970s, feminist historians had spent a lot of time thinking 'We've got to rethink the marxist historians, we've got to rethink class as the only dynamic'. This took us to sexual difference and to gender. But, then, coming to see how nation, empire, race and ethnicity were also critical meant a huge amount of new thinking, new reading, new understandings. That was all happening, for me, in the late 1980s and 1990s and was part of the postcolonial moment in Britain. It all fed into what became my book on England and Jamaica, *Civilising Subjects*.

And then there was your work, Bill.

Bill

In terms of thinking about *The White Man's World,* I particularly remember two occasions when the ideas for my argument were rooted in my teaching.

First, I was giving a lecture on the end of the British empire and thinking about Rhodesia. It was like a revelation when I suddenly saw, which I should have seen all along, the degree to which white Rhodesian politics were operating inside Britain, in the sense that there was a huge mental traffic between colony and metropole. It's obvious of course, but it didn't seem so at the time. I remember I could see on the horizon the intoxicating figure of the white man moving to the centre of the stories I was telling about England. I was both delivering the lecture and succumbing at the same time to a kind of internal reverie, which later developed into a fat book.

On the same course, secondly, there was a troubled, smart but anxious student. He offered to do a talk on Enoch Powell. Although it never became clear, he seemed to embrace a degree of sympathy for Powell. It couldn't quite be spoken, which I regretted at the time and since. But what stayed in my mind was the ambivalence in play.

He showed a short film clip in the aftermath of Powell's 'rivers of blood' speech outside the House of Commons when the dockers were demonstrating for 'Enoch'. One of them – they'd all packed away a few pints by the look of it – pointed to the House of Commons and says, 'He's the only white man in there'.

I fell over backwards when I heard that. 'The only white man in there'! In London, in 1968. He didn't even have to name him. The great symbolic figure of the colonial past, in that very moment, was transported back to England. It signalled a powerful moment in the reinvention of ethnicity. Whiteness was not epidermal (there were in Westminster many men with pale skins), but a disposition which had to be earned. It could be won or lost. Whiteness was itself a symbolic reality. That organised the themes of the book for me. From that point on I could see exactly what story I had to tell. Later I tried to tell the student how important it had been for me. But it didn't work out and proved too difficult.

Sally

Well, I think what that reminds me of – to stick with race for a moment – is the moments of epiphany that came, most insistently from students, but also from the readings. Staying awake all night to finish Toni Morrison: it was life-changing, if life and psyche can be changed in your forties!

The self-consciousness I'd developed as a feminist – not to speak for others, just for yourself and people like yourself – inhibited me from thinking actively as a historian about race, and racial thinking. I struggled to think about whiteness. It just was a blank to me. 'I don't know what it means, I don't know what that means': that's what I thought. It was years before I began to see whiteness everywhere.

So, I can't pretend that there was more – for me – than glimpses or flashes of insight into race in British history, or in British intellectual traditions.

Ken Parker invited David Dabydeen to speak, and on another occasion Jackie Kay. He gave me a book, *The Healers,* which took me into a completely other ethical world of aesthetics and belief. In fact, he was simply saying, 'Don't think you can understand everything about other cultures. We can recognise a common humanity, but other cultures, we won't necessarily understand'. Historians on *History Workshop Journal* were writing into that tension, addressing questions of race, racial thinking and racial difference. Bodil Folke Frederikson's essay in *HWJ* 65 on the debate between Jomo Kenyatta, Marie Bonaparte and Bronislaw Malinowski on clitoridectomy in Kenya, for instance, resurrected a moment in the 1920s when European intellectuals attempted – and only partially succeeded in – a meeting of minds across continents.

Bill

There's one last thing going through my head. The practice which I bought from the Cultural Studies Centre in Birmingham – with Richard Johnson, Greg McLennan and others – was that we were explicitly reading history books conceptually. Our primary purpose was to uncover the conceptual architecture which allowed the books to work as history books. We got into much trouble, from E.P. Thompson in particular, for reading *The Making of the English Working Class* in ways which he didn't like.

Sally

We all did that, didn't we? We all read him in ways he didn't like.

Bill

Yes, indeed!

Catherine

From different perspectives.

Bill

It was a partial way of working, and perhaps a perverse one. We were approaching history books as in some ways practical philosophical texts. It was a curious way to proceed, and we never set out to think along these lines. But in retrospect I believe it wasn't without its virtues.

Sally, I co-taught with you, for maybe three or four years, the MA in Cultural Studies: Theories and Histories. Couze Venn took the theory component, and you and I the historical. We read an eclectic range of authors: Macaulay, Luisa Passerini, Natalie Zemon Davis, Foucault, Carlo Ginzburg and so on. I found it such a productive way of reading a history book: we weren't reading Passerini because we needed to find out what happened in Italy in 1922. We were thinking, 'Well, how can we use Passerini to help us understand our own historical problems?', and to ask as well how historical inquiry itself should be recast.

Sally

I want to say two things. You've reminded me that we were reading, or I was reading, Freud's *Thoughts for the Times on War and Peace* with his later exchanges with Einstein in the way you describe. I was asking both 'Why was this written then? What was Freud thinking about in Vienna through the 1920s and 1930s?' and, alongside this, 'How can we use these writings now, how can we use this thinking?'.

The other thought, Bill, is remembering the brilliant and innovative course you constructed around *Black Jacobins* and C.L.R. James, which was to reconstruct at least three temporalities globally: Haiti in the 1790s, the Caribbean in the twentieth century and our own times at the end of the twentieth century, in Britain.

Bill

Yes. The ambition was extraordinary, but looking back I'm not persuaded that I had the intellectual capacity to place all these questions together.

Sally

You explored San Domingo and Paris in the 1790s-1810s, England (and the world!) in the 1930s, when James was writing, and then the 'conjuncture' of the 1990s, which was when the course was taught, asking how we read the book in this very different historical time. You thought first years would learn from reading one history book about the making of the modern world thoroughly, and understanding the political contexts which produced it.

There were plenty of other examples we might take, but this particularly sticks in my mind as a means critically to bring the past 'historically' into the present.

Conclusion

It is strange looking back on this shared experience. It seems to suggest a time which was radically different from university life today.

But there may be reason to be more circumspect. Much of the toil and frustration may have slipped out of memory. And maybe we should concede the degree to which our collective ambitions were unrealistic or unrealisable. The endeavour was of its time and, as we've sought to explain, it was the product of a particular history which can't now be repeated, although new opportunities arise.

In part, also, success and failure existed inside the other. In this regard the arrival of the Research Assessment Exercise (the RAE, the forerunner of the Research Excellence Framework) was telling. Hard though it is to recall, initially we welcomed the RAE as a democratic policy, seeking to distribute national research funds more equitably, giving institutions like NELP greater access to research money. This laudable intention soon was to collapse under its own reliance on metrics as the dominating arbiter of intellectual quality.

But more than that, as much as we welcomed the arrival of the RAE, it also worked to individualise research reputations and to encourage the migration of scholars from poorer institutions to richer, creating concentrations of research in the traditional, more privileged locales. Each success served to undermine the collectivity we worked hard to create. The RAE was not alone in the decomposition of the intellectual world we have been describing. But it worked as an agent in the larger dissolution. We were all implicated.

CHAPTER TWELVE

Independent study

Derek Robbins

Introduction

This is a personal account of the pedagogical innovation which was, to a large extent, the hallmark of the university in its first twenty years as North East London Polytechnic (NELP). I try to give an account of the place of this innovation in my social and intellectual trajectory, deliberately specifying my referents, in order to show that 'independent study' was not a maverick development in one institution but was an attempt to respond to general issues concerning the nature of higher education in mass democracy.

Having received an education in the humanities in privileged institutions, I came to NELP in the year in which it was instituted and spent the whole of my career there until retirement in 2014. The challenge was to relate my kind of intellectual formation to the supposed educational needs of the whole population. After almost half a century, this same challenge remains. In the early 1970s, 'independent study' spearheaded the institution's attempt to revolutionise higher education. With the abolition of the 'binary divide' in the early 1990s, the institution reneged on its polytechnic vision in order to situate itself as the University of East London (UEL) in the market of universities and, simultaneously, reneged on its commitment to 'independent study'. The demise of a mode of study coincided with the deformation of the institution.

My partisan retrospection is an attempt to pose questions which are relevant to our current situation. Was, for instance, the emphasis on the acquisition of 'transferable skills' rather than knowledge accumulation a contributory factor in degrading intellectuality and in generating our contemporary malaise in relation to specialist expertise, or did it accurately anticipate the extent to which information exchange now supersedes knowledge possession? For all its apparent radicalism, was ‘independent study’ a last throw of modernist ‘Bildung’ in that it sought to allow the articulation of hitherto excluded cultural dispositions just at the moment when the mass media were beginning to actualise a post-modernist obliteration of the notion of indigenous cultural identity? Could the institution have retained its original social mission if it had sustained its commitment to independent study? Whatever our response to these questions might be, is a recovery of that historical moment desirable or feasible? The questions are inextricably linked to my part in the evolution of ‘independent study’ and its part in my career, both before and after. Other participants saw the development differently at the time and would now see it differently in retrospect. The excitement of those years was that ideological differences were vigorously expressed but largely suppressed in the interest of encouraging practice. I am not now in the business in retrospect of seeking unilaterally to impose one interpretation of events which had diverse meanings for those involved.

My acquired cultural capital: before NELP/UEL[1]

My parents both left school at the age of fourteen in the mid to late 1920s. They were determined that their two sons would have life chances through educational achievement which had not been open to them. I won a scholarship to my local grammar school at the age of eight and remained at that school until eighteen, when I won a state scholarship to study English at Clare College, Cambridge. My familial culture was nonconformist, entailing detailed biblical knowledge, strict Sunday observance and total abstinence from alcohol. My school culture was scholastic, particularly involving initiation into the ‘humanities’ which did not appear to be in conflict with domestic values. My career was promoted by parental aspiration, achieved by O-, A- and S-level and Cambridge entrance examination performance, and effected through local authority and state funding. I was part of the 'grammar-school boy' phenomenon analysed sociologically shortly before by A.H. Halsey.[2]

My school still measured its success in terms of the number of its students who gained entry to Oxbridge. I 'chose' to study English at Cambridge because I was aware of the tradition of the Cambridge English school, which emphasised the study of the relations between 'literature' and its social 'background', as most exemplified in the texts of Basil Willey[3] who was still King Edward VII professor of English literature in my first years as an undergraduate, as opposed to the Oxford tradition which tended to concentrate on the analysis of literary texts as autonomous aesthetic phenomena. By complete accident, I was admitted to Clare College where some of the English tutors were among the few remaining disciples of F.R. Leavis. His influence was still significant in several ways. Leavis thought that his ideal of the social function of the English school was challenged by the kind of technological 'culture' represented by C.P. Snow. Rather in the tradition of Matthew Arnold, Leavis's assumption in the 'two cultures debate' of the 1960s was that Snow's achievements should not be regarded as 'cultural' at all.

My undergraduate career at Cambridge was one of initiation into an accepted critical discourse about literature, but this was in a context which constantly raised questions about the nature of literature and of discourse about it. I have discussed elsewhere the implications of the class profile of my fellow students at Clare.[4] There was a sense in which there was a divide between the dominant discourse of public school entrants and the alternative perspective of grammar school entrants. Within the English school the balance of power was shifting with the arrival of Raymond Williams in 1961,[5] and I was able to benefit from following courses which he was responsible for introducing into the tripos. The system of tuition suited me in that specific subject teaching was provided in college in preparation for examinations while it was also possible to pursue personal interests by auditing lectures in any faculty. I attended lectures in moral sciences (philosophy), such as those given by a Nietzschean, Michael Tanner,[6] and in the divinity school, such as those given by Donald MacKinnon.[7] Access to fellows in college enabled cross-disciplinary discussion with, for instance, the dean, Maurice Wiles,[8] an expert on gnosticism, and the émigré existentialist, Paul Roubiczek.[9] I graduated in the summer of 1966. My proposal for doctoral research was accepted for commencement in the autumn. I proposed to study 'Literature and science, 1770-1800 with particular reference to Samuel Taylor Coleridge and Joseph Priestley'. My main supervisor was Raymond Williams in the English faculty but I was also assigned to Mary Hesse[10] and Robert Young[11] in the recently established Department for the History and Philosophy of Science.

This intellectual and institutional background to my doctoral research is significant in respect of what subsequently occurred. I had selected for study the relationship between the work of Priestley and Coleridge as a case study of the relations between literary and scientific creativity at a particular period of time. The object of study was the transition in Coleridge's early thought from allegiance to a philosophical *system* similar to that developed by Priestley, one which sought to reconcile a Unitarian theology with an empirically derived understanding of the material universe, to an interest in a vital physical world, one immanently constituted by an ideal, Neo-Platonic spiritual presence. I explored the extent to which Coleridge reconciled the opposing world views within a poetic artefact such as *The Rime of the Ancient Mariner,* establishing an alternative and autonomous aesthetic discourse. There was an affinity between the problem studied and the process of undertaking the study. In spite of the multidisciplinary supervisory team, I was constrained to produce a thesis which would be acceptable to the English faculty. The organisation of knowledge embodied in the faculty structure of the institution impinged on my capacity to articulate an analysis of the phenomena. Similarly, the final product of my research was influenced by the interests of my main supervisor. What had started as a philosophical enquiry into the truth claims of competing intellectual discourses at the end of the eighteenth century became much more sociological. The historical dimension became more dominant, focusing on the *social* conditions of possibility of different discourses.

I did not complete my thesis within three years and, in 1969, I needed paid employment. I applied for jobs in departments of

English in universities. I can give three reasons for my lack of success – obviously, first, the fact that I had not yet gained my doctorate but, also the facts that the boom for employment of new young lecturers had just passed as the 'new' universities had become fully established, and that there were few English departments willing to accommodate what was becoming known as the 'sociology of literature'. I was appointed to a temporary post in September 1969 to teach English on the University of London BA General course offered at the Barking Regional College of Technology. In January 1970, Barking became one of the constituent colleges of the newly instituted North East London Polytechnic (NELP) and my post was confirmed. I taught English literature 'traditionally' for several years. For the first time I experienced the tension both of teaching a curriculum expressing a dominant culture to students who were relatively uninitiated into that culture, and of being an instrument in the transmission of knowledge which was predefined and then adjudicated by an external body over which I had no control and in which I had no representation. I reflected on this experience in the preface to my doctoral thesis, which was examined and accepted in 1972. 'There is a need', I wrote, 'to "demythologise" past literature and to rationalise the relation which we accept or impose between the past and the present'.

My early years at NELP: 1969-74

Working at NELP made me realise very quickly that the structural discrimination I had experienced intellectually at Cambridge was integrally related to the social discrimination exercised by the institution. It was a relief when it became an almost immediate policy of NELP to discontinue subordination to the University of London external degree system and to develop its own degree courses. I was slower to recognise that challenging the domination of universities would involve a transformation of the philosophy of course design. In 1972-73, I was given the task of developing a proposal for a new degree in communication which would accommodate elements of existing teaching in literature and linguistics. I now realised that the emphasis of 'practical criticism' which I had imbibed as a student was predicated on a shared discourse within a socially privileged minority, and that concern with communication within a mass democracy necessitated the articulation of different premises.[12] I tried to develop a degree course based on the pragmatic analysis of communication processes rather than one which merely extended 'literary' values and judgement.

Shortly after the institution of NELP, Eric Robinson had been appointed deputy director (academic). As political advisor to Anthony Crosland, Robinson had been instrumental in proposing the 'binary divide' in English higher education, separating the purposes of universities and polytechnics in the system, but he was not an advocate for the peaceful co-existence of the two types of institution. His *The New Polytechnics*[13] was a call for a new kind of higher education institution altogether, a kind which would offer education to the whole population rather than sustain the privileged few and would subvert existing universities. He took the view that the liberal universities maintained social distinction and that the curriculum developments in the 'new' universities of the 1960s had provided staff with the opportunity to innovate with 'cross-disciplinary' course content which was, however, an expression of their interests rather than responsive to the interests of a wider constituency of admitted students. The 'innovations' euphemised the perpetuation of prior distinction. Robinson argued, instead, for a 'systems approach' to course design. Course designers should not begin by devising innovative course content but should begin by identifying the characteristics of the likely student 'input' to the proposed course and the 'output' likely to be desired by future employers. The proposed content of the curriculum should function as a means to enable students to travel from 'input' to 'output'. Robinson established a course development unit (CDU) to scrutinise internally all new course proposals at NELP and ensure that they would adhere to his principles of course design.

The proposed communications degree was rejected by the CDU in 1972-73. It was thought to remain too intellectualist, without reference to the needs of the rapidly developing communications industry. With a selected group of staff, Robinson had already been working on a course proposal which he hoped would fulfil his intentions for the whole institution and, in turn, for the whole educational system. With political opportunism, Robinson responded to the James report, published on 25 January 1972, which contained the findings of the work of a committee appointed at the end of 1970 by the then secretary of state for education and science, Margaret Thatcher, to study the education, training and probation of teachers. The report recommended that teacher training should occur in three cycles, the first of which would either be a degree course or a new two-year course for a Diploma of Higher Education (DipHE). Mrs Thatcher's higher education white paper of December 1972, *A Framework for Expansion*, approved the introduction of two-year courses leading to a DipHE and envisaged that this might have a function in the system much wider than simply within the field of teacher training. Robinson established a working party during the period between the publications of the James report and the white paper to make proposals for a new two-year course which could be introduced at NELP, and which might be a blueprint for the national development of the new DipHE award. It produced an interim report in October 1972. An extended working party continued this work in the spring of 1973 and, in July, the academic board agreed to the establishment of a DipHE development unit for the following year, comprising some staff seconded internally from the institution's faculties. This unit met for the first time in September 1973, with the task of adapting the original interim report to constitute a course proposal to be validated by the Council for National Academic Awards (CNAA) in time to enable a first intake in 1974-75.

Following the rejection of the communications degree proposal, I was seconded to the DipHE unit. This was a full-time internal secondment but I was also given permission to study part time at the London School of Economics. In 1972-73, I received my Cambridge PhD, and it was the suggestion of Raymond Williams that I should secure a formal qualification in sociology to advance the study of the sociology of literature. In the first year I satisfied the qualifying requirements to be registered for an MSc (Econ.) and I pursued this course part time in 1973-75. In the year of the DipHE development unit, therefore, sociological work at the LSE was also consolidating my move away from the study of literature towards a more general interest in the sociology of knowledge.

The DipHE unit operated with a core group of about six staff which met weekly with a wider working party of staff representing the faculties of the institution. It inherited two main emphases from the interim report, and from these it was required to develop a course submission to be approved by the CNAA. The first was that the course should not be restricted to entrants possessing traditional A-level qualifications, but would provide for applicants who could demonstrate the 'capacity to benefit' from higher education rather than exclusively for those who had already satisfied standard assessments. The second proscription on planning was the argument that the future employment needs of students would be best served by designing a course which would inculcate 'transferable skills' rather than enable the acquisition of accumulated knowledge. During the year, the unit developed a course framework which would try to actualise the objectives of the interim report. Tyrrell Burgess was appointed to lead the DipHE unit. He was an Oxford history graduate who had an established reputation politically as a member of the Greater London Council, and intellectually as, previously, a member of Richard Layard's research centre on higher education at the LSE. He was also already well known as an advocate of 'student-centred learning' in primary and secondary education. He was also a known disciple of Karl Popper. His leadership of the unit introduced two key components into the process of course design. He argued that the way to actualise opportunity for 'non-standard' entrants was to ensure that the proposed curriculum would follow from the objectives articulated by the students. He also argued that skill acquisition and knowledge accumulation could be rendered compatible by accepting that both derive from the practice of problem-solving, particularly from a Popperian recognition that skills and knowledge advance by a process of hypothesis formulation and falsification.

There were three key components of the DipHE proposal which was submitted to the CNAA in spring 1974 and which was formally approved on 18 June. First, the introductory six weeks of the course were to be a 'planning period' when students would be guided in a process of locating themselves as 'input' and identifying their goals as 'output'. In other words, the process of *course* design recommended by Robinson became an integral part of the proposed course, allowing students to propose their own curriculum. The other two key components were structural. Students were required to propose their individual 'programmes' of study within the constraints that half of their time would be devoted to 'central study' and the other half to 'special interest study'. Students were to be encouraged to define their own objectives within the course but they would be required to meet these objectives by prescribed means. In 'central study', students would be required to realise their personal objectives by working in groups, developing and implementing activities which would enable the acquisition of skills in processes of cooperative social action. In 'special interest study', students would be required to undertake placement with any member of staff in the institution. The aspiration was that students would be encouraged to use attachment to specialist staff as a means to meeting their personal objectives rather than with the purpose of imbibing the totality of the disciplinary knowledge possessed by staff. Specialist knowledge was to be seen as instrumental in the development of skills.

It is clear from this brief outline of the intentions of the DipHE course designers that they represented a challenge to the assumptions underlying the existence of the CNAA. The council had been established to validate course proposals submitted by polytechnics in order to guarantee their quality equivalence with degree courses in universities. Typically, the CNAA operated with disciplinary panels predominantly comprised of academics from universities. The CNAA set up a new panel to deal with national proposals for the DipHE but the choice of its chair – James Porter, head of Bulmershe College of Education – significantly situated its brief within the field of education and teacher training. The epistemological challenge posed by NELP's DipHE proposals was barely recognised and, of course, the further challenge was that it appeared that the NELP course proposal was defying the evaluation of its *course* by arguing for procedures which would internally legitimise what *individual* students would propose to study by the end of their 'planning period'. The NELP proposal seemed to be seeking approval for a carte blanche. As a consequence, 'validation' became a crucial issue in seeking approval for the course. In effect, the CNAA agreed to approve the course, initially as an experiment, on condition that the staff administering it would establish a 'validating body' which would scrutinise all the programme proposals submitted by students at the end of their planning period. The CNAA devolved its authority to the institution while maintaining its right to monitor the institution's exercise of that authority.

The School for Independent Study, 1974-1990

The Dip HE

'The School for Independent Study' (SIS) was the unit within which the new course was to be delivered. The first intake to the DipHE was in autumn 1974. The seventy-two students were assigned to groups of twelve, each led by a dedicated member of staff. Within these groups, the students wrote small autobiographies and carried out assessments of their levels of skill; these were exercises designed to enable them after six weeks to write a detailed statement of their objectives and the processes they would embark on within the constraints of the course to meet these objectives and submit themselves to assessment on their performance.

Influenced considerably by Tyrrell Burgess's contacts and reputation, SIS invited powerful people to constitute the validating body for the course. These included Lord James of Rusholme, the leader of the earlier report, Sir Toby Weaver, a former permanent secretary at the department of education, Cedric Price, an avant-garde architect in the East End, and Lady Plowden, author of an earlier (1967) report on primary education. These were 'establishment' figures, most of whom were associated with education and education policy. They were not primarily academics but were prominent for their actions. This orientation implied that they would attempt to scrutinise the totality of what students proposed to undertake in their individual programmes of study in terms of the likely acquisition of their capacity to *act* rather than to possess knowledge.

The process of validation and, subsequently, that of assessment, highlighted some of the ideological tensions within the school. There was a constant difficulty in seeking to reconcile the course's commitment to the transmission of transferable skill and its equally strong commitment to student self-determination. The ambivalence was present in the choice of 'independent study' as a title for the innovation. Independence was seen as both a personal competence and also the essence of cognitive individualism. There was a tension between vocationalism and libertarianism, which I tried to resolve by recommending an enactment of Dewey's instrumentalist theory of knowledge.

For my part, my understanding of independent study derived from several key texts of the late 1960s and early 1970s. These were *The Social Construction of Reality,*[14] *Deschooling Society,*[15] *The Structure of Scientific Revolutions,*[16] *Beyond the Stable State,*[17] and *Knowledge and Control: New Directions in the Sociology of Education.*[18] The process implemented in SIS was 'constructivist' in that it emphasised that students should construct their own curricula rather than be in receipt of prescribed content. The 'group work' component of the course sought to encourage students to perform 'real-life' tasks collaboratively within the local community and to evaluate them and, as such, sought to challenge the social detachment of the educational institution. The 'special interest' component sought to actualise scientific revolutions in that it was an attempt to regard established knowledge ('normal science') as provisional and pragmatic, and to allow students to be change agents in developing new paradigms. Critically, these orientations all meant that existing institutional structures should go beyond stability, should not be ossified or reified. Treating education as an ongoing process necessitated both an opposition to already dominant structures and also resistance to any tendency to allow independent programmes of study to generate institutionally normalised new courses. M.F.D. Young's editorial introduction to *Knowledge and Control* specifically drew attention to the controlling function of the CNAA in respect of polytechnic innovation in the UK system of higher education. Staff in SIS were agreed that, within the circumscribed field of 'education' to which their pedagogical innovations were assigned, they were in sympathy with the thinking within the department of sociology at the Institute of Education, London, in clear opposition to the rival position adopted there by R.S. Peters and P.H. Hirst in its department of philosophy.[19]

The BA/BSc by Independent Study

The course for the DipHE at NELP was one of two courses for the new award approved by the CNAA for commencement in 1974. Other course approvals followed quickly, largely in colleges of education. Staff in SIS were instrumental in establishing an Association of Colleges Implementing the DipHE (ACID) with a view to ensuring that the NELP model for the award would be secured nationally. This was a time when, post-1968, West European governments were experimenting with the introduction of short-course qualifications as levers for transforming their higher education systems. The Diplôme des études universitaires générales (DEUG) was introduced in France at the time when the 'experimental university' at Vincennes was also established. West Germany was attempting to pioneer, at institutions such as Kassel and Bielefeld, a 'Gesamthochschule' concept which would integrate technological and humanities educational traditions.

In the UK there were working parties which tried to recommend that the new DipHE would receive recognition across the binary divide, ensuring that diplomates would secure advanced entry to degree courses if they wished to pursue their studies beyond the diploma level. In spite of these discussions, it became clear by the end of 1974-75 that the first intake of students to the NELP DipHE would receive little recognition at the end of their course. NELP was one of the few institutions arguing for the 'transferability' of its DipHE qualification between institutions and disciplines. The argument that the emphasis of the NELP DipHE was on problem-solving rather than accumulated knowledge, and that this was a skill which enabled late entry to any single-subject degree course, was almost completely dismissed within the higher education system, even within NELP itself.

Nationally, the DipHE became a subordinate exit point from structured three-year degree courses, lacking any independent currency. To ensure that the first intake of students at NELP would not become disadvantaged as a result of their pursuit of an innovative course, SIS moved quickly to seek approval for a one-year post-DipHE course to provide the opportunity for its diplomates to progress to degree qualification. The academic board gave SIS formal responsibility for the establishment of post-diploma opportunities in the polytechnic, and it also ensured that a working party of faculty representatives was established to liaise with SIS. The aspiration was to devise a course which would meet the needs of students completing the DipHE and of those who might want to complete their taught course degrees 'by independent study' in their final year. The intention was that this accessibility would not be confined to NELP students. I had begun to think that a key issue for the future development of independent study was the nature and status of university *institutions*.

Related to my allegiance to Dewey's epistemology, I submitted an MSc thesis in 1975 at the LSE on 'The context of Chicago sociology'[20] in which I explored the social conditions for the emergence of the University of Chicago in 1895 and the consequential *institutional* impact on the contemporary development of sociological research. This was an objective correlative for reflecting on the limits and possibilities for independent study within NELP. The proposal for a BA/BSc by independent study differed from that for the DipHE in important respects. It retained the idea that students should plan personal programmes of study but it proposed that this planning should take place in a 'pre-course' which would precede admission to the course. In developing their individual programmes, students would be required to justify their use of the academic institution for the advancement of their projects. Whereas the DipHE instituted a 'validating board' which scrutinised proposals made by students in the first weeks of the course, the BA/BSc instituted a registration board which would assess proposals to ensure that they demonstrated that students could argue why and how they would require the specialist tuition offered by the university to fulfil their intentions. Progression from the NELP DipHE was not automatic but, rather, was dependent on the capacity of students to demonstrate in their proposals the intellectual skills which the course providers had argued would be the generic characteristics of all diploma holders. It was clear that, in effect, the decisions of the registration board for the degree would be offering a judgement of the claims made for the DipHE.

Some staff in SIS thought that the degree submission subordinated the values of the DipHE to those of conventional degree course specialists. The establishment of the degree created a rift within SIS between those involved in the delivery of its two courses. The intention had been that the whole institution should own the degree by independent study, and the course proposal argued for an internal registration board comprising representatives of each of the faculties. It proposed that there should be one external examiner sitting in an advisory capacity on the registration board to establish the necessary link between registration and assessment. After several extensions to approval subject to course revisions, the degree course was fully approved in September 1979. During this period, NELP resisted the CNAA's contention that the registration board should be external to the polytechnic, established by the council itself. In concession, NELP agreed that each faculty of the institution would have a sub-registration board attended by one external examiner and that proposals from students would come for decision to a full registration board, attended by faculty representatives and all external examiners, including one overall chief external examiner. The registration board would be chaired by the course leader of the degree, preserving the position that this was the institution's board.

During the period in which the degree was receiving full approval, SIS also gained approval to run a part-time DipHE course. The full-time DipHE was finally approved in the autumn of 1976 for five years and, with it, the part-time DipHE for the same period. By the beginning of the 1980s, all three courses were firmly established.

The 1980s

Early in the 1980s, SIS proposed a further course development. An MA/MSc by Independent Study was approved by the CNAA with a first intake in January 1985. The School for Independent Study was expanding and was a significant element in the course provision of the institution. In autumn 1983, the new head of the school, John Stephenson, projected that by November 1986, populations of 518 full-time and 390 part-time students, including 280 pre-course students, could be expected. Expansion exacerbated ideological tensions. The emphasis of the DipHE on skill acquisition became inter-personal and affective, heavily influenced by counselling and co-counselling orientations, and it seemed to follow that there was a disjunction between the products of the DipHE and the entrants to the degree. In November 1984, an internal polytechnic review of the degree course pointed out that 'the balance of registered proposals in June 1984 was such that NELP DipHE holders would be slightly in the minority on the course' (NELP academic programme committee, quoted in Robbins, 1988, p95). The first intake to the MA/MSc of twelve students comprised only two graduates from the NELP BA/BSc by independent study. The BA/BSC and MA/MSc courses were served by excellent chief external examiners who elevated the profile of the courses nationally as a result of their sympathetic involvement. The BA/BSc was served, for instance, in sequence by professors Donald MacRae and Paul Halmos, and the MA/MSc by professors Tony Becher, Oliver Fulton and Peter Scott. In June 1985, the course committees for the BA/BSc and the MA/MSc agreed a paper which argued that the operation of their two courses should be undertaken by an autonomous Independent Studies Unit, separate from the School for Independent Study. As course tutor for the MA/MSc, I wrote, in May 1985, that 'Whereas the BA/BSc and the MA/MSc have both concentrated upon the issues involved in the engagement of independent study with the rest of the higher education system, the DipHE has tended to concentrate upon the value of its "independent study" practice in itself' (quoted in Robbins, 1988, p96).

Abolition of the School for Independent Study

The attempted secession of the post-DipHE courses from the DipHE failed. The consequence was that the assessment of the school made by HM Inspectors at the end of the decade failed to differentiate between courses in its general condemnation. It was not then clear, and is not now clear, what precisely were the machinations that led to the downfall of the school. As director of NELP from 1982 until 1992, Professor Gerry Fowler, a former Labour junior minister of education at intervals during the 1970s, had always been supportive of the intentions of SIS. At the end of the decade, he was supplanted by a new director, Frank Gould, who, perhaps, used the shortcomings of independent study practice to undermine the authority of his predecessor. This coincided with changes in the nature of the institution, shortly to be made formal nationally in the designation of the polytechnics as 'new' universities. The intervention of HM Inspectors seemed authoritarian and indicative of a new central government control over local higher education practices. There was now a perceived need for NELP/Polytechnic of East London/University of East London to acquire a new brand image in the market of higher education institutions and, as a consequence, courses designed to enable individual students to pursue personal objectives were inconveniences.

Reflections

In 1988, I published *The Rise of Independent Study.*[21] It was an attempt to justify the practices of the school in such a way as to save its reputation. In 1986 I had received an Economic and Social Research Council (ESRC) research grant to assess the contribution of Pierre Bourdieu to the analysis of higher education. In the second half of the 1980s I deployed his conceptual apparatus to try to analyse the extent to which independent study had enabled students to overcome the mismatch between the indigenous cultures of disadvantaged students and the cultures transmitted by privileged staff, which Bourdieu and his research colleagues had considered in the 1960s to be the key factor in explaining the way in which French universities perpetuated inequalities in French society.[22] In the final chapter of *The Rise of Independent Study,* I tried to draw conclusions from my experience which were inspired by my reading of both Bourdieu and Habermas. I argued that 'The process of registration becomes the model for institutions' (Robbins, 1988, p177), acting as an intermediary between 'system' and 'life' worlds. I thought that maintaining this balance between these competing worlds would enable institutions to be instrumental in recreating a 'public sphere' of a whole society. It seems likely, however, that this vision was a function of my own social and intellectual trajectory and, also, similarly of many of my colleagues. In reflecting on the past practice of independent study at NELP, the question is whether a new generation feels the need for this balance and whether higher education institutions feel the need to try to offer it.

Notes

1. For further detail see Derek Robbins, *On Bourdieu, Education and Society*, Bardwell Press: Oxford, 2006, pp1-47.
2. A.H. Halsey, *Education and Social Mobility with Special Reference to the Grammar School since 1944*, unpublished PhD thesis, University of London, 1954, and Chapter 2 in J. Floud, A.H. Halsey and F.M. Martin (eds), *Social Class and Educational Opportunity*, Heinemann: London, 1956.
3. See, for instance, Basil Willey, *The Seventeenth Century Background: Studies in the Thought of the Age in Relation to Poetry and Religion*, Chatto & Windus: London, 1934; Willey, *The Eighteenth Century Background: Studies on the Idea of Nature in the Thought of the Period*, Chatto & Windus: London, 1940; Willey, *Nineteenth Century Studies: Coleridge to Matthew Arnold*, Chatto & Windus: London, 1949.
4. Robbins, 'Cambridge in the 1960s: intellectual debate as a form of institutional *méconnaissance*', *Cambridge Anthropology*, 29, 2, 2010, pp73-90.
5. Williams had already published, most significantly, Williams, *Culture and Society, 1780-1950*, Chatto & Windus: London, 1958; and Williams, *The Long Revolution*, Chatto & Windus: London, 1961.
6. See his subsequent M. Tanner, *Nietzsche: A Very Short Introduction*, Oxford University Press: Oxford, 2000.
7. See his subsequent D. M. MacKinnon, *The Problem of Metaphysics*, Cambridge University Press: Cambridge, 1974.
8. See his subsequent M. Wiles, *Archetypal Heresy: Arianism through the Centuries*, Oxford University Press: Oxford, 2001.
9. P. Roubiczek, *Existentialism: For and Against*, Cambridge University Press: Cambridge, 1966.
10. See M. Hesse, *Science and the Human Imagination: Aspects of the History and Logic of Physical Science*, SCM Press: London, 1954.
11. See his subsequent R. M. Young, *Darwin's Metaphor. Nature's Place in Victorian Culture*, Cambridge University Press: Cambridge, 1985.
12. I argued this in an essay which appeared a few years later (Robbins, 'Culture and Criticism. Willey, Richards and the Present' in A. P. Foulkes (ed.), *The Uses of Criticism*, Herbert Lang: Bern, 1976).

13. Eric Robinson, *The New Polytechnics: The People's Universities*, Penguin: Harmondsworth, 1968.
14. Peter L. Berger and Thomas Luckmann, *The Social Construction of Reality*, Penguin: Harmondsworth, 1967.
15. Ivan Illich, *Deschooling Society*, Harper & Row: New York, 1971.
16. Thomas S. Kuhn, *The Structure of Scientific Revolutions*, University of Chicago Press: Chicago, 1962.
17. D. Schon, *Beyond the Stable State*, Penguin: Harmondsworth, 1973.
18. M.F.D. Young (ed.), *Knowledge and Control: New Directions in the Sociology of Education*, Collier-Macmillan: London, 1971.
19. See, for instance, R. S. Peters and P.H. Hirst, *The Logic of Education*, Routledge & Kegan Paul: London, 1971; and P. H. Hirst, *Knowledge and the Curriculum*, (2nd edition), Routledge & Kegan Paul: London, 1974.
20. This considered the career of Robert E. Park – the development of his urban sociology and his involvement in producing reports on Chicago race riots – and also the relationship between Jane Addams's Hull House community project and the work of the sociology department in the new institution.
21. Derek Robbins, *The Rise of Independent Study. The politics and the philosophy of an educational innovation, 1970-87*, SRHE & Open University Press: Milton Keynes, 1988.
22. See, in particular, P. Bourdieu and J.-C. Passeron, *Les héritiers, les étudiants et la culture*, Minuit: Paris, 1964.

CHAPTER THIRTEEN

Innovation studies and its roots

Alvaro de Miranda and Tony Hargreaves

Introduction

In the late 1980s, in the dawn years of what later became known as the information society, an innovative interdisciplinary degree with the title of BSc (Hons) New Technology was developed and launched by a group of North East London Polytechnic (NELP) staff from various disciplinary backgrounds, based in different departments, led by those who had been teaching previously in the area of science, technology and society (STS).[1] The degree was primarily aimed at mature students, particularly women, without formal educational qualifications, and its aim was to widen access of these students to information and communication technology (ICT) skills at a time when such skills were becoming essential for employment. Until then, the development of these skills had been the preserve of highly technical computing degrees requiring A-levels in mathematics and science subjects aimed at the production of computers and their software. The new technology degree pioneered the concept of the development of user-centred technical skills in the context of an understanding of the relationship between social and technical change at a time when information and communication technologies were changing at an extremely fast rate. Students were told at the outset that the ICT skills that they acquired in their first year of study would probably be out of date by the time they completed the degree. An understanding of the relationship between social and technological change was, therefore, essential in order for them to be able to follow the direction of change and keep their skills relevant and up to date.

The degree eventually led to the creation of a new department to house it, the Department of Innovation Studies. A number of new course developments were undertaken by this department, most notably a Europe-wide master's degree in society, science and technology undertaken in collaboration with ten other European universities. Innovation studies was rooted in the radical science movement of the 1960s and 1970s, facilitated by the liberal ethos under which the new polytechnics were developed at the start of the 1970s. We start by tracing these developments.

Liberal studies in the polytechnics

The 'new polytechnics' were created in the late 1960s by Tony Crosland, education secretary in the Wilson government.[2] They were part of the trend initiated by the 1963 Robbins report which had argued for a considerable expansion of higher education and had led to the creation of the 'new universities' (Sussex, Essex, Warwick, East Anglia, etc.). The report itself was the product of a rising tide of liberalism in education fuelled by the social, cultural and political changes of the 1950s and 1960s. The institutions it created were, by and large, committed to liberalising education and freeing it from the traditional academic structures and disciplines. The 'new polytechnics' were both a product and an extension of this.

The rise of liberalism in education in the early 1960s had been accompanied by a critique of the narrowness of scientific and technical education. This critique gradually became the orthodoxy. The worries about the excessively early specialisation, narrowness and obsolescence of such education were publicised in both the Dainton and Swann reports of 1968. The Dainton report, which became known as the 'Swing away from science' report, investigated the reasons why the numbers of science and engineering students entering higher education was declining.[3] The Swann report investigated the flow into employment of scientists, engineers and technologists, and the allocation of government resources for research and development.[4] This concern with the narrowness of scientific and technical education was rooted in part in the high liberal critique of the 'two cultures' developed by C.P. Snow in an influential Rede lecture at the University of Cambridge in 1959 entitled 'The Two Cultures and the Scientific Revolution'.[5] In the mid-1970s it became mandatory for all vocational courses in technical colleges to include an element of 'liberal or general studies',[6] which were supposed to broaden the mind of the students and open them to the 'higher things in life'. These early experiments were, at best, a partial success. Liberal studies were often resented and ignored by the main subject teaching staff and by the students.

The rise of the radical science movement

Almost at the same time as the polytechnics were being created, the universities were rocked by the student rebellion of 1968, a movement rooted in a critique of academic institutions which saw the university both as an elitist institution denying access to the disadvantaged members of the society but also as being totally tied to the interests of the ruling class of capitalist society.[7] A passionate argument of this case was given by the historian E. P. Thompson in what became his resignation statement from Warwick University, published by Penguin as *Warwick University Ltd.*[8] The 1968 student movement largely denied the possibility of reform of the system and argued for revolution.

The student rebellion grew to a large extent out of the anti-Vietnam war movement. For the first time, the brutal images of a high-tech war being waged by a superpower against a poor people had been brought into people's homes via television.[9] The anti-war movement in the US, in which many, mainly young, scientists participated, examined in detail the inter-relationships within the scientific-industrial-military complex that created the weaponry used in the genocide of the Vietnamese people, building on the earlier work of the anti-nuclear weapons activists of the early 1960s CND. The later work uncovered the powerful political forces that shaped the direction of scientific and technological research. 'By the mid-60s, by far the greatest proportion of university science was being done on federal contracts, often for the Department of Defense, and the linkage was most powerful in the élite, high science, ivy-league colleges'.[10]

A radical science movement arose around the idea that science and technology were themselves socially constructed, and therefore not neutral. The capitalist system created a capitalist science and technology. In Britain this understanding was expressed mainly through the work of the British Society for Social Responsibility in Science (BSSRS), its magazine *Science for People* and the *Radical Science Journal*.[11] BSSRS started life in 1968 as a mainstream liberal organisation of concerned scientists. Its inaugural meeting in 1968 on 'The social responsibility of the scientist' was held in London at the Royal Society and was sponsored by sixty-four Fellows. Its president was Maurice Wilkins, a Nobel Laureate. It evolved into a radical body whose work linked into that of the trade unions and the shop stewards' movement, rather than professional scientific organisations. This was particularly true during the early 1970s, through the health and safety at work movement and the *Hazards Bulletin*.

Another aspect of the 1960s radicalism that influenced the radical science movement was what might be described in the language of the time as 'third worldism'.[12] This was the belief that the main positive changes for humankind were taking place in the countries fighting to free themselves from colonialism and imperialism. It arose partly out of the anti-Vietnam war movement, but also out of other solidarity movements with anti-colonialist and anti-imperialist struggles, such as those with the Cuban and the Chinese revolutions. A related theme was anti-racism and solidarity with the Black Power movement of the US.[13]

In Britain this concern centred mainly around two overlapping strands. The anti-Vietnam war movement was led by the far left. The organisation that led the campaign against the war was the Vietnam Solidarity Campaign, set up under the auspices of the well-known philosopher Bertrand Russell, but with the activists that came to dominate it coming from far-left Trotskyist groups. Tariq Ali, then a member of the Trotskyist International Marxist Group (IMG), became its best-known leader and described his experiences in his memoir of the times.[14] The other strand grew out of the earlier movement to support the anti-colonialist struggles in the British colonies, mainly organised by the Movement for Colonial Freedom, in which the British Communist Party played a significant role. As the bulk of the British colonies achieved independence, the focus gradually shifted to support the struggle in Southern Africa, mainly in South Africa and in the Portuguese colonies of Mozambique, Angola and Guinea-Bissau. Anti-imperialism was allied to anti-racism. The radical science movement developed a critique of the allegedly scientific basis of the connection between race and IQ introduced in the work of right-wing psychologists Eysenck in Britain and Jensen in the US,[15] and a more general critique of reductionism and biological determinism which was also influential in discussions of women and science.

The women's movement of the 1960s and 1970s[16] also made a strong contribution to the radical science movement. Two influential themes were: women and science, a critique of how science contributed to the stereotyping of women and increased control of them by men (for instance, how the medicalisation of health placed control of women's bodies in the hands of male experts); and women in science, an attempt to understand why there are so few women in science and technology, one strand of which argued that science and technology are themselves constructed as masculine.[17]

Concern with the effects of science and technology on the environment also added to the generally negative image that these subjects developed in the late 1960s and 1970s. The systematic and widespread use of pesticides and herbicides by the US in the Vietnam war greatly contributed to this and spilled over into a critique of the use of the same chemicals in the green revolution, and a general critique of intensive agriculture.[18] The 1974 oil crisis contributed to the revival of the concept of the energy crisis and fuelled opposition to the ideology of growth, where science and technology play such a central role. Environmentalism and green ideology became influential right across the political spectrum and contributed to the general scepticism about the positive role of science and technology.

STS at NELP

At NELP, as at many other polytechnics, the group which eventually developed science, technology and society as a distinct area of study had its roots in the earlier liberal studies tradition of the technical colleges, which has been previously discussed. With the formation of NELP in 1970 out of the amalgamation of the West Ham College of Technology, Barking Regional College of Technology, the Anglian Regional Management Centre and South West Essex College of Technology (Waltham Forest), the process of developing courses under the aegis of the Council for National Academic Awards (CNAA) began. The philosophy of the CNAA expressed the prevailing liberal ethos and implicitly enshrined the critique of the narrowness of science and technology education. Principle 3.2 stated: 'The primary aim of any programme of studies must be the development of the student's intellectual and imaginative skills and powers. Not only increasing knowledge, but also increasing intellectual and imaginative development, must be presumed by the content of the programme and the way in which it is taught ...'.

And 3.4 stresses: 'A programme of studies must stimulate an enquiring, analytical and creative approach, encouraging independent judgement and critical self-awareness ...'.

But perhaps most fundamental to the development of STS studies in polytechnics was the C. P. Snow 'two cultures'-influenced principle 3.7 which asserted:

> The student must be encouraged to appreciate the nature of attitudes, modes of thought, practices and disciplines other than those of his or her main studies. He or she must learn to perceive his or her main studies in the broader perspective. As part of this process he or she must be enabled to develop an informed awareness of factors influencing the social and physical environment.

It was as a result of this principle that every CNAA science and engineering course in the country was obliged to have some element of liberal studies. Though many institutions stuck with traditional models of liberal studies, some staff at NELP began to reject what they saw as arbitrary and unsuccessful grafting of social sciences or humanities subjects on to science and technology courses in favour of a more deep-rooted approach.

In 1970, Tony Hargreaves, a chemistry graduate from the University of Leeds who had developed an interest in science and society, was hired to join what was shortly to become the

Department of Applied Philosophy at NELP, incorporating the existing liberal studies structures. Some of the staff had already been doing what might be called proto-STS liberal studies. These, consisting of the history of science and technology, and the philosophy of science, were taught in a wider and deeper way than the traditional biographical 'great man' approach to the history of science, but contained little that might be called critical, analytical or even descriptive of the contemporary practice of science and technology.[19]

The various CNAA and polytechnic statements of liberal educational policy were very useful in supporting the insertion of STS into science courses, as were two new polytechnic course development rules. First, that a member of applied philosophy had to be on all course development teams, and second, that all course components must be assessed. As new science courses were developed or old ones came up for revision, more applied philosophy staff were recruited to teach STS. Internal appointments included philosophers and sociologists plus several staff from the science faculty. External appointments were mainly of lecturers from a diverse range of science backgrounds, with additional expertise in the science and society nexus.

While in the earlier courses the STS philosophy had remained peripheral to the main ethos of the course, the main faculty of science modular degree course, BSc Science, which embraced all the sciences from maths and physics to psychology, was constructed around the notion of STS. The core curriculum, largely consisting of STS, became the only subject which all students were compelled to take, accounting for nearly one-quarter of their assessment. Tony Hargreaves led the team that developed the STS component, and members of the science faculty, including Alvaro de Miranda, also contributed.

Politically, academic STS represented a compromise between the far left-oriented radical science tradition represented by BSSRS, and the Communist Party tradition with its roots in the left-scientist movement of the 1930s, in which J. D. Bernal and J. B. S. Haldane took leading roles. This had its post-war continuation in a broad-left alliance, mainly within CND and the anti-cold war Pugwash scientist movement, with liberal elements in the C. P. Snow and

Bronowski 'two-cultures' tradition. In the 1970s, contrary to the earlier 1950s progressive science coalition, the common element was a critique of the neutrality of science and technology.

Radical science-oriented activists were organised nationally around BSSRS. In NELP David Albury, another member of NELP's STS team, was an active member of BSSRS, a one-time member of its national committee and of the 'Science for People' collective. Albury was also a member of the collective which edited the *Radical Science Journal*, precursor of *Science as Culture*. The broad left/liberal strand was organised within the Science, Technology and Society Association (STSA), an association of teachers of STS of which Tony Hargreaves was a leading member. This was linked to the earlier national Science in a Social Context (SISCON) project, which was set up in 1973 with £50,000 from the Nuffield Foundation. SISCON published a series of STS study guides aimed at science students in schools, universities and colleges around the main STS themes, and organised annual conferences during the 1970s at Harlech.

The Thatcherite years

STS was never popular with most mainstream science and technology staff. Within BSc Science, the STS team was subject to a constant attack by many of the science staff, who carried this opposition into an open attempt to turn the students against the subject. The prevailing liberal ethos, however, sustained STS with the support of the CNAA. An influential figure within the CNAA was David Edge, editor of the prestigious journal *Social Studies of Science*, who participated in many CNAA panels validating science courses in polytechnics to monitor the broadening of curriculum content beyond science, in accordance with CNAA principles. However, as the liberal 1970s came to a close, the position of STS became more and more difficult to maintain. When the BSc Science degree came up for re-submission in 1980, the centre of gravity within CNAA had already shifted significantly and the erosion of its liberal principles had begun. An alliance of traditional scientists within the visiting external validating panel with some hostile members of the component BSc Science course teams would have sunk the STS component at its core if had not been for the powerful presence of David Edge conducting its strong defence within the visiting validating party.

This, however, proved to be only a temporary respite. In 1984 Sir Keith Joseph, who was Thatcher's secretary of state for education and science, singled out STS for attack as it poisoned young minds destined to contribute to the nation's revival in science and technology with left-wing ideology. He prohibited the setting of any questions on the social repercussions of scientific decisions in science examinations.[20] From then on, STS gradually withered, starved of funds in the universities, of support by the CNAA in the polytechnics and viewed with increasing scepticism by a student body for whom the social and political concerns of the 1960s and 1970s were historical quirks.

Throughout the country, supporters of STS who had reached senior academic positions retreated from the broader critique into policy studies and the management of innovation, often in the wake of the growth of business studies. At NELP, the STS team gradually dwindled and dispersed to teach in other areas.

In 1986, two inter-related events were eventually to halt this general decline. The first was David Albury's launch of the idea of the new technology degree through a three-page paper which contained the outline of the course. The proposal recognised that STS could no longer be sustained as an appendix of science and technology education in Thatcher's Britain through the liberal ethos of the 1970s. It implicitly rejected the very term STS as a term of the 1970s and replaced it with the 1980s concept of innovation, which had already become accepted elsewhere. It attempted, however, to resist the general drift into a subdivision of business and management studies by defending the need to develop a critical approach in students. Survival in the 1980s required either reorienting into the ideologically acceptable growth areas of business and management studies, as many other centres were doing, or the development of its own independent centre by harnessing those local and national factors which could be used to its benefit. The main factor thus used was the government's (and specifically Keith Joseph's) desire to reverse the drift away from science into the social sciences (which was reflected locally at NELP as a severe shortage of physical sciences and technology students)[21] and the skills shortage in IT. The degree found an echo both locally and nationally with its implicit critique of traditional computing education as being technology- rather than people-oriented, thus echoing the STS concerns of the 1970s. There was support for this view even in the world of business, except that in this world 'people' meant 'business'.

The core team that directed the development of the new technology degree was led by David Albury, with Alvaro de Miranda, then still in the Department of Physics, involved from the start. Shortly afterwards we were joined by Angela Glasner from the Department of Sociology, who had recently completed a master's degree in the area of computing. At the behest of rector Gerry Fowler, all of us were substantially relieved from our teaching duties in order to undertake the development of the degree. This was not unusual then. From its formation, NELP had supported course development by seconding staff from all or part of their teaching duties in order to undertake course development as members of its course development unit. In the same academic year, the STS Unit became the Innovation Studies Unit (ISU) with David Albury as its head, later to be succeeded by Angela Glasner.

The concept of the new technology degree was strenuously opposed by senior staff in science and engineering, particularly those in the Department of Systems and Computing. The head of the mathematics department commented acerbically that it was the tail (STS) starting to wag the dog (science and technology). However, the degree had the strong support of Gerry Fowler. This became essential to ensure that it was validated. One of the great attractions of the new technology degree for the institution was that it promised to increase its numbers of technology students. These carried a higher level of funding than social sciences and humanities students and were in short supply. The mixture of social science and technology in the curriculum raised doubts in the Higher Education Founding Council, and we were the subject of a special enquiry which concluded that there was enough technology in the degree for it to warrant technology funding. We were no doubt helped in this by the fact that the government itself was under pressure because of the declining numbers of science and technology students in the country as a whole.

The study of the relationship between technical and social change formed the basis of the concept of innovation studies (the title eventually given to the department that emerged from the new technology degree when student numbers grew enough to justify its creation as a separate academic unit). This study was a requirement for all students and formed the core of the degree. The core took up a third of the curriculum in the second and third years. In the first year, students spent a third of their time developing purely technical ICT skills, a third in studying the relationship between social and technical change from a historical perspective, and a third integrating the two by studying the technical and economic history of computing from the time of Babbage. Much of the technical knowledge was acquired through the study of this history. In the first year a lot of attention was paid to the development of study skills and to supporting students who had been out of education for a long time. In their second and third years, students had a choice of different context areas in which to develop their skills. Two-thirds of the curriculum covered these areas. The context areas offered were social policy, taught by members of the Sociology Department, and computer-aided design and manufacturing, taught by staff of the Department of Mechanical Engineering and Manufacturing. The core of the degree was taught by staff in the Department of Innovation Studies. A contextual area, media and communications, was developed in collaboration with cultural studies. Additional staff required to teach the degree were newly appointed to the Innovation Studies Unit.

Also situated in Innovation Studies were the staff who developed and taught a particular area of specialisation with different characteristics and aims from the others. It was called women and new technology. This area was designed to create a friendly environment in which mature women could develop high-level IT software design skills. It was a unique endeavour at a time when women were virtually excluded from all computing and engineering courses, most of which had entry requirements that few women possessed and developed a culture which was off-putting to women. The women and new technology area was staffed entirely by women, and developed technical skills in the context of exploring the gender relations of technology.

As the degree took in its first intake of students, new staff were appointed from outside NELP in order to help with the teaching of the first year and to organise the delivery of the specialist subject areas women and new technology, media and communications, and manufacturing.

The new technology degree was successful in attracting a considerable number of students. At its height the degree had an intake of about eighty students. More than 80 per cent were mature and without formal qualifications, recruited via access courses or through the accreditation of prior learning, and more than 50 per cent were women. Access courses directly linked to it were developed in local further education colleges.

The Department of Innovation Studies and after

The new technology degree grew rapidly and the growth in student numbers was sufficient to support the appointment of enough new staff to justify the Innovation Studies Unit becoming the Department of Innovation Studies with David Albury as its head. Further academic developments were also undertaken by the department. Gavin Poynter had joined innovation studies from the education department of the Trades Union Congress to take charge of the manufacturing area. In the wave of media enthusiasm for the European Union that accompanied its creation in 1993, he designed an innovative four-year sandwich degree entitled New Technology and European Studies, in which students developed knowledge of one of three European languages, French, German or Spanish, and spent their third year at a partner institution in France, Germany or Spain working on a thesis that would be completed in the final year back at what by then had become the University of East London (UEL).

Another innovative development took place at postgraduate level, directed by Sally Wyatt, who had been recruited from the University of Brighton to lead the department's research. The department joined the European Inter-University Association for Society, Science and

Technology (ESST), a consortium of ten European universities jointly offering a master's degree in society, science and technology. The structure of the master's, offered over two semesters, required each university recruiting students primarily from their own country to study there for the first semester. The curriculum taught in the first semester by all universities was common and had been developed over a number of years with funding from the European Union. Besides following the common curriculum during the first semester, students were required to study a European language other than the one in which they were studying. Each of the member universities offered a specialisation area for the second semester. Students during the first semester chose their specialisation area for the second semester and travelled to the university offering this, supported by European Erasmus funding. Second semester teaching was carried out in English and the final master's thesis in the specialisation area was also written in English. The Department of Innovation Studies offered a specialisation on 'Europe in the information society'. Alvaro de Miranda and Sally Wyatt later served terms as presidents of ESST, and Sally Wyatt also became the overall director of studies of the ESST master's for a period.

In collaboration with cultural studies, a new specialisation subject area entitled 'multimedia' was developed. This eventually became the area which recruited most students, particularly school leavers, as it developed skills in web design, making up in part for the decline of student numbers in specialisation areas which relied primarily on the recruitment of mature students, such as women and new technology. As the enthusiasm for widening access to higher education and the numbers of mature students declined, the new technology degree became increasingly dependent on the two specialisation areas that recruited significant numbers of school leavers: media and communications, and multimedia, the two areas in which it collaborated with cultural studies. The department set up within the multi-subject DipHE the subject area of information technology, adhering to the philosophy of developing user-oriented technical skills. This proved highly successful in recruitment and became a full degree as the multi-subject DipHE evolved into UEL's modular programme. By 2000, when the Department of Innovation Studies joined cultural studies to form the School of Cultural and Innovation

Studies in whose development we had jointly collaborated, the information technology subject area and degree had become the main provider of student numbers. Its first-year modules attracted up to 300 students as it also became a popular area for students undertaking combined studies degrees. This was relatively short lived as the ICT industries made user-friendliness the main development priority and technical skills in use became unnecessary. User-centred technical skills were no longer required.[22]

Conclusion

The new technology degree and innovation studies were radical attempts to row against a tide that had been set in motion in the Thatcher years. That tide had engulfed the concept of liberal education and replaced it with an ideology in which the purpose of education, including higher education, was to prepare young people for the employment market. That ideology was internalised to a large extent by young people themselves, a process that was facilitated by the great increase in unemployment that took place from the early 1980s. The 1970s had seen growth in the polytechnics centred mainly on the critical social sciences. Growth in the 1980s took place mainly in business and management studies. The new technology degree, in targeting mature students whose traditional employment skills had been deemed redundant and promising to give them skills in the areas where growth in employment was not only predicted but was even being hyped as determining the future,[23] was responding to the new demand. Yet the degree attempted to maintain the element of critical thinking which the social sciences provide and gave the students the intellectual tools to understand the direction of technical change, the socioeconomic forces driving this and their own fate in the jobs market. A key second year module of the degree was entitled 'New technology, work and the economy'.

The historical conditions which brought about the success of the degree and of innovation studies were of limited duration. Political enthusiasm for widening access of mature students to higher education waned as unemployment subsided and the proportion of school leavers entering higher education greatly increased. The expectations of the school leavers in the new millennium were mainly of job-related skills, an expectation which was greatly reinforced by government education policy with its emphasis on employability.

Notes

1. The authors would like to thank our colleagues Judy Greenway and Denis Cattell for their very useful comments and contributions.
2. The rationale for the creation of the new polytechnics and the process leading to it were well described in an early book by Eric Robinson, a first deputy director of North East London Polytechnic, Eric Robinson, *The New Polytechnics*, Penguin: Harmondsworth, 1968. Another prominent NELP educationalist, Tyrrell Burgess, described the rationale for the polytechnics thus: 'There are two longstanding traditions in higher education which are typified by the universities and the technical colleges. Put crudely, almost to the point of parody, the universities are independent bodies, concerned with the preservation, extension and dissemination of "knowledge for its own sake"; concentrating on full-time students and maintaining their exclusiveness by rigid and ever stiffer entry requirements. Under the recommendations of the Robbins Report the technical colleges were to be a permanently depressed sector. The best colleges would move over periodically into the university sector and neglect their own distinctive tradition in a fruitless aping of the other. The plan for polytechnic was meant to prevent this.' (Tyrrell Burgess, 'Education: Optimism is not enough', Tyrrell Burgess *et al.*, *Matters of Principle: Labour's Last Chance*, Penguin: Harmondsworth, 1968, p88.)
3. F. S. Dainton, (chairman), *Enquiry into the Flow of Candidates in Science and Technology into Higher Education*, HMSO: London, 1968.
4. M. Swann (chairman), *The Flow into Employment of Scientists, Engineers and Technologists: Report of the Working Group on Manpower for Scientific Growth*, Cmnd. 3760, HMSO: London, 1968.
5. C. P. Snow, 'The Two Cultures and the Scientific Revolution', Rede lecture delivered at the University of Cambridge, 1959: https://doi.org/10.1017/CBO9780511819940.002. For an interesting analysis of the issues relating to the C.P. Snow lecture and ensuing debate with Michael Polanyi, see S. Jacobs, 'C. P. Snow's "The Two Cultures": Michael Polanyi's Response and Context', *Bulletin*

of Science, Technology & Society, 31, 3, 2011, pp172–8: http://dx.doi.org/10.1177/0270467611406052.

6. R. Simmons, C. Waugh, M. Hopkins, L. Perry, R. Stafford, 'Liberal and General Studies in Further Education: Voices from the "Chalk Face"', *Teaching in Lifelong Learning: A Journal to Inform and Improve Practice,* Vol 6, No. 1, 2014, pp32-42: http://dx.doi.org/10.5920/till.2014.6132
7. For an expression of the ethos of the student movement edited by two participants, see Alexander Cockburn and Robin Blackburn, *Student Power: Problems, Diagnosis, Action,* Penguin: Harmondsworth, 1970.
8. E. P. Thompson (ed.), *Warwick University Ltd: Industry, Management and the Universities,* Penguin: Harmondsworth, 1970.
9. An influential collection of the type of images of the war which greatly influenced young people was published as a Penguin Special by the documentary film maker Felix Greene, F. Greene, *Vietnam! Vietnam!*, Penguin: Harmondsworth, 1966.
10. Hilary Rose and Steven Rose, *The Radicalisation of Science,* Macmillan: London, 1976, p15.
11. D. Albury and J. Schwarz, *Partial Progress,* Pluto Press: London, 1980, although published in 1980, provided a good synthesis of this kind of view of science and technology. The view was not in itself new. Some of the marxist scientists of the 1930s held similar positions, but on the whole they projected a positive view of science being misused by capitalism. The 1960s radical science movement, by seeing modern science as a construct of capitalism, projected a largely negative image of science. The moral implication was that to practise science was to serve capitalism, and some supporters of the movement consequently felt compelled to leave the practice of science.
12. For a discussion of the concept of third worldism see A. Nash, 'Third Worldism', *African Sociological Review,* 7,1, 2003: http://dx.doi.org/10.4314/asr.v7i1.23132; and R. Kiely, *The Sociology of Development: the Impasse and Beyond,* Taylor and Francis: Hoboken, 2014.
13. The positions held by the Black Panthers and their struggles in the United States are well represented in the collection edited by P. S. Foner, *The Black Panthers Speak,* Haymarket: Chicago, 2014. A. Haley, *The Autobiography of Malcolm X,* Penguin Classics: London, 2001 was another reference text of the times.
14. Tariq Ali, *Street-Fighting Years,* Verso: London, 2005.
15. Steven Rose, 'Scientific Racism and Ideology: The IQ racket from Galton to Jensen', Hilary Rose and Steven Rose (eds), *The Political Economy of Science,* Macmillan: London and Basingstoke, 1976, pp112-141.

16. An influential text expressing the main themes of this movement was *Beyond the Fragments: Feminism and the Making of Socialism* by Sheila Rowbotham, Lynne Segal and Hilary Wainwright, first published in 1979 and reissued in 2013 (Sheila Rowbotham, Lynne Segal and Hilary Wainwright, *Beyond the Fragments - Feminism and the Making of Socialism*, Merlin Press: London, 2013).
17. On the question of the gender relations of science and technology, a key reference text was *Alice Through the Microscope* by the Brighton Women's Group (L. Birke *et al.*, Brighton Women and Science Group, *Alice Through the Microscope*, Virago: London, 1980). Discussion of the history of STS, with a focus on theoretical issues and debates, including an article by Donna Haraway, a significant early contributor on feminism, science and technology, can be found in K. Asdal, B. Brenna and I. Moser (eds), *Technoscience: The Politics of Interventions*, Oslo Academic Press: Oslo, 2007, available at: http://www.academia.edu/download/30572223/AsdalBrennaMoserTechnoscience.pdf#page=329.
18. A contributor to the debates in this area was the British Society for Social Responsibility in Science Agricapital Group. Its history and the issues it dealt with have more recently been described by two of its participants (C. Clutterbuck and E. Millstone, 'The BSSRS Agricapital Group: History and Legacy', *Science as Culture*, 25, 3, 2016, pp400-414, DOI: 10.1080/09505431.2016.1164403).
19. T. Hargreaves, 'STS at NELP', unpublished paper given at visit to NELP of STS delegation from Thailand, 1981.
20. H. Higgs, 'Self-conscious science: Is this peace education?', *Cambridge Journal of Education*, 17, 1, 1987, pp25-34: https://doi.org/10.1080/0305764870170104, p28.
21. In NELP and its successor institutions, physical sciences departments dwindled in size and were eventually closed, including physics and chemistry. Biological sciences, which survived for longer, eventually were reincarnated in the form of vocational education, such as nursing, physiotherapy and sports science.
22. Early personal computers of the period in which the new technology degree was set up required a considerable amount of technical knowledge and skill in order to operate. After PCs adopted graphical user interfaces with the introduction in 1990 of Microsoft Windows 3.0 (the first version of Windows to be successful), manufacturers and software developers gave great priority to increasing user-friendliness and reducing the amount of technical knowledge required to use PCs. The need for people with skills that could bridge the gap for users dwindled and eventually disappeared altogether.

23. A. de Miranda and M. Kristiansen, 'Technological Determinism and Ideology: The European Union and the Information Society', paper delivered at the third Policy Agendas for Sustainable Technological Innovations (POSTI) international workshop at the University of East London, 1-3 December 2000: https://www.researchgate.net/publication/328695801_Technological_Determinism_and_Ideology_the_European_Union_and_the_Information_Society; A. de Miranda, 'Technological Determinism and Ideology: Questioning the Information Society and the Digital Divide', J. Burnett, P. Senker and K. Walker (eds), *The Myths of Technology – Innovation and Inequality,* Peter Lang: New York, 2009, pp23-37: https://www.researchgate.net/publication/252087059_Technological_Determinism_and_Ideology_Questioning_the_'Information_Society'_and_the_'Digital_Divide

CHAPTER FOURTEEN

A radical law school?

John Strawson

Introduction

In early October 1975 at the first lecture, the thirty-seven new students were warned that the degree that lay ahead would be challenging, offering, quoting Marx, 'no royal road' to knowledge and, referencing Freud, that self-knowledge would be painful. Despite this perhaps unsettling beginning, the students stayed and the law school[1] was born.

The school was founded by South African lawyer Edwin Lichtenstein[2] who had been an activist against the racist regimes in South Africa and then Southern Rhodesia. His background in academic philosophy, human rights legal practice and political commitment was to play a significant role in creating an open, internationalist and critical Law School. His leadership team included John North and Mike Slade. The latter (who was to be Lichtenstein's successor) projected a 'liberal education through law' with the aim of using the study of law to understand society and, in particular, the role of power and legitimacy in society's relationship to the state. In this Slade was very much in tune with the debates about the direction of legal education. He was to play a significant role beyond East London, as we shall see. The school's initial staff were small but had a high proportion of migrants, including three South Africans and the Ghanaian lawyer and scholar Offerwiwa Augustine and others who had worked or been educated outside the UK. This underlined an internationalist theme which was to be a continuous feature of the school. Many of the staff in 1975 were involved in political activism beyond the school[3] and most were members of the Haldane Society of Socialist Lawyers, which reinforced a radical approach to legal practice. This chapter will explore the contribution and work of the school in the context of broader concerns about legal education. It will consider the context in which it was created, its ethos and the work that it has undertaken.

Context

Higher education in the 1970s was lived in the wake of the revolutionary events of Paris in 1968. Les évenements, it was thought, presaged general revolutionary social change. This promise did not materialise and, despite the overthrowing of the fascist regimes in Portugal, Spain and Greece in the mid-1970s, the European state system remained intact. Nonetheless, radical ideas certainly were in currency in every sinew of society and this was markedly evident in legal education. Contemporary legal education began with William Twining's inaugural lecture, 'Pericles and the Plumber' published in the *Law Quarterly Review* in 1967.[4] It challenged law schools to think through their role and decide how to balance legal education between the philosophical tradition represented by Pericles, the lawgiver, and the technical character of law represented by the plumber. He begins by referring to an issue that has been raised by all critics of universities, its seems from time immemorial: 'From outside the ivory tower there has always been pressure, varying in intensity at different periods, to make university education more obviously useful and vocational'.[5] However, he points to a survey of UK legal education carried out by John Wilson[6] which concluded that: 'The general view of university teachers and practitioners alike was that law degree courses should provide the student with a liberal education and train him [*sic*] to think like a lawyer rather than give him a vocational training'.[7]

The question was, therefore, how to think through what it meant to provide a liberal education and, equally, to make a distinction between vocational training and thinking 'like a lawyer'. In doing this Twining drew on the example of the United States, which had explored these issues as law schools had been established in universities and which, especially in the 1920s and 1930s, had produced some highly original results. This led Twining to conclude that:

> We need to break free from the extraordinary rigid stereotyped thinking that has come to dominate legal education: that the cosmos is irrevocably divided into fields of law such as contract and torts; that the only mode of classification to be used in curriculum planning is that of fields of law; that examinations must be of three hours in length; that examinations only can test knowledge of legal doctrines and ability to apply rules to hypothetical fact situations; that all courses must be given equal weight; that every course must have a textbook; that every textbook must conform to a standard pattern; that legal doctrine *is the* subject matter of legal studies; that every lawyer is a private practitioner of law; that there should be a uniform pattern of qualifications for law teachers; that there are accepted and fixed criteria of the suitability of a subject of study in a university – and so on.[8]

His lecture coincided with the creation of the new law schools at Warwick, Kent and Sussex – in the new universities of the 1960s. These schools were to produce a nucleus of the young core staff in the Law School of the North East London Polytechnic (NELP) in the 1970s.[9] The intellectual influences of the times combined not only radical thinking about the curriculum but also about the role of lawyers in society.[10] Law schools up to the 1960s had often been bastions of conservativism replete with gender and racial discrimination. This reflected the white male-dominated legal profession and the judiciary of the times. The new law schools were to disrupt this establishment phenomenon, and NELP was to become an interesting tributary in this process.

In 1971 the Ormrod report on legal education[11] recommended dividing legal education into three phases: an academic stage, the LLB degree; a skills stage under the supervision of the profession; and then a practical phase before qualifying. The committee thought a lawyer needed a 'sufficiently general and broad-based education', and this meant students 'must also cultivate a critical approach to existing law, an appreciation of its social consequences, an interest in and positive attitude to, appropriate development and change'.[12] The academic stage was to provide both 'much teaching of substantive law and a general liberal education'.[13] It should be noted that the Ormrod committee made no distinction between law degrees from universities and polytechnics.[14] This fact perhaps indicates the contradictory roles that polytechnics were supposed to play. As John Pratt reminds us, when conceived by the then secretary of state for education, Anthony Crosland, the polytechnics were to offer 'vocational, professional and industrial based courses'.[15] Indeed, Pratt appears to be under the impression that polytechnic law schools were distinctive in offering a different type of education from the universities,[16] including offering clinical legal education.[17] However, law clinics were first established by university law schools; Kent in 1973 and Warwick in 1976. In reality, law degree programmes at both the universities and the polytechnics were remarkably similar, as indeed the Ormrod report intended, in providing the academic stage of legal education. There were differences between institutions in what the programme consisted of, for example, what was compulsory and the range of optional subjects. However, these differences were not between universities and polytechnics. For example, Roman law, which had been a compulsory course in most universities up until the 1960s, was beginning to disappear, although Kingston Polytechnic still required students to take it in 1971.[18]

The big difference between the university and polytechnic law schools was size (and no doubt resources in general). In 1970 there were twenty-nine law schools in the United Kingdom with 5000 students enrolled. However, the intake of the polytechnic law schools in 1971 was only 318 with a total of 107 graduates.[19] By 1975 there were forty-eight law schools, a massive expansion in the teaching of the subject. However, it should be pointed out that by 1978, the first year of NELP law graduates, there were only a total of 938 Council for National Academic Awards (CNAA) law graduates in the entire country.[20] East London reflected this pattern, beginning with thirty-seven enrolments in 1975. However even seven years later when the law degree was well established, there were only 152 students in each of the three years and the academic staff totalled thirteen, a staff:student ratio of 1:12. This situation undoubtedly created a community atmosphere where staff knew each other quite well and also knew their students. It might also suggest that law as a subject was seen as marginal to most polytechnics at the time. Certainly at NELP, law did seem quite cut off from the rest of the institution. This sense of distinct identity was reinforced by the control the school exercised over the programme – not only its structure and content but also its assessment regulations. It was a paradox that despite, or perhaps due to, the supervisory role of the CNAA, the school could set its own regulations relatively untrammelled by the institution. After 1992 this was to change. By that time the school had expanded dramatically and its 1992 third year undergraduate students alone exceeded the total enrolment for all years in 1982.

Ethos

In setting about offering a law degree in the mid-1970s, the challenge was to provide a course that would appeal both to those wishing to become lawyers and to those who were only interested in the subject as such.[21] As has been pointed out, the legal profession and judiciary of the time were overwhelmingly male and white.[22] One early decision was to encourage the recruitment of women and ethnic minority students. This meant ensuring that the law degree was advertised in relevant publications and that all applicants were interviewed. The number of applicants for law far exceeded the places offered in law schools.[23] As a result, the vast majority of successful applicants had A-levels, a minority had BTech qualifications and a very small number were admitted under an access scheme. There was a degree of success in recruiting women and students from ethnic minority backgrounds, although the school was highly conscious that those who wanted to enter the profession were likely to encounter discrimination.

Despite this stance on student recruitment, the law degree itself in its design and structure appeared like most others. Law degrees at the time were normally four courses a year with the first two years almost entirely taken up with subjects required by the profession: constitutional and administrative law, contract, torts, criminal law, land law, equity and trusts. The third year tended to consist of optional topics, although jurisprudence and legal theory were usually compulsory. NELP worked within this framework with some interesting finesses. Since 1945 there had been a massive increase in the role of the state in British society, for example through the NHS, welfare, planning controls and nationalised industries. Even in the mid-1970s this trend seemed to be continuing. As a result, some university schools, such as LSE, put a heavy emphasis on public law. Indeed NELP received very helpful advice from Professor John Griffiths of LSE and also decided to teach public law over two years – the first year to focus on constitutional law and the second to offer an in-depth study of administrative law. Within four years, with the arrival of the Thatcher government the assumption on which this was based was to be somewhat challenged! However, this focus laid the basis for the subsequent emphasis on human rights education and research. Instead of teaching a traditional jurisprudence course we opted for a broader course called law and society. This did include key elements of jurisprudence but also allowed students to study the sociological aspects of law in society, including case studies on law in apartheid South Africa and in the Soviet Union. Even in the traditionally more 'technical subjects', such as contract and torts, there was an attempt to study them through the lens of economic analysis of law. At the heart of the first year was an apparently anodyne-sounding course, 'English legal system'. However, as delivered by Anne Bottomley, Jeremy Roche and Stuart Vernon it became a radical insight into class and patriarchal power in British society.

The school was very keen to provide students with a choice of developing their specialist interests. By 1982 the options offered reflected staff expertise and research interests, and comprised: public international law, family law, social security law, criminology, equity and trusts, labour law, consumer law, law of the EEC, competition law, law of business associations, and law and scientific development.[24] Despite Britain's membership of the then EEC, EEC law was an option but much championed by Maurice Moore,[25] who was keen to enthuse the students with an interest in the European project. Part of his approach was to organise study tours to the EEC institutions.[26]

It would of course be erroneous to think that the staff had a uniform approach. Indeed, it was quite the opposite. Once allocated a course, much freedom was given to those who taught it, and there were differences and sometimes passionate disagreements, even within teams. It was striking how patient and supportive Edwin Lichtenstein and Mike Slade were in dealing with such situations, and experimentation was encouraged. Slade played a major role in developing the ethos of the school and set many challenging tasks to the staff to transform legal education. By the 1980s, Mike Slade's focus on legal education extended beyond the school and his edited collection *Law Higher Education in the 1980s*[27] fortuitously contains many of the views that informed the way in which the NELP school developed. In his introduction, Slade argued that:

> We still have difficulty in arguing that our courses deal with the acknowledged and inherent abrasive effects of law on people and bonds of community, for all the tools for insolation are built into the legal mystique and into the traditional mode of legal training. If we want to convince others of our role beyond elite technicians we must have a frame of mind that that takes seriously the modern dilemmas of providing within a complex society progress with the security of living conditions, freedom with equality, planning with autonomy, democracy with efficiency in resource allocation and reconciling rules and principle in the action of lay people in a stressful environment.[28]

Mike Slade's radical assessment of what he regarded as the failures of legal education to be rooted in an understanding of how society operated is underlined as he continues:

> As law teachers we have generally lacked the imagination and the sympathy for the in-depth investigation of legal phenomena required in contemporary society. If we have not been well served by other disciplines and if simplistic ideological positions ride too easily to the surface, legal academics have an

> even more daunting task ahead. The fascination with law is that there is an endless agenda of unfinished business. It is an institution that should be on the periphery but which exists as a central component of the social fabric.[29]

In his chapter he expands on the problems of providing high-quality legal education. Slade says: 'We often lose sight of general educational objectives in law teaching, partly due to our equating a "specialist" education with information gathering'.[30] This in part is the result of highly traditional and hidebound ways in which legal education developed, with an obsessive focus on abstract rule learning. As a result, he argues:

> A distinction needs to be made between knowledge acquisition and the range of competences that may be acquired in the course of learning. Classroom technique and assessment methods often reveal a preoccupation with knowledge acquisition. How can we teach the level or degree of competence desired with the existing institutional settings and staff expertise? Surely before we attempt the transfer of high-level 'lawyering skills' more basic achievements must be established? The ability to think, communicate, to plan, assess risks, identify choices, find information and invent solutions must stand as primary definitions of competences. These skills above all will allow the student to be released from the regulatory quagmire that is modern law.[31]

This restlessness with the task of creating a more adequate legal education was Slade's enduring legacy to the school. His comments at the beginning of the collection are representative of his approach to the department and its staff. It was not just a question of providing a law course, it was a question of providing a course that answered the challenges of society, not just the needs of the CNAA and the legal profession.

Slade's openness to science and technology as well as to legal philosophy led him to conduct ground-breaking research on the application of online resources to legal education, funded by a grant from the British Library research and development department.[32]

As a result, the school had a terminal that linked it to the Lexis legal database.[33] His report of the project, jointly written with Rosemary Gray, was prescient about the direction of future legal education – and indeed legal practice – into the contemporary period. Chapter eight of the report has a detailed account of the manner in which NELP students were part of the research project during the academic year 1982-83. It records 'an integrated legal research skills course was offered to law students ... One of the explicit aims of the course was to facilitate practical search experience of the Lexis system'.[34] In order to do this the course offered 'a broad-based understanding of the nature of legal information'.[35]

The report offers an intriguing insight into the open and innovative atmosphere at NELP at the time – and that the department was in many ways a pioneer of an aspect of legal education which is now commonplace. Traditionally all law students are introduced to the law library, which is composed of primary sources, such as law reports, consolidated statutes and secondary legal commentaries, and works of jurisprudence and socio-legal studies. The Lexis database transformed the ways in which lawyers and law students could access the primary sources and created new ways of searching for material. Since the creation of the internet and emergence of Google as the main search engine this now sounds rather tame, but in 1982 this was quite revolutionary. Over 100 first- and second-year students participated, and five students taking on Mike Slade's optional course, law and scientific development, also received instruction. Students responded well to the course, being overwhelmingly in favour of all having formal instruction on using online resources, and were particularly keen to have special workshops in the third-year optional subjects, such as international law, family law, criminology, EEC law or labour law, 'which required them to become familiar with a broad range of legal, political, commercial and social information sources'.[36]

In concluding the report, the authors considered that the reception of online retrieval systems:

> Must generally be considered a success and a worthwhile improvement both in the information services offered to support the curriculum but more especially in the catalytic

> effect it has had in focusing attention on critical issues of information handling, the perception of knowledge in the legal world and the behavioural requirements of the learning and researching process. Access to a wider selection of materials is an important by-product of the more important change, a perceived shift in the notion of the quality applied to legal education. The department is now in a better position to develop its future curriculum and teaching patterns on a firmer foundation.[37]

These comments had implications for all law degrees. Slade saw that the possibilities of reducing the time that students spent in information gathering opened the space for much greater theoretical analysis of legal texts and the effect of those texts on society. In this he was very much in the tracks of Twining's arguments in *Pericles and the Plumber.* Mike Slade's turning around of the reference to 'liberal education' by Twining, and indeed in the Ormrod report, into a 'liberal education through law' cleverly re-centred law and raised the question of what work the school should be doing in advancing the understanding of law in society.

Work

This ethos was very ambitious and placed a heavy burden on the staff to realise it. In the early phase a great deal of energy went into creating rich courses. However, the more difficult task was to generate the new research which would be needed to sustain the programme and the project more widely. It also raised the question of methodologies, destination of outputs and relationships with other scholars. These questions were difficult to address, and in the first decade the school lacked a collective research culture. In the 1980s there were attempts by members of the school to reach out to activist audiences and to the profession. Anne Bottomley with Katherine Gieve, Gay Moon and Angela Weir published *The Cohabitation Handbook: A Women's Guide to the Law*[38] in 1981 from an explicitly feminist perspective. The authors described themselves as 'all active members of the women's liberation movement and are members of the Rights of Women collective. They are variously single, married, divorced, separated, heterosexual and gay'. The text was explicitly aimed towards women with the aim of empowering readers with an understanding of how law worked, with very good advice of when professional help would be needed. In the same period, Howard Levenson and Fiona Fairweather (then Hargreaves) published *A Practitioners Guide to the Police and Criminal Evidence Act 1984.*[39] This was a highly detailed account of a very complicated piece of legislation which seemed at the time to possibly change the relationship between the police and the public. As the title implies, its audience was the legal profession. It was published by the Legal Action Group, which had been created in the early 1970s with the aim of creating better legal services to the wider public. This text was undoubtedly a helpful tool in the hands of defence lawyers.

In its first decade, many in the school tended to see law as a tool for social change. The focus was very much on social change rather than law itself. The staff were divided between those who subscribed to various forms of marxism and others who had a more reformist outlook. Both groups, however, saw law instrumentally. This situation created a tension between these positions and Mike Slade's aspiration for legal education in which law itself was central. This was not appreciated at the time. However, as Tim Murphy has observed, from the late 1970s legal scholars subscribing to marxism were 'hit' by the translations of Foucault and Derrida: 'Between them they transformed the scene in terms of intellectual influences and future directions, and this led to a collapse of Marx as a reference point'.[40]

The process of reading and engaging with these scholars took many years and their influence did not become immediately apparent.[41] Both scholars offered legal academics new ways of thinking about law through deconstruction and critique. This opened the way for releasing legal scholars from the marxist theory when law was both marginal and merely a tool in the hands of the ruling class. Foucault's view of power as exercised in discursive forms had profound implications for an analysis of law. Derrida offered a methodology which particularly appealed to those engaged with the law. As Murphy writes: 'The reception of Derrida encouraged critique as etymology, as word play and as symptomology. This was ideally suited to legal studies'.[42] As a result, there was a shift away from instrumentality toward a concentration on the way in which law operated through discursive power, and an interest in understanding how legal narratives were constituted. In Britain this process took shape through the creation of the critical legal conference in 1984. It was to have a significant impact on the development of a research culture in NELP. As can be seen in its formative statement, it posed the development of a critical legal studies movement in a way that possibly straddled different intellectual traditions:

> The central focus of the critical legal approach is to explore the manner in which legal doctrine and legal education and the practice of legal institutions work to buttress and support a pervasive system of inegalitarian relations. Critical theory works to develop radical alternatives and to explore the role of law in the creation of social, economic and political relations that will advance human emancipation.[43]

The critical legal studies movement was to transform the way in which many legal academics engaged with law. It addressed in many ways the space that had opened through technical advances that Mike Slade had alluded to. The movement re-centred law as a site of intellectual inquiry with the application of deconstructive methodologies to legal materials, cases, statutes, textbooks. At the same time, it gave rise to an interest in images of law in literature, history and the humanities more generally.[44] These developments had a major influence in NELP, and participation in the critical legal conference and the conferences of the Association for the Study of Law, Culture and the Humanities was to be a feature in the embedding of a research culture. Derrida in particular, by removing Marx from a central place, also opened the door to other writers whose work could enlighten the critique of law. This was evident in the work of many in the school; Said for myself, Bhabha for Mirza and Lacan for Collins. Critical legal studies thus provided a direction for much research and, over the years, a significant proportion of staff engaged with these developments, including

Anne Bottomley, Kate Green, Hilary Lim, Patricia Tuitt, Jeremy Roche, Bill Bowring, Barry Collins, Qudsia Mirza, Roshan de Silva Wijeyeratne, Jeremy Gilbert, Edel Hughes, Dimitrios Kivotidis and myself. It provided an important research network and opened the way to many successful collaborations.[45]

This involvement in the legal studies movement highlights another of the contradictions inherent in the polytechnic idea – and not just, I suspect, confined to law. In referring to the question of research Pratt, having made a distinction between universities as autonomous institutions and the polytechnics as a service tradition, argues that: 'The service tradition does not, on the whole, claim to pursue knowledge for its own sake. Human knowledge may advance as much through the solution of practical problems as through pure thought. "Research" in these institutions is typically directed to some external problem, often in the form of consultancies for companies'.[46]

This notion of applied research was particularly problematic given the way that the critical legal studies movement was established by both university and polytechnic law schools. The publication of Fitzpatrick and Hunt's edited collection *Critical Legal Studies* was highly significant in confirming the parallel research interests of legal academics in both universities and polytechnics. Out of the seventeen contributors, six were from polytechnics (including Anne Bottomley from NELP) and eight were from new university law schools. Indeed, critical legal studies was in many ways a coalition between scholars drawn from the new law schools of the 1960s and the polytechnics. Alan Hunt, one of the editors, was at the time at Middlesex Polytechnic and had been at Manchester Polytechnic in the 1970s. Peter Fitzpatrick,[47] then at Kent University, was to play a major role in the developing interest of law and postcolonialism, which had an impact on NELP (Lim, Collins,[48] Mirza, Strawson, de Silva Wijeyeratne,[49] for example). The other major contributors were Costas Douzinas and Ronnie Warrington, both then at Middlesex Polytechnic, who produced ground-breaking work which established critical legal studies as a formidable intellectual movement.[50]

Within the school, the construction of a research culture was highly complex. However strong the collective environment, to a high degree outputs are dependent on individual efforts or particular collaborations. This in turn is affected by staff churn. In the second decade (1985-95) the shift toward critique did assist the development of a more resilient research culture. This was reinforced by the hire of new academics in the early 1990s, particularly Bill Bowring, Qudsia Mirza and Barry Collins. The period also saw the publication of a series of works on public interest law, children's rights and social work law.[51] Kate Green published a well-received textbook *Land Law.*[52] It was also accompanied by a marked increase in presentations at conferences and in the organisation of panels. There were also a number of important initiatives. A PhD programme on the theme of women, law and development, between NELP/UEL and the University of Dhaka in Bangladesh, funded by the Department of International Development, was established under the direction of Kate Green. Jeremy Cooper created a link with the Brooklyn Law School in New York, which led to staff research collaboration and student exchanges. I engaged in a research project on the constitutional reform in communist Bulgaria, funded by the British Council and the Bulgarian Academy of Sciences.[53] Bill Bowring and myself created a joint workshop between NELP and Moscow State University on legal reform, funded by the British Council.[54]

The 1980s marked the beginning of the Research Assessment Exercise (RAE) which, in contradictory ways, had a positive impact for academics in the polytechnics. While law did not perform well in the 1980s it did focus attention on the significance of research. Despite the increasing productivity and the development of interesting projects, the school had no academics holding senior titles such as professor or reader. In 1995 the school decided that it needed to appoint professors. Colin Sumner from the Cambridge University Institute of Criminology became the first professor in that year.[55] His arrival also heralded the creation of the BA Criminology and Criminal Justice.[56] The following year Mike Slade was awarded a chair but decided to retire that year. Colin Sumner became the head and a second professor, Beverley Brown from Edinburgh University, joined the school. Both appointments were critical in developing a stronger research culture. Beverley Brown, who had a background in publishing and the women's movement as well as academia, was especially helpful in launching the research careers of many younger members of staff. She was also insistent on holding regular research seminars and discussion of new books, and ensured that that the school was working with scholars outside the university, especially through the London legal theory group.

Although a turning point for the school it was in fact a brief period, and by 2000 it had lost both professors. In part this highlighted the relative fragility of the environment and underlined the necessity of building a more robust research culture from within. However, with the appointment of Fiona Fairweather as head in 1999, the advances made in that period were consolidated though just such a project. The results were rewarded in the RAE 2001, where the school rose by two grades with all its work classified of national standing. The submission, led by Hilary Lim, set a standard for the future.[57]

The millennium began with a threat to close the school altogether due to an alleged fall in student recruitment. However, Fiona Fairweather led a brilliant campaign to save the school and it certainly brought out the best in staff. As head and later dean, despite the burden of administrative duties, she always insisted on teaching so that she could remain in contact with the daily challenges of the job. This closeness to the staff was key in not merely saving but in building the school. In fact, student numbers were relatively stable, and after 2001 undergraduate recruitment to both the law degree and BA (Criminology and Criminal Justice) increased. The LLM, which had been launched in 1993, dramatically increased its intake, which has been, with fluctuations, sustained. Under Fairweather's leadership, research became normalised and much more integrated into the life of the school, and saw a high level of productivity.[58]

The 1990s had seen a growing interest in Islamic law, which was to remain a theme in the school's work. The work began with a focus on British colonialism and the construction of images of Islamic law.[59] An important contribution was made by Qudsia Mirza who became an active participant in the debates about Islamic feminism.[60] After 11 September 2001, this aspect of the work assumed a greater importance. During this period, Hilary Lim and Siraj Sait carried out work on a UN Habitat-funded project on Islamic law and land issues.[61] Work around these issues has continued, and the relationship between UEL and UN Habitat has become a feature of the school's work. As a consequence of my work on colonialism and Islamic law, I became a visiting professor at Palestine's Birzeit Law Centre (now Institute) between 1996 and 2006. Qudsia Mirza's work on Islamic feminism was recognised with a fellowship at the International Institute for the Sociology of Law at Onati, Spain in 2003 and by her appointment as the Kate Stoneman visiting professor of law at Albany Law School in the United States in 2004.

The consolidation of the research culture created conditions in which professorial appointments could be considered again. Given the long-term commitment of the school to human rights, it was decided to establish a chair of human rights. In 2005 the American scholar Chandra Lekha Sriram, then at St Andrews University, was appointed and in 2006 she established the Centre on Human Rights in Conflict (CHRC).[62] The centre focused on the protection of human rights and the role of international humanitarian law in conflicts and conflict resolution. From the start, Chandra Sriram's energy and enthusiasm had a huge impact on the school as a whole. She quickly recruited two research fellows, Olga Martin-Ortega and Johanna Herman, and began the arduous task of applying for research funding. In the course of her campaign, grants were won from the British Council, the EU, the US Institute of Peace, and the Economic and Social Research Council (ESRC). The first successful British Council grant looked at the role of law in conflict resolution in Africa.[63] Chandra Sriram carried out research in the field often in difficult and dangerous situations in Colombia, Sri Lanka, Sierra Leone and Sudan.[64] She was the author or editor of thirteen books, and her untimely death in 2018 at the age of forty-seven was a loss to the school and, more importantly, to the field of transitional justice.

As the fourth decade of the school began, the various strands in its past began to solidify. Staff were actively working internationally tackling major issues and engaging in debates about them, encompassing the Balkans, West Africa, Kenya, Ireland, Palestine, Israel, Colombia, Sudan and Sri Lanka. This was reflected in the submission to the RAE 2008. It saw a marked improvement in the school's research rating, with 80 per cent of its work rated of international standing or above.[65] In that submission the creation of the CHRC and the work on the UN Habitat project were prominent in demonstrating the strengths in international law and human rights. Other themes that were also important included work on law in Africa led by Kofi Kufuor, whose own work has continued to be significant.[66] Another key area of work was on terrorism studies which was centred on the work of Andrew Silke.[67] In due course he was joined by three other scholars who worked in the same area: Anthony Richards,[68] John Morrison[69] and James Windle.[70] The sustained work in the areas of international law, human rights and terrorism studies, which contained discrete areas of Islamic and African law, provided the basis for the research excellence framework (REF) 2014 submission. Despite the changes in evaluation and the inclusion of 'impact', the school saw a further improvement with 99 per cent of work rated as of international standing or above with 57 per cent in the two top grades.[71] A good result, as especially under the selective system of the time the research of some 40 per cent of staff was submitted. Significantly, 90 per cent of the staff had published their work in the census period. It represented the results of a huge amount of creative energy nourished by an empowering culture.

Conclusion

The question mark in the title hangs over this chapter. Was, or is, the NELP/UEL Law School radical? Certainly, it has attracted radical individuals over the years. Of course, not all the staff would want to identify in this way. However, the difficulty comes when you attempt to assess this description for the institution itself. A further difficulty is that radicalism needs to be constantly renewed. This necessary undermines the task of institution-building, which relies on the consolidation of mores, habits and procedures. However, within that limitation the school has shown tremendous adaptability to the times, sometimes to reinvent itself while it constantly renewed its commitment to scholarship in the service of justice.

The creation of the school in the mid-1970s inevitably meant it was the product of a moment which combined radical social and political change, the creation of the polytechnics, and new departures in legal education and legal practice. What is important about NELP/UEL is the way in which it assumed a distinctive agency to take advantage of those times. Its participation in the critical legal studies movement, its contribution to conflict resolution, and its promotion of human rights education and research[72] demonstrates a trajectory to disrupt an unjust social order. Edwin Lichtenstein's openness encouraged academic and pedagogic creativity, while the ethos that Mike Slade created was based on challenges to staff and students to do the unexpected. In a sense he was never satisfied that the school had really reached its potential and was always keen for it to rethink its mission. This sense that there was yet more to be achieved has contributed to the dynamics of the school's culture. At the same time, it has contributed to a sense of endless possibility. Perhaps that is where its radicalism lies.

Many of the school's graduates have gone on to contribute to the changes in society that a 'liberal education through law' can provide. Imran Khan became the solicitor for the family of the murdered teenager Stephen Lawrence at the inquiry into his death and helped argue for the legal concept of institutional racism. Mark Stephens became a leading solicitor in London and has made a major contribution to media law – and became chair of the governors of UEL. Urfan Khaliq has become a professor of international law and is currently the head of Cardiff Law School. Although Gina Miller spent only a year at East London, she has shown how the rule of law can be a force for decent constitutional government by upholding the power of Parliament over the executive.[73]

The legal profession is about to change its approach to legal education, in particular ending the qualifying law degree which has been a feature of the system since 1971. As the school contemplates its future in such new circumstances, it is to be hoped that the spirit of openness, internationalism and critique that marked it out at the beginning and nourished it since will stand it in good stead.

Notes

1. I am using the term 'law school' throughout in its generic sense, although the exact designation has been through many configura-

tions; a law department in the Faculty of Business in the 1970s then a department in the Faculty of Social Sciences in in the 1980s, as an independent law school in the mid-1990s, then in a school of law and sciences a decade later and, after 2015, a department of law and criminology in the School of Business and Law.

2. Edwin Lichtenstein 1923-2004. In the early 1960s he had been a national leader in the briefly united nationalist movement in South Rhodesia. During the Smith regime his office was bombed, and he was injured.
3. Some were members of far-left organisations or the Communist Party of Great Britain and many were active in trade unions and the women's movement, or members of the Anti-Apartheid Movement and CND.
4. William Twining, 'Pericles and the Plumber', *Law Quarterly Review,* Vol 83, Issue 3, 1967, pp896-426.
5. *Ibid.,* p 898.
6. See John Wilson, 'Survey of Legal Education in the UK', *Journal of the Society of Public Teachers of Law,* New Series, Vol. IX, No. 1, June 1996. The statistics in this article were drawn from the Ormrod Report, see below.
7. Quoted by Twining, *ibid.,* p899.
8. *Ibid.,* pp420-421.
9. Anne Bottomley, Sussex; John Strawson and Jeremy Roche, Kent; Fiona Fairweather, Warwick.
10. This was a period in which law centres were being created to offer free legal services to working-class communities. It was also marked by the creation of more informal and radical organisations providing legal and social services to particular communities, such as Release and Street Aid (founded by the future UEL professor of cultural studies, Phil Cohen – and for which the author worked in the early 1970s).
11. Report of the Committee on Legal Education, HMSO: London, cmnd. 4595, 1971.
12. *Ibid.,* p41.
13. *Ibid.,* p43.
14. The committee included two heads of law schools in polytechnics, S.D. March from Manchester and G.A. Seabrook from Trent.
15. Quoted in John Pratt, *The Polytechnic Experiment,* Buckingham: Open University Press, 1997, p7.
16. *Ibid.,* p111.
17. Clinical legal education was pioneered by US law schools in the 1920s and 1930s and offers students some experience of dealing with legal advice, under the supervision of a qualified lawyer. UEL established such a law clinic in 2013.

18. Report of the Committee on Legal Education, p125.
19. *Ibid.*, p107.
20. Ella Rule, 'Prospects for Women Law Graduates', Michael P. Slade (ed.), *Law in Higher Education: Into the 1980s,* Association of Law Teachers: Stoke-on-Trent, 1980, p40.
21. The Ormrod committee had noted that probably 35 per cent of law graduates had no intention of practising, Committee on Legal Education, p104. That number had increased significantly and now is almost reversed, with only about 40 per cent of law graduates entering the profession.
22. For example, only 7.1 per cent of practising barristers were women in 1975, see, Ella Rule, *Prospects for Women Law Graduates,* p37. Despite more women than men reading law by 2014, only a third of practising barristers were women, see, Nikki Godden-Rasul, 'Portraits of Women of the Law: Re-envisioning Gender Law and the Legal Profession in Law Schools', *Legal Studies,* Vol. 39, No.3, 2019, p415. The article demonstrates that even after four and a half decades and many advances, it is still necessary to discuss gender in law schools and the profession.
23. This was a pattern noted by the Ormrod committee; in 1970 there were 5400 applicants for 2076 places, Committee on Legal Education, p104.
24. This list was to grow as the school developed with options such as, the law of evidence (Beverley Brown), medicine and the law (Sharon Levy), law and postcolonialism (myself) and law and film (Barry Collins).
25. Maurice Moore was to become central to the leadership of the school and was adept at leading it through the labyrinth of quality procedures.
26. He began a pattern of international study tours for undergraduates which grew to include tours to the United States, the Soviet Union (then Russia), Turkey and South Africa. Alan Wilson continues the tradition today.
27. Michael Slade, *Law Higher Education into the 1980s,* Association of Law Teachers: Stoke-on-Trent, 1980.
28. *Ibid.*, p4.
29. *Ibid.*
30. *Ibid.*, p170.
31. *Ibid.*
32. Michael Slade and Rosemary Gray, 'The Impact and Potential of On-Line Legal Research Systems on Academic Legal Education', British Library Research and Development Report 5812, North East London Polytechnic: London, 1984.

33. At the time of the research project, fifteen institutions offered students some access to online resources (nine polytechnic and six university law schools), see *ibid.*, p263. However, the report suggests that three-quarters of law schools did have some access overall to online resources, see *ibid.* p267. One constraining issue was the cost; for Lexis it was £1200 for ninety-five-hours access.
34. *Ibid.*, p195.
35. *Ibid.*
36. *Ibid.*, p207.
37. *Ibid.*, p337.
38. Anne Bottomley, Katherine Gieve, Gay Moon and Angela Weir, *The Cohabitation Handbook: A Women's Guide to the Law,* Pluto Press: London, 1981.
39. Howard Levenson and Fiona Hargreaves, *A Practitioners Guide to the Police and Criminal Evidence Act 1984,* Legal Action Group: London, 1985. A second and expanded edition appeared as Howard Levenson and Fiona Fairweather, *Police Powers: A Practitioners Guide,* Legal Action Group: London, 1990.
40. Tim Murphy, 'BritCrits: Subversion, and Submission, past, present and future', *Law and Critique,* Vol. 10, Issue 3, 1999, p255.
41. Indeed it was to be in the 1990s that some of the most critical developments were to take place. For example, Jacques Derrida's influential contribution on law, the 'Force of Law,' was first circulated at a colloquium at the Cardozo Law School in New York in 1989 and appeared in print in 1992; Jacques Derrida, 'The Force of Law: the Mystical Foundation of Authority,' Drucilla Cornell, Michel Rosenfeld and David Gray Carlson (eds), *Deconstruction and the Possibility of Justice,* Routledge: New York and London, 1992, pp3-67.
42. *Ibid.*
43. Quoted in Peter Fitzpatrick and Alan Hunt (eds), 'Critical Legal Studies: Introduction', *Critical Legal Studies,* Basil Blackwell: Oxford, 1987, pp1-2.
44. In due course this led to the creation of the Association for the Study of Law, Culture and the Humanities, based in the United States with a significant input from Britain, especially Birkbeck and Kent law schools – and a high participation of UEL scholars.
45. In 1996, Qudsia Mirza and Barry Collins organised the annual Critical Legal Conference at UEL.
46. John Pratt, *The Polytechnic Experiment,* p10.
47. See for example Eve Darian-Smith and Peter Fitzpatrick (eds), *Laws of the Postcolonial,* University of Michigan Press: Ann Arbor, 1999.
48. See Barry Collins, 'The Belfast Agreement and the nation that

"always arrives at its destination"', *Penn State Law Review*, Vol. 2, No. 2, 2002, pp385-413.

49. See Roshan de Silva Wijeyeratne and John Strawson (eds), 'Tracking the Postcolonial in Law', *Griffith Law Review*, Vol. 12, No. 2, 2003.
50. See for example Costas Douzinas and Ronnie Warrington, *Justice Miscarried: Ethics and Aesthetics of law*, Harvester Wheatsheaf: New York and London 1994.
51. See for example: Jeremy Cooper, *Key Guide to Information Sources in Public Interest Law*, Mansell: London, 1991; Stuart Vernon, *Social Work and the Law*, Butterworths: London, 1993; Wendy Stainton Rogers and Jeremy Roche, *Children's Welfare and Children's Rights: A Practical Guide to the Law*, Hodder and Stoughton: London, 1994; Stuart Vernon, *Social Work and the Law*, Butterworths: London, 1993.
52. Kate Green, *Land Law*, Palgrave: London, 1993.
53. With the fall of communism at the end of 1989, Hilary Lim and I made a memorable trip to Sofia in February 1990 to interview many of those involved in the radical changes taking place, among them the deputy prime minister. We also witnessed the formation of the new constitution as our host Dencho Georgiev discussed amendments to the text over the dinner table and then would rush the results to the state council building.
54. The first workshop took place at UEL in autumn 1991 in the last days of the Soviet Union; the second was held in Moscow in 1993 in the new Russian Federation.
55. While at UEL he co-founded the journal *Theoretical Criminology*.
56. Ably overseen by Elizabeth Stokes.
57. See: https://www.rae.ac.uk/2001/Submissions/Form.asp?Route=2&HESAInst=H-0058&UoA=36&MSub=Z (accessed 7 September 2019).
58. See for example: Jane Pickford (ed.), *Youth Justice: Theory and Practice*, Cavendish: London, 2000; Susan Scott-Hunt and Hilary Lim (eds), *Feminist Perspectives on Equity and Trusts*, Cavendish: London, 2001; John Strawson (ed.), *Law after Ground Zero*, Cavendish: London, 2002; Kofi Oteng Kufuor, *World Trade Governance and the Developing Countries: The GATT/WTO Code Committee System*, Royal Institute of Foreign Affairs: London, 2004.
59. See John Strawson, 'Islamic Law and English Texts', *Law and Critique*, Vol. VI, No. 1, 1995, pp21-38.
60. See Qudsia Mirza Islam, 'Hybridity and the Laws of Marriage', *Australian Feminist Law Journal*, Vol. 14, No. 1, 2000, pp1-22.
61. See Siraj Sait and Hilary Lim, *Land, Law and Islam: Property Rights in the Muslim World*, Zed Press: London, 2006.

62. See: https://www.uel.ac.uk/research/the-centre-on-human-rights-in-conflict (accessed 14 September 2019).
63. See Chandra Lekha Sriram, Olga Martin-Ortega and Johanna Herman (eds), *Peacebuilding and the Rule of Law in Africa: Just Peace?,* Routledge: London, 2011.
64. One of the results of this was an excellent edited collection, see Chandra Lekha Sriram, Olga Martin-Ortega and Johanna Herman (eds), *Surviving Field Research: Working in Violent and Difficult Situations,* Routledge: London, 2009.
65. See: https://www.rae.ac.uk/submissions/submission.aspx?id=57&type=hei&subid=2906 (accessed 20 September 2019).
66. See for example: Kofi Oteng Kufuor, *The Institutional Transformation of the Economic Community of West African States,* Ashgate: Farnham, 2006; Kofi Oteng Kufuor, *The African Human Rights System: Origin and Evolution,* Palgrave Macmillan: Basingstoke, 2010.
67. See for example: Andrew Silke (ed.), *Terrorists, Victims and Society: Psychological Perspectives on Terrorism and its Consequences,* Wiley: Chichester, 2003; Andrew Silke, *Research on Terrorism: Trends, Achievements and Failures,* Frank Cass: London, 2004.
68. See Anthony Richards, *Conceptualizing Terrorism,* Oxford University Press: Oxford, 2015.
69. See John Morrison, *The Origin and Rise of Dissident Irish Republicanism: The Role and Impact of Organizational Splits,* Bloomsbury: London, 2013.
70. See James Windle, *Suppressing Illegal Opium Production: Successful intervention in Asia and the Middle East,* I. B. Tauris: London, 2016.
71. See: https://results.ref.ac.uk/(S(2yeysw5nrkzj4kx3tvyqemnd))/Results/BySubmission/2459 (accessed 20 September 2019).
72. A contemporary example of this can be seen in the results of a CHRC workshop, see: Kalliopi Chainoglou, Barry Collins, Michael Phillis and John Strawson (eds), *Injustice, Memory and Faith in Human Rights,* Routledge: London and New York, 2018.
73. Most recently see: https://www.supremecourt.uk/cases/docs/uksc-2019-0192-judgment.pdf (accessed 24 September 2019).

CHAPTER FIFTEEN

Physiotherapy: a story of change

Sarah Beeston

Introduction

This chapter considers the effects of the integration of the School of Physiotherapy at the Royal London Hospital and North East London Polytechnic (NELP), a newly designated polytechnic to the east of it. The merger led to the establishment of the first BSc Honours degree in physiotherapy in England, and the subsequent expansion of the physiotherapy subject area as postgraduate courses were validated and as research activity grew and prospered: each in turn providing unforeseen opportunities to collaborate with other institutions in the UK and further afield. Without the radical move from a hospital base in Whitechapel to that of the polytechnic in West Ham, these changes would not have been possible.

Background

The formal integration between the London Hospital School of Physiotherapy (LHSP) and NELP took place in 1981 and was the culmination of preparatory work undertaken during the mid-to-late 1970s. By 1981 a BSc Honours Physiotherapy degree course had been validated jointly by the Council for National Academic Awards (CNAA), the Chartered Society of Physiotherapy (CSP) and the Council for Professions Supplementary to Medicine (CPSM).

The course was well-established by 1988 when the school transferred from the Royal London Hospital at Whitechapel to become the Division of Physiotherapy within the Department of

Paramedical Sciences led by Professor John Neville. It was located in the newly completed Arthur Edwards Building on the Stratford campus: only a few miles down the road but a world away!

What ensued was the result of a change in context, in culture and in connections.

The LHSP had been established in 1936 in the then newly completed department of physical medicine, adjoining the outpatient department in Stepney Way. In the 1970s it remained above the outpatient physiotherapy treatment rooms, which included the consulting rooms of specialist doctors of physical medicine. Despite good working relationships between medical and physiotherapy staff there was little opportunity for shared teaching and learning across the divide, or with the school of nursing located nearby. In short, the school was somewhat isolated, probably having closer links with the CSP than with the rest of the Royal London Hospital. This isolated context and medically dominated culture meant that there were few connections with external educational groups or institutions, other than with the CSP's education department and with special interest groups (SIGs) within the profession.

Physiotherapy had come into being as an adjunct to medicine. In an attempt to differentiate itself from other professions allied to medicine, early definitions of its role had expressed its concern with the treatment of disease, injury or deformity by physical methods such as massage, heat treatment and exercise, rather than by drugs or surgery. This depiction had defined its identity and determined its core curriculum and scope of practice. The goal of training had been to produce competent practitioners of these skills, largely within the context of acute care and under the authority of medical doctors who specified the treatment required for their patients. However, the shift towards primary health care and the advancement of technology during the 1970s and 1980s was leading to an expansion of the role of physiotherapists.

Drivers of change

During the 1970s the CSP began advocating the development of degree courses for physiotherapists, most of whom were entering training with A-levels commensurate with university entrance. Its calls were amplified by those of the CPSM, which had become an additional gatekeeper for physiotherapy and the other professions supplementary to medicine in 1960.

It was in 1970 that the CPSM, under the chairmanship of Dr J.A. Oddie, recommended that: 'opportunities must be given for practitioners either to acquire higher and recognised qualifications, or for the institution of a degree course for a selected number who are likely to be the future leaders of the profession'.[1] On the heels of this came another recommendation; this time from the advisory board of the Department of Health and Social Security (DHSS) concerned with oversight of the training of health professionals and the promotion of health research. This board expressed the view that there would be substantial benefit gained from greater integration between universities and the current training schools for health professionals. It saw this as leading to greater access to an increasing knowledge-base in the sciences and to more varied approaches to teaching and learning. The call appeared to be twofold: a higher level of qualification and a new curriculum, demonstrating the necessary breadth and depth of knowledge, and taught in a way that would encourage a spirit of enquiry.

This growing pressure for more professional autonomy was the context in which the LHSP found itself when contacted by NELP, and within which the potential for partnership was discussed.

Having been designated as a polytechnic in 1970, NELP was keen to increase student numbers and to expand its partnerships within the local area in order to serve the needs of the surrounding community. Its first director, George Brosan, had determined that the polytechnic should adopt a 'matching function' which brought together a learner's knowledge and skill and the need for that knowledge and skill within society. Its first directors were committed to: 'the idea of making the *application* of knowledge the central theme of the polytechnic philosophy'.[2] What better match could there be than to encompass a physiotherapy course to accompany the existing health studies and post-basic nursing courses which were already offered within the Department of Paramedical Sciences? To that end, NELP approached the LHSP on the advice of the CSP and began negotiations with Joan Piercy, head of the school.

Foundations for change

In order to achieve the goal of providing an honours degree course, considerable change was needed and would have to be agreed by a number of parties, namely the CSP, CPSM, NELP and CNAA. The essential requirement was a new curriculum that demonstrated greater depth and breadth in the science subjects which underpinned practice, and a more challenging and innovative approach to teaching and learning which introduced students to basic methods of enquiry, research and clinical reasoning. Lecturers from NELP were called upon to provide more depth in physiology, physics and statistics, and more breadth through the inclusion of aspects of psychology and sociology. Physiotherapy staff would continue to teach anatomy, human movement, physiotherapy skills and theory, and to encourage reflexive and critical thinking through the process of clinical reasoning and decision-making. Importantly, the course would include small-scale student research projects within the final year: a challenge to staff as well as students.

Considerable time and effort were expended before the course was validated in 1981 by the CNAA, CSP and CPSM. As previously stated, it became the first BSc Honours Physiotherapy course in England, and as before still attracted students from all over the country. Most were female school-leavers with A-level qualifications, and with little if any ethnic diversity. The Northern Ireland School of Physiotherapy at the Ulster College Belfast had begun its first undergraduate course in 1976. Scotland followed in 1982 with an ordinary degree at Queen's College, Glasgow. The momentum was under way and the pressure was on for an all-graduate profession!

This pressure was also felt by teaching staff at the LHSP, and by the mid-1980s all physiotherapy teaching staff were in possession of a first degree in addition to their professional and teaching qualifications, and eight would gain higher degrees during 1986, one of which was a doctorate.

Between 1981 and 1988 the course was run on a split-site basis with students spending two days each week at each institution. Science-based subjects were taught at the polytechnic by relevant staff: anatomy, human movement, physiotherapy skills and theory were also taught at the polytechnic by physiotherapy staff. Blocks of clinical practice were interspersed with teaching throughout the course. Team teaching, bringing together staff from both institutions, occurred only for clinical observation seminars. The seminars were held at the hospital. This pattern served to familiarise students and staff with the polytechnic environment.

Meanwhile resources were being developed at NELP for the eventual transfer of the school as a whole. Thanks to the wise and experienced oversight of Joan Piercy, several cohorts of students had graduated before she retired in 1987, to be replaced by myself, a physiotherapy teacher with an MA in Curriculum Studies from London University's Institute of Education. A year later the school in its entirety moved to West Ham.

Adjusting to change

The move into the top floors of the Arthur Edwards Building on The Green at Stratford offered premises and resources far superior to those left behind in the ageing buildings of the outpatient department at Whitechapel. Student teaching was well catered for with a number of dedicated lecture rooms and laboratories for the learning of professional skills. In addition, technical staff were designated to support the course. Staff were provided with offices, also on the fourth floor at The Green: a light and airy environment. Staff and students alike had easier access to the increasingly well-stocked library resources pertinent to physiotherapy at Maryland House. More importantly, this change in our environment was a further major step in our transition to a very different system: that of higher education as opposed to the National Health Service.

Student adjustments

Despite some familiarity with the premises on the part of all but the new intake of students, it took time for them to adjust to their new environment. Those already on the course were accustomed to being a close-knit body of students with a clear-cut purpose and an identical curriculum and timetable. They now found themselves part of a much larger body of students who were more self-directed and following more flexible pathways through their studies. Moreover, their study location had changed, but their social circles had not: these were still rooted in the Royal London Hospital.

Inevitably, the pathways followed by physiotherapy students were still clearly defined and directed, although there had developed a greater expectation on them to take more responsibility for their own learning. Within the new degree course it was incumbent on staff to provide resources which would enable students to complement lectures and seminars with their own reading and study. With the reduced number of hours available for the teaching of manual skills, it had become essential for students to give time to practise in small groups in their discretionary time. As students progressed within the course they were required to present their ideas in seminars, working as small groups, and in so doing learning to work within a team. By their final year they were expected to have initiated ideas for small-group projects which would be supervised by individual members of staff. These were changes which had been implemented from the start of the degree course: however, they were still a work in progress. We were still in transition!

When it came to specific curriculum issues, one which had already reared its head was that of relevance. The focus of students was on their future role as physiotherapists. They were hungry for what they perceived of as being the most relevant areas of study and, for some, these did not include the social sciences. Perhaps one reason for these difficulties was the fact that students were still largely school-leavers with little life experience: another may have been that most entered the course with science A-levels.

As the course continued in the new context and culture of the polytechnic, a wider diversity of students entered it. By the early 1990s, student numbers were being increased and more physiotherapy degree courses were being validated, providing more choice for potential students. At the same time, more local students were applying to the University of East London (UEL). The philosophy of welcoming mature students and accepting a more open access route had begun to rub off on staff responsible for admissions to physiotherapy. There began to be more balance in terms of age, entry qualifications, gender and ethnicity. This was in keeping with the values espoused by the polytechnic: those of widening access to local students.

Staff adjustments

In some respects the adjustments of staff were similar to those of students. They had also been a small close-knit group of physiotherapy teaching staff, with clear-cut roles within the school. Now they were part of a much larger body of lecturers, sharing the West Ham site with the departments of life sciences and psychology. Good working relationships between the two groups had already been established, but there was still room for better understanding on the part of each regarding the application of theory to the skills and practice of physiotherapy. Being together on one site enabled this to happen to a greater extent,

With the retirement of some previous members of the physiotherapy staff, several key appointments were made between 1988 and 1991 which strengthened the existing team significantly. Christine Bithell, previously deputy principal of the School of Physiotherapy at King's College Hospital London, joined our staff in 1988. Having obtained an MA in Curriculum Studies at the Institute of Education at London University, she had recently held a unique advisory role within the CSP, supporting physiotherapy schools as they developed degree courses. She brought with her a wealth of experience and, as the physiotherapy subject area grew, she took on the role of course leader for the BSc Honours Physiotherapy course.

In order to provide for a wider range of learners we also appointed Susan Ryan to our staff in 1991. Susan had just gained a master's degree in gerontology and occupational therapy at Columbia University, New York. Her interest in qualitative research and in looking at professional practice contributed significantly to the learning of students who were to be recruited to our post-experience and postgraduate courses.

Another important appointment was that of Dr Oona Scott who moved to NELP from the Hammersmith Hospital in 1991, having been one of our external examiners since 1988. She was one of the first physiotherapists to gain a doctoral degree while working within a basic neurophysiological research group at University College London (UCL) led by Professor Gerta Vrbova. Having earlier studied postgraduate biomechanics at the University of Surrey, Oona Scott brought with her the ability to design and build equipment and establish methodologies to combine neurophysiological investigations and clinical tests. She was responsible for the development of research, including the recruitment and oversight of PhD students within the physiotherapy subject area, and for our contribution to the Research Assessment Exercise (RAE) submissions. Designated a reader in 1994, she was appointed a professor in 2003 and made emeritus in 2004.

There was a widening of horizons for all staff as we were actively encouraged to take on new responsibilities within our new context. Perhaps this was more apparent for our more senior staff who soon became aware of their responsibilities to the department as well as to the division. There were far more committees on which our subject area needed to be represented. Christine Bithell and I were quickly involved in the process of validation across the polytechnic. This proved a valuable learning experience and training ground for course development which was to come within the physiotherapy subject area. Similarly, Oona Scott was quickly able to connect with other researchers across the polytechnic as she became part of the research community within NELP.

For some others the adjustments came as more of a dislocation from the old order of things. The committee which most clearly exposed remaining divergence of thinking among the staff as a whole was the BSc Physiotherapy assessment board. Historically the over-riding course aim had been to produce competent practitioners with professional attitudes and standards of behaviour. The previous approach to teaching and assessment had been patient-centred, especially in the area of skills teaching. Assessment requirements within the course had tended to be demanding and fairly rigid, and some elements had remained so. Given the reduced number of hours allocated to the teaching of skills within the new curriculum, it could have been predicted that a number of students would fail one or other of the skills elements of the course.

Under the new assessment regulations such failures could substantially alter the profile of individual students. Over time the lengthy debates over issues of safety and clinical competence gradually gave way to an acceptance that student potential as well as student performance was important to consider, especially in the case of students in the early years of their course, before they had been able to gain much clinical experience.

Perhaps this is one example of the need which we as a staff team still had: to move from a training approach to a broader educational perspective. This was not something done quickly or easily. It was all part of the gradual move towards a more student-centred approach to teaching and learning, and also to the reality of working in partnership with clinical supervisors who assessed the clinical competence of students in their placements. The balance between the needs of students and the safeguarding of patients remained an issue of debate; we were still accountable to our professional and regulatory bodies.

Clinical supervisor adjustments

In the midst of change, what had remained relatively constant from the polytechnic's perspective were the arrangements for clinical placements throughout East London. These were well-established and expertly managed by Susan Neville, who ran regular clinical supervisor days at NELP for discussion and mutual updating between clinical and polytechnic staff.

Visits to the students on placement were still made by NELP physiotherapy staff. The changes consequent upon a broadening definition of practice had already affected the curriculum of NELP students but the application of these changes had to be learned in practice. This responsibility fell to a large extent on clinical supervisors responsible for them during placements. This aspect of their role was supported through the work done by Susan Neville during clinical supervisor days. In association with others she also produced a book *Teaching and Learning: A Guide for Therapists*, with the aim of providing a broad and practical guide for busy clinicians.[3]

Accelerating change

As these and other adjustments were still taking place, the pace of change accelerated during the 1990s as the physiotherapy subject area expanded to include more courses and the beginnings of a growing research culture among staff and students.

Course development

In 1986 the CNAA began promoting the development of post-experience courses whereby members of the professions allied to medicine (PAMs) could accrue credit towards a BSc degree in their own particular profession. We were one of the six institutions which gained funding for the development of a 'credit accumulation course for professions allied to medicine' (CAPAM). This afforded us the opportunity to provide for the needs of a range of PAMs, and we recruited occupational therapists, radiographers and orthoptic practitioners, as well as physiotherapists, to our first course. The experience of designing and running this course was pivotal to our further development. Not only did it demand a more multidisciplinary perspective, but it also required a more critical and evaluative stance towards professional practice.

The course comprised two elements: the first was a certificate in evaluation of practice and the second a certificate in research methods. The focus of each was on practice; its nature, its effectiveness and the evaluation of its effects. Recruitment was enthusiastic and it was encouraging that a number of the clinical supervisors of the students on our BSc Physiotherapy course were among the first cohort. The course was relatively short-lived but it served the purpose of preparing some already experienced practitioners to pursue postgraduate studies.

From the point of view of our own development, it also helped prepare us for teaching at a postgraduate level. The focus on practice achieved through this course permeated course development and research as we began to offer more postgraduate opportunities.

In addition to the route to a BSc by credit accumulation, the following courses were also validated during the early 1990s.

- Postgraduate Diploma in Orthopaedic Physiotherapy (1990) in association with the orthopaedic special interest group of the CSP.
- MSc Physiotherapy (1991) – again the first MSc course in the country specific to physiotherapy.
- MSc Occupational Therapy (1991).
- MSc Physiotherapy Practice (Orthopaedics) (1993).
- MSc Physiotherapy Practice (Neurology) (1993) – in conjunction with the National Hospital for Neurology and Neurosurgery at Queen's Square in London.

Research development

Concurrent with our curriculum development came the growth of our research development, without which these courses could not function. It was thanks to the strong support of Professor John Neville who found space for us, and the vision and skill of Dr Oona Scott, that we were able to establish the first of three research laboratories. Funding was made available for a research assistant Mary Cramp, who was also a physiotherapist, and a small team of staff keen to pursue research in the area of muscle physiology and human movement developed.

Alongside this research group was another small group of staff whose interests focused upon qualitative approaches to research. Members of this group explored and published in the areas of clinical reasoning, perspectives on practice, and on the process of learning and teaching in the clinical context. For example, I used in-depth interviews with expert physiotherapists working in the field of neurological physiotherapy to explore their perceptions of their practice.[4] Christine Bithell and Julie Baldry Currens examined perceptions of clinical educators and students regarding a new model of supervision which they had proposed, both as a learning experience and with regard to practical aspects of its management.[5]

Both groups supported and supervised student projects at undergraduate and postgraduate levels, and both groups were able to publish findings in relevant journals. The aim of each was to address questions that emerged from physiotherapy practice. In the case of what became known as the 'human movement performance group', important links with clinical researchers in our local hospitals were made by Oona Scott and others.

Following our submission for the RAE in 1991, the polytechnic chose to support us over a four-year period from what it had designated as its research development funding (DEVR). The required submission of a definitive research plan had provided the impetus for setting up basic research structures and a small departmental research committee was established. This led to some successful bids for external grant funding, and there began to be tangible evidence of ongoing research and publications.

International development

By 1990 John Neville was dean of the Faculty of Health and Life Sciences and was keen to involve what had become the Department of Rehabilitation Sciences in the initiatives afforded through the European Commission. This opened up many opportunities for physiotherapy staff to engage with developments in Europe through a consortium of institutes of higher education in health and rehabilitation (COHEHRE). In February 1990 NELP became one of eight founder members of the consortium with John Neville as its first president. Its purpose was to work towards harmonising education for health professionals across European countries. This involved regular conferences, opportunity for student exchanges and enhanced opportunities for gaining funding for short-term projects.

Between 1993 and 1995 physiotherapy staff from NELP contributed to the curriculum development of degree-level physiotherapy education at the University of Ljubljana in Slovenia, and provided a series of short courses for its staff. This project included visits to NELP by the Slovenian staff, several of whom subsequently joined our MSc programme, with one becoming a research assistant for a time. Further funding was forthcoming through the Socrates programme, and between 1998 and 2000, staff were again involved in a curriculum development project; this time with physiotherapy staff at Uppsala University in Sweden, working in partnership with staff from the Helsinki Polytechnic in Finland.

These opportunities of working with European partners from several countries prepared the way for the ensuing challenge resulting from a visit to UEL in 1998 from some Russian doctors from the St Petersburg State Medical University, named after Pavlov. Their interest in developing rehabilitation services in St Petersburg had led them to a programme of visits to key specialist areas of excellence in rehabilitation in the UK. Their visit to UEL was prompted by their desire to develop a physiotherapy course in St Petersburg, with the long-term aim of promoting physiotherapy as a profession in Russia.

Initial uncertainty on our part gave way to a preliminary visit to St Petersburg, followed by a series of short courses for groups of doctors with an interest in this development, all funded by a Russian charity. Subsequent regular visits and short courses between 1998 and 2000 and again between 2002 and 2004 by UEL staff were funded respectively through the know-how fund of the Department for International Development (DFID) and through DFID's health and social care partnership scheme.

Reflecting on change

Becoming part of NELP had resulted in more change for the physiotherapy subject area than we could have imagined, making a radical difference to the students and staff of LHSP between 1980 and 2000. As well as enhancing the education of physiotherapy students, it was a life-changing move for staff which opened doors on both professional and personal levels.

It had been a gradual change and a timely one for both institutions. Solid foundations had been laid and had served well from the beginning. However, the change in context from hospital to polytechnic in 1988 represented a further vital step in our transition to a very different system: that of the higher education sector as opposed to the National Health Service.

This changed our perception of ourselves and of our students. As adjustments were made on the part of staff it was evident that the somewhat narrow roles which characterised the traditional context of physiotherapy teaching were being broadened. We had come into a community where there was an academic climate which offered space to grow and to make a contribution. We were now in an educational context as opposed to a clinical one: students, rather than patients, became our first concern. There were possibilities for staff as well as students to further their education, to engage in research, as well as in teaching and mentoring their students. There was also the possibility to design and run courses at a variety of levels. We were actively encouraged to take initiatives and supported in doing so.

The context of NELP had provided a greater depth and breadth in the curriculum through its teaching contribution in different subject areas. This encouraged a closer consideration of the ways in which we claimed the application of physiology and physics, for example, to the modalities used in practice. It prompted staff and students to question our claims and contributed to a greater degree of critical thinking and clinical reasoning. As a result it could be described as a better 'match' between students' knowledge and the application of that knowledge within clinical placements: a principle dear to the first directors of the polytechnic.

There was a research culture within NELP which attracted a number of staff to become involved. Within the physiotherapy subject area there was a desire to examine questions arising from physiotherapy practice and this group stimulated the interest and involvement of students. Oona Scott was encouraged and supported by NELP's research committee and others in her work to develop the human movement performance group. In 1998, she organised and hosted a residential conference on 'Human motor performance: the interaction between science and therapy', which attracted over 300 participants from a wide range of clinical and non-clinical scientists.

Another facet of NELP's culture was that of widening access to its courses, in particular to local students. Our gradual assimilation of this principle resulted in the recruitment of a greater proportion of mature students from the local area who were able to identify more fully with the patients in their care. It was encouraging to learn that the retention of our students in employment in the area where they graduated was extremely high. It is unlikely that there would have been such a widening of access had it not been encouraged by the philosophy of NELP.

This same culture of collaboration allowed us to continue to work in partnership with the CSP and with our professional colleagues in clinical settings. Several of our staff became external examiners for other physiotherapy courses in the UK and further afield. Christine Bithell was appointed as a subject advisor for Quality Assurance Agency for Higher Education (QAA) subject reviews. She also sat on the editorial advisory board of *Physiotherapy Research International* and was appointed scientific editor of the professional journal *Physiotherapy*. In 1996, Oona Scott was a key contributor in a successful joint application with the Homerton University Regional Neurological Unit for North Thames Regional Health Authority funding, resulting in a fruitful partnership, one among several collaborations.

The very fact of being in the higher education sector opened doors to our international involvement through COHEHRE and allowed us to gain wider experience and influence. Graduate status put us on a more equal footing with physiotherapy education in the United States, Australia and some European counties where graduate and postgraduate courses already existed. This enhanced our ability to connect with physiotherapy lecturers and researchers from other countries, a number of whom visited UEL. It also opened more career possibilities for students, offering a variety of postgraduate opportunities, including research and managerial positions.

The period from 1980 to 2000 had seen many changes within the subject area. Connections made were stimulating and challenging, and encouraged staff to network quite extensively. Their time at NELP/UEL had equipped them to participate in the ongoing development of physiotherapy research and education.

Three members of staff went on to take head of department roles: Christine Bithell in the joint Faculty of St George's, University of London and Kingston University; Fiona Coutts at Queen Margaret University, Edinburgh; and Susan Ryan at University College, Cork. Dr Mary Cramp, our first research assistant, moved to the University of the West of England where she continues her research and is associate head of the Department for Allied Health Professions. Wendy Drechsler completed her PhD in 2002 and moved to the University of Essex. Julie Baldry Currens continued to develop her interest in practice-based learning and peer learning, begun in association with Christine Bithell. This formed the basis of her doctoral studies at the Institute of Education, University of London. She remained at UEL where she designed a BSc (Honours) Physiotherapy course by situated learning, unique in the UK, and then went on to hold the role of director of academic practice and student experience at the University of East London between 2007 and 2013.

This was a unique period and an exciting time of change, producing significant growth for all concerned. The merger between NELP and LHSP put the latter in the forefront of the change that was beginning for all schools of physiotherapy in the country. The support of NELP, and later UEL, and its staff provided both the stimulus and the safety net within which we were enabled to develop our ideas, our courses and our research. We were the benefactors of that change, both professionally and personally.

Notes

1. Dr J.A. Oddie (chair), *Report and Recommendations of Remedial Professions Committee,* Council for Professions Supplementary to Medicine (CPSM), 1970, paras10.6, 10.7.
2. T. Burgess, M. Locke, J. Pratt and N. Richards, *Degrees East: The Making of the University of East London 1892–1992,* The Athlone Press: London, 1995, p70.
3. S. French, S. Neville and J. Laing, *Teaching and Learning: a Guide for Therapists,* Butterworth Heinemann: London, 1994.
4. S. Beeston and H. Simons, 'Physiotherapy practice: Practitioners' perspectives', *Physiotherapy Theory and Practice,* Vol.12 No. 4, 1996, pp231-242.
5. Julie Baldry Currens and Christine Bithell, 'Clinical Education, Listening to different perspectives', *Physiotherapy,* Vol. 86, No.12, 2000, pp645-653.

CHAPTER SIXTEEN

Sixty years of innovating in applied psychology

Mark R. McDermott, Dave Harper, John Radford, David Rose and Aneta Tunariu

Introduction

2012 marked the fiftieth year of psychology being taught as a subject at UEL and in its predecessor institutions, namely West Ham College of Technology (WHCT), North East London Polytechnic (NELP), the Polytechnic of East London (PEL). Now in its sixth decade, we can look back and notice UEL psychology's many successes and innovations.

To begin with, it is worth noting that our academic psychology department in the 1960s was the first to be formed in what was not a university, that is, to be established in the pre-1992 polytechnic sector. So arguably the birth of the school was a radical move in and of itself. Many of those who have spent time in psychology at UEL/PEL/NELP/WHCT, whether as staff or students, know they have internalised a distinct educational experience, one typified by psychology as an applied, demand-led subject with real-world relevance, as evidenced in recent years by the nationally outstanding impact of the school's research. The ethos of the school is one typified by social justice, multiculturalism, and the importance of giving opportunity to and nurturing students from marginalised social groups, a democratised, transformative, inclusive education that seeks to promote learning and excellence in all.

Those who have passed through the corridors of the school will also know it to be an exemplar in terms of offering students a complete trajectory from undergraduate BSc level through to postgraduate doctoral training as professional psychologists. The proximal delivery of these courses offers a uniquely and powerfully motivating context of possibility and opportunity. This has been a distinctive feature and a key to understanding the school's longevity and continued success. We chart here the history of the school, its innovative responses to changing times and circumstances; we highlight its watershed moments, and follow the golden thread of its distinctiveness in terms of teaching, theory, research and practice.

The first thirty years – 1962 to 1992

West Ham College began as part of the nineteenth century movement to make higher education much more widely available than ever before in the UK. Nationally, there was an increasing need for science and technology; locally, municipal authorities and individual philanthropists did much to meet this. The college developed notable strengths in biology, chemistry and chemical engineering. By the early 1960s, however, student demand for these was falling off. Among West Ham's courses was an external general honours science degree of the University of London. In this, three subjects were taken in the first year, two thereafter. It was relatively easy to add psychology – a very novel subject then – initially for the first year, then the remainder.

As it proved popular, the next step was a single honours course. To teach it, eight psychology staff were in post by 1965. Several innovative steps were taken. First, all applicants were given a standard test of intelligence (to ensure selection on the basis of ability rather than just exam results), two separate interviews and a rating based on all other information available (such as extra-curricular activities, testimonials and so forth). GCE grades were not prioritised. Second, all students had a minimum of one tutorial a week in a group of no more than five, with a dual function, academic and pastoral. Third, staff were deliberately chosen with a shared commitment to teaching rather than to the university priority of research first and foremost, and with wider experience than simply academic.

An accidental but beneficial 'innovation' was that as a latecomer psychology found itself occupying two successive annexes to the main college. As one ex-student, George Butterworth (later to become a distinguished professor), remarked: 'the whole place buzzed with psychology'. Staff and students perforce (but happily) met together and ate together.

As psychology at West Ham (and later NELP) developed a national reputation, members of staff (in particular the head of department, John Radford) were instrumental in two major national innovations. One was the introduction of psychology as a GCE A-level subject, from 1970 on. This proved exceptionally popular and increased the demand for degree courses nationally, and of course at the polytechnic. This continues. The other was the work of the Council for National Academic Awards (CNAA), which validated degrees in the non-university sector as this became independent of the universities. John Radford was the first non-university chair of the Psychology Board and held this post for six years, and was able to push forward the valuable interactive, cooperative validation processes characteristic of the CNAA. Unfortunately, the CNAA was discontinued in 1992 in the interests of increased central control of the whole higher education system, a change that was intended to be and remained permanent. In 1992 NELP, in common with other polytechnics, became a university, creating and validating its own degrees. For psychology, this meant continuing and developing its programmes as formerly regulated by the CNAA.

The nineties and noughties

Between 1994 and 2010 there was dramatic expansion in higher education (HE) nationally but, at the same time, greatly increased government scrutiny of how HE funding was being used. One of the highest profile manifestations of this was the Research Assessment Exercise (RAE), a periodic evaluation of research activity in HE, which became firmly established during this period. It was an added pressure for all disciplines, especially in the post-1992 universities, but other Higher Education Funding Council for England (HEFCE) measures had a disproportionate effect on psychology. Moving psychology between funding bands represented a significant funding reduction for the departments. So too did the HEFCE decision to withdraw funding for teaching students doing 'equivalent or lower qualifications' (ELQ), which was a real problem for departments with mature part-time students who already had a degree but were seeking to change careers. A particular 'hit' for psychology at UEL was withdrawal of HEFCE funding for students on external psychology-related courses validated by the university. During this period there were also non-governmental pressures to contend with, for example, the university league tables started by *The Times* (soon followed by *The Guardian*), which had a profound negative influence on student recruitment in post-1992 universities.

These developments certainly focused the collective mind on the financial 'bottom line' but also increased acceptance that, whether we approved of it or not, we had to learn to 'play the system' in a way that had not previously been all that apparent at departmental level. Further, it provided useful preparation for very positive internal changes which occurred in 2001 when Mike Thorne became our vice-chancellor. He replaced the existing eleven schools (which had, in turn, replaced the faculty and department structure) with eight schools, each with a non-negotiable target of a minimum of 1000 students. Crucially, he also introduced a devolved budgeting system in which all the income generated by a school (teaching, research and consultancy) was allocated to that school. Out of its total income, the school had then to purchase services (HR, library, IT services) using a clearly defined series of cost drivers, based mainly on student and staff numbers and space occupied. Whatever was left could then be spent by the school to develop its plans. Deficits, however, had to be met by the school – no safety nets. The contrast with the previous system in which deans allocated funds to departments was notable, with the greater autonomy enhancing departmental morale and facilitating a 'can-do' approach. Mike Thorne's estates strategy also helped enormously. Once the main development of the Docklands campus had been completed, there was real investment in the Stratford campus, including a major refurbishment of the Arthur Edwards Building, psychology's home. The School of Psychology benefited not just in terms of improved teaching and office accommodation, but also in much-improved dedicated research space. The scene had been set for expansion, diversification and innovation. Student numbers increased markedly, new courses were developed (both internal and through external organisations), research initiatives were supported and the school significantly increased its consultancy activities.

A UEL kind of psychology

Through much of its sixty years of development, psychology at UEL and its predecessor institutions has been distinctive in terms of its identity and values. Though now methodologically pluriform, from the 1970s onward, psychology at UEL became known for its critical approach to research, theory and practice. Arguably, the UEL School of Psychology has, over several decades, established a reputation for attracting psychologists who ask troubling but much-needed questions about the discipline, in recent times focusing on the need to 'decolonise' it. Between the 1980s and early 2000s, its psychologists were asking questions about the history of the discipline. For example, John Radford and David Rose examined psychology as a liberal science,[1] and Graham Richards in the first edition of *Putting Psychology in Its Place*[2] evaluated psychology in its historical context, while in *Race, Racism and Psychology*[3] he took a critical look at how psychology has engaged with race and racism since the late nineteenth century. They were questioning psychology's epistemological assumptions, influenced by a range of traditions, including positivism, social constructionism, post-structuralism, feminism and critical race theory. Other notable work in this vein was produced by former UEL colleagues Bipasha Ahmed, Pippa Dell, Clive Gabriel, Harriet Marshall, Celia Kitzinger and Paul Stenner, with this tradition continuing today among its current cohort of academic staff.

Successive generations of trainee and qualified psychologists have experienced the distinctive orientation of psychologists at UEL. For example, Mary Boyle and Richard Hallam provided challenging critiques of psychiatric diagnostic categories such as schizophrenia[4] and anxiety.[5] They argued that it was important to examine the social context and functions of psychological distress and behaviour that troubled social norms. Those who had trained on the UEL clinical psychology training programme had a distinctive way of looking psychologically at the world. In the 1990s this was one of the few such programmes taking seriously criticisms of conventional psychiatric and clinical psychological practice, and thinking through how one might take a different approach. As a result, some NHS clinical psychologists, a number of whom had trained at UEL, continue to draw on ideas from community psychology, and from social constructionist and systemic therapy approaches. This remains a refreshing counter to the individualising and de-contextualising focus of traditional approaches to understanding human misery and distress.

By the turn of the millennium, the approach of what had then become the clinical doctorate course had broadened even further with Nimisha Patel and colleagues critiquing clinical psychology's approach to 'race' and culture, and suggesting alternative approaches to practice.[6] Mary Boyle revised her book on schizophrenia, focusing more attention in its second edition on how psychiatric diagnosis served a range of social and cultural functions and was sustained by a medicalised assumptive framework and language.[7] Following Mary's retirement, the late Mark Rapley became programme director and continued this critical tradition, most notably through the two edited *De-medicalizing Misery* collections.[8]

One of the strengths and innovative qualities of psychology at UEL has been the way in which it has combined a critical approach to the 'psy' disciplines with a commitment to changing professional practice,[9] particularly through its professional psychology programmes. This approach has also been reflected in different ways in the School of Psychology's other public sector-oriented programmes, notably the professional doctorates in counselling psychology and educational psychology. Often, innovations developed in professional psychology training at UEL have moved from the margins to the mainstream. For example, the late Sheila Wolfendale, who was programme director of the educational psychology programme at UEL, championed the need to focus on children's early years and the importance of schools working collaboratively with parents years before these ideas became mainstream practice.

Innovating in courses and pedagogy

Since 1965, when the Psychology Department was established by John Radford, several examples of pioneering programmes of study at UEL have emerged, with each being part of leading an emerging trend at the time. The development of a wide variety of applied postgraduate training programmes has been a distinctive feature of the School of Psychology over many years. Few other academic departments in the UK have been able to offer in one location such an extensive range of professional postgraduate courses.

In the early 1970s, educational psychology training began at what was then NELP, led by Sheila Wolfendale, starting out as an MSc but later developing into a taught doctorate. In 1975, Andree Liddell, Martyn Baker and Richard Hallam set up one of the earliest clinical psychology training programmes in the UK – it likewise starting out as an MSc and thereafter morphing early into the now familiar three-year taught doctorate model. This was followed closely in 1978 by the opening of psychotherapy training. Ten years later in 1988, occupational and organisational psychology training started and today is the fourth oldest programme of its kind nationally as accredited by the British Psychological Society (BPS). In more recent times, as a result of the visionary leadership of the school's then head, David Rose, the first Master's in Applied Positive Psychology (MAPP) in Europe opened its doors at UEL in 2007, led by Ilona Boniwell.

The programme retained its leading flag status for several years, establishing a position as a hub for thought leadership and practice in this area of psychology internationally. Student numbers in the school reflect the vibrancy of this reputation, with a steady upward growth of on-campus and distance-learning student numbers – currently in the region of 350 students enrolled. Mindful of positive psychology's complementary relationship with coaching psychology, the two fields of psychological study were integrated into one programme at UEL in 2015, this being the first-ever such deliberate co-provision internationally. In keeping with this ethos for trendsetting, the school was an early provider of the now ever-popular MSc conversion programme, providing graduates with non-psychology first degrees a time-efficient pathway for obtaining recognition with the BPS and, thereafter, access to practitioner training. In similar vein, in 2019 our new MSc Integrative Counselling and Coaching was awarded professional accreditation from the British Association for Counselling and Psychotherapy (BACP), successfully demarcating itself thereby as the first and only such programme in the UK and Europe. Since the turn of the millennium, both positive psychology and coaching have delivered a remarkable boost to public awareness of the utility of psychology. In their own distinct ways, they have contributed to debates about epistemic justice: that is to say, who decides (wittingly or unwittingly) what gets to constitute 'proper' knowledge, and who and what is in or out in terms of accessing and defining such knowledge.

In all this, psychology at UEL has been an active architect in opening up the subject to the lay reader and to the professional non-psychologist. In part this has been because of abundant free-of-cost e-sharing of novel, user-friendly applications for optimising performance and skills for personal flourishing. Concepts such as resilience, emotional intelligence and character strengths are now deep in the fabric of (particularly western) social and professional dialogues. Teachings on our programmes have disseminated lifestyle options underpinned by the tangible habits of self-reflection, analytic reasoning and skills for deploying strengths, while recognising shortcomings, thereby promoting well-being, self-acceptance and greater readiness for optimal productivity. Arguably, UEL's cutting-edge courses have been at the forefront of changing the lexicon and substantive content of many ongoing national and international psychological conversations, and will continue to do so.

Critical clinical psychology at UEL – a case study in distinctiveness

Psychology at NELP began running the UK's first three-year master's degree in clinical psychology in 1975, others at the time being two years in duration. The programme has always been innovative in its intellectual approach and in pioneering novel ways of delivering training. On many clinical psychology courses, trainees had relatively short placements. So the NELP programme instituted a 'base placement' in the NHS with which trainees remained engaged over a two-year period, combining this with shorter placements in other specialties. By the early 1990s, when clinical psychology training programmes nationally moved to a model of three-year professional doctorates, UEL was in a good position to argue that it had, in effect, been running such a programme for some time. Mary Boyle recalls (personal communication) that the wider school and university were supportive both of the clinical psychology programme and, more generally, of a diverse approach to the teaching of psychology. From the beginning of the 1990s, following a major curriculum review, the training programme was critiquing psychiatric diagnosis and supporting the use of qualitative research methods – features which were felt to be radical by some outside the university. Moreover, when the programme applied to become a professional doctorate, Mary Boyle observed that university staff were energised by the idea, leading to intellectually stimulating debates about the role of universities in national life.

However, many challenges have been encountered when clinicians attempt to practise from a more critical and social perspective in the NHS. This has been the case because the medicalisation of human misery is still a dominant perspective in mental health care provision, and because ongoing policy incentives tend to privilege individualistic and reactive approaches (such as psychiatric medication or individual therapy) rather than ones which work at the level of the population or seek to address the structural causes of psychological distress.[10] Navigating these challenges has been an important theme in training at UEL. Managing the inevitable tensions which arise from this is a key task for trainees as they move through the programme.

Another challenge addressed by the course team is how to recruit a clinical psychology workforce that more closely resembles the populations it serves. At a national level, undergraduate psychology students are still predominantly white and female, while middle-class young people may be more financially able to acquire voluntary experience or undertake further study to improve their chances in a highly competitive selection process. This has been a long-running concern at UEL,[11] and has led to recent innovations, such as the introduction of online assessment of applicants, including a task requiring them to consider how best to respond to a series of vignettes presenting practical and ethical dilemmas.

A key aspect of professional clinical psychology training at UEL is the way in which it has been, to use a contemporary phrase, co-produced by staff at the university, practitioners and supervisors, those using psychology services and trainees, who, through their research and wide reading, alerted staff to important new methodological and conceptual resources. Through the 1990s, NHS clinical psychologists in Newham (UEL's borough) – with whom the programme had a close connection – developed a social constructionist systemic approach.[12] This offered a counter to psychology's engrained individualism by providing consultations which included the client's wider social network. This was particularly culturally appropriate given Newham's ethnically and culturally diverse population in which the Stratford campus and School of Psychology is situated. [13]

More recently, the clinical psychology programme, after another curriculum review, has consolidated specialised teaching on systemic family therapy and community psychology, and introduced an ethics and epistemology component examining their conceptual foundations and focusing on a range of 'protected characteristics' identified in the 2010 Equality Act. Staff on the programme continue to reflect on how best to address issues of 'race' and culture in clinical psychology teaching.[14] The programme's 'people's committee' (a group of service users and carers) continues to develop innovative ways to involve experts by experience in teaching, selection and assessment.

Still perturbing the discipline

UEL psychologists continue to ask questions of the discipline in a range of collaborative projects with colleagues both inside the university (such as through the Centre for Narrative Research, see Chapter 5) and outside – for example, proposing alternative approaches to the teaching of psychology.[15] Members of the school's mental health and social change research group have worked with colleagues in changing professional practice through BPS publications which have outlined an alternative approach to psychosis,[16] and in the 'power threat meaning framework', an alternative to medicalised approaches to distress and troubling conduct.[17] Rachel Tribe has been involved in developing a number of professional practice guidelines with the BPS, building on her interests in working with interpreters[18] and ethical issues.[19] John Read's work with colleagues in highlighting the problems of withdrawing from anti-depressants has led to a recent change in National Institute for Health and Care Excellence (NICE) guidelines.[20] Nimisha Patel continues to develop a distinctive human rights-based approach to applied psychology.[21]

A number of staff and students have become involved with groups such as Psychologists for Social Change (http://www.psychchange.org/) to increase public awareness of the links between psychological distress and social inequality.[22] Indeed, with the combination of deepening social inequality and psychology's tendency to avoid issues of social context and power, a critical approach to psychology and the development of alternative ways of practising it are needed perhaps now more than ever. UEL psychology continues to provide a lead forward into these issues and a challenge to the status quo in terms of teaching, research, theory and practice. It continues to speak its truth to power about questionable taken-for-granted psychological truths, whatever they may be and by whomsoever they are spoken. Reasoned debate imbued with carefully considered dissent has been a touchstone marker of UEL psychology.

Auditing research – quality matters

Contrary to the effects of the rose-tinted spectacles of biographical memory, progress in the school has not all been plain sailing. Since the periodic evaluation of the quality of research was instigated by Margaret Thatcher's government in 1986 as a way of allocating funding to UK universities, it has been only in the last two audits of research in 2008 and 2014 that UEL psychology has fully realised its potential within this domain of activity. In the most recent quality exercise, 100 per cent of its submitted research outputs were judged to be of two-star quality or above, with 60 per cent rated as of international quality (three-star or four-star). In 2008, 85 per cent of submitted outputs were rated as of two-star quality or above. In terms of the impact of research outside of academia, in 2014 UEL psychology research received a 100 per cent rating – an exceptional and outstanding result which testifies to the real-world practical utility of the work carried out in the school. Proportionate levels of funding council support followed on from these two sets of results, which for the last decade has made a significant difference to the buoyancy of psychology research at UEL. Before that though in 1992, 1996 and 2001, the results were disappointing, with perhaps overly optimistic numbers of staff submitted, with the consequence that the school on those occasions just missed out on the funding council's allocations.

The breadth of psychology in the school, however, has proved to be its saving grace, presenting both challenges and opportunities, with other UEL psychology staff being submitted to the audit's units of assessment for health, sociology, social policy and education, from where funding was secured during the 1990s and 2000s. At a national level, the perception was that the psychology unit of assessment (UoA) appeared to privilege quantitative, positivist research traditions, given the composition of the UoA panel. Fortunately, colleagues in a range of other schools across the university welcomed the inclusion of psychology staff whose work followed other epistemological traditions. Thereby, the School of Psychology adopted an approach which ensured that research outputs were submitted to the UoA most likely to judge the work on its own terms. As a result, psychology staff research has been submitted variously across five UoAs. The wisdom of this strategy has been evident when funding arose from these additional submissions, while on occasion it did not from the psychology UoA.

Nevertheless, lessons were learned from previous audits and subsequently concerted efforts made to secure better results from the psychology UoA submission. In 2003, Mark McDermott was appointed Brian Clifford's successor as school research leader. He worked determinedly for eight years in that role alongside other psychology colleagues (most notably Derek Moore, David Rose and Mark Davies) to ensure that the outcome of the 2008 and 2014 assessments properly reflected the quality of research ongoing within the school. Ian Tucker now leads UEL psychology into the 2021 research assessment submission, with the national rules of engagement having changed once again. So, as before, preparations are under way, with the outcome known in due course. We remain realistically optimistic.

Past, present and an informed future

At the time of writing, in the latter part of 2019, the School of Psychology at UEL offers twenty-one academic programmes, approximately half undergraduate and half postgraduate, including three professional doctorate programmes. All of these courses are taught by experts in their field, with academic staff numbering nearly 120. Arguably the ethos of psychology at UEL still embodies the aspirations of its founders – higher education as vocational, personally transformative and concerned with things-that-matter. This applied emphasis endures and preoccupies our collective efforts ongoing. So, we look to the past and our beginnings to inform continuity into the future, with awareness of our heritage, capturing this in the 'root to rise' theme of our first annual pop-up museum (September 2018) curated in the school's research laboratory suite in our home, Arthur Edwards Building – a building that owes its existence in large part to the efforts of one-time deputy head of school, Ernie Govier. At the university level, the school's values find consonance with and expression in the current vice-chancellor's 'Vision 2028': to become over the next decade the leading careers-focused, enterprising university in the UK. At school level, this vocational focus is reflected through high-calibre academic and professional training programmes that are intentionally oriented to prepare graduates to contribute to current social, economic and industry located needs. Our commitment to systematic and scholarly-informed applications of psychological knowledge to address real-life issues is also a conspicuous feature of the school's portfolio of research projects, psychosocial interventions and commissioned work.

Throughout our history, since 1962 when psychology was first taught at UEL's forerunner, academic rigour and psychological application through the lens of civic engagement have enabled the flourishing of the school's identity and continues to shape its future trajectory. As we continue to dwell inexorably in the age of the digital revolution, old important philosophical and existential questions necessarily will resurface. What does it mean to be human? From what do we most derive meaning? How does the confluence of nature and nurture continue to reconstruct the human condition and our experience of it? How effectively psychology as a human science responds to such questions in the years ahead will be a pivotal test of its character and ingenuity. Doubtless, UEL psychology, as part of that response and given its track record to date, will continue to reinvent itself, pushing at the boundaries of the subject, finding new ways to prepare successive generations of students to contribute, to make a difference, to lead and innovate in the face of the challenges that lie ahead.

Notes

1. J. Radford and D. Rose, *A Liberal Science: Psychology Education Past, Present and Future,* Open University Press: Milton Keynes, 1989.
2. G. Richards, *Putting Psychology in its Place – Critical Historical Perspectives,* Routledge: London, first edition, 1996.
3. G. Richards, *Race, Racism and Psychology: Towards a Reflexive History,* Psychology Press: London, first edition, 1997.
4. M. Boyle, *Schizophrenia: A Scientific Delusion?,* Routledge: London, 1990.
5. R. S. Hallam, 'Some constructionist observations on "anxiety" and its history', T.R. Sarbin and J.I. Kitsuse (eds), *Constructing the Social,* Sage: London, 1994, pp139-156. R. Hallam, 'Agoraphobia: Deconstructing a clinical syndrome', *Bulletin of the British Psychological Society,* 36, 1983, pp337-340.
6. N. Patel, E. Bennett, M. Dennis, N. Dosanjh, A. Miller, A. Mahtani *et al., Clinical Psychology, 'Race' and Culture: A Resource Pack for Trainers,* BPS Books: Leicester, 2000.
7. M. Boyle, *Schizophrenia: A Scientific Delusion*? Routledge: London, revised second edition, 2002.
8. J. Moncrieff, M. Rapley and E. Speed (eds), *De-medicalizing misery II: Society, Politics and the Mental Health Industry,* Palgrave MacMillan:

Basingstoke, 2014; M. Rapley, J. Dillon and J. Moncrieff (eds), *De-medicalising Misery*, Palgrave Macmillan: Basingstoke, 2011.

9. See for example: R. Bayne and I. Horton (eds), *Applied Psychology: Current Issues and New Directions*, Sage: London, 2003; R. Bayne and G. Jinks (eds), *Applied psychology: Practice, training and new directions*, Sage: London, second revised edition, 2013.
10. D. Harper, 'Beyond individual therapy: Towards a psychosocial approach to public mental health', *The Psychologist,* 29 June 2016, pp440-444: https://thepsychologist.bps.org.uk/volume-29/june/beyond-individual-therapy.
11. M. Boyle, M. Baker, E. Bennett and T. Charman, 'Selection for clinical psychology courses: a comparison of applicants from ethnic minority and majority groups to the University of East London', *Clinical Psychology Forum*, 56, 1993, pp9-13.
12. I. Ekdawi, S. Gibbons, E. Bennett and G. Hughes, *Whose Reality is it Anyway? Putting Social Constructionist Philosophy into Everyday Clinical Practice*, Pavilion Publishing: Brighton, 2001.
13. K. Partridge, E. Bennett, A. Webster, I. Ekdawi, 'Consultation with clients: An alternative way of working in adult mental health', *Clinical Psychology Forum*, September 1995, pp26-28.
14. K. Berg, M. Castro Romero, D. Harper, N. Patel, T. Patel, N. Rees and R. Smith, 'Why we are still talking about race?', *Clinical Psychology Forum*, 323, 2019, pp8-12.
15. J. Cromby, D. Harper and P. Reavey, *Psychology, Mental Health and Distress*, Palgrave Macmillan: Basingstoke, 2013; S. Peacock-Brennan, D. Harper and N. Patel, 'Developing policy-relevant skills in clinical psychology training', *Clinical Psychology Forum*, 301, January 2018, pp 9-14.
16. A. Cooke (ed.), 'Understanding psychosis and schizophrenia: Why people sometimes hear voices, believe things that others find strange, or appear out of touch with reality, and what can help', British Psychological Society Division of Clinical Psychology: Leicester, revised version, 2017: http://www.bps.org.uk/networks-and-communities/member-microsite/division-clinical-psychology/understanding-psychosis-and-schizophrenia
17. L. Johnstone and M. Boyle, with J. Cromby, J. Dillon, D. Harper, P. Kinderman, E. Longden, D. Pilgrim and J. Read, 'The Power Threat Meaning Framework: Towards the identification of patterns in emotional distress, unusual experiences and troubled or troubling behaviour, as an alternative to functional psychiatric diagnosis', British Psychological Society: Leicester, 2018: www.bps.org.uk/PTM-Main

18. R. Tribe and H. Raval (eds), *Working with Interpreters in Mental Health*, Routledge: London, 2002.

19. R. Tribe and J. Morrissey (eds), *Handbook of Professional and Ethical Practice for Psychologists, Counsellors and Psychotherapists*, Routledge: London, second edition, 2015.

20. E. Rhodes, 'When we look back in 20 years' time, this will be a turning point', *The Psychologist*, 32, November 2019, p17: https://thepsychologist.bps.org.uk/when-we-look-back-20-years-time-will-be-turning-point.

21. N. Patel, 'Human Rights-Based Approach to Applied Psychology', *European Psychologist*, 24, 2019, pp113-124: https://doi.org/10.1027/1016-9040/a000371.

22. C. Jones, V. Griffin, S. Peacock-Brennan, R. H. Tribe, C. O'Mahony and J. Cheetham (Psychologists for Social Change), 'The social and political origins of wellbeing: A critique of Action for Happiness', D. Frayne (ed.), *The Work Cure: Critical Essays on Work and Wellness*, PCCS Books: Monmouth, 2019; L. McGrath, V. Griffin, E. Mundy, 'The psychological impact of austerity: A briefing paper', Psychologists Against Austerity: London, 2015: https://psychagainstausterity.files.wordpress.com/2015/03/paa-briefing-paper.pdf

CHAPTER SEVENTEEN

The emergence of psychosocial studies

Barry Richards and Joanne Brown

Context

Psychosocial studies is now a recognised niche in the division of academic labour. Since 2013 it has been represented by a scholarly body, the Association for Psychosocial Studies, which is UK-based but has members globally, and which publishes through Policy Press the *Journal of Psychosocial Studies*. Academics in PSS, as we will call it here, believe that psychology and the social sciences have different objects of study but that these can and must be conjoined or integrated in some way if we are to achieve the best and most useful ways of understanding human experience and behaviour. It is therefore an interdisciplinary project, which aspires to influence understandings and practices in a wide range of professional areas, and to generate innovative research agendas on many important social issues. It is now represented in a number of undergraduate programmes in British universities, and it is seen as their intellectual 'home' by academics from many disciplines teaching and researching in widely different contexts on many topics.

The term 'psychosocial studies' first appeared on an undergraduate programme in 1983, in an area of post-industrial, pre-redevelopment desolation in East London: to be precise, in an abandoned cigarette factory situated just off a roaring main road into Central London. Livingstone House was an outpost of the North East London Polytechnic (NELP), one of several disused buildings in the Stratford area acquired when NELP was stitched together from a number of pre-existing institutions in the 1970s. The nearest tube station was a fifteen-minute walk away along the bleak arterial road.

NELP's larger buildings in West Ham and Barking (and for a while Waltham Forest) were more suitable and better placed, but some of its departments were housed in the smaller re-purposed buildings of its scattered estate. Sociology and cultural studies were together for much of the 1980s in Livingstone House – interrupted by a period in a nearby Victorian primary school building formerly occupied by the Psychology Department. This period began abruptly one morning when staff were told to evacuate Livingstone House immediately because asbestos (at risk of releasing pathogenic fibres as it deteriorated) had been discovered in its structure, and had to be removed. Some months of resilience and improvisation later, normal service was resumed at Livingstone House, but the episode illustrated the makeshift and impoverished infrastructure inside which some of the creative NELP versions of undergraduate education were being developed. In this inhospitable context there developed strong staff teams, committed to social justice and to addressing social inequality.

In the 1980s, students paid no fees and were given maintenance grants, but by the late 1980s, when the psychosocial studies programme was beginning to recruit significant numbers of students, the erosion of grants had begun and the introduction of fees was on the horizon. Fortunately, in 1990 a new building was erected on a field at the Barking site and the occupants of Livingstone House transferred there. It was admittedly a short-life modular building, but provided an agreeable space to work, on a campus. So as the financial pressures began to bear more heavily on students, they at least escaped the shabby and insecure environment which the first seven cohorts of psychosocial studies students had endured.

Yet in that environment, the Sociology Department had been offering a thriving undergraduate programme, one which was intellectually rich while also bearing a strong professional orientation, as mentioned in the Introduction, towards the welfare sector.

Its students included many first-generation undergraduates from the working-class and ethnically mixed populations of the London region who could see around them in the 1980s and 1990s growth in the social services broadly speaking, including the expanding voluntary sector. As well as growth in qualified social work itself, new agencies and roles were appearing in the fields of mental health, youth and community work, housing, drug and addiction services, and the emergent counselling profession. In these areas they could see possibilities for upward social mobility which did not necessarily involve leaving their own communities, and which – as we will discuss further – addressed their own personal identities and aspirations. This was the specific basis for the opportunity to develop an undergraduate programme in psychosocial studies, since new courses then as now had to be justified in terms of their potential market.

Another factor necessary for the development of PSS was that the Sociology Department had a small number of psychologists (Margaret O'Brien, Barry Richards, Anna Witham) who were involved in teaching on the social work professional option, and had also been involved in a freestanding social work course and various post-qualifying nursing courses offered by the polytechnic's Department of Health and Social Studies, which at one time had also occupied Livingstone House. There had always been a basic psychology course as part of the first-year core of the sociology degree, one feature of its intellectual breadth. Overall then, there existed a combination of factors favourable to the emergence of something like PSS: students looking for careers in the helping professions; an expanding and diversifying welfare sector; and a body of psychological expertise inside a department which was in the business of blending a social science education with professionally relevant trainings.

Curriculum and faculty

The three psychologists were all eager to identify with the rubric of 'psychosocial studies'. They were not comfortable in mainstream academic psychology, and had deep interests in the social, cultural, political and organisational contexts of individual experience, seeing themselves as interdisciplinary academics. All also had clinical trainings and experience as part of their CVs, which helped to ensure that the ethos of the course, while as academically intensive as any other, was closely influenced by agendas and preoccupations outside of academia. This coupling of the academic and clinical became a core feature of PSS. On the sociology side, the main contributors were Mike Rustin and Mike Smee, a sociologist of education. Units across various iterations of the course included: 'accounts of the individual', examining the history of attempts at psychosocial syntheses (Richards, Smee); developmental psychology (Heather Price), comparing Piagetian and other classical accounts of development with the psychoanalytic; family studies (Margaret O'Brien, Shelley Day Sclater), combining the social history of the family with systemic and other theoretical approaches to family dynamics; love, intimacy and modernity (Joanne Brown), comparing different conceptions of romantic love from psychoanalytic to sociological; psychoanalysis, culture and society (Amal Treacher); humour (Iain MacRury); film (two units, led by Caroline Bainbridge and Candida Yates); and crime (David Jones).

The term 'psychosocial' had previously been used mainly in the context of theoretical approaches to training health and welfare professionals (as in 'psychosocial nursing'), but had also been used, on a grander scale, to address the heart of human civilisation by the psychoanalyst and social theorist Erik Erikson. It seemed a good fit for the aspirations of the new venture. It had associations with psychodynamic approaches, but not exclusively so. It was important that the new 'subject area', as it became called when a modular system was introduced, was to some degree pluralistic, to reflect staff interests and to maximise potential student interest. Social psychology (Alison Thomas), systemic (Rabia Malik) and humanistic approaches were other presences in the curriculum. Counselling skills units were taught in a basically integrative mode (Caroline Hickman, Stephen Briggs *et al.*), and mental health (David Jones *et al.*) introduced students to the history of psychiatry and the service user movement. Work discussion groups were conducted using different approaches, including psychoanalytic. Qualitative and quantitative research methods were taught (Phil Bradbury).

However, the strong influence of psychoanalytic approaches within the curriculum was always present, and as the area expanded and more posts were recruited, there were strong applicants with psychoanalytic interests. Many staff had also had long personal analyses and their interest in psychoanalysis was, therefore, also rooted in an effort to understand the unfolding of their own lives.

The development of links with the Tavistock Clinic (see Chapter 20) also added to the psychoanalytic work of the PSS team. While Tavistock courses were not directly linked to the psychosocial programme, some PSS staff were active in the Tavistock, mainly in the MA Psychoanalytic Studies, launched in 1992 and co-led with a Tavistock clinician, at different times by Richards, Brown and Price. This immersion in the clinical field at the Tavistock inevitably affected how psychoanalysis was taught on the BA. In the other direction, Stephen Briggs of the Tavistock became a part-time lecturer in PSS, and Andrew Cooper became the UEL/Tavistock professor of social work.

The first 'Psychoanalysis and the public sphere' conference was organised in 1987 as a joint venture between UEL (then still NELP) and the psychoanalytic journal *Free Associations*, and had PSS students as the conference hospitality team. (There is another article to be written, which would overlap a little with this one, about UEL's role in the creation of psychoanalytic studies, seen either as an overlapping area of research and teaching or as a specialism within the territory of the psychosocial.) These annual conferences ran until 2001, and brought together PSS academics and clinicians interested in applied psychoanalysis. Clinicians also came to give annual lectures to PSS students.

In parallel with the psychoanalytic base, a group of staff was building up with a common interest in narrative methods (Molly Andrews, Shelley Day Sclater, Corinne Squire, Maria Tamboukou), which led to the formation of the Centre for Narrative Research in 2000 (see Chapter 5). A second major presence within the PSS curriculum was thus established, distinct from the psychoanalytic though linked in various ways, initially through the life histories unit developed by the sociologist and poet Carole Satyamurti. Perspectives brought by colleagues initially trained in cultural studies, another important element in the area's academic heritage, could also feed into both psychoanalytic and narrative work. PSS at UEL, therefore, allowed for differences of opinion and a robust conversation between a more social constructionist narrative studies approach and some of the universalist and essentialist claims of psychoanalysis. It also allowed for some creative diversity in the field of new research methods reflecting psychosocial principles (in which the work of Wendy Hollway,[1] one of the external examiners of the PSS degree, has been influential).

Colleagues from all sides of the PSS team at UEL have been researching and writing since its inception. As the Research Excellence Framework (the REF, formerly the Research Assessment Exercise, RAE) became established on the British university scene, the works of UEL's PSS academics were valued parts of its submissions to the broad church of the sociology unit of assessment (UoA) (though at other universities PSS work has been submitted to other UoAs). A collection of the main writings of those who have been in the team over the years would be a very thick volume, and would be an important reader covering large areas of the psychosocial territory.[2] Much of it extends far beyond the welfare-oriented agenda, which was at the heart of the early development of the educational offer, into studies of culture and politics.

The emergence of British 'cultural studies' as an academic specialism had strongly influenced the Sociology Department from its NELP days onwards, with a number of its lecturers having been researchers at the Birmingham Centre for Contemporary Cultural Studies. As described in Chapter 6, the work of that centre had also shaped the UEL cultural studies degree, and its influence flowed on into psychosocial studies, in teaching on film and consumer culture. A link with the neighbouring Department of Cultural Studies led, in 1994, to the setting up of the Centre for Consumer and Advertising Studies, with a historical and psychosocial research agenda, which in turn led to the development in 2000 of UEL's undergraduate programme in advertising and media.

The theoretical and empirical richness of cultural studies in the 1980s and 1990s meant that both the psychoanalytic and narrative strands of PSS could connect with it. However, there was inevitably a tension between the necessary vocational, applied agenda of PSS and the tendency in cultural studies towards 'deconstructive' critique of practices and institutions, which did not always sit comfortably with commitments to practice, nor with the essentialist tendencies in psychoanalysis. Among some academics there is also disquiet with the employability agenda in HE, sometimes seen as intellectually limiting, perhaps especially in relation to the relatively low-status professional sectors of care and welfare. In our experience, PSS combined a commitment to practice and employability with intellectual substance. Its interdisciplinary nature means that staff and students have to move between different academic terrains as well as requiring reflexive academic work. Opportunities for supported placement work have, therefore, been available within the psychosocial studies programme for much of its existence, often linked with a Tavistock model of 'work discussion' sessions, in which careful observation and self-reflection have been encouraged as tools for understanding both the dynamics of the workplace and the student's relationship to it. As student:staff ratios have increased, this kind of input becomes very hard to sustain. Still, the 'employability' agenda that characterised PSS protected it from the sharper falls in recruitment which affected some courses after the raising of student fees to £9000 per annum in 2012.

Students

At first psychosocial studies was a pathway added to the sociology degree, and as an unfamiliar novelty it struggled to recruit many students. An early staff-student party for the course team and all students was easily accommodated in the living room of a staff member's small flat. However, it slowly consolidated its place in the department and was well placed to benefit from the rapid expansion of student numbers nationally at the end of the 1980s. Two institutional shifts also enabled its student numbers to grow, and so strengthened its economic base.

One was the introduction of a modular framework. This was firstly in the form of a 'Multi-Subject DipHE', a programme within the university which, as the name suggests, offered various combinations to DipHE level of certain subjects. This established PSS as a subject area separate from the sociology degree. Second, in the early 1990s, there was a recasting of the university's entire undergraduate offer within a modular framework. Most subjects could then be taken to degree level as single honours courses or in combined honours with another subject as major, joint or minor. The flexibility this offered was attractive to many students, and it gave new or marginal subjects the chance of broadening their recruitment base. PSS was able to recruit between 100 and 220 students each year for much of the 1990s. While not large by some of today's standards, this intake was a serious contribution to the university's numbers, and it underpinned the creation in 1995 of a new department, the Department of Human Relations, which separated off from sociology taking with it PSS and the free-standing social work qualification (the Diploma in Social Work).

The second shift was in the national abolition of limits on student numbers and the consequent loosening at UEL and many other institutions of admissions criteria, such that the gateway of entry to the PSS degree became almost fully open. 'MNQ' students (mature non-qualified, that is, twenty-five and over with no A-levels, and possibly no formal educational qualifications) became a majority. Many came from what would now be called 'widening participation' postcodes. The borough of Newham, for example, which lay between the Stratford and Barking sites of UEL, ranked highly on the 'Jarman' index of deprivation. And many had little post-sixteen educational experience apart from an access to higher education course at a local college.

The student population was always predominantly female, to varying degrees, and (like many other metropolitan 'modern' universities) with much higher proportions of black and minority ethnic recruits than in the HE sector as a whole. There have also been much lower proportions of the traditional 'middle-class' undergraduate, with very few having university-educated parents. Significant numbers struggle with personal problems, so referral rates and attrition rates have been high. Especially in the earlier years, UEL offered little in the way of the social and cultural pleasures and rewards of a lively university community. But the aspirations towards upward mobility, and the hunger for greater understanding of the social world and for greater self-knowledge, were powerful motivators.

One feature that was typical of most PSS students, whatever their ethnicity and geographical home, was a sense of preoccupation with personal identity and personal experience. This was partly anxiety-driven; these were often young people who did not feel fully at home in their families or communities of origin, but were not sure where or how they might find themselves. Many of them were engaged (often knowingly) in 'identity work', at various levels of intensity. The PSS curriculum offered something distinctively helpful in that work, with its 'psycho-' emphases on reflexivity, life history and emotional development linked to close '-social' study of how differences in experience can be determined by societal structures around gender, race, class and sexuality.

At the same time, there was a different kind of identity-driven motive to study PSS, an assertive social identity and consciousness of social injustice, whether the identity was as black, mixed race, gay, British Asian, female, Muslim, single parent, or whatever 'intersectional' combination of these and other identities an individual felt themselves to have. For this consciousness, the PSS curriculum offered support in the search for a voice: academic sources of help in legitimating that identity, understanding its origins and its present predicaments. The turn to identity that helped to drive recruitment to PSS was part of a wider socio-political shift, which was to an important extent an individualising one. The rise of identity politics is often linked to the decline of class-based politics, a connection expressed at UEL in the way that as PSS student numbers rose, so those in sociology, which had thrived nationally as an undergraduate subject choice from the 1960s through to the 1980s, were in decline. The key principle ceases to be attachment to the particular collective of the 'working class', and is replaced by commitment to whatever particular identity/ies an individual might experience as theirs. However it should be noted that a preoccupation with identity is often closely linked to an assertion of belonging (typically, in many of the contexts where identity has become salient, to a group that is seen as marginalised).

No doubt many other curricula in the humanities and social sciences offer something to undergraduates (narratives, ideas, models and so forth) to support their efforts to define themselves. So PSS was not unique among undergraduate subjects in providing this resource, but it did so with a particular intensity and, in its more reflective modes and its focus on personal development, with an explicit address to the individual experience of each student. Moreover, the inclusion of psychoanalysis in PSS and the influence of the UEL-Tavistock partnership was distinctive. Brown and Price took Freud's 1919 paper 'Should psychoanalysis be taught at the university?' as a starting point for thinking about the emotional effect of learning and teaching about psychoanalysis at a university and not in the consulting room.[3] Freud said that psychoanalytic thought brought students 'nearer to the problems of life in general', and a psychoanalytically inflected PSS did this too. That is, the material itself could act as a mirror to oneself. Inevitably we were introducing students to the influence of our early lives on our present life, and to theories of loss, psychic pain, sociological suffering and conflict. Of course, there was also a discourse of emotional strength, of discovery and repair, and of the deep pleasures of popular culture, but the material had the capacity to stir us all up.

As Wittenberg (1983) said, any learning experience can trigger 'an agony of helplessness'[4] as we confront newness and not knowing, but we were adding to this a subject which invited deep reflexivity about the nature of the self. Of course, in this respect, a reflective psychoanalytically informed PSS could be seen as an example of the 'dangerous rise of therapeutic education' lambasted by Ecclestone and Hayes.[5] For them, therapeutic pedagogy infantilises us, rendering us all vulnerable learners who must be protected from robust academic challenge. But, as already stated, PSS conjoined a reflective capacity with rigorous academic scholarship.

The preoccupying question in the 1999 paper cited above was whether the university setting offered containment and security for identity work, and for the emotional experience of learning and teaching in PSS. For example, for many PSS students doing the degree was an attempt to rewrite the narrative and trajectory of their lives. Being attentive to this emotional aspect of learning became particularly difficult when PSS expanded and classes could be 250-plus. Staff then had less mental space to respond to the volume of need, exemplified by office hours seeing queues of students along the length of corridors. And for this emotion work, staff also needed holding. For this reason, we employed a Tavistock organisational consultant (Tim Dartington) to consult with PSS staff about the emotional challenges of teaching and learning in the context of HE mass expansion, and in a subject area which 'disturbed the world's sleep'. Hence there was a strong element of reflective practice which informed the teaching and learning in UEL's PSS.

The belief of some staff in the value of the reflective approach to placements, and indeed to the curriculum as a whole, has been matched in the enthusiasm and seriousness with which some students have taken it up. They can use it to understand, for example, the ways in which their own (often difficult) life experiences can enable them to empathise with the various client/service user groups they may be in contact with, and also to be alert to the risks of over-identification with clients. They could benefit from experiencing the very sophisticated and personal educational experience which it offered. Whether interested in its professional dimensions or not, some students have developed very strong identifications with PSS, finding what may have been an unexpected academic 'home'.

This 'homeness' is of course true for staff too. Graduates of PSS at UEL are now at the forefront of expanding and leading the area at UEL (Darren Ellis, Lurraine Jones) and second and third generations of PSS staff (such as Angie Voela, Nicola Diamond, Helen Powell) continue the work which started in 1983. It isn't possible to list all of the many who have been involved up until now, and their distinctive contributions, but we hope to have pointed to the continuing growth and creativity of PSS.

Significance and influence

Psychosocial studies at UEL is still a going concern, so any attempt at overall assessment of what it has contributed to higher education and to the wider society must be provisional. However, it was already possible in its early years to understand its significance in some ways which are still true of it today.

First, it was part of the democratisation of higher education in Britain, a process begun in the 1960s post-Robbins report major expansion of the university sector, continued with the establishment of polytechnics in the 1970s and then turbocharged in the 1980s and 1990s with government targets for higher participation rates. As student numbers rose it was uplifting to see classrooms filling up with unprivileged young people presenting themselves with hope and ambition, their horizons stretched beyond those of their parents. At times, this was also unsettling for staff, when we were not meeting some of their expectations, or when we did not have the resources to meet their needs. With hindsight, the downsides of the unmanaged expansion of HE have become more visible. Without going here into the complex sociological and economic debates around that, we can say that the opportunities for personal development afforded by a university education should be universally available: everyone should have in adolescence or early adulthood an invitation to wider social and cultural experience, and a supportive environment for self-discovery and to contribute to society's understanding of itself and to change. There should be other gateways to those benefits, outside of HE. However, insofar as universities are a major provider of those opportunities, they should be offering, *inter alia*, curricula and pedagogic approaches which are particularly designed to support personal development. The emergence of PSS was, therefore, among initiatives across the whole sector which qualitatively and quantitatively contributed to the beneficial effects of higher participation in undergraduate studies.

Second, psychosocial studies has been a very small part of the broad cultural transformation which is still under way, and which is the development of what has been called 'therapeutic culture'. This term refers to a complex set of trends seen globally in recent decades. An interest in psychology has become a mass phenomenon, higher levels of emotional expressivity have become the norm, and a belief in the possibility of improving life through self-awareness and self-reflection has become widespread (as see in, for example, the influence of concepts such as emotional literacy and emotional intelligence). The therapeutic is a major phenomenon in contemporary popular culture, and has appeared in the social sciences and humanities as the 'turn to affect'. The psychoanalytic and the narrative approaches which the UEL PSS curriculum has promoted are important intellectual drivers of both of these developments, and its students are certainly asked to consider the potential benefits of psychotherapeutic work for both individuals and society. However, PSS also hosts a debate between the more positive views of the therapeutic, and the critiques of it as promoting narcissism and sentimentality. Thus it is reflexive about its own location in this cultural trend.

What we will turn to finally is the question of what influence PSS's existence at UEL has had, beyond its effects on the lives of its thousands of students, and the families, friends, colleagues, clients and others whom they have gone on to live their lives with. Those are, of course, its most important effects, but we don't know enough about them to generalise. Institutionally, we have already noted some cases of its value to UEL in successive REFs, in supporting the Tavistock link and in seeding the creation of another innovative undergraduate programme. Members of the Centre for Narrative Research, in particular, have also had significant success in generating research income.

With regard to its impact within wider academia, it is tempting to claim that, as the site of the first course in psychosocial studies, UEL played a catalytic role in the development of other programmes, and that the research outputs of the UEL team have been founding contributions to the development of PSS as a recognised zone on the map of international research in the social sciences and humanities. A research project on the networks and chronologies involved would be necessary to back up such a claim, but whatever the exact chains of influence and effect have been, we can take satisfaction in the fact that UEL played a major pioneering role. PSS has gone on to become formally established in various ways (in curricula, course titles, job titles, research agendas, etc.) in several British universities (such as Birkbeck, Essex, University of the West of England, University of Central Lancashire, Brighton), and to become the explicit 'home' for many researchers from a range of disciplinary backgrounds and with interests in widely different topics.

Conclusion

UEL has not always been the most facilitating of institutional homes for PSS. It has, over the years, had more than its share of chaos, and PSS staff have rarely felt cherished by its senior management. In the 1980s, the Sociology Department was frequently under threat of closure, and a proposed reorganisation in 2011-12 would have seen the end of PSS. Like many other subject areas and departments in many other institutions, it has not been able to see itself as adequately resourced within a containing organisational environment.

But it has much more than survived, as have some other academic projects initiated in the pre-'92 polytechnic sector, as this book shows. Like many of the polytechnics, NELP/PEL followed a path of development which subverted the plan for polytechnics to provide degree-level education of a kind differentiated from that of universities by a clear orientation towards a vocational/professional course portfolio, and less emphasis on research. The unification of the sector in 1992 was in part an acknowledgment that the differentiation had failed to hold, mainly because many academic staff in the polys wanted to teach more academically based curricula, and wanted to do research and to publish. UEL was a strong example of an ex-poly which had achieved outstanding excellence in some academic fields, particularly cultural studies, where because of its recent emergence there were no established strengths in older universities and so no existing hierarchy of institutions. In the case of psychosocial studies, there was not even a pre-defined field with any consensus among its occupants as to what it should contain and why. And as the field has expanded, the scope for dissensus has increased. The Association for Psychosocial Studies is vital to the continuation of the field as an academic specialism, yet has to manage some competing visions of its priorities and purposes. Hopefully at UEL, on its purpose-built Docklands site since 2003, the PSS area will continue to embody and promote the kinds of work with which it has been associated since it first poked through the cracks in an old factory building in East London.

Acknowledgments

Many thanks to David Jones and Heather Price, key PSS team members for many years, for informative comments on an earlier draft of this chapter.

Notes

1. See, for example, W. Hollway and T. Jefferson, *Doing Qualitative Research Differently,* Sage: London, 2012.
2. At the end of this note we list a very small number of the outputs involving UEL PSS academics, as authors and editors. This is simply an indicative sample of the large and diverse body of work produced across the last four decades in monographs, edited books and journals. M. Andrews, S. Day Sclater, C. Squire and A. Treacher (eds), *Lines of Narrative: Psychosocial Perspectives,* Routledge: London, 2000; S. Day Sclater, D. Jones, H. Price and C. Yates (eds), *Emotion: New Psychosocial Perspectives,* Palgrave: Basingstoke, 2009; C. Bainbridge, S. Radstone, M. Rustin and C. Yates (eds), *Culture and the Unconscious,* Palgrave: Basingstoke, 2007.
3. J. Brown and H. Price, 'Teaching psychoanalysis: an impossible art?', *Psychoanalytic Studies,* 1(1), 1999, pp87-102.
4. I. Wittenberg, *The Emotional Experience of Learning and Teaching,* Routledge: London, 1983.
5. K. Ecclestone and D. Hayes, *The Dangerous Rise of Therapeutic Education,* Routledge: London, second edition, 2019.

CHAPTER EIGHTEEN

Refugee studies – the East London experience

Philip Marfleet

For almost 350 years, East London has been a place of refuge for people displaced by repression, war, civil conflict and economic crisis. In the seventeenth century, the first people formally recognised as *réfugiés*, the Calvinist Huguenots of France, settled in large numbers in Whitechapel. An increasingly diverse and rapidly expanding East End subsequently received refugees from across Europe and, by the twentieth century, from proliferating crises worldwide. By the 1990s London was widely seen as the 'refugee capital' of Europe – one compelling reason for the University of East London to establish the city's first dedicated course in refugee studies.

Since the 1970s, the University of East London (UEL) had admitted 'non-traditional' students – those who had not passed through phases of secondary education that usually provided qualifications for university entry. Among these were refugees whose education had been disrupted or deferred as a result of displacement during conflicts in Africa, Asia and the Middle East, many associated with the final collapse of colonial regimes. By the 1990s these students were joined by those displaced during new crises in Latin America and Eastern Europe, and by young people from refugee families – young Londoners with complex experiences of diasporic life across the continents. It was engagement with these students that in 1997 prompted a small group of academic staff to establish a dedicated postgraduate programme in refugee studies.

This was an unusual initiative, especially at a time of increasing hostility to refugees – the enactment of exclusionary policies and the construction of a 'Fortress Europe'. It was facilitated by existing multidisciplinary initiatives at the university, especially programmes in the social sciences which undertook critical analyses of culture, 'race', ethnicity, gender and human rights. Benefiting from the independent critical culture fostered at UEL, the programme soon attracted large numbers of students and became established internationally as a centre for the study of forced migration. This chapter examines the distinctive character of refugee studies at UEL – a focus on migrants' lived experience and social agency which continues to challenge increasingly hostile discourses on migration and policies of exclusion in the UK and worldwide.

Refuge

The refugee is a creation of the modern state. The idea of sanctuary under the authority of national governments emerged in the seventeenth century as the power of religious bodies in Europe diminished. Protection of fugitives, escapees, and victims of feuds, local conflicts and wars had for centuries been a privilege of the church. Buildings and estates of the church had divine protection: according to canon law they were inviolable and people in need could claim sanctuary within churches, monasteries and shrines or within a certain radius of the *sanctum*, usually the altar. In certain states, however, church privileges were contested by other centres of power, notably by the absolute monarchies of England and France.[1]

When in the 1680s Louis XIV of France expelled hundreds of thousands of religious dissenters, the Protestant Huguenots, the English state – eager to capture their skills, capital and commercial energies – offered them 'an asylum'. For the first time large numbers of people received formal guarantees of protection from a nation-state – the English parliament assured their safety and raised funds widely to support them. Some 100,000 *réfugiés* settled in London – the Huguenot elite in Soho, and the craftspeople and artisans, who made up the majority of migrants, in Whitechapel.[2]

The refugees made an important mark upon the east of the city. Their chapel in Spitalfields, La Neuve Eglise, built in 1743, was to be an institutional site for successive migrant communities. In 1891 it became Machzike Hadath, the great synagogue, serving Lithuanian Jewish refugees. In 1976 it was re-consecrated as the Jamme Masjid, the congregational mosque of the Bangladeshi community – a further expression of the complex migration histories of the area.

Throughout the nineteenth century, refugees arrived in East London from across Europe. Most were then known as 'political exiles' – people escaping repression that followed political upheavals, notably the revolutions of 1848. The East End was often their place of arrival: London's docks were concentrated in the east and the area was already home to a diverse population that reflected the reach of imperial networks and maritime routes. Jewish refugees from the Russian empire settled in Whitechapel; activists from Western Europe favoured Clerkenwell, popularly described in mid-century as 'little Germany'.[3] The Germans also made their mark on the city, establishing several Lutheran churches and the German Hospital in Hackney. When at the end of the nineteenth century an intensification of antisemitism in Russia and Eastern Europe brought larger movements of refugees, the immigrants settled more widely across the east of the city.

Hidden from history

These repeated migrations made their mark on people of the East End but not upon official narratives. In official histories – constructed by professional historians, archivists and writers – refugees were largely absent. This was consistent with practices that went back to the earliest years of the modern state. Although emergence of the nation-state was everywhere associated with processes of exclusion and selective inclusion, as in the case of the Huguenots, refugees remained outsiders who were seldom allocated a place in the national narrative.

When in 1914 over 250,000 refugees from Belgium entered England as result of military offensives during the first world war, over a third were allocated to temporary homes in London. They too were rendered invisible by mainstream historians – a practice that American historian Ali Behdad describes as the 'disremembering' of migrants in the service of narrating a 'unified imagined community'.[4] In specific circumstances refugees were treated differently, notably when Jewish refugees from fascism were reluctantly granted asylum in Britain in the late 1930s, and when in the 1950s and 1960s refugees from the Soviet Union and its allied states were welcomed as 'defectors' from the eastern bloc.[5] These were rare exceptions: refugees in general had no role in nation-centred accounts that dominated assessments of the past. In the 1970s and 1980s, global developments brought new refugees from the global south. Their circumstances and experiences were also largely ignored: the revisionist historians Tony Kushner and Catherine Knox observe that if the presence of refugees is one of the hallmarks of contemporary society, 'historians have hardly noticed it'.[6]

For over three centuries refugees had been arriving in London, and specifically in the East End. Scholarship largely ignored them: notwithstanding the growth of the social sciences, of migration studies and of urban studies, none of the city's many universities had systematically examined their lives past or present. When UEL established a course in refugee studies it addressed a striking deficit in the study of forced migration and its implications, both global and local.

Refugee studies

Until the launch of the UEL programme, only one institution in the UK addressed refugee issues by means of dedicated teaching and research. The Refugee Studies Centre (RSC) at Oxford University was initiated in 1982 within the Department of International Development to undertake research on displacement and humanitarian relief in Africa. In 1986 it began a foundation course in refugee studies, focusing on relief and aid in the global south, and in 1988 established the *Journal of Refugee Studies* – the first publication to focus on forced migration and its impacts.

An editorial in the first issue of the *Journal of Refugee Studies*, published from the RSC, observed:

> 'Refugee' constitutes one of the most powerful labels currently in the repertoire of humanitarian concern, national and international public policy, and social differentiation ... [it] both stereotypes and institutionalises a status.[7]

Refugees had become highly contentious figures in international affairs and in the domestic politics of states of the global north, the journal noted. It aimed to provide a multidisciplinary forum in which academics and others could explore the complex, sometimes contradictory phenomenon of forced migration and those it affected.

This important development was associated with crises in Asia, Africa and the Middle East in which large numbers of people were being displaced repeatedly across borders and wider regions. In the 1970s, wars of national liberation vis-à-vis the colonial powers had coincided with a global economic crisis that prompted European governments to revise policies which, since the end of the second world war, had focused upon maintaining 'labour' migration. For decades people forcibly displaced by repression, civil conflict and war, and who had become 'long-distance' refugees, had moved as part of mass migrations encouraged – and sometimes stimulated – by European states. After the world recession of the mid-1970s, European governments attempted to restrain – in some cases, to halt – migrations from the south. Immigration control became a key issue within domestic politics, and refugees – who often arrived uninvited in abrupt mass movements – became problem people said to require special regimes of exclusion.

Ideas about 'race' were embedded in European society: in the case of Britain, immigration policy had been shaped by concern to maintain labour recruitment from former colonies *and* by racist exclusions that periodically inhibited movements from the south. From the mid-1970s, as mass displacements in the south grew in number and in scale, historic prejudices against black and minority ethnic people were directed increasingly towards refugees. Following the second world war the refugee had been associated primarily with an 'escapee' from Stalinist regimes of the eastern bloc. These migrants were embraced by governments in Western Europe – their movement from east to west presented as confirmation of the latter's liberal democratic values. But as the pattern of refugee movements moved from an east-west to a south-north axis, refugees were increasingly the object of official hostility and, by the 1980s, of sustained attempts at exclusion.

'Aberrant' people

Refugee studies at the RSC emerged at this conjuncture, initially attracting a small circle of academics in legal studies and international affairs, together with 'practitioners' – aid workers, development professionals and others engaged in humanitarian relief and the management of holding centres, refugee camps and transit centres. Dominant approaches to forced migration had specific impacts on their work. Refugees remained primarily an *object* of study: in a world of nation-states, forced migrants were seen as people who violated arrangements among and between governments and international agencies. They were seen overwhelmingly as aberrant people, challenging norms and, in particular, legal arrangements based upon the sovereign power of the modern state – and much early work in refugee studies focused on means by which states and agencies addressed crises of displacement and applied asylum policy. Matters of law, notably the complexities associated with instruments and agreements governing access to sovereign state territories, were high on the agenda. Significantly, the pioneering *Journal of Refugee Studies* was soon followed by another new publication, the *Journal of International Refugee Law*.

A second problem lay in the assumption by states that the authentic refugee was a person formally identified and acknowledged as such by governments and international agencies. Forced migrants were viewed as problem people who should be controlled by means of 'encampment' – relocation in camps and holding centres. In the global south these were placed routinely in rural locations. People 'encamped', and who were enumerated and registered with the authorities, usually through the office of the United Nations High Commissioner for Refugees (UNHCR), were properly refugees: others, even displaced people in the same area but who were not registered, were not viewed as refugees and could not access aid or legal protections.

It was already clear, however, that the majority of the world's refugees were not encamped in the countryside under the authority of governments or migration agencies. Millions of people were on the move or living in cities that had become regional hubs within complex migration networks. Many were undocumented migrants – people without passports or formal means of identification, and who had crossed borders by informal ('illegal') means. They were invisible to bodies such as the UNHCR, which argued that they pursued illicit strategies and were potentially or actually a threat to states and international agencies. This approach – which amounted to a denial of the realities of forced migration at the global level – had its impact on academic researchers. The concerns of policy-makers in government, and of the UNHCR and other international agencies, limited their agendas for research, publication and for teaching.

East London – new racisms

Economic globalisation was prompting more, and more severe, crises of mass displacement: at the same time, changes in means of communication and transport facilitated long-distance migration. States of the south constructed during the colonial era and marked by the European powers' principle of *divide et imperia* were vulnerable to sudden changes brought by movements of global capital, especially by speculative initiatives launched in the global north. 'New wars' involving conflict between ethnic groups, religious currents and regional factions produced extensive zones of crisis – in the Horn of Africa, Central Africa, Central America, the Arab East – in which millions were displaced. In the early 1990s the break-up of states across the eastern bloc produced similar movements in and from Central Asia and the Balkans.

Millions of refugees were moving to regional migration hubs such as Mexico City, Johannesburg, Nairobi, Tangier, Cairo, Beirut, Moscow, Mumbai, New Delhi and Bangkok. Here, many sought onward movement to the more stable states of the global north.

Assisted by networks originally established by the former colonial powers during their search for migrant labour, they travelled to cities of Western Europe and North America, establishing complex diasporic networks that facilitated further migrations.[8] In London, refugee communities grew rapidly as migrants arrived from crisis zones by all means, formal and informal. Official records show that between 1985 and 2000 over 300,000 refugees entered the city: many others arrived unrecorded. East London was a key destination: by the 1990s the borough of Newham was home, officially, to some 20,000 refugees; other areas of East and North London, notably Hackney and Haringey, accommodated comparable numbers.[9] Hundreds of thousands of people who entered the UK by clandestine routes, meanwhile, lived 'under the radar'.

In East London, refugee community organisations were proliferating. Some represented collaborations among people of a common national origin; others expressed the interests of regional groups, religious currents and political parties. As in earlier centuries, religious practice was of special importance. Churches with dwindling attendances found their congregations fortified by the migrants. At the same time, new churches, mosques and temples, some in modest terraced houses, were established widely. As before, the refugees were making an emphatic mark upon the area. As before, their reception might be sympathetic or intensely hostile. East London had a long history of organised racist activity – from the antisemitic British Brothers League of the early twentieth century, through Mosley's New Party and his British Union of Fascists, to the National Front of the 1970s. The Newham Monitoring Project, established in 1980 as a grassroots anti-racist organisation, noted increasing hostility towards refugees in the area, now made to carry more and more of the burden of historic racisms.[10]

First steps at UEL

UEL's policy of admitting 'non-traditional' students accommodated people whose education had been disrupted by displacement, journeys of flight, and the complex experiences of arrival and engagement with a new environment. A younger generation, among whom some had been forcibly displaced or had joined relatives on the basis of family reunion, had been schooled in Britain and was also entering higher education. At UEL they contributed much to understanding both the global and local dimensions of forced migration, in particular on courses in the departments of sociology and cultural studies, in which issues of class, 'race', gender, colonial history, imperialism, globalisation, critical historiography, identity and representation came to feature prominently. Of special importance were initiatives taken by the Centre for New Ethnicities Research (CNER). From 1991, its director Phil Cohen developed research on issues of cultural hybridity, diaspora, and links between local cultures and communities of East London and global patterns of immigration, settlement and national identity. CNER encouraged interdisciplinarity and practical interventions in anti-racist work and inter-cultural education with young people. This provided opportunities for students and academic staff at UEL to explore forced migration and its implications for the city. In discussions initiated by the centre it became clear that refugee studies could be advanced most effectively by addressing forced migration as a systemic global phenomenon and by viewing those affected as *subjects* of complex processes of change – people who were social agents rather than passive objects of study.

UEL colleagues who established the postgraduate programme in refugee studies in 1997 committed to a multidisciplinary approach that combined law and legal studies, sociology, anthropology, cultural studies and international development. The three core members of staff – Alice Bloch, Patricia Tuitt and myself – came, respectively, from departments of sociology, law and cultural studies, each of which for years had encouraged independent critical thought, fostering radical social and cultural theory, and developing critical legal theory. Liaising with the Refugee Council, the leading body in the UK advocating for refugees, the team initiated a master's course that attracted refugees, independent researchers and many professionals active in the refugee field – teachers, social workers, community workers, counsellors, legal practitioners, and workers in aid and development. Significantly, of the seventy students admitted during the first two years of the course, almost a third were refugees or people whose families or communities had experienced forced migration and its impacts.

Fortress Europe

The UEL initiative came at an important conjuncture. During the 1990s there had been sustained efforts by British governments and states of the European Union (EU) to inhibit refugee movements from the global south. On 1 September 1997, days before the refugee studies course at UEL held its opening session, the Dublin convention on asylum was implemented. This specified that among member states of the EU a 'Dublin regulation' would obtain, preventing an applicant for asylum from submitting a case in more than one state of the union. The convention established the principle of a 'first country of asylum', under which an application for refugee status would be restricted to the state in which an initial claim was made. This 'first country' had authority to accept or to reject a claim and its decision would be binding for the EU: applicants could not make claims in any other member state. Decisions taken by states with the most exclusionary policies would be binding for the union, so that many refugees would be unwelcome across the continent.

The 'Dublin regulation' formalised by the convention had been years in the making, having been agreed in principle by states of the European Community (EC) in 1990. Changes then affecting the Soviet Union and its satellite states had profound implications for Western Europe and especially for the EC, which had its origins in post-war agreements to support states that contested the communist east. After decades of cold war hostility, borders between east and west were being reshaped, notably by German unification and by the wish of governments of the former eastern bloc to accede to the community. In the absence of cold war enemies, states of Western Europe sought new reference points for their solidarities and collaborations. They were strongly influenced by warnings about global cultural conflict issued by academics and policymakers in the United States. Samuel Huntington, who played a prominent role in debates about foreign policy following the collapse of the Soviet Union, proposed that challenges to 'the west' would now come primarily from the global south – from people who, he argued, posed a fundamental challenge to the shared cultures of the global north. It was the threat presented by such people, he maintained, that should shape strategic decisions among western states: 'We know who we are', Huntington maintained, 'only when we know who we are not and often only when we know whom we are against'.[11]

These ideas found a ready audience in Western Europe. It was already clear that migration policy could be a key area of collaboration among governments often engaged in highly charged, competitive relations within the EU. Now immigration took on new significance. In the absence of cold war enemies, states of the union found common cause in collaborative efforts vis-à-vis displaced people of the global south. Regions earlier viewed by European governments as reservoirs of cheap labour had become zones of instability from which opportunistic migrants, it was said, travelled north to exploit credulous European populations, threatening the integrity of the continent as a whole. States acceding to the union were required to write new laws on immigration and asylum: those located at the eastern and southern edges of EU territories were required to fortify their borders with fences, radar, watchtowers and patrols.

The Dublin convention was followed by Dublin II and Dublin III, and by a cluster of further measures aimed to intensify monitoring using biometric records. Across Europe, refugees were officially under suspicion. Mobilising discourses and practices of historic racism, mass media in many states viewed them not only as a threat at the border but as an enemy within. Currents of the extreme right drew confidence – assaults on refugee centres, hostels, businesses and places of worship, notably mosques, proliferated.

Gendered perspective

Refugee studies at UEL attempted to comprehend these fast-changing processes. Both mass displacement and policies of exclusion had become systemic features of the global order. Scores of millions of people were being displaced: in the global north new barriers inhibited their movements. At physical borders, fences and walls sealed national and supranational territories. In social and political discourse, refugees were made to play the role of threatening 'others'. People who had escaped existential crises, undertaking long, risky journeys to find security, were targets of official hostility, often driven to the margins of a 'host' society.

Students on the refugee studies programme at UEL were encouraged to address the structural aspects of the global refugee crisis while considering impacts on the lives of refugees and those with whom they interacted. The UEL course emphasised the importance of displacement, journeys of flight, arrivals and destinations, legal frameworks, diasporas and refugee agency. To the extent that refugees had appeared at all within academic research they had been seen as people rendered helpless by their experiences. Typically, refugees were the collateral damage of wars and civil conflicts, driven by forces that evacuated them of capacities to make choices and to act upon them. Social and cultural theorists at UEL, however, had already developed a body of work in which people silenced by dominant narratives and historiographical practices were addressed as social actors – people with expectations, aspirations and capacities to develop strategies and to act upon them.

UEL researchers had undertaken pioneering work in women's histories, black histories, LGBTQ histories, and working-class and labour history. Influenced by the history workshop movement, they developed critical assessments of dominant professional history, emphasising history from below, lived experiences and the lives of those rendered marginal or invisible by mainstream academic practice. Of special note was the work of Catherine Hall and of Bill Schwarz, who addressed issues of class, race and gender in the colonial encounter and in the European imagination, and of John Marriott, who examined labour and trade union struggles in East London.[12] Complementary work in oral history, emphasising the importance of lived experience, memory and reflection on events past and present, highlighted the circumstances, experiences and insights of those silenced by dominant narratives. Feminist historians in the global south were making similar breakthroughs – in particular, Indian researchers were revising approaches to partition of the colonial state. Engaging with the experiences of refugee women, they demonstrated the close relationship between mass displacements of the past and contemporary structures of exclusion.[13] At UEL these initiatives helped to shape a distinctive approach to refugees' lives in East London past and present.

A gendered perspective was of critical importance to the new refugee studies programme. The more that gender relations were unequal in societies affected by involuntary migration the more likely that, as refugees, women and girls would experience disadvantage, abuse and violence. The more that exclusionary barriers were erected in the north against migrants from the global south, the more likely that women and girls would be exploited within migration networks and in border zones. The Dublin convention of 1997 had been established, according to its authors, to inhibit persistent applications for asylum across states of the EU. Its effect was to greatly increase the activity of clandestine networks in which migration agents, often seen as 'facilitators' or 'smugglers', moved refugees along irregular routes by land and by sea. Those using the networks were vulnerable to all manner of dangers: most vulnerable were women and girls, among whom many were raped en route or at the border and/or forced into prostitution or sexual slavery in countries of destination. The architects of Fortress Europe had constructed new means of oppression for some of the world's most vulnerable people.

Gendered perspectives also provided insights into the lives of refugees in destination states and across diasporas. Here, UEL provided further invaluable resources. Its programme of psychosocial studies, initiated in the 1980s, combined psychological, social and cultural perspectives (see Chapter 17). Mobilised in the study of forced migration, they facilitated understanding of experiential aspects of repression, conflict, displacement, encampment, journeys, arrivals and the process of 'settlement'. Medical professionals had long viewed refugees collectively as people with reduced capacities, usually said to be the result of trauma. Psychosocial perspectives assisted in revising this approach. Although some forced migrants underwent profoundly damaging experiences, many passed through challenging episodes by mobilising both individual and collective resources. Rather than medical attention, they sought opportunities, options and the space to make choices. The psychosocial framework enabled better understanding of lives constrained by involuntary migration but within which human capacities could also be stimulated and expanded.[14] Here too gender was a key issue, notably where women refugees in 'host' countries were able to advance in education, employment and social networking. Male counterparts, especially those raised in societies strongly marked by patriarchal relations, experienced greater disadvantage – apparently a reversal of the gendered inequality intensified by displacement. Forced migration, it was clear, was a complex and sometimes contradictory phenomenon.

Legal regimes

Early additions to the core teaching team at UEL included specialists in psychosocial approaches, in gendered analysis – and in human rights. UEL's School of Law made a key contribution to the refugee programme (see Chapter 14). It had long highlighted issues of rights – their origins and meanings, formalisation in legal instruments and agreements, and application in contexts, including forced migration. The school encouraged critical assessment of efforts by states and agencies to shape ideas about rights, notably in the case of the refugee convention of 1951, the 'Geneva convention'. This agreement, sponsored by the United Nations, for the first time defined the term 'refugee' in precise terms, outlining the rights of displaced people and the obligations of states to protect them. Pioneering work by legal scholars at UEL, notably Patricia Tuitt, demonstrated how partisan interventions by key states had shaped the convention and subsequent international agreements, producing a legal regime that both facilitated and inhibited refugee movements. They also identified the gendered character of the convention, its later protocol and related regional agreements, with their assumptions about the character of the normative refugee.

These insights played a key role in identifying the many obstacles faced by people making claims for refugee status. By the 1990s, applicants in the United Kingdom faced state authorities that adopted a posture of high scepticism vis-à-vis refugee claims, part of a 'culture of disbelief' in which officials and judicial authorities assumed that migrants' accounts of their experiences were inaccurate or simply invented. Applications were delayed for years as the asylum system in the UK all but collapsed. Tens of thousands of people were marooned, neither accepted nor finally rejected. Many refugee communities dedicated their sparse resources to legal costs, repeated appearances in courts and before appeal judges. In London the relative security of life in a diverse global city offering new opportunities was accompanied by uncertainty and the possibility of new forced migrations in the form of detention and deportation.

Global and local

The initiative taken at UEL was ambitious. It attempted a holistic approach to forced migration, viewing refugees as central figures around which multidisciplinary perspectives could be developed. Some important issues bearing upon migration received less attention, however. Political science, international relations and policy studies had long addressed migration in the context of relations between states and international organisations. The emergence of refugee studies brought these disciplines into the study of forced migration, with the emphasis on states as the principal actors. This important area of work had a lower profile in the UEL programme: in effect, UEL undertook a refugee-centred approach in which the status of institutional actors was set alongside the circumstances and experiences of migrants.

The UEL programme sought to address global dimensions of migration as experienced in specific local contexts. In an early initiative, students on the programme were invited to join a study visit to Cairo, Egypt, organised annually by UEL's international development team. This presented an unusual opportunity to visit a major hub within global migration networks, drawing refugees from across Africa, the Middle East and Central Asia. Since the 1970s, Cairo had become a 'magnet city' for refugees, especially from the Horn of Africa, where persistent conflicts had displaced millions of people. A number of migration agencies had located there, notably the UNHCR and the International Organisation for Migration (IOM), variously involved in processing claims for refugee status and arranging admission to programmes of refugee resettlement in the United States, Canada, Australia and a handful of European states. Few applicants were accepted for resettlement but the city gained a reputation as a gateway to the global north. By the late 1990s it accommodated over two million refugees – most from Sudan, with large groups from Ethiopia, Eritrea, Somalia and some thirty other states – among whom there were many active community organisations. The city's churches played a key role in refugee advocacy and welfare, providing food programmes, legal advice and schooling.

The UEL visit combined lectures and seminars at the American University in Cairo with talks from refugees and support workers at church centres, and visits to key migration agencies. It provided insights into global patterns of forced migration, the role of migration networks, the lives of urban refugees in the global south, and the experiences of people who had often undertaken multiple journeys and were now living at the margins of a society which barely recognised their presence. The opportunity to consider refugee lives in Cairo vis-à-vis those in London and other 'destination' cities in Europe was a valuable addition to the UEL programme.

Research initiatives

For more than twenty years, academic staff on the programme produced a stream of publications on global migrations, community life, gender, psychosocial issues and legal matters. Global networks of scholars who addressed forced migration were at last expanding and other specialist centres had appeared, stimulating debate and gradually addressing the deficit in research and published material. UEL students undertook particularly innovative work. Many who were refugees, or from communities with experiences of forced migration, wrote theses on personal and family experiences – displacement, journeys of flight, exclusion, settlement, legal barriers, diaspora, discrimination, issues of identity, concepts of home, political activism and cultural initiatives. A number undertook doctoral research as students on the programme won a series of awards from research bodies, including the Economic and Social Research Council, the Arts and Humanities Research Council and the British Academy. As a programme unique in Europe, the course attracted increasing numbers of international students.

The programme had maintained links with the Refugee Council, agreeing to host the organisation's archive on refugees at UEL's Docklands campus. The archive had been established in the 1940s and consolidated over the decades by addition of books, journals, reports, press cuttings, 'grey literature', films and photographs – a unique collection that provided rich materials for students at UEL and attracted researchers from around the world. Archivists at UEL have since developed a living refugee archive which builds upon and extends the Refugee Council collection by linking to community archives, digital collections, oral history recordings and multimedia collections: http://www.livingrefugeearchive.org

The archive has revealed a hidden history of refugee initiatives, especially in the area of cultural production. Refugees and those who advocate for and show solidarity with them have produced a wealth of written literature and materials in the visual arts, the plastic arts, performance and, most recently, in multimedia. UEL students have also created a remarkable range of work embracing short stories, poetry, film, photography, installation, painting and sculpture, performance and multimedia projects.

Refugee studies at UEL has been associated with two productive research centres. The Refugee Research Centre and the Centre for Research on Migration, Refugees and Belonging (CMRB) have provided bases for advanced study.[15] Among notable initiatives, a series of conferences on refugee lives in the city, on migration, racism and religion, and on borders and bordering have brought scholars worldwide to East London. They have been accessible to a wide audience, especially refugees and those working with and for them. Here the university has played a role as citizen and public intellectual, opening debate about issues that can be contentious and highly charged but which are profoundly important as forced migration continues apace.

The university's long engagement with refugees has facilitated a ground-breaking initiative. In 2017, UEL joined with universities and migrant organisations in Europe to provide the open learning initiative (OLive) programme, introducing refugees and asylum seekers to higher education. OLive offers opportunities for students to discover what skills and knowledge are needed in order to apply for and succeed in higher education in the UK, providing information about pathways and opportunities. The course provides modules and workshops in English language and academic writing, research skills, academic tutoring and introduction to academic discussions. It is co-funded by the Erasmus+ programme of the EU, together with University of East London's civic engagement fund, and organised in partnership with the Central European University in Budapest, University of Vienna and the European Network Against Racism (ENAR).

Why UEL?

For more than twenty years, the refugee studies programme has made a significant contribution to analysis of a key feature of contemporary affairs, hitherto largely ignored by scholars. What accounts for the success of this initiative at UEL – a university in an underprivileged area in which resources for advanced study have been particularly thin?

If material resources at UEL were limited, intellectual resources were rich. Academics who in the 1980s and 1990s encouraged independent critical approaches in the social sciences provided space for multidisciplinary projects, such as innovation studies, women's studies and psychosocial studies. The proposal for a programme on forced migration, which would have made little progress in most British universities at this time, was consistent with an emphasis on new thinking about people marginalised in the wider society. Without radical social and cultural theory, critical history, historiography and legal studies, and new approaches to international development, the refugee studies programme could not have been envisaged – and without commitments of the university's academic staff to advance social justice it could not have progressed. At the same time, without the realities of life in East London, and without its long history as a place of destination for refugees, refugee studies would not have had the relevance and purpose required to address forced migration past and present.

Acknowledgements

Thanks to the staff and students, especially many refugees from far and wide, who have brought insights in understanding a key feature of the modern world. Special thanks to Michael Rustin and Gavin Poynter for their encouragement and strong support during the early years of the programme.

Notes

1. Philip Marfleet, 'Understanding "sanctuary": faith and traditions of asylum', *Journal of Refugee Studies,* Volume 24, No 2, 2011.
2. For a comprehensive account of Huguenot settlement see Bernard Cottret, *The Huguenots in England,* Cambridge University Press: Cambridge, 1991.
3. Rosemary Ashton, *Little Germany: Exile and Asylum in Victorian Britain,* Oxford University Press: Oxford, 1986.
4. Ali Behdad, *A Forgetful Nation: On Immigration and Cultural Identity in the United States,* Duke University Press: Durham, NC, 2005, p23.
5. Throughout the 1930s, British governments resisted calls to provide sanctuary for victims of fascism in Europe. It was only after years of campaigning that refugees from Spain, and later Jewish refugees from Germany and Central Europe, were admitted, principally as an outcome of sustained campaigning by Jewish organisations and by trade unionists and communists. The 'rescue' of such refugees by British authorities is often inflated in official narratives: see Ari Sherman, *Island Refuge: Britain and Refugees from the Third Reich 1933-1939,* Frank Cass: London, 1994, and Louise London, *Whitehall and the Jews,* Cambridge University Press: Cambridge, 2003. On representation of refugees from the Soviet Union and the Eastern bloc in the post-world war two era, see Patricia Tuitt, *False Images,* Pluto Press: London, 1996.
6. Tony Kushner and Catherine Knox, *Refugees in an Age of Genocide: Global, National, and Local Perspectives During the Twentieth Century,* Routledge: London, 1999, p4.
7. Editor Roger Zetter in the first issue of the journal. Roger Zetter, 'Refugees and Refugee Studies – A Label and an Agenda: Editorial

Introduction to the Journal of Refugee Studies', *Journal of Refugee Studies*, Vol 1, No 1, 1988, p1.

8. These global patterns of forced migration are addressed in Philip Marfleet, *Refugees in a Global Era*, Palgrave: Basingstoke, 2006.
9. Martin Bardsley and Marian Storkey, 'Estimating the number of refugees in London', *Journal of Public Health Medicine*, Vol 22, No 3, 2000, p409.
10. Newham Monitoring Project/Campaign Against Racism and Fascism, *Newham – the Forging of a Black Community*, Newham Monitoring Project: London, 1991.
11. Samuel Huntington, *The Clash of Civilizations and the Remaking of World Order*, Simon and Schuster: New York, 1996, p21.
12. See, for example, Leonore Davidoff and Catherine Hall, *Family Fortunes: Men and Women of the English Middle Class 1780–1850*, Routledge: London, 1987; Bill Schwarz, '"The only white man in there": The re-racialisation of England, 1956-1968', *Race and Class*, Vol. 38, No. 1, 1996; and John Marriott, *The Culture of Labourism: The East End Between the Wars*, Edinburgh University Press: Edinburgh, 1992.
13. See in particular the work of Urvashi Butalia, *The Other Side of Silence: Voices From the Partition of India*, Penguin Books India, 1998.
14. See for example the work of Giorgia Dona, an early member of the refugee studies team at UEL: Giorgia Dona and John Berry, 'Acculturation Attitudes and Acculturative Stress of Central American Refugees', *International Journal of Psychology*, Vol. 29, No. 1, 1994.
15. Nira Yuval-Davis, a sociologist with a long record of research on gender, nation and nationalism, expanded work on forced migration at UEL with a leading role in establishing the CMRB and initiating projects on refugees and theatre, race, and the phenomenon of bordering.

CHAPTER NINETEEN

Sociology @ East London

Tim Butler and Barbara J. Harrison

Overview

This chapter focuses on sociology as a discipline and department at the University of East London (UEL) and its predecessor colleges.[1] Sociology and departments of sociology were ubiquitous in the new polytechnics and new universities that sprung into existence in the 1960s; this was not the case in the older-established universities which were slower to embrace the social sciences.[2] At North East London Polytechnic (NELP), as elsewhere, departments and disciplines were not seamlessly aligned, and there were many sociologists and much sociology (or quasi-sociology) across the institution – for example, teaching 'liberal studies' on business, science and technology courses. While the discipline of sociology continues to be taught at UEL, the Department of Sociology has undergone many name changes and restructurings with the name itself even disappearing at times – often as a consequence of a hostile environment in national, local and institutional political discourse towards social sciences in general, and sociology in particular. While not in any way wishing to underestimate the extent or nature of the threat, it could be seen as having had the consequence of forcing sociologists to have engaged with the huge social and economic restructurings that have marked the past half century. It is more than an ironic coincidence that sociology not only continued to thrive as one of the institution's most successful disciplines in terms of external benchmarks, such as the successive Research Assessment Exercises (RAEs) but also that many of the original staff saw out most or all of their careers at the institution. It is probably not too much to claim that social scientists were disproportionately influential in driving the institution in its commitment to widening educational opportunity in a geographical area that traditionally had the lowest age participation ratio into higher education in the UK.[3] The extent to which this is likely to continue, however, remains moot.

We will not trace every twist and turn of curriculum development or organisational restructuring that has taken place since the 1970s, which would be both tedious and probably invidious. Rather, we will focus more on the early years of the North East London Polytechnic, during which time sociologists embraced the challenge of building a different type of higher education institution that not only met the needs of contemporary society but also catered to a 'client' group that had not traditionally been educated at university level. In so doing, we focus on the original conception of a wide-ranging sociology programme in the founding years of the polytechnic. We then move on to describe a series of cognate developments – some of them successful while others have fallen by the wayside. Separately, we discuss how a distinctive research agenda emerged at the university and has been remarkably successful in engendering an ongoing culture of research and scholarly activity. Long before 'research' became legitimised by Research Excellence Framework (REF)-funding, colleagues in sociology at UEL were writing about the application of sociology.[4]

Finally, we consider how sociology as a discipline has seemingly survived despite being perceived as a thorn in the side of a sometimes 'gung-ho' management who, over time and with greater or lesser degrees of success and determination, tried to manage an apparently unruly set of staff and temper the perception of their often unflavoursome views.

Context

At this stage, it is worth reflecting on the context within which sociology as a discipline and department developed. The early 1970s was a period of considerable social and political conflict in the UK. The staff were, for the most part, young and, for many, the experiences of 1968 and the protests against 'the bomb' and the Vietnam war had been formative. Despite slowly rising unemployment and other tensions, the period was still characterised by social and political consensus and economic growth, which would last until the election of Margaret Thatcher's Conservative administration at the end of the decade. There remained a solid commitment to the expansion of the state both in welfare and industrial interventions – although the portents of the future were clear in so-called Selsdon man and Edward Heath's threats about how there were to be 'no lame ducks'.

It was these assumptions about the role of the state that particularly informed the thinking behind the BA Sociology with Professional Studies programme – to produce a cadre of professionally qualified state workers in the welfare sector. The role of the polytechnics, as the subalterns in the binary system of tertiary education of the day, was to provide avenues of upward mobility into the lower end of the new middle classes and to train a new cadre of state workers. The expansion of the state sector thus both provided services for the increasingly displaced working classes, as deindustrialisation and technical change began to cut a swathe through traditional forms of industrial production, and new employment opportunities. Such a training also served to support the growth of a new social grouping that could sit alongside the more traditional middle-class professions – albeit below the old professions of medicine, the law etc. Perhaps unsurprisingly, these were seen as the semi-professions in the contemporary literature. Expectations from young people in particular for greater equality/social mobility were rising, and it was acknowledged that these institutions needed to do something different by developing a kind of education that was more embedded in linking theory with practice and engaging with local and national communities in their widest sense. Crudely, there was no point in simply replicating what was on offer in the traditional universities.

The development of a sociology programme

When NELP was founded as a polytechnic in 1970 it inherited from the constituent colleges a solid, if conventional, base that was laid down for sociology by the London external degree. This had sociological theory, the social structure of modern Britain, research methods and various options as its structure. We were required by the director, George Brosan, and deputy director, Eric Robinson, to do something different, and sociology with professional studies was the 'vocationalist' outcome of their demands. Nevertheless, the external (essentially London School of Economics) degree remained an important foundation for us and provided a link with mainstream sociology. The BA (Hons) Sociology with Professional Studies was validated by the Council for National Academic Awards (CNAA) in 1972 and enrolled its first students in the following September. The first enrolment was approximately 100 students with a high proportion (at least in terms of the prevailing norms) of mature students.[5] It was approved as a four-year programme with the 'professional studies' component justifying the additional year of study compared to the normal (for England at least) three-year undergraduate programme. Initially, four pathways were approved – in social work, vocational guidance, personnel management and sociological research. While the first three were professionally recognised qualifications, that in sociological research was an academic CNAA validation by the polytechnic.[6] In the new polytechnic sector so-called 'sandwich' degrees, which played to its 'applied' mission, were not uncommon – particularly in science, engineering and business, and increasingly with applied social studies programmes, which were in effect social work degrees.

What distinguished the BA Sociology with Professional Studies programme was the way in which academic and professional study and practice were integrated, with both parts of the programme talking to each other throughout the four years – although the compulsory fieldwork placements in social work presented both professional and practical problems. Nevertheless, the use of often jointly taught seminars and a programme of residential away-days and/or weekends ensured a close integration throughout the degree.[7] This model was unusual and not without its tensions, but was appreciated by students and helped to ensure a 'critical' understanding of their role as (essentially) state professionals with multiple (and often conflicting) loyalties and obligations. This basic model of a sociology programme run out of a sociology department bringing together professional and academic training was remarkably resilient. It lasted for the next twenty years or so with minor modifications, although student numbers became a problem towards the end when the pool of mature students had largely exhausted itself, and as the post-war demographic transition began to work its way through the school-age population. One major innovation in the 1980s was to introduce a part-time variant (the BA Sociology with Vocational Studies), but in the long term it failed to recruit sufficiently in order to remain viable.

These pressures contributed to the decision in the late 1990s to revise the single honours degree programme. Social policy research had been closed as a single honours offering but it was felt that some policy, as well as research methodology, expertise could provide a useful route through a sociology degree, following a common foundation year. The European Studies degree had a similar trajectory, as being originally a component part of the Sociology with Professional Studies programme with an emphasis on learning a European language and drawing on the European Union-funded Erasmus programme, in which we had students going to and coming from universities in France, Germany, Italy and Spain. It was uneconomically small, but attracted good incoming students, who had been well prepared and who enjoyed the fact that we offered more contact with teachers than usually happened in their home universities.

The second impetus for change, which reflected a changing staff group, was to design a programme that better reflected key aspects of the social world – crudely speaking, there was a view that the original programme was too ordered around so-called structural issues of class inequality to the detriment of those of diversity and identity. These had always been popular as optional subjects within the old degree, and the proposal was now to focus on them as core course concerns in addition to providing options offering greater specialisation. Over time, the changing demographics of East London were reflected in our student body, with growing numbers of black and minority ethnic groups studying at UEL, giving rise to pressure for a curriculum that made sense of this changing context. This development, and an insistence that issues of colonisation and race should be given greater recognition, was not without its tensions at the time. A curriculum review resulted in a course that linked local and global issues, and embedded research methods in East London, using it as a laboratory for methods training drawing on the wide body of sociological research, from Booth's poverty studies to Young and Willmott's *Family and Kinship in East London*. Focusing the curriculum around themes of globalisation and multiculturalism was ahead of its time, although it is now commonplace across higher education.

Globalisation was a concept that was sufficiently malleable ('slippery') to inform the development, while retaining the idea that both theory and research were key to what counted as a basic sociological education/training. A further innovation was in relation to pedagogy, especially in the first year, in which students were to learn through utilising the London environment by undertaking practical projects. In one course on consumption and popular culture, students constructed and then displayed an 'identity box' in which they put six items that represented themselves. In this course, and in researching East London, visits with associated tasks were made to cultural institutions such as Tate Modern and the Imperial War Museum. Researching East London oriented students to the idea of London as a laboratory for a history of social research. Much of this has remained in the subsequent iterations to the curriculum, with globalisation, modern Britain and researching East London remaining core foundational subjects in which field trips remain as key features.[8]

Along the way were innovations and developments that failed. Several attempts were made to offer taught postgraduate programmes – one of them, the MA in Social Research, did survive for several years. In the late 1990s, an MA in New Social Movements recruited a few committed students but after three cohorts it was considered not viable. Location was probably a dominant factor in this difficulty. Until 2004, sociology was based on the Barking campus on the Becontree estate, and it was reluctantly concluded that this was not somewhere to which part-time students often in full-time employment could anticipate travelling at the end of the day. Social sciences moved to the Docklands campus in 2004 and sociology appeared quite vulnerable, with declining numbers on the single honours sociology course and a virtual collapse of numbers on the European studies and social policy research pathways. A review of sociology resulted in the development of a single honours sociology course alongside a new sociology (professional development) course. The former offered a more theoretically informed approach, continuing its focus on globalisation and multiculturalism while more effectively incorporating gender and class, which continued to utilise East London as a 'laboratory' for quantitative and qualitative methods training – capitalising on our expertise in narrative research. In a strange irony, this reflected earlier sociological iterations with a strong applied focus. Students were able to combine sociology with specialisms in a wide range of areas, such as health and education, along with practical skills in line with twenty-first century concerns, such as fundraising and leadership. At the time, those validating the programme commented on UEL's strength in managing to find ways to ensure the continuing relevance of sociology. The focus on field trips and practical experience continued under the guise of 'flipping the classroom'.

In the early 2000s, responding to resource constraints and recruitment pressures, staff from sociology, anthropology, politics and psychosocial studies (all themselves 'spin-offs' from the original sociology programme) regrouped to offer four new degrees that drew upon staff research interests and what were perceived as emerging areas of student interest (in a situation where 'student choice' was becoming the primary currency). (See also chapters 1 and 17.) With a common first year, which was largely thematic and hopefully attractive as a form of deferred choice as far as students were concerned and resource efficient as far as senior managers saw it, there followed a specialisation in one of: visual culture, travel and tourism, consumption, and people and the planet. At validation there was considerable external peer enthusiasm, but this sadly was not reflected in recruitment. It may have been that we went too far down the 'fun' route of trying to articulate our programmes with what we understood as emerging interests of the school-leaving cohort, and underestimated the influence of the traditional A-level sociology syllabus. Ultimately, it failed to promote a sense of discipline identity like more traditional well-established cross-disciplinary degrees, such as criminology and development studies. Programmes such as tourism have always been rather fickle, appealing at first sight to those attracted to a life on the beach but which, in the cooler light of day, become seen as simply too hedonistic and self-indulgent.

Research and public engagement

Recently, most of UEL's sociologists have been recruited with doctoral research behind them, while many staff hired in earlier years acquired doctorates by part-time study. Even in the early years, while there was an emphasis on course development and the curriculum, staff were encouraged, as we have already noted, to engage in research and to be intellectually active through varied forms of scholarly activity. For example, in the teaching domain these interests were accommodated by the development of options within the degree programmes – prime examples perhaps being anthropology and cultural studies. With the onset of the RAE in the early 1990s, the emphasis on developing and supporting a research culture among existing staff and appointing new staff who had an active research profile became more important. The RAE/REF imperative served to broaden the boundaries of what might be seen as sociology in research terms compared to the boundaries for teaching purposes. The sociology unit of assessment took in staff not only from anthropology, social policy and politics and social psychology but also from other outposts around the university. The 'turn to research' had the potential to create in- and out-groups of those eligible for the kind of support that enabled them to be intellectually and scholarly active. In practice though, the relative success of sociologists in the RAE provided a more secure financial basis for supporting research efforts than would otherwise have been the case in a climate of growing resource constraint, and the benefits were spread beyond the contributing group. Crucially, we were able to finance a number of one-term sabbaticals from teaching (buying in replacement part-time staff), provide some support for research centres and for those wishing to enter research – by funding PhD fees for example. In recent years, when the RAE became the REF and other criteria came into play in addition to peer review of research quality, UEL sociology outranked some major top-league universities, in terms of 'impact' and community engagement.[9]

As with the evolution of the teaching programme and curriculum, research focus was an ever-changing landscape, partly determined by a shifting staff group but also as new priorities emerged. As mentioned, there was often a synergy between research interests and emerging curriculum areas – some of which sadly did not last long but others that did and achieved an enviable national and international reputation – refugee studies being a prime example (see Chapter 18). Increasingly staff were successful in winning UK Research Council funding. The Centre for Biography in Social Policy was home to the seven-nation EU-funded 'social strategies in risk societies' (Sostris) research project as part of its targeted programme on social exclusion. For its part, the Centre for Narrative Research (see Chapter 5) had its base within psychosocial studies but drew in staff and postgraduate students from a number of disciplines. Sociologists within the East London research group examined issues around regeneration (such as gentrification), the place of global cities and the relationship between Olympic Games and their cities, something which UEL was well-located to investigate when the 2012 Olympics came to its doorstep at Stratford. All these centres developed an international focus/participation and achieved a national and international reputation.

Research has been one of the means by which UEL sociologists have been involved in the wider sociological community, collaborating with colleagues on numerous projects, conferences and workshops. In addition, a number of staff have served as trustees on the executive of the British Sociological Association (BSA) and editorial board members of its journal *Sociology* and, in 2007, four of them were the organising committee for the BSA annual conference 'Connections: identities, technologies and relationships' at the Docklands campus of UEL.

Creative destruction: evolving responses to threats to the discipline and department

Over the last five decades, sociology at UEL has undergone countless reconfigurations and restructuring, sometimes being part of smaller management units, such as a department, and other times becoming part of larger units, such as a school. Mergers and separations have been the order of the day – sometimes for self-protection, other times by management fiat. This meant that at various times sociology was contiguous with many other subjects, some of which were conducted by fellow social scientists (anthropology, politics, psychosocial studies and social work). At other times, it has found itself combined with humanities, cultural and media studies, innovation studies as well as with law; some disciplines were carved out and moved elsewhere – for example, social work moved to education. Name changes (re-badging) inevitably accompanied this, and sociology sometimes disappeared from view altogether, such as at present in which it is located in a Department of Social Sciences and Social Work located in the Cass School of Education and Communities, which in turn is one of two schools in the College of Professional Services – so much for slimming down!

On balance, these restructurings were always in some measure disruptive and demoralising, since some at least were accompanied by what staff perceived to be a threat to the survival of their discipline, to social sciences more generally and to their jobs. On some occasions, other subjects were targeted too. In the early 1980s, the governors and founding director, George Brosan, determined to 'excise' four departments (including sociology). Eventually, following both informed academic arguments and a strident trade union campaign, the threat was seen off and the director resigned to be replaced by Gerry Fowler, who was much more sympathetic to what the social scientists were trying to achieve. A major restructuring in 2006 led once again to lobbying of governors on securing the future of social sciences more generally. We think it is not unfair to say that sociology and social sciences have often been a 'thorn in the side' of management and suffered more attention to what they were doing than elsewhere in the institution. This no doubt contributed to some of these problems with senior managements and governors. But also, management control was thought necessary to reduce the autonomy of academics in a wish to make universities into more managed institutions, with much greater attention paid to the bottom line and the perceived needs of private sector employers. Nevertheless, over the years many senior managers have also been supportive or at least neutral – not least because the social sciences and humanities have been among the most successful at 'delivering' in the new performance culture.

In retrospect

The sociology programme of the 1970s proposed a new model for social science education which was not only designed to provide a university-level of education to those who had not progressed through the school system to university the 'first time around',[10] but also proposed a melding of academic and professional training to provide new cadres for the welfare state society of the time. At the time of writing this, of course, has changed out of recognition, with a society dominated by social media and what has now become known as neoliberalism, in ways that would probably be unrecognisable to those of us who joined NELP in the early 1970s and whose careers journeyed across this massive social, economic and cultural transition. However, a number of things remain. It is notable that many of those who began their careers at NELP in the 1960s and 1970s ended them with retirement from UEL well into the twenty-first century. Many may not have expected to have lasted it out, given the serial threats to job security, but it is perhaps testament to their tenacity, organising skills but above all their imagination and flexibility that they managed to continue to design and teach courses and, more recently, undertake research that was attractive to students and of sufficient high quality to survive in a world devoted to comparative performance metrics.

In reflecting on this, values (such as a commitment to equality of opportunity and social justice) were crucial, but we were also fortunate to have had consistent and principled disciplinary and managerial leadership which encouraged not only intellectual curiosity but also a communal spirit that embraced intellectual disagreements as a positive. To end on an overtly self-congratulatory note, it seems to those of us who are members of the welfare state generation that the basic idea of providing an education and a training that meets the needs and aspirations of those struggling to enter the middle mass of British society and to transform it has continued to be a winning formula. It remains the case that, despite all the transformations that have occurred in the British state over the last fifty years, publicly provided services, together with the non-governmental sector, have been and will continue to be the market, much as we might cringe at the word, of our consumers, and we have by and large successfully addressed that as teachers and researchers.

Post-1992 universities are increasingly struggling with agendas around value for money, league table performance and graduate outcomes, and while East London is a very different place from fifty years ago, it continues to embody the contradictions of our time: concentrated poverty alongside extreme wealth, and regeneration that trickles up rather than down. Finally, it is to be hoped that there is as much contemporary resonance in the approach applied at NELP/UEL as a model for thinking about sociology today as there was when it was founded – turning theory into practice and enabling staff and students to embed themselves meaningfully in the community. One irony of London's gentrification is that today staff are much more likely to live in the area than fifty years ago when they lived in now unaffordable places such as Hackney, Camden, Islington and Haringey!

Notes

1. We would like to acknowledge the helpful comments made by Penny Bernstock, Judith Burnett, Michael Rustin and Lionel Sims (all former members of staff) on an earlier draft. We have incorporated many but not all of their suggestions, for which we are very grateful.
2. See M. Savage, *Identities and Social Change in Britain since 1940: The Politics of Method*, Oxford University Press: Oxford, 2010.
3. It is also worth noting the influence of one of the editors of this volume. Michael Rustin was the head of sociology during the period of frenetic course development under the CNAA during the early 1970s; he subsequently became head of school and dean of faculty, and influenced or mentored many of the new areas of study and/or departments, as well as fighting off successive threats to the social science 'project' at the university over a forty-year period.
4. Noel Parry, Michael Rustin and Carole Satyamurti edited *Social Work, Welfare and the State*, Edward Arnold: London, 1979, which explored some of these issues. Carole Satyamurti wrote a fine anthropolog-

ical study of a social services department from her PhD (published as *Occupational Survival,* Blackwell: Oxford 1981), which described the extreme stresses of social work, which remains to the point today. Sociologists in Polytechnics (SIP), founded at NELP, organised conferences and produced a series of working papers, mainly about vocational applications of sociology, in town planning, social work etc. George Brosan delivered a stunning welcoming talk at one of these conferences, at which he talked about the value of sociology as a demystifying subject, to the amazement of colleagues from other polytechnics! Janet Finch (one of our early external examiners) and Michael Rustin edited a Penguin collection, *A Degree of Choice: Higher Education and the Right to Learn,* Penguin: Harmondsworth, 1986, about widening opportunities. One chapter, 'Education is Ordinary', by Alan White, a former student and subsequently a member of staff, wrote about his great sense of liberation and pleasure in becoming a sociology student. He brought together very nicely what it meant to do sociology in relation to his previous experience working as a shop assistant before studying sociology at NELP. Bill Schwarz, David Page and Jenny Shaw from UEL also contributed chapters to this book.

5. Mature students were, at that time, defined as those aged over twenty-five with experience of work or similar activities, which were taken as equivalent to the two A-level entry normally required for university entry. Over the years the definition was progressively relaxed both in terms of age and work experience, particularly as further education colleges developed 'feeder' access courses.
6. The model here was to produce graduates with the skills necessary to undertake 'action research'. This was being pioneered by the Roy Jenkins' Home Office-inspired community development programmes. One of its pioneering projects was located down the road in Canning Town with its research wing somewhat uncomfortably perched in NELP's Centre for Institutional Studies. Whatever the local difficulties, the model was for sociologists who could deploy their (quantitative and qualitative research) skills in deprived communities not only to map and chart that deprivation but support those communities and state agencies in devising a regeneration strategy – particularly in relation to jobs and housing.
7. An example of this would be the role of the dissertation undertaken by all students in their fourth year, which drew on their placement experience in the third year; the dissertation was supervised by a member of the sociology academic staff and had to reflect sociologically on an aspect of professional practice. To this end, the sociology

dissertation tutor visited students at least once during their placement at their place of work.

8. If the residential and awayday was central to the ethos of the original programme, then it might be argued that (learning from art history and human geography programmes) the field trip became a key methodological device in the revised programme. In a sense, of course, financial stringency became the mother of invention. Nevertheless, the idea that the city was a resource and that London, at the cusp of the twenty-first century, occupied a not dissimilar position to Chicago in the first decades of the twentieth provided a key focus, not just to what was taught but how it was taught.
9. In 2014, UEL was the top-ranked modern university (i.e. ex-poly) in London overall, the second best modern university in the UK for sociology, and the top university in London for 'impact' (this term refers to the Research Excellence Framework's measure of the social, economic and cultural benefits of the knowledge gained from research).
10. It is worth remembering that approximately 5 per cent of young people aged eighteen went to university in the early 1970s compared with nearly 50 per cent today.

CHAPTER TWENTY

The Tavistock-UEL partnership

Michael Rustin

Introduction

The academic partnership between the Tavistock Clinic – now formally the Tavistock and NHS Foundation Trust – and the University of East London (UEL) began in the late 1980s. It came about in part because of intellectual and professional orientations shared by members of staff in the two institutions, but also because of an unexpected convergence of their institutional interests. The Tavistock was then at the beginning of seeking academic accreditation for its professional training programmes and had an advanced social work course, some of whose students – already experienced and innovative social workers – wished to undertake research in their professional field. At that time, we in social sciences at UEL were at the beginning of a major development of our research and doctoral degree work, and the opportunity to encourage and supervise professionally well-qualified PhD students at the Tavistock was attractive.

Thus a link was established in 1989 between an advanced professional course in social work (led by Joan Hutten, a senior Tavistock social worker), which had no academic accreditation, and a linked option for PhD registration with UEL.[1] Five or six advanced social work students registered with UEL for PhDs, and three of them completed their doctorates successfully, two of their theses finding publication as books.[2] This was the beginning of a substantial link between the two institutions; the Tavistock[3] with its high reputation as the leading institution in the field of community mental health, and UEL, which was keen to develop its own postgraduate portfolio and to support high-quality vocational education, a commitment which had continuities with UEL's earlier 'polytechnic' origin.

During the 1980s, the Tavistock had come under governmental pressure to obtain academic accreditation for its work. It was (since 1948) and remains a National Health Service institution, providing free treatment and services to its patients and clients, and it held (and still holds) a national training responsibility in several of its professional fields. Such demands on it from the state had to be taken seriously. The Tavistock had explored the possibilities of academic accreditation with several universities. While links were established with two London area universities in relation to specific subject areas (for example, the family systemic master's course was accredited by Brunel University before it came to UEL), these links were limited and the usual response of universities to these approaches was cool. It seems that the kinds of professional work for which the Tavistock gave training – a significant part of it was psychoanalytic or family systemic in its orientation – was not welcome to most of them. Perhaps this resistance came from established mental health disciplines, averse to professional competition, and perhaps from a belief that the Tavistock's approach was out of line with that of mainstream mental health services, and might thus do nothing to support a university's scientific reputation. While influential in its own fields of work, the Tavistock had since it was founded taken up a radical and challenging position in the broader ecology of therapeutic and community mental health provision.[4] It had favoured a multidisciplinary rather than a predominantly medicalised approach to mental health, and was committed to a range of 'talking therapies' rather than, as the preferred option, pharmaceutical treatments.

Psychoanalytical approaches, especially in their broader applications (for example, short-term and less intensive therapies) had always had a significant place in its formation, but the validity and value of psychoanalytic treatments remained matters of public contention. By the 1980s, however, a changing intellectual climate had led to some interest in these perspectives in the social sciences and cultural studies, including at UEL, and the Tavistock's orientation did not discourage UEL from exploring an engagement with the clinic.

Developing the partnership

The two Tavistock programmes which were first considered for academic accreditation at UEL were an advanced social work course, arising from the doctoral cooperation mentioned above, and a long-established two-year course, colloquially known as the observation course, and whose full title was the Postgraduate Diploma/Master's Course in Psychoanalytic Observational Studies. A formal academic partnership between the institutions was established in 1990. The observation course was the first that became ready to be submitted for validation. It had since its inception in the early 1970s consisted of three concurrent modules, in psychoanalytic theory, infant and young child observation (conducted for one hour per week over two years, in the natural setting of the infant's family, or in a day nursery), and a practice known as 'work discussion'. There were, in addition, one-year units on child development research, and on personality development. In the weekly infant or young child observation seminars, students were expected to present, reflect on and discuss with a supervisor and seminar group their observations and their experience of them. The purpose of 'infant observation', as it was called, which was the core practice of this course, was both to enhance students' understanding of babies and their relationships with their mothers and families, and also to deepen understanding of their own states of mind and feeling, since it was recognised that the experience of an observer regularly visiting an infant in its family over two years was usually an emotionally intense one. Infant observation had been designed by Esther Bick in 1948[5] as a first-stage introduction to the kinds of emotional experiences most relevant to the understanding of a psychoanalytic perspective. Because infant observers were required to be essentially passive in their role in a family during their weekly visits, and because they were supervised, within their seminar groups, on a weekly basis, this procedure was designed to be 'safe', that is to be without risk to the families being observed. Indeed it has been found over many years that many of the mothers who received observers in their homes came to enjoy their visits as a regular time in what could often seem a long week alone with a small child, in which they had sympathetic company from someone interested in their child. The role that has evolved for the students and trainees who have undertaken these observations over many decades is a remarkable one, a distinctive 'form of life', to use Wittgenstein's term, in that an infant observer is not there as a professional, nor as a personal friend, but someone whom a family accepts as a regular visitor to an intimate sphere, in response to an initial request to contribute to a student's experience of learning about infancy.

The observation course, like many others taught at the Tavistock, was found to be an intense experience by students, even though most of it, apart from the observational visits to families, took place on a single day per week during term time. In the decades since infant observation began, there have been thousands of such observations conducted in arrangements set up through the Tavistock, although students are usually expected to use their own initiative in finding a family setting in which to observe. (Sometimes networks of acquaintances, sometimes ante-natal classes and the like make this possible.) Infant observation has become an element of many courses (for example in social work) other than the observation course itself, and has also been extended as a practice to many other settings of psychodynamic education, both in Britain and in many other countries of the world. It has given rise to a substantial literature, concerned with its educational practice, as a genre of qualitative research, and in its modified use as a form of therapeutic intervention to support troubled relationships between mothers and their infants. There is a journal (*Infant Observation*) devoted to this and its adjacent practices, young child observation and work discussion, which has been published since 1997, together with many books.[6] It is noteworthy that despite what one can imagine could be a context of risk, with observers regularly visiting the homes of hitherto unknown families over a lengthy period, there seem to have been exceedingly few serious mishaps, still less scandals, arising from this practice over all these decades.

The two modules offered in parallel to infant and young child observation, from early in the observation course's development, have been work discussion and psychoanalytic theory. Work discussion requires students to be working, or to be in a work placement, in a setting concerned with children or adolescents. Their task was to reflect on the meanings of their day-to-day experience to them, taking account of the fact that there, unlike in an infant's family, their roles are as active participants in a working practice, not merely as passive observers. The chosen settings for work discussion might be a classroom, day nursery, children's home, hospital ward or university department. The third parallel course, in psychoanalytic theory, was intended among its broader purposes to provide conceptual resources with which to reflect on these infant, young child observation and work discussion experiences and their meanings. The frame of reference for these observational and reflective practices has always been primarily concerned with the domain of feelings – those aroused, and especially those found troubling, in the situations in which students are placed.[7] These invite attention to be given to 'unconscious' aspects of experience, and thus introduce students to the psychoanalytic conception of unconscious mental life, as involving unrecognised anxieties, desires and beliefs of different kinds. But while students are being introduced, while they are undertaking observations, to theoretical concepts and ideas, through a psychoanalytical theory course and in later years through a parallel course in developmental psychology, the primary focus of observation and work discussion seminars is not mainly theoretical. The aim is that students should learn in the first instance from the detailed particulars – one could say the phenomenology – of their experience. That is, to differentiate feelings and states of mind from each other, using the ordinary language of emotions. It is only at a later stage of the course, when observational visits have ended or are near completion, that students are required to formulate some unifying meaning in what they have observed, and to make use of theoretical conceptualisation to give a name and definition to this in a written paper. While the entire procedure gives much of its attention to qualities of feeling, it is nevertheless notably particularistic, and observation-centred in its method. One can characterise it as empiricist in its style (with affinities to the British philosophical tradition of empiricism) while taking emotional states as its principal object of attention. This conjunction is also to be found in practices of education in English literature, in its methods of 'close reading' and its attention to the specific qualities of texts. Some of the formative figures in the development of infant observation (Martha Harris, Margot Waddell and Lisa Miller, for example) believed literature to be a more relevant source of emotional understanding than could be found in most mainstream psychological science.

The observational studies programme had originally been designed, and nearly fifty years onwards retains, two purposes. The first is to enable practitioners in various settings concerned with children and adolescents to enhance their understanding and capability in their everyday work, especially in regard to the dimensions of feelings and relationships with others. The work in question might be teaching, nursing, social or youth work. It was sometimes the case that students from more remote occupations – for example business administration or law, or students finding themselves between careers – would choose to make use of the course to explore the ambience of a new field of work. This required them not only to attend the classroom sessions on a weekly basis, but also to find an infant to observe and a placement in which they could undertake some kind of work with children or adolescents.

But second, the observation course has always been a mandatory pre-clinical qualification for admission to the four-year NHS-recognised professional training in psychoanalytic psychotherapy with children and adolescents. On average about a third of students on the observation course have proceeded to apply for this clinical training. It is striking that this programme has successfully provided over many years both for the needs of prospective child psychotherapists, and for the larger number of students whose purpose has not been to change their profession, but rather to enhance the quality of their experience and understanding within their existing field of work. With this dual purpose, the course has always had a primarily psychoanalytic orientation, and has been taught in nearly all of its modules by qualified child psychotherapists.

So here was a course that had already been established in a secure form for about twenty years when in 1990 it was proposed that it be accredited by UEL as a postgraduate diploma and master's level degree course. This posed interesting and challenging problems for the university's system of course validation. In many respects, the course was quite dissimilar to – one might even say fell short of – what was normally required of a course validated at this level. While supervision of the students, and their regular observational reports, was unusually close, taking place in the favourable but now almost unheard-of context of a two-year long seminar composed of a single tutor and only five students (this was to enable each of them to present two observations in each term), it prescribed little formal written work, and there were few procedures for assessing it. (However, the infant, young child observation and work discussion reports for seminars did require a lot of writing up.) Great importance had always been attached to the students' final observation essay, in which they were expected to describe their experience of observation, and in particular the development of the 'infant in the family' whom they had observed for nearly two years. This paper had always been taken as a significant measure of what a student had learned, and similar papers are used elsewhere to assess a student's aptitude for clinical training. However, it was also recognised that students could be sensitive and perceptive observers while not being accomplished writers, or could be more capable as writers than as observers of infants. Furthermore, the procedures of infant observation and work discussion were different from most academically accredited methods of learning, and were unfamiliar to the university's academic assessors. How, therefore, was the university to respond to this course proposal?

The capability which UEL brought to this task had been developed during its own transition from the licensed degree structure of the London external degree to the transitional academic jurisdiction of the Council for National Academic Awards (CNAA). The University of London had allowed colleges to register students for 'external' versions of its own degrees, both in British colonies overseas and in the UK itself, fully prescribing syllabuses and maintaining full control of assessment. College staff members could become 'recognised teachers' of London University. This was how the degree courses offered by the three colleges of technology that combined to form the North East London Polytechnic in 1970 were initially provided. But when the polytechnics were formed, responsibility for the award of degrees was assigned to a new institution, the CNAA, and under this arrangement, responsibility for proposing and designing degree courses for validation was assigned to the polytechnics themselves.

As described in other chapters of this book, this new polytechnic – at first familiarly known as NELP – took an exceptionally innovative view of the task of renewing and expanding its curriculum. CNAA itself adopted an enlightened approach (although it seems that not everyone experienced it in this way) which gave the initiative to the polytechnics to define and propose the programmes they wished to put forward for validation. Course proposals were required to specify what were termed their 'aims and objectives' (it was never clear what the distinction between these near-synonyms was supposed to be!), and to set out the design through which these were to be delivered.[8] This design needed to include a full specification of a proposed course – its curricula, teaching and learning methods, form of assessment, internal governance, provision for student complaints, and most other operational matters. Precedents and templates were soon established which initiators of courses could follow, so that submissions could be made in a relatively standard and thus comparable form. One version of a submission – often its longer version – was written for the scrutiny of the validation panel dispatched by CNAA to consider a course for prospective approval. Another version of it, usually shorter, was designed as a 'student handbook', and was intended to set out the specification of a course as both a description of it for students, and also as a kind of contract with them, setting out what they were entitled to expect and what could be expected of them.

Panels were assembled by the CNAA from subject-specialists (drawn in early years largely from the older universities). In many fields those who volunteered and were appointed to take these roles were committed to the development – sometimes even to the initial academic recognition –of their subjects. This situation, and the considerable expansion of higher education which was then taking place, facilitated innovation, just as had the setting up of an earlier generation of new universities (Sussex, Warwick Essex etc.) in the 1960s. It sometimes takes a major institutional shake-up to bring about intellectual change.

Since all of these new institutions were required to have their programmes set out and validated, this became an enormous undertaking. There were more than thirty polytechnics in England and Wales when the 'binary divide' was abolished in the 1992 Further and Higher Education Act, and they were reconstituted as universities, under an explicitly corporate form of governance which regrettably excluded elected local authorities. CNAA course validation procedures were notably deliberative, even though they had prescriptive authority. An appointed panel, in a specific subject area, would receive the written documentation describing a proposed course, and would meet with staff at their institution to discuss their course proposals with them. This was usually in a day of scheduled meetings, with members of the course team. In conclusion, following a private meeting, they would then come to a decision. This might be to approve a course without conditions, or approve it with conditions (mandatory) or recommendations (advisory), or reject a proposal entirely. The appointed chairs of these subject panels usually had a highly influential role, and as one might expect CNAA visits could be occasions of high drama, with their own rituals.

At the North East London Polytechnic and no doubt in most such institutions, a specialist apparatus – here called the course development unit or CDU – was set up to support and manage this process of validation. For several years, this administration, supported by committees of academics within faculties, had the role of mediating between subject departments and course teams within the university, and the CNAA, assisting them in developing and presenting their proposals.

In effect, this experience involved the 'internalisation' within the polytechnic and university of the norms and practices which had been developed by the CNAA. Its essence was, you (the proposers of a course) must tell us what your purposes are, and we will advise you on how these might be met in ways which are acceptable to CNAA. The senior staff of the CDU developed an ongoing relationship with the capable administrative secretariat at CNAA, and with the polytechnic's senior management. Before a course proposal ever got as far as being submitted for validation, it was subject to an internal procedure called 'initial approval', on which the CDU gave its advice. Decisions on 'initial approval' were made with regard to issues of potential student recruitment, possible duplication of programmes and broader educational desirability, related to the priorities of the institution. At the beginning, under the leadership of director George Brosan and deputy director Eric Robinson, NELP had a strong commitment to innovation, and an astonishing number of new programmes were submitted for CNAA validation in a short period. To a considerable degree this encouragement of innovation continued under subsequent vice-chancellors, as is shown in other chapters in this volume.

When the power and responsibility for validating and awarding degrees was transferred to the polytechnic from CNAA, an approach, very similar to that which had been established by CNAA, was followed within the university. Course approvals (and periodic mandatory re-approvals) involved the same kinds of documentation, regulatory structures and externally moderated validation panels as the CNAA had developed. By the time the first Tavistock course (the observation course) was submitted for validation, the CNAA was no longer involved, and the entire procedure was conducted by the then polytechnic.

One of the striking facets of course validation procedures, and the deliberations which they involved at this time was how 'content rich' they were. Issues of subject content and teaching and assessment method were explicit matters for debate. This was a context in which the expansion and proliferation of courses (and the engagement with new institutional partners like the Tavistock) facilitated innovation. The deliberative practices of the CNAA were to a degree internalised within the university. At this time, the development of new degree programmes was the preoccupying task of academic staff, at a time before research became a priority. This began when, in 1992, the polytechnics were redesigned as 'new universities', and were authorised to take part in the periodic 'research assessment exercise' (RAE), which was a competitive evaluation of portfolios of published research submitted by universities in designated subject areas, giving rise to differential funding and positioning in 'league tables' held to denote comparative 'research excellence'. The Tavistock was later able to submit some of its research in these exercises, and also to gain credit for the substantial professional doctorate programmes which it had developed in partnership with UEL.

This was the situation which was encountered by the Tavistock when it first submitted for validation its proposed course in psychoanalytic observational studies. This process was commenced in 1990, but the validation itself was undertaken by the university in 1992, after it had taken on this authority from the CNAA. It first had to be agreed in principle that the course was appropriate for validation at postgraduate diploma and master's level. This decision was no doubt made easier by the fact that the course had been operating successfully for decades, and had long been a mandatory pre-qualification for an NHS-recognised professional training. The issue then was to build on to the existing course design the full specification of curricula, teaching methods and assessments which was appropriate to a postgraduate degree. This involved devising written forms of assessment, including a master's-level dissertation which equated in its volume and criteria to those expected of postgraduate courses. While the effect of this was to add substantially to the academic requirements of the course, it had the benefit of generating more high-quality written work by students. Assessment methods were designed to be consistent with the commitment of the course to close observation and its description and conceptualisation. It seems that the atmosphere of learning and development which characterised the course was not significantly damaged by its development for academic accreditation. Just one significant curriculum revision was called for by the validating panel, which was to give increased importance to the unit in developmental psychology, to broaden the disciplinary range of the programme beyond psychoanalytic approaches. A benefit of the academic development was to enhance the value of the course in the eyes of potential students, and also of employers who might be asked to authorise a one-day-per-week attendance on it. A two- or three-year course of this kind can hardly now be competitive in its recruitment without an academic accreditation of this kind.

The Tavistock model

The observation course was the largest as well as the first to be accredited at UEL. This was not only because of the size of its first-year intake at the Tavistock itself – this reached well over fifty in some years – but also because the course was offered in various locations elsewhere (known as 'outlying centres'), not only in the UK but also in Italy. The centres in the UK at different times included Birmingham, Oxford, Liverpool, Bristol, Exeter and Belfast, and, in Italy, Rome, Florence and Genoa. This outreach served to extend the geographical range and influence of the Tavistock's work. The curriculum and assessment for the centres whose work was validated by UEL were managed centrally from the Tavistock. Its annual assessment board at its largest had 350 student candidates to consider, from as many as six different centres. Validation panels were from time to time dispatched from the Tavistock to each of these centres to assess their suitability. Validation visits to Italy had special interest and attraction for panel members, for obvious reasons. Other centres in the UK offered a 'Tavistock model' observation course, but arranged academic validation through a local university, as in Leeds and Glasgow. The university showed commitment and courage in supporting this widely spread programme, since it had reason to be concerned about possible risks it might be running, given problems, financial and other, which had been experienced with some UK university courses operated overseas.

Around twenty postgraduate programmes followed the MA in Observational Studies in obtaining validation at UEL, with at its maximum nearly 1000 postgraduate students enrolled. These courses were in many areas of professional education, including social work, systemic family[9] therapy, child and adolescent psychotherapy, emotional factors in teaching and learning (provided mainly for teachers), and consultation to organisations. The pattern of academic development of these programmes had many similarities with that of the observation course described, with a good deal of 'learning from experience' taking place at the Tavistock and UEL. Two of the programmes involved a significant contribution by teachers from both institutions. One of these was in the field of social work, in which UEL had its own longstanding presence. The other was a Master's course in Psychoanalytic Studies, which was unusual for the Tavistock in not being specifically vocational in its purpose, but rather offering a substantial introduction to psychoanalytic ways of thinking, with elements of observational as well as academic study of psychoanalytic theory and its applications.

Before long, after 1990, several professional doctorate programmes were added to this portfolio, in the fields of systemic family therapy, social work, child and adolescent psychoanalytic psychotherapy, and consultancy to organisations. These were part of a project to enhance the qualifications and capabilities of professionals trained at the Tavistock, and to add to the body of research in their fields. An associated aim was to meet the increasing demands for a stronger evidence-base for mental health treatments. These doctorates, which were largely oriented towards professional practice, gave an opportunity to generate and validate qualitative forms of research into clinical processes, countering the predominance of quantitative outcome studies and randomised controlled trials. But it still proved difficult to bid successfully for grants for clinically based research projects. Academic staff from the university and staff holding joint appointments at the Tavistock and UEL were able to provide necessary expertise in research teaching and supervision. In child and adolescent psychoanalytic therapy alone, over eighty-five professional doctoral theses have been completed.[10] The social work master's and doctoral programmes were part of an initiative to develop forms of 'relationship-based practice' in a professional field in which this had become weakened in recent decades. The programme supported the formation of the Centre for Social Work Practice and the *Journal of Social Work Practice* and significant book publications.[11] Most of the Tavistock-UEL courses gave rise to publication in professional journals and in the Tavistock Clinic Book Series, which since its launch in 1997 has published over fifty titles. In addition to the many professional doctorate degrees, the degree of PhD by published work was awarded to sixteen members or former members of the Tavistock's staff during this period, giving academic recognition to the clinical research work previously undertaken at the Tavistock.

At the time the partnership began, links in Britain between universities and psychoanalytic and family systemic professional trainings were few. This partnership was a pioneer of what soon became a considerable development of others in this field, involving many universities and reducing the isolation of psychoanalysis and systemic psychotherapy from the academy. (Several substantial links of this kind now exist, for example at UCL, Birkbeck and the University of Essex). It was UEL's liberal and enabling approach to educational development, and the fact that at that time it was willing to allow approaches that challenged dominant orthodoxies, which made this possible.

Up to the level of master's courses and after a first phase of development, the university allowed considerable autonomy to the Tavistock in conducting their joint programmes. After their initial validation, most responsibilities for teaching and assessment were devolved to the Tavistock, which was encouraged to develop its own academic management capabilities. The procedure for assuring that academic standards were being met was largely retrospective, through the periodic inspection and revalidation of each course. Unfortunately, equal responsibilities were not delegated to the doctoral programmes, where the university insisted on forms of micro-regulation of registrations. research proposals – which required three separate committees to approve them – ethical approvals, etc.), difficulties with which would eventually lead to disenchantment at the Tavistock with the partnership itself.

The liaison lost

In 2014, the greater part of the large portfolio of UEL-validated Tavistock and Portman NHS Trust was transferred to the University of Essex, and revalidated there with few substantive revisions to the programmes deemed necessary. Only a joint qualifying Master's degree in Social Work, founded on the two institutions' strong commitments to 'relationship-based' approaches, survives of the previous academic partnership.

There were some significant limitations to the extent of joint work achieved between the two partners during their connection over twenty years. Only a small number of academic staff from UEL, mainly from the fields of sociology, psychosocial studies, social work and cultural studies, engaged in joint activities with the Tavistock, although there were memorable joint initiatives. Among these were the annual conference, 'Psychoanalysis and the public sphere' held between 1987 and 2001, in which the radical psychoanalytic journal *Free Associations* was a third partner, and three conferences on the theme of 'Culture and the unconscious',[12] which linked academic and clinical approaches to psychoanalysis. The systemic family therapists at the Tavistock had good links with the Centre for Narrative Research (CNR) at UEL (see Chapter 5), which supported the setting up and recognition of the Tavistock's Centre for Family and Systemic Research (FRSRC). Many publications accompanied this work.[13] Following the move of family therapy (and most other taught programmes) to the University of Essex, FRSRC lost its formal university link, although it retains good connections with the CNR. As we have said above, social work was a field in which there was and still is substantial collaboration between the two institutions. But there were UEL faculties which might have been expected to take a more active interest in the partnership with the Tavistock than actually transpired. Perhaps there could never have been an easy synergy between a specialist postgraduate community mental health institution, like the Tavistock, and a university whose main work then was the teaching of undergraduates.

The University of Essex is, of course, an entirely suitable academic partner for the Tavistock, but then so, in my view, was UEL. One has learned that such partnerships can be placed in jeopardy if those holding their most senior positions allow their attention to be diverted from what is needed to maintain them.

Notes

1. The late Carole Satyamurti and I were responsible for this initiative at UEL.
2. Brynna Kroll, *Chasing Rainbows: Children, Divorce and Loss*, Russell House: London, 1994; Katie Prince, *Boring Records? Communication, Speech and Writing in Social Work*, Jessica Kingsley: London, 1996.
3. On the history of the Tavistock, see M. Waddell and S. Kraemer (eds), *The Tavistock Century*, Phoenix: London, 2020.
4. Eric Trist and Hugh Murray (eds), *The Social Engagement of Social Science, Vol. 1 The Socio-Psychological Perspective; Vol. 2. The Socio-Technical Perspective; Vol. 3. The Socio-Ecological Perspective*, University of Pennsylvania Press: Philadelphia, PA, 1990.

5. Andrew Briggs (ed.), *Surviving Space: Papers on Infant Observation,* Routledge: London, 2002.
6. Books include: E. Miller, M. E. Rustin, M. J. Rustin and J. Shuttleworth (eds), *Closely Observed Infants: Case-Studies in Psychoanalytic Observation,* Duckworth: London,1989; S. Reid (ed.), *Developments in Infant Observation,* Routledge: London, 1997; Stephen Briggs, *Growth and Risk in Infancy,* Jessica Kingsley: London, 1997; Andrew Briggs 2002 *op cit.*; M. E. Rustin and J. Bradley (eds), *Work Discussion: Reflective Practice in Work,* Routledge: London, 2008; and S. Adamo and M. E. Rustin (eds), *Young Child Observation: a Development in the Theory and Method of Infant Observation,* Routledge: London, 2013.
7. M. J. Rustin, 'Learning about Emotions: the Tavistock Approach', *European Journal of Psychotherapy, Counselling and Health,* Vol. 6, No 3, September 2003, pp187-208.
8. Stefan Collini (*Speaking of Universities,* Verso: London, 2017), who has written an important critique of recent developments in higher education, has referred to 'aims and objectives' and their like as deadening formulations, stifling of creativity. It must be said, however, that at this innovative stage of new course development, they could focus thought in valuable ways.
9. Charlotte Burck and Andrew Cooper have each given valuable advice on this chapter in regard to systemic family therapy and social work.
10. Recent books related to this programme are M.J. Rustin, Researching the *Unconscious: Principles of Psychoanalytic Method,* Routledge: London 2019, and M.E. and M.J. Rustin (eds), *New Discoveries in Child Psychotherapy: Findings from Qualitative Research,* Routledge: London, 2019.
11. Such as: A. Cooper and J. Lousada, *Borderline Welfare,* Routledge: London, 2005; A. Cooper, *Conjunctions, Social Work, Psychoanalysis and Society,* Routledge: London, 2018; G. Ruch, D. Turney and A. Ward (eds), *Relationship-Based Social Work: Getting to the Heart of Practice,* Jessica Kingsley: London, second edition, 2010; and C. Parkinson, L. Allain, H. Hingley-Jones, *Observation in Health and Social Care: Applications for Learning, Research and Practice with Children and Adults,* Jessica Kingsley: London, 2017.
12. C. Bainbridge, S. Radstone, M. J. Rustin and C. Yates (eds), *Culture and the Unconscious,* Palgrave: Basingstoke, 2007.
13. For example, A. Vetere and E. Dowling (eds), *Narrative Therapy with Children and their Families,* Routledge: London, second edition, 2016 and C. Burck and G. Daniel, *Gender and Family Therapy,* Routledge: London, 2019.

Experiences of Former Students

CHAPTER TWENTY-ONE

Bloody snobs

Tanya Frank

University, like avocados or caviar, was something I knew I'd never have the chance to sample. It was costly, and middle class, and no one in my family had been to one. The first time I came across the grand five-syllable word was when Mum accidentally flicked the telly to the wrong channel, and scholars from Corpus Christi College Oxford and King's College Cambridge were answering questions on a programme called *University Challenge*.

As the years went by, I told Mum it might be useful for me to get some further education, not university but maybe college, a trade, just so I could make a few bob, and treat us to a curry from time to time. Mum would just say, 'not now, Tan', and pat my tummy: she was getting desperate for me to have a baby. I was twenty, and all my friends had nippers already.

I knew not to tackle Mum. I also knew if I had been born in North Chingford on the boundaries of Epping Forest where the Queen Elizabeth I hunting lodge still stood, I might have gone to private school with the posh kids who spoke like they had plums in their mouths, kids who were prepped to go to university. Mum called them 'bloody snobs', and said they looked down on us. Mum knew best, and I wanted to please her. I would have babies and I might even end up raising them on my own. It was no big deal. Mum had been a single parent, and most of the mothers I knew on Chingford Hall Estate parented alone. I could claim income support and work the odd shift at the London Rubber Company on the North Circular Road, making condoms for men, and Marigold gloves for women. It was decided.

The council housing estate where we lived had been my home from the time I was three. Built in the 1960s, it comprised three tower blocks, four maisonette blocks and a few houses around the perimeter that were snapped up in the 1980s under Thatcher's right-to-buy scheme.

People outside of Chingford Hall called it a shithole, and in a sense they were right. The place had been a sewerage farm before it became our home, and just a few feet beneath the concrete foundation, excrement still festered and bubbled, and rats ran amok.

Our address was 49 Yew Court, Marigold Way. No one knew why this dismal block of council flats was named after a tree, or the street for a flower. Wishful thinking, perhaps, because aside from a square patch of grass that was used as a dog toilet, nothing much grew there at all.

Still, I might have been content with two babies, a common-law husband, and a couple of Certificates in Secondary Education (CSE) from McEntee Senior High were it not for three things.

One: Auntie Betty in America.

Two: The eighteen months I spent volunteering abroad.

Three: The big banner that hung from the façade of Waltham Forest College in 1988, advertising an access to higher education course in cultural studies.

Auntie Betty had been an almost mythical creature during my childhood. She lived in a large Moorish house in the Hollywood Hills, renting out the basement level to some aspiring actor at the time called Patrick Swayze. This fantastical aunt worked for Irwin Allen, the master of disaster, helping to make *Towering Inferno* for the big screen, and *Land of the Giants* and *Lost in Space* for TV. For my tenth birthday she sent me a ViewMaster with a series of slides so I could see Los Angeles for myself in Technicolor.

Auntie Betty was my mother's aunt, her foster aunt in fact, since she had found Mum, mute, scabies-ridden and malnourished, at Norwood Jewish Orphanage after the second world war. Betty, whose real name was Elizabeth Emanuel, was from wealthy Jewish stock, a family of philanthropists. She fostered Mum for a time – but wasn't able to adopt her. Auntie Betty was gay, and in those days the law prohibited homosexuals from adopting children. Unable to live the way she wanted to in this country, Betty left in 1958 for New York, taking with her a good measure of guilt and a promise to help my mother, even from afar. Once I came of age, Auntie Betty wanted to educate me, to encourage my love of writing, my curiosity.

In her queen's English she told me I might want to travel and that she would help defray the cost. I volunteered first at a kibbutz in Israel, then I spent six months in Andhra Pradesh, India at a rural development project run by Oxfam and Action Aid. I met people who spoke like Auntie Betty, who sounded just like the kids from North Chingford, but they didn't look down on me. They had exciting ideas about society and had all been to university. Andhra Pradesh changed me, but not as much as what happened upon my reluctant return, when I forgot to take my contraceptive pill and got pregnant with Dale. It was 1987. I was about to turn twenty-two.

Back home, I tried to compensate for my reverse culture shock by connecting with family, but I felt adrift in the sea of new motherhood and in my relationship with my baby's father. I didn't fit in with the other mothers at the mums and tots group at the community centre, women who breastfed with ease, whose babies were thriving, and sleeping through the night, while I was struggling to get Dale to latch on, to make enough milk, to get more than two hours' sleep at a time.

Dale was eight months old when I saw the open enrolment sign on the stripped-down classicist façade of Waltham Forest College. I hauled his buggy up the many steps to the entrance – and took the admission test for the access to higher education programme in cultural studies, a course for people like me who had left school with few if any formal qualifications. Anne Thompson, a tall, straight-backed woman who would become my tutor, offered to hold the whimpering Dale, pat his back, and walk him up and down the corridor to pacify him, while I sweated in the August heat over the paper that would change the course of my future.

The Waltham Forest College access programme had forged links with Middlesex Polytechnic and NELP: North East London

Polytechnic, as the University of East London was then known, so folks like me, who were classed as mature students, could progress to these institutions with just a little form-filling and an orientation day, provided we passed the access course.

I knew I wasn't clever enough to get a fully-fledged degree. My teachers at McEntee High had known it too, telling me I wasn't college material. But I started to toy with the idea that I could maybe get a diploma in higher education. It would take two years of study at the polytechnic. The words diploma and polytechnic were less formidable to my ears. Encouraged by my tutors at Waltham Forest, and by the confidence I'd gained from recent forays into feminist and cultural studies writing, I decided to give it a go.

But by the start of the spring term at Waltham Forest College, I was pregnant again. Gordon, Dale's father, and I bickered more than we didn't, as he berated me for applying to polytechnic, reminding me that I would never earn as much as him, and that women's studies would turn me into a lesbian. The only lesbians I knew, apart from Auntie Betty, were big Pam and Ricky, who drank barley wine and fought outside the Greyhound pub on the estate. I had children. I was a mother. I didn't like the reptilian sounding word. I would never become a lesbian.

Mum agreed wholeheartedly with Gordon that I should stay home and look after the children. A short access course was one thing, but leaving the kids in order to study for a diploma, and heaven forbid getting a full-time career afterwards, would risk causing them irreparable harm. The vice-principal of North East London Polytechnic leaned closer to Mum's sentiment than my own, suggesting I might consider postponing full-time study for a year to focus on my domestic responsibilities.

But I knew differently, intuitively, despite the loud noise to the contrary. I knew that I needed something under my belt, for not if, but rather when Gordon and I would go our separate ways, and I would have to become everything to the boys. I took driving lessons. Just in case. In case of an emergency, in case I needed to do a big shop at the weekend, and secretly in case I might dare to really take up the course. Thinking about gears and a clutch on top of everything else was overwhelming, so I took my test in an automatic, my balloon of a belly wedged behind the steering wheel. And just a few weeks after Zach was born, I found her – a cheap mud-brown Triumph Toledo. Manual. I decided I would get the hang of it.

In the autumn of 1989, I clunked through the gears and stalled at every stop on my way to the main site of the polytechnic in Barking, Dagenham, hoping I wouldn't get pulled up. I dropped Dale at the on-site crèche, and took newborn Zach with me into the classroom. The polytechnic was modern and spread out. A double grey portakabin housed the student union and bar, and sat smack bang in the centre of campus. The place was more Chingford Hall than Oxbridge, and I felt immediately at home.

I chose classes in women's studies, third world studies (later renamed development studies) and anthropology. In that first semester I sat at the back of the lecture theatre and breastfed Zach, learning from women's studies professor Maggie Humm how that nameless feeling which had been sitting heavy in my stomach for years, that sense of displacement and subjugation, was not just peculiar to me but had been written about and interrogated even before I was born by Betty Friedan in *The Feminine Mystique.* The units for women in the third world helped me conceptualise what I had witnessed in Andhra Pradesh, and to understand the gender politics at work in the community of Bangladeshis close to where I had lived, where a rising trend of termination of female foetuses had hit the headlines and caused international alarm. Theories of class and race, ideas that had shaped my life without ever consciously crystallising became suddenly as clear as the view from my tower block window – the North Circular Road, and beyond it the illegal caravans squatting near the perfectly round reservoir.

The access course had kept our learning local. We studied at The Vestry in Old Walthamstow, which had once been a workhouse for the poor, the industrial revolution, the suffragists, the miners' strike, and Britain's role in the first world war. But now, as part of my lessons at the polytechnic, I was learning things on a macro scale, global concepts of neo-imperialism, second-wave feminist writing from both sides of the pond.

In the buzz and fervour of it all, I started to find my voice, to read critically, to pin myself on the map, to know where I stood politically. Although I was attending the polytechnic part time, two days a week rather than three, in my heart and mind, in my gut that now churned with excitement and novel ideas, I was more than part-time, more than full-time; I was a whole new me. It must have been visible, somehow, this transformative moment, because in the second year – as I sat in anthropology discussing the late stone-age matriarchal community in Catalhoyuk – I felt her eyes on me. Kelly was a lesbian with flaming orange hair and strong opinions. She was from Birkenhead, and her singsong accent and belly laughter was a tonic. I had never met anyone like her and I drank in her affection, her passion, her independence like it was nectar.

Gordon left soon after I fell in love with Kelly. Although our union was short-lived, it changed my life. For the first time I embraced being different, being other, being loved.

In the aftermath of this relationship, I was no longer the single mother I assumed I would be. I had a tribe. There was strength in the students in my cohort: Meena, a young divorced mother of five; Barbara, a florist old enough to be my mother; Michelle, a burned-out Afro-Caribbean nurse who worked on an intensive baby care unit. These women buoyed me up, talking to me late into the night about postmodernism, poststructuralism, post-everything. I finally found the confidence to stay on beyond the two-year mark and the diploma, and study for my degree.

North East London Polytechnic became the University of East London. I loved that something about my East End working-class roots was still there in the title of the university, and I loved that I was attending a real university now. By the time I graduated, I had learnt to craft ceramics, paint, do needlework, take photographs and make an audio-visual tape-slide project in my women in art unit, to examine the slave trade and the impact of colonialism in my women in third world development, but it was the opportunity to tell my story in the women in autobiography unit that would reshape my story forever.

For the final semester of the degree, Professor Humm set us an assignment to write 3000 words about our life history. In the margin of my early draft, she noted that my writing was like Virginia Woolf's desk, with too many ideas cluttering it up. It was true; like so many other writers who had been silenced, there was *so* much I was bursting to say.

In 1993 I earned my BA Hons degree. I was the first student in the country to receive a named women's studies degree. The Women's Press came to our class and presented me with a certificate and a book token to celebrate my newly won status. That year my name appeared in *The Guardian* along with the other students up and down the country who had won first-class degrees with honours.

Mum was proud in the end. 'That's my Tan,' she shouted when I walked on to the stage in my cap and gown at the Barbican. Afterwards when we posed for photos, I insisted that she wear my gown and mortarboard, and I snapped her by the fountains, Mum with a pseudo-degree, smiling like a giddy teenager.

Later when I got a position as a lecturer for the Open University and had to teach evenings and summer school, she watched the boys for me. And, always a bit of an exhibitionist, she especially liked it when I went on to write about her in a short film I made for Anglia Television. When I got paid my commission fee, the first thing we did was to splash out on a curry.

I had the bug after my women's studies degree. I acquired a postgraduate certificate in further and higher education, from the University of Greenwich, and a master's in creative writing at the University of California, Riverside. The latter I completed after packing up my life, and escaping with thirteen-year-old Dale, and eleven-year-old Zach to live with Auntie Betty in America. None of these further studies changed or challenged the core of me as much as that first degree.

I am an author now, splitting my time between the UK and the USA. My book *Zig-Zag Boy* is forthcoming from Harper Collins in the spring of 2021. I am not saying that without my women's studies degree I wouldn't have embarked upon this path. It is impossible to know what my life might have looked like. Maybe writing was always in my blood, and Auntie Betty recognised it as a writer herself. But I will always be grateful to the University of East London for the way it nurtured me in those early days as a mother, accommodated me as I searched and grew and changed, recognised me as someone who was worthy of the chance to learn and tell my story, and to enable it all without landing me in thousands of pounds of debt.

Today, thirty years to the date from when I started at North East London Polytechnic, things are different. I know that so much of what defined my experience at the time is now a thing of the past. I know I am lucky. Sometimes I think back to the very first women's studies class that I attended. Professor Humm went around the room and asked us what our mothers and what our grandmothers were doing at our age. My mother had been a single parent at my age, like me. My grandmother, also a single parent, unable to provide for her children, was getting ready to relinquish them to the Jewish orphanage. We were the same, all of us, three generations of single mothers.

But there was one difference, small at first, then big enough to change everything. It was the radical thinking, new ideas and freedom of expression in that first glimpse of higher education that gave me the confidence to take those first steps into my new life.

CHAPTER TWENTY-TWO

The air vibrated: anxiety, excitement and intellectual endeavour

Amal Treacher Kabesh

I was interviewed for a place to undertake a cultural studies degree as a mature student (I was twenty-seven at the time and working as a psychiatric nurse). I vaguely remember a group interview but the content and the atmosphere has been lost in the mists of time. I remember, however, vividly my individual interview with the late Ken Parker that was acerbic and challenging. Ken and I had a robust altercation over the novel that I was reading at the time – *The Sea, The Sea* by Iris Murdoch (it turned out that Ken Parker's wife was an expert on the work of Iris Murdoch). The interview finished with Ken Parker telling me that he was making me an unconditional offer. When we left the room he said to two lecturers, the late Peter Horne and Bill Schwarz, that he had no idea why he was offering me a place. I do not have an O- or A-level to my name as a consequence of a broken family history, and I have never known whether Ken meant that it was because of my lack of educational qualifications or something more personal about who I am. In any case, I had no idea what was meant by an 'unconditional offer' and it was only when the papers arrived from the university that I gathered from the content that I had gained a place.

I arrived on the first day nervous and apprehensive as I had absolutely no idea what undertaking a degree would entail. I found the room where my first lecture was held without much difficulty. I remember it as spacious and airy. There were many young people milling around talking together. I found a place to sit and I looked around me feeling overwhelmed and out of place. Across the blackboard was written 'history is about the present' and if I remember correctly, the name of the late American historian Hayden White was written under the quote. I stared at the board feeling bewildered, confused and had the first inkling that my belief system was about to be thrown off its axis. In walked the historian Bill Schwarz who provided the first lecture, elaborating on the interwoven web of temporalities, events and the dominant narratives of occurrences that had apparently taken place. It may have been the first lecture but I was already thrown into a cultural studies approach to knowledge and understanding.

This lecture focused on the complexities of understanding the web of events, time and dominant historical narrative. Through lectures on history we were introduced to the seventeenth and nineteenth century (I cannot remember if we covered the eighteenth century), Cadbury's and the Quakers in Birmingham, the first and second wave of feminist activity. I was introduced to E.P. Thompson's majestic book *The Making of the English Working Class* and Keith Thomas's *Religion and the Decline of Magic*. I studied Richard Hoggart's *The Uses of Literacy* and through engaging with the work of the Birmingham Centre for Contemporary Cultural Studies I discovered the importance and value of subcultures that, thankfully, undermine the dominant culture. Raymond Williams was the benevolent and generous figure that seemingly hovered over all of us. His notion of 'structures of feeling' seemed, and remains, pertinent and apposite.

I learnt to think through structural matters and how prevalent discourses of historical events set the foundation for what is perceived as 'fact'. I learnt how to think through the inextricable web of the economy, the workings of the state and the official media. Alongside this valuable understanding I also began to understand more fully that lives are not made up of facts alone, indeed, that all subjectivities are jagged and contradictory. I was introduced to psychoanalysis and history through a particular strand of feminist theory, and was gripped by the notion of listening for absences, silences, gaps and the fissures of dominant historical accounts, the narratives that are spoken and adhered to and the relentless workings of the unconscious.

It is important to say that it was all much more messy, confusing and incomprehensible than this account provides. I am at risk of making this personal narrative too clean and overly coherent. To be honest, I spent much of my time feeling baffled emotionally, intellectually, politically. My first seminar lecturer – David Chalmers – was a philosopher who was sharp, did not suffer fools gladly, gave no leeway to us as first-year undergraduates and new to really thinking through whatever opinion or belief we held dear. I appreciated his wit, his depth and extent of knowledge, and the way he challenged us simultaneously with warmth and a clear firmness. The few seminars that he delivered laid the foundation for my desire to understand and to engage with knowledge.

Needless to say this account is reliant on my memory and to provide this account my undergraduate past has had a firm grip on my present life over the past few weeks. I have been thrown back to an important part of my history and I have recollected that time viscerally through recalling the rooms and the senses that the various buildings evoked: sounds and smells primarily. I have remembered lecturers who remain important to me and who persist vividly in my tapestry of intellectual endeavour. Having said that, most of the time they are in the background as part of the texture of my lived experiences. I am grateful to my lecturers and the generosity, kindness and support that they provided (I was a particularly needy and demanding student), and they never betrayed the inevitable irritation and frustration that they must have felt when I intruded on their time and space.

I began to realise that the capriciousness of human beings could not be reduced to false consciousness and needed (needs) to be taken seriously. These matters continue to inform my thinking, and attempts to conceptualise my current preoccupations to understand more closely poses the rather impossible question: why we do insist on acting against our best interests? This essay is being written in the lead-up to a general election to be held on 12 December 2019, the perpetual aftermath of the vote to leave the European Union, and yet another bout of hysterical nationalism as England reached the final of the rugby world cup (South Africa beat England comprehensively). However, the narratives from the media are never straightforward or homogenous – some TV commentators did refer back to South Africa's victory in 1995 when Nelson Mandela attended, and they commented on the importance for South Africa of winning the rugby world cup. I am thrown back to thinking about Gramsci's political analysis of domination, coercion and consent. I remember a lively disagreement among the lecturers that focused on the applicability or not of Gramsci's analysis in relation to Thatcherism and the Falklands crisis. I cannot remember the precise lines of divergence but I learnt that disagreement could sharpen up intellectual thought and political engagement, can be fun and enliven self and others. Above all, and this is personally important, that disagreement could be survived. The air vibrated with intellectual endeavour and excitement.

At this particular troubling political period I find myself turning back to Gramsci to try to make sense of the turbulent political landscape that we inhabit, through trying to understand matters of common sense, consent and coercion. I now work and live, part of the time, in the East Midlands, and I am persistently puzzled as to why so many people (frequently underpaid, struggling to make ends meet and who have no chance to sit at the table of success and status) have such a strong attachment to the Conservative Party and to leaving the EU (most people in the deprived East Midlands voted to leave). I remain profoundly bewildered and troubled, and the theoretical frameworks learnt when I was an undergraduate prove enduring and invaluable. Here I am thinking of Althusser and his conceptualisations of state apparatuses, the work of Foucault and governmentality, as written above Antonio Gramsci, and the work on representations and power through Stuart Hall and the Centre for Contemporary Cultural Studies that was located at University of Birmingham before it was shamefully closed in 2002.

The experience remained exciting, giddy-making and overwhelming, especially when I attempted to tackle psychoanalysis, feminism and sexual difference. I read second-wave feminist theory and was confronted by my attachments to patriarchy and the ties that bind me so closely into the sociopolitical order. I worked my way through Simone de Beauvoir, Kate Millett, Juliet Mitchell, Adrienne Rich, Gayle Rubin, Jacqueline Rose and Sheila Rowbotham (this is a partial list), and French feminist theory, and was challenged to truly understand that sexual difference and gendered identities are made through the sociocultural spheres. Feminism as a theory and as a political stance has remained an essential part of my identity.

None of us, however, are immune from the inexorable effects of the societies and histories that we inhabit. At that time we could choose from one of three pathways on our course – literature, popular culture and philosophy; I chose philosophy. I have frequently wondered about my choice, and it was partly based on being completely intrigued and wanting to know more about the philosophical canon. On reflection, I now think there was another, and perhaps more pertinent, motivation. Contemplating this more closely, I now realise that I choose philosophy, after all the most 'conservative' of the three pathways, so that I would be acceptable, be the right thing and to garner intellectual respectability. I have, and remain, insecure about my intellectual capacities and frequently feel that my right to belong in academia is precarious. My troubled history during my secondary school education has always endured. Moreover, I am dual-heritage (Egyptian/Muslim father and English/Christian mother) and this history also, inevitably, persists and pulses away.

Philosophy as a pathway introduced me to Thomas Hobbes, Immanuel Kant, John Locke, John Stuart Mill, and I still remember clearly a lecture delivered by Peter Horne that concentrated on elaborating David Hume's conceptualisations of taste. But herein lies the rub, for while I was introduced to radical thought and learnt to locate philosophical thought in relation to time and history, we were never introduced to thinking through philosophical thought in relation to differences of place. The philosophical canon was firmly Eurocentric. There was then a complete lack of engagement with matters of how colonialism impacts on, and forms, the philosophical canon. I do not know if this is true of the other two pathways but I do know that other ways of thinking, other engagements and preoccupations and, above all, other knowledges were rendered completely absent. I regret that I could not find my voice to challenge this and that I was overly attached to being acceptable, to being a good student and that in order to belong more securely I shunted any criticism firmly under wraps.

My undergraduate degree underlined my fascination with

matters of gender and subjectivity and after graduating (I did well enough) I embarked on a PhD under the supervision of professors Barry Richards and Michael Rustin. I was ill-equipped to undertake a PhD, and in retrospect perhaps should have done an MA before embarking on a doctorate, but I rarely take the sensible path and instead I rushed headlong into postgraduate studies. I was ill-prepared emotionally for the isolation of working in libraries, barely speaking to another person for hours at a time (I worked mainly in the British Library, then located in the British Museum). The room was full of books, it was dark and smelled musty, and was occupied with people bent over books – I fondly imagined that they were undertaking sophisticated scholarship with ease. I loved it and I miss it, even though the new British Library is lighter, there is more space and it is far more user-friendly. It is still full of academics bent over books and I still imagine they are undertaking sophisticated scholarship with a lightness of touch (I also know this is a foolish fantasy!).

But back to the past ... I worked hard on my PhD, became confused, attempted to find my theoretical frame, struggled to keeping going, became lost in the data and had no idea how to analyse it, and found the whole endeavour emotionally testing. It was challenging intellectually and emotionally as I endeavoured to answer the following question: why had independence become the new moral virtue for women? I endeavoured to understand female identity, representations of femininity in women's magazines and became engrossed in women's problem pages. I doubt that I met a deadline throughout the whole process, except for the final deadline of submission (but that really was a case of the thesis being wrenched away from my computer). I learnt again the value of ideas, the benefit of intellectual endeavour and of hanging on in. Psychoanalytic theory was central as I read articles on the unconscious, the complexities of subjectivity with a specific focus on female identities, and attempted to bring together feminist theory with psychoanalysis. I finally finished the thesis and embarked on an academic career that initially consisted of part-time lecturing in various institutions as I built up my CV. I remember with some shame the first lecture that I delivered when I hit undergraduate students over the head with heavy Foucauldian theory – I really did not know what I was doing – and as the students sat becoming more and more confused, I blithered in panic as I sensed that the students were not with me at all.

I am now more experienced as a lecturer, and hopefully I engage students more fully and provide them with a sense of the excitement of ideas and the worthwhile attempt to engage in thinking anew. I am an academic in the School of Sociology and Social Policy at the University of Nottingham, where my interests have come together in an interlinked web. In no particular order these include diversity, identities, postcolonial subjectivities, gender, and this has widened out to include masculinities, and an engagement with the inter-relationship between the UK and Egypt. I am fortunate as my administrative role, teaching responsibilities and research interests form an interconnected labyrinth.

In this last paragraph I want to concentrate on my ongoing research concerns as I find myself back to that moment of staring at the board and attempting, again, to understand closely what is transmitted and absorbed of the past into the present, but now in a different geopolitical location as I concentrate on Egypt and as I return to my own biographical past. It is challenging personally, theoretically, politically as I attempt to understand the intricacies of the formation, and lived experience of Egyptian female subjectivities. I am nearing the end of my academic career and I discover through writing this essay that my personal history, the theoretical foundations gained through undertaking an undergraduate cultural studies degree and a PhD and my present life (I have a home and family in Cairo and also a home in Nottingham) are interlinked in which one aspect of my life reverberates across other facets. As Susannah Radstone (also a graduate of the cultural studies degree and now based at Monash University in Melbourne, Australia) argues cogently in an essay entitled *Theory and Affect: Undivided Worlds,* theory and affect are intertwined and cannot, should not, be separated out. This is also an argument made by Robyn Wiegman in her book *Object Lessons,* who writes that ontological matters always underpin and are persistently woven through our theoretical investments. I do not know who I would be without the knowledges and understandings that I gained so valuably as an under/postgraduate student and what I absorbed intellectually, emotionally, politically. I am grateful.

CHAPTER TWENTY-THREE

Object lesson

Francesca Hughes, interviewed by Christine Hawley

C.H. *Your undergraduate education in architecture was at Edinburgh University, an institution with a prestigious reputation and a good (if rather conservative) architecture school. What motivated you to move after three years and why did you choose UEL?*

F.H. My education at Edinburgh was blessed by the presence of Iain Boyd-Whyte and the late Izi Metzstein. Otherwise, with the exception of the extraordinary Deborah Howard with whom we had very little contact, the faculty was, as you intimate, composed of very kind and very conservative old white men deep in their comfort zone and what I was to discover was my discomfort zone. My fellow students were, unbelievably, all also English, white and middle class – we later collectively figured out that there must have existed an unwritten carve-up deal whereby Scottish students applying to Edinburgh's schools were offered places at Heriot Watt, and English at Edinburgh University – so any peer education was homogenous and limited. Izi and Iain did not get on, one of the many foolish tragedies of academic life. But their two singular and often opposed voices – Izi, the Jewish Berliner adopted by Glasgow and of course the Mac, and Iain, who'd rowed for Cambridge and fallen for Berlin (a very different Berlin from Izi's but nonetheless still Berlin) – constituted all my lasting 'education' from Edinburgh. I could not have asked for better, but after three years I needed more. I needed not just two voices but a whole chorus of dissenting voices that I might become part of: I needed a more diverse set of fellow students to learn from.

In my third year and with Iain's incredible support, and much eye-rolling from Izi (though I knew I had his backing too), I organised a conference at the school with fellow student Natasha Nicholson on women in architecture, including speakers such as Jane Drew and Alison Smithson. Through this process I'd learnt of Christine Hawley becoming head of school at what was then North East London Polytechnic. (The conference was the beginning of what would later lead to a book I edited for MIT Press, *The Architect: Reconstructing her Practice,* to which Christine contributed the only chapter by a British architect.)

I pored over every bit of information I could find about this architecture school in an old Victorian primary school building in East London (with the very same beer-coloured tiles on the stairs that had adorned the stairs of my Camden primary school), where students were making crazy devices in the old playground loos converted into a fabrication workshop and where, apparently, you were allowed to use architecture to talk about *any*thing and in *any*way. I glimpsed the full polysemous possibility I was being denied and was hooked. I went to my director of studies and told him I was thinking of bailing out of my four-year honours degree at year three, and leaving with a humble BSc instead, because I had to go to be part of these experiments in an East London polytechnic. He made no bones about expressing his utter horror. His disdain sealed my decision. Despite Izi and Iain's brilliance I had to get out of there.

Edinburgh is one of the grandest historic cities in the UK and it has always been argued that urban context will teach you as much about cities and their history as anything you can be taught within a university. The context of Holbrook and Plaistow is very different and fairly removed from the cultural and historic 'hotspots' of London. How did the characteristics of the area influence (if at all) the work that you did?

When I was a master's student at UEL I lived in George Orwell's flat on Canonbury Square. Every day I would train or drive from well-heeled Georgian splendour – the same splendour Orwell had described as 'squalid slums' in *Down and Out in Paris and London* – to the two-ups and two-downs of Holbrook Road. The cross-section the journey cut across London and its demographic canyons was my history and theory curriculum – the way in which the city makes concrete and physical all that is virtual: the legislative, economic and social architecture that was Thatcher's legacy. From the window of the overground train a different cross-section was drawn as Islington's manicured rhododendron and wisteria planted gardens gave way to an ad hoc landscape of buddleia growing out of rubble, of scrapyards with rusting hulks piled like carcasses, of canals with dirty swans floating amongst semi-submerged shopping trolleys. The contrast between the Georgian grammar and the aesthetic lexicon of Hackney and Stratford's then *terrain-vague* was riveting. (This, before the arrival of the great Olympic tidy-up or the emergence of hipster and Instagram visual clichés.) More riveting still was the fact that I was not required to leave these train window lessons at the school door but found that when I drew upon their compositions and juxtapositions in my studio work, not only were they were accepted as valid as visually quoting Carlo Scarpa or Giancarlo di Carlo had been in Edinburgh, but also they were deeply understood and responded to. We were all exploring the development of the latent aesthetic language of UEL's immediate environs that had existed in a kind of visual, and indeed scholarly, lacuna, and that allowed our designs to talk differently about contemporary urban existence.

Of the many beautiful models that were built in the school I remember yours as being quite distinctive. I imagine that very little of this type of work was done in Edinburgh; was this a refreshing challenge and did it influence the way you developed your architectural narrative?

At Edinburgh I had always felt frustrated by my inability to find a way of drawing that could really articulate my intentions, could really act as a vehicle for the alchemical unfurling of the design process. The drawings we were producing all felt like traps, cul-de-sacs. Rather than interrogating their authors they simply confirmed expectations. Entering UEL I found myself suddenly surrounded by students producing drawings that took their thoughts elsewhere, that answered back, disrupting the design process in fertile ways. I also found students up to their elbows in plaster, casting and then carving out complex voids; others drawing in space by soldering great long piano wires into a set of tensioned arcs; or dragging into school objets trouvé from the very landscapes around us we were designing for and then incorporating them into their models. I jumped in. This was my duck-to-water moment.

I had never made anything before but discovered that this I really could do, god knows how. Perhaps I was back making mud pies in my childhood garden. I let my hands think first, my eyes and then mind could follow later. I found Albert, the technician in the converted loos, and he taught me how to check alignment of joints not by sight but by a stroking caress, with the intelligence of finger tips. He taught me to be patient and to improvise in the making of all things. I had found the medium that would make my 'pleasure flow', as Jennifer Bloomer counsels, and the traps of representation that had thwarted me so became trapdoors that opened on to a myriad of unexpected possibilities.

How much of the work in other parts of the school were you aware of – and, if so, did it influence your own thinking?

At UEL we were all aware of everything going on around us. Now that I run a school of architecture I return to the question of why this was so, how this worked? The intimate scale certainly made this possible, but also the Victorian primary school plan: a cluster of brown-tiled classrooms used as studios around what had been the also beer-tiled and parquet-floored assembly hall/gymnastics space. Nat Chard was in one classroom with a cohort of piano wire solderers, welders and casters. The late and much-missed Pascal Schöning was in another making architecture through film. C. J. Lim was in another painting shards. In another, members of the Laboratory for Primary Studies in Architecture were returning from Le Corbusier's Unité in the French forests of Briey.

It was in many ways a space of miraculous fertile exchange. Everyone and everything was learning from everyone and everything else. There was no inside and outside to different bodies of knowledge. In an echo of Jacques Rancière's poetics of knowledge, all intelligence was valid. And the building itself was complicit (confirming again the paradox that the best architecture schools are always in not-designed-for-purpose buildings). We saw each other's crits as we walked through the hall to the loos. We swapped tips on the very generous old school stairs. We dipped into each other's classrooms to steal a soldering iron or drill bit. In so doing we also 'stole' the edge of an idea, the crank of a line, the twist of an argument. The resulting 'influence' was not from any identifiable sources *per se* but from the whole ecology, its fluidity and its generosity.

I have always felt that teaching should be supportive rather than purely instructive and that students should be given the intellectual freedom to mine their own imagination, and always question the status quo. My, perhaps nostalgic, memory was that the school was fairly liberal in what it allowed the students to do. The best teaching as I remember was where there was a mutually creative dialogue between staff and students. What was your commentary on teaching style?

The teaching ethos in the school, as you describe it, made the diversity of its student body its gold. This is what I am now working to install, protect and cultivate at UTS in Sydney, where we have an even more extraordinarily diverse community of students. Their different experiences and frames of reference drive the studio work and conversations – you legitimised this pedagogical approach at UEL, pedagogy without pedantry. The compulsion to instruct is difficult to dismantle and the students have an enormously important role in educating the educator. This is not to say that expertise must not be disseminated, but that there must be complex feedback loops in the dissemination process. Ultimately the creative process draws on the self. I forget whom MIT Press's Roger Conover once quoted to me when he said, 'the personal is always a catastrophe',' but what I took from it, and what confirmed what I had learnt from UEL, was to always not install but *translate* the personal in my work. It is these analytic and methodological skills of translation that reside in the teacher and must be imparted to the student, so that they might then use their own personal experience in a way that is not cloying or self-indulgent – catastrophic. In turn it is the witnessing of the students' testing of the imparted translatory tools against their own experiences that allows the teacher to further refine their abstract tools for themselves.

Looking back at some of the work produced well over thirty-five years ago (with absolutely no digital input) it still looks amazingly fresh. Perhaps this was because it captured a formal language that was not explicit and not clearly relatable to historic precedents. I felt that many of the finished pieces had different ways to be interpreted. Perhaps that was the point – to try and get students to realise there are no black and white answers, just possibilities. What do you think? What role does abstraction play in the development of an idea?

Like all really good architecture schools, at UEL the central lesson was how to think. Abstraction, its strategic ambiguity (and its strategic specificity in terms of rigour) played a very important role in this process. As you say, as students we had to accept that there were no right answers, nothing was black and white. We had to learn to navigate nuance and articulate a complexity of conflicting conditions. Within the many representational registers you always insisted on specificity – this I later realised *was* the crucial rigour that prevented ambiguity simply becoming a swamp of uncertainty. But the specificity was not necessarily a reference to an instance in the canon, a precedent, but to an instance or condition that existed anywhere, that we had encountered already or were still to encounter, out there in the world. That is, it was precisely abstraction that not only legitimised but also facilitated the possibility that architecture could speak about anything and everything. This liberation was nothing short of intoxicating. I maintain to this day, and to the continued disgruntlement of the seemingly continuous supply of conservative voices in architecture, that no topic owns architecture and no topic is outside of architecture.

You have taught and examined in many schools of architecture internationally and obviously have good judgement about the way architectural education has developed. Are you optimistic about what you see?

Yes and no. I have a horror of the metricisation of education that has descended upon us worldwide and the mediocrity it promotes, whether intended or not. Systems of measure change what they measure, and we have to be very judicious about how we design and employ them. The most insidious perhaps is the measuring of research which has led to a very narrow definition of 'curiosity' and its partitioning away from everything that feeds it: the studio, imagination and processes that need not be teleological-, 'goal'- or 'outcome'-focused. Joan Ockman writes of the need to protect the 'unfettered desire' of the studio. We also must protect the 'unfettered desire' of research. In the research auditing climates both in the UK and in Australia this is increasingly under threat and worries me greatly: I fear that 'research' as newly defined under these regimes risks destroying real research; what Mark Cousins cleverly refers to as 'study'.

However, as someone who grew up under Thatcher, I also know the most repressive regimes generate the most radical responses. And this I hope will be timely: architectural education – the learning of how to think, how to harness curiosity and imagination – will play an important role in addressing the extraordinary challenges we now face. Given the anthropocene is the only logical conclusion of capitalism and the fallacy of infinite growth, how we design for different models of society, economies of sharing, of post-work and of de-growth is a question that falls squarely into the lap of architecture. It will require radical imagination, radical argumentation and radical communication. So perhaps all this repression will come to good use when it provokes precisely the radical reactions that we now need for so much more than research purposes.

You are considered to be one of the most perceptive philosophical critics of your generation and someone who writes in order to ask many of the questions we rarely hear. Would you say your architectural position (political or otherwise) was influenced by your own education)?

I am flattered and must protest!

Yes of course, everything I do was and remains shaped by the incredible education I received. The combination of Izi's rigorous, didactic modernist rule book, and your gifting of the intellectual and methodological crowbar with which to break or at least question all rules, with no less rigour. It was a potent recipe. All the more augmented by the extreme contrast between the environments in which the two lessons took place. I was incredibly lucky. And this education was for free.

Do you see education as a ring-fenced prescribed process at a certain time in your life or do you see it as part of a continuum? What should the aspirations of an educational degree be and how should this prepare young people for what appears to be a much more uncertain employment landscape?

I don't know why I find this often-asked question so hard to answer. I feel I should say yes, education is now a lifelong pursuit; yes, the university as a project may be over, learning and research will take place in all forms and in all contexts, corporate included. But I remain worried about what we might lose when the distinction between when you are entirely focused on being formally educated in life and when you are not collapses, as it surely will. I fear we will miss the extraordinary process of those three-plus years when pragmatic reality is suspended and when we can focus on the pleasure of a pursuit of knowledge free of instrumentality. We have all seen how the seamless connectivity procured by technology has led to not more leisure but more work, not the liberation for parents we hoped, but the erosion of our private and family hours by a continuous state of distraction by screens, pings and buzzing notifications. Similarly I fear that learning distributed across a lifetime, a continuum of what in Australia we call 'short courses', taken in breaks or at the weekends, not protected within the three-year walls of the university, will lead to the end of the sanctuary of learning and its protection from the fiscal and metricised world of the labour market, and what Samuel Beckett might call its 'filthy logics'.

As the 'boot is now on the other foot' and you are now the head of architecture at UTS, what comments can you make looking down the other end of the telescope?

I love that you remind me in this question to remember being a student myself in the running of a school now. I think when you were running UEL you remembered every day what it was like to be a student which for you was in a very different environment: the Architectural Association, before it became fee-paying, but an elite institution nonetheless. I remember you coming back to studio from a presentation at the AA one day and saying: 'God, I had forgotten how much I hate that place!'. What you established in UEL kept the best of the AA (its experimentation) and eliminated the worst (the egos, the arrogance, the pretension and yes, elitism). For myself now at UTS I endeavour daily to instil everything from UEL in those days, above all the informal generosity of the school and its community, a property that seemed to leak in through the windows and doors from its surrounds – East London always was a part of London that put people and their relationships first. There is nothing from my student memory at UEL that I want to eliminate or reject in the school I am making now. That was all left in Edinburgh. I remain eternally grateful.

Notes on Contributors

Sally Alexander is Emerita of Modern History at Goldsmiths, University of London, a founding editor of *History Workshop Journal*, and is writing two essays on mid-twentieth-century social democracy. She is a member of 'Who Cares in Europe?', a COST EU research project.

Molly Andrews is Professor of Political Psychology, and co-director and co-founder of the Centre for Narrative Research at the University of East London, and Jane and Aatos Erkko Visiting Professor at the Helsinki Collegium for Advanced Studies at the University of Helsinki, 2019-2020. Her books include *Lifetimes of Commitment: Aging, Politics, Psychology; Shaping History: Narratives of Political Change* (both Cambridge University Press), and *Narrative Imagination and Everyday Life* (Oxford University Press).

Sarah Beeston MA, FCSP, Dip.TP was head of the Division of Physiotherapy and subsequently head of the Department of Health Sciences between 1988 and 1999. In addition to initiatives in curriculum development at NELP, she served as external examiner for BSc physiotherapy courses in the UK and Zimbabwe during their early years; going on to lead several funded projects on curriculum development within Europe.

Penny Bernstock is head of Education and Society at the University of West London. She was previously head of Sociology and Social Policy at UEL and Director of the Centre for East London Studies. She has published extensively on East London regeneration, and is co-chair of the East London Communities Organisation Olympic Strategy Committee, a member of the academic advisory board of the Institute of Community Studies at the Young Foundation, and sits on the London Prosperity Board.

Sara Bowman is an artist, film maker and fashion historian, currently completing her film *The Man Behind* the *Camera*. Principal Lecturer, Art and Design Fashion Contextual Studies 1979 to 2002, her research focused on the hidden world of artists and craftspeople in haute couture and fashion, and includes her book *A Fashion for Extravagance: Art Deco Fashion and Textiles*. Sara's textile art has been exhibited internationally. She is a practising SGI Buddhist.

Joanne Brown began lecturing at Nottingham Trent University in 1988. She worked at UEL as a senior lecturer in Psychosocial Studies from 1992 until 2004, when she joined the University of Southampton (until 2018), as a senior lecturer in Mental Health. She combines academic work with a psychotherapy practice. She is the author of *A Psychosocial Exploration of Love and Intimacy* (2006).

Tim Butler worked in Sociology at UEL from 1974 until he moved to King's College London in 2003, where he is now Emeritus Professor of Human Geography. The main focus of his work in both institutions was on gentrification and the changing nature of London's middle classes and more recently on the geography of educational choice. Whilst at UEL he edited the journal *Rising East*.

Alvaro de Miranda is of Portuguese origin, trained as a physicist at the University of London. He taught at the University of East London and precursor institutions from 1965, until retirement in 2010, initially in physics and later in Science, Technology and Society. He was a founder member of the Department of Innovation Studies in 1988 and its head from 1992 to 1999. He was president of the European Inter-University Association for Society, Science and Technology (ESST) from 1994 to 1997. His research has included the areas of the ideology of the information society, European science and technology policy, the history of technology in East London and the role of the 2012 Olympics in the regeneration of East London.

Tanya Frank holds a BA in Women's Studies from the University of East London, and an MFA in Creative Writing from the University of California. Her work has featured in the *New York Times* and the *Washington Post*. She is currently working on her memoir, *Zig Zag Boy: A Mother's Reckoning with her Son's Psychosis* (Harper Collins UK, forthcoming 2021). She lives between Los Gatos, California, and her native city of London, with her wife.

Jon Griffith did a year of independent study, then temporary and part-time teaching, research and consultancy contracts at NELP/PEL/UEL from 1982 to 2002, when he became a permanent lecturer, until escaping in 2016. His main interest was in the management of not-for-profit organisations. He now walks a lot in Sussex, and writes occasional letters to *The Guardian*.

Catherine Hall is Emerita Professor of History and the chair of the Centre for the Study of the Legacies of British Slave-ownership at University College London. She is currently working on a manuscript, *Making Racial Capitalism: Edward Long and the History of Jamaica*, is an associate editor of *History Workshop Journal* and, with Bill Schwarz, General Editor of *The Writings of Stuart Hall* for Duke University Press.

Tony Hargreaves was born into a Catholic, socialist working-class family in Liverpool, and survived education by the Christian Brothers. He graduated in Chemistry/History of Science at the University of Leeds. After teacher training, he worked in schools, teaching science with elements of Science, Technology and Society. He was appointed to the North East London Polytechnic in 1970, and designed and taught various STS courses, heading the Science Faculty STS group from 1974 to 1984. He obtained an MSc in the History of Science at Imperial College, London. He moved to Independent Study in 1984, and then to Innovation Studies in 1991, where he continued to teach STS. Having retired from UEL in 2004, he now lives in rural Lancashire looking after ex-feral ponies.

David Harper is Professor of Clinical Psychology and Programme Director (Academic) of the DClinPsych at UEL. He is a member both of the Mental Health and Social Change Research Group in the School of Psychology and of UEL's Centre for Narrative

Research. He has co-authored and co-edited a number of books, including *Psychology, Mental Health and Distress* (Palgrave Macmillan, 2013).

Barbara Harrison joined UEL in 1996 as Professor of Sociology and head of the Department of Sociology and Anthropology. In 2001 she became deputy and subsequently head of the School of Social Sciences, a position she held until 2004. She retired, and until 2011 continued as Professor of Sociology on a part-time basis. She now works part-time with former UEL partnership organisation the Tavistock Clinic on professional doctorate programmes, mainly supervising students in Child and Adolescent Psychoanalytic Psychotherapy. Her academic work in recent years has been in fields of Life Story methods and Visual Sociology.

Christine Hawley CBE was Professor of Architectural Design at the Bartlett UCL. Between 1993 and 2009 she held the posts of Dean of the Bartlett School of Architecture and head of the Faculty of Building Environment at UCL, the first woman to have done so. She has lectured, exhibited and published throughout the USA and the Far East. Her built work as an architect includes teaching and exhibition space for the Städel Academy in Frankfurt, exhibition pavilions at the Osaka and Nahoya Expo, and commissions to devise new forms of social housing in Berlin and Kitigata. She has curated exhibitions including the Hong Kong Architecture Biennale in 2015, and advised on the future of architectural education in the UK, Europe and Australia.

Peter Howells joined Barking Regional College of Technology in 1969, becoming Principal Lecturer and later Professor of Economics at UEL. In 1997 he joined the Bristol Business School as Professor of Monetary Economics and retired as Professor Emeritus in 2011. He has been a member of the Royal Economic Society for many years and has edited the Society's newsletter since 1998. He holds degrees from the University of Kent and LSE.

Francesca Hughes is Professor and Head of School at UTS, Sydney. She is author of numerous publications, including *The Architecture* *of Error: Matter, Measure and the Misadventures of Precision* (MIT Press, 2014) and *Architectures of Prediction* (ARQ DOCS, 2019).

Maggie Humm, Emeritus Professor UEL, is author/editor of fourteen academic books, lately on Virginia Woolf and the arts, the topic of *Talland House*, her debut novel, published August 2020. *Talland House* was shortlisted for the Impress and Fresher Fiction prizes (as *Who Killed Mrs Ramsay?*) and the Retreat West and Eyelands prizes. She is completing *Rodin's Mistress*, about the love affair of the artists Gwen John and Auguste Rodin. http://www.maggiehumm.net/

Michael Locke was with the Centre for Institutional Studies from 1970 until 2008, eventually becoming Reader and, from 2001, its Director. He left in 2008 for Volunteering England (later NCVO). Mike chairs the Advisory Panel of the Institute for Volunteering Research at the University of East Anglia, and is Honorary Visiting Fellow with the Centre for Philanthropy at Kent University.

Mark McDermott is Professor and has been a lecturer at UEL for over thirty years, since 1989. During this time, he has been the School's Research Leader, the PhD Programme Leader and a university staff governor. He trained as a clinical psychologist and has led undergraduate modules on health psychology and mental health for over twenty-five years. His published research focuses on the psychology of individual differences.

Philip Marfleet is Emeritus Professor of Migration Studies at the University of East London. He has published widely on migration, refugees, globalisation, and social and political change in the modern Middle East. Among his books are: *Globalisation and the Third World* (1998), *Refugees in a Global Era* (2006), *Egypt: the Moment of Change* (2009) and *Egypt: Contested Revolution* (2016).

Alan O'Shea joined UEL in January 1980 following postgraduate work at the Centre for Contemporary Cultural Studies at Birmingham University, and was head of the Department of Cultural Studies for seventeen years. His overarching research interest has been on the political significance of popular culture.

He was editor and contributor (with M. Nava) of *Modern Times: Reflections on a Century of English Modernity* (Routledge, 1996). He retired in 2002, but continued to teach an MA course on cinema at Goldsmiths, University of London, for five years.

David Page lives, paints and writes on the Norfolk/Suffolk border. He went to Oxford from Southend High School for Boys, read English, with post-grad B.Litt and Dip.Ed. He taught at the University of Marburg, Hornsey College of Art and NELP. He contributed to *The Hornsey Affair* and generally to the debate on art education. He wrote and illustrated *Ferocious the Puppy-Dragon* (Puffin). He is active in community politics.

Gavin Poynter joined the University of East London from the Trade Union Education Department of the TUC in 1988. He was head of the Department of Innovation Studies (1998-2000) before becoming head of the School of Cultural and Innovation Studies (2000-2004) and head of the School of Social Sciences, Media and Cultural Studies (2004 to 2007). In 2008 he became Professor of Social Sciences and is now Professor (Emeritus). He has co-edited several books and published widely on the London Olympics and the economy and society of East London.

John Pratt was Professor and Director of the Centre for Institutional Studies at UEL from 1972 to 2001. Although his degree was in engineering, he undertook numerous research studies into higher education policy, and was a consultant for local, national and international organisations. His books include the history of British polytechnic policy, and OECD policy reviews of higher education in Austria and Finland.

John Radford is Emeritus Professor and was the founding head of the Department of Psychology at UEL (then West Ham College). He led the introduction of psychology at GCE 'A' level, and was joint founder of the Association for the Teaching of Psychology. He is a Fellow and Honorary Life Member of the British Psychological Society, and recipient of its Lifetime Achievement in Psychology Education award. He has published twenty books on varied topics.

Barry Richards began lecturing at UEL (then NELP) in 1977. He became Professor and head of the Department of Human Relations in 1994. He joined Bournemouth University in 2001, where he is now Professor of Political Psychology. His books include *Emotional Governance* (Palgrave, 2007), *What Holds us Together* (Karnac, 2018) and *The Psychology of Politics* (Routledge, 2019).

Derek Robbins was employed at NELP/UEL from January 1970 until his retirement as Professor of International Social Theory in 2014. He has published extensively on twentieth-century French social theory, particularly on the work of Pierre Bourdieu. His most recent book is *The Bourdieu Paradigm: The Origins and Evolution of an Intellectual Social Project* (Manchester University Press, 2019). He is currently translating, editing, and introducing *Vers le style du XXe siècle* (1945) by the 'équipe d'Uriage', for publication by Peter Lang.

David Rose is Emeritus Professor at the University of East London. He gained a London University external BSc degree in Psychology before completing a PhD at University College London. He has published extensively on recovery from brain damage. In 1994 he moved from Goldsmiths College to become head of the Department of Psychology at UEL, a post he held for fourteen years.

Michael Rustin has been associated with the University of East London since he joined it in 1964, and has had an active role in its development. He was head of the Department of Sociology, and Dean of its Faculty of Social Sciences for twenty-five years, and continues in part-retirement as a Professor of Sociology. He has written and edited many books, in the fields of politics, culture and psychoanalysis, developing new approaches to the social application of psychoanalytic ideas. He is a Visiting Professor at the Tavistock Clinic, and an Associate of the British Psychoanalytical Society. He is a founding editor of *Soundings*.

Alice Sampson led the urban regeneration research team at the Centre for Institutional Studies from 1997 and was director of the Centre from 2008 until 2013, researching East London urban regeneration initiatives and violence prevention programmes nationally and internationally. Alice is currently visiting the Mannheim Centre for Crime and Criminology at the London School of Economics and Political Science and has published in leading academic journals including the *British Journal of Criminology* and *British Journal of Social Work*.

Bill Schwarz teaches in the School of English and Drama at Queen Mary, University of London, and is currently writing *Memories of Empire*: *Vol. II: The Caribbean in England*. He is an associate editor of *History Workshop Journal* and, with Catherine Hall, General Editor of *The Writings of Stuart Hall* for Duke University Press.

Lionel Sims is an anthropologist specialising in cultural astronomy, archaeology and mythology. His research focuses on interpreting the prehistoric monument complexes at Stonehenge and Avebury. He is Vice President of the European Society for Astronomy in Culture (SEAC). A film of his research was commissioned by National Geographic. He led the anthropology programme at UEL from its inception in 1993 until his retirement in 2010.

Frank Skuse joined NELP in 1971. He holds a degree in Economics from the University of Melbourne and a Masters from Monash University, where he taught from 1966 to 1969. He has also taught economics at Civil Service College, London, and IUT Dijon. He became head of Economics at UEL from 1997-2001. His few publications are in post-Keynesian economics.

Corinne Squire is Professor of Social Sciences and Co-Director of the Centre for Narrative Research. Her research interests are in HIV and citizenship, refugee politics, popular media and subjectivities, and narrative theory and methods. Recent publications include *Stories Changing Lives* (OUP, 2020), *Voices from the 'Jungle'* (Africa et al., Pluto, 2017) and *What is Narrative Research?* (Bloomsbury, 2014).

John Strawson is honorary Professor of Law at the University of East London and is Co-Director of the Centre on Human Rights in Conflict. He works in the areas of international law and Middle East Studies. He joined the law department in 1974.

Amal Treacher Kabesh (Dr) is an Associate Professor in the School of Sociology and Social Policy at the University of Nottingham. Amal's research is underpinned and informed by a Cultural Studies approach that she absorbed as an undergraduate at NELP. She has published on matters of identity (gender, ethnicity) and currently is focusing on analysing the formation of Cairene women's identities.

Aneta D. Tunariu is a Professor of Applied Psychology. She joined UEL in 2004 and has been the Dean of the School of Psychology since 2017. Aneta graduated with a BSc in Psychology (1st Class Hons) from London South Bank University in 1999, and in 2003 was awarded her ESRC-funded PhD for research on relational well-being. Her ongoing work focuses on developing and implementing existential positive psychology and coaching interventions across professional, educational and community contexts.

Acknowledgements

We would like to express our thanks to Brenda Kirsch and Katharine Fletcher for their patient and excellent work in editing the text of this large book, and to Lynda Dyson and Lawrence Wishart for their support for this project.

We also thank the many contributors to the volume for the time and commitment which they have given to their writing, and to the collective initiative of producing this book. We have found its editing an enjoyable experience, from which we learned that the richness and variety of work that had taken place in the North East Polytechnic and the university was even greater than we had previously imagined.

Although there are many chapters in this book, covering a wide range of subject areas, we are aware that there are fields of original work at UEL which we have not been able to include. We hope there may be an opportunity for future contributions to this history to be made, and discussion of it to take place.

Finally, we would like to express our gratitude to Dame Rachel Whiteread DBE, sculptor and artist, for giving us the fine cover image for this book, and also to Lynne Whiteread for her help. Their father, the late Tom Whiteread, was head, first of Humanities and then of the School of Art in the polytechnic and university, and was greatly admired and respected for his enabling work in these roles, and for his unvarying support of his colleagues.

Michael Rustin
Gavin Poynter

Index